T0357014

Get the eBook FREE!

(PDF, ePub, Kindle, and liveBook all included)

We believe that once you buy a book from us, you should be able to read it in any format we have available. To get electronic versions of this book at no additional cost to you, purchase and then register this book at the Manning website.

Go to https://www.manning.com/freebook and follow the instructions to complete your pBook registration.

That's it!
Thanks from Manning!

Praise for the first edition

The thinking engineers guide to Go, replete with examples, pitfalls, and scalable approaches worthy of apprentices and architects alike.

—Zachary Manning, senior DevOps engineer at Zillow

An invaluable reference resource for Go developers seeking to refresh their knowledge of core concepts or enhance their understanding of testing, logging, and microservices.

—Jonathan Reeves, software engineer at EQL Games

An essential read for Go enthusiasts, offering practical tips and deep insights to harness Golang's true potential in modern programming.

—Sergio Britos Arevalo, senior software engineer at Schwarz Global Services

The book to improve your Go, practically!

—Leonardo Taccari, cloud architect at faire.ai

Go in Practice,
Second Edition

NATHAN KOZYRA
MATT BUTCHER
MATT FARINA

MANNING
SHELTER ISLAND

For online information and ordering of this and other Manning books, please visit www.manning.com. The publisher offers discounts on this book when ordered in quantity. For more information, please contact

> Special Sales Department
> Manning Publications Co.
> 20 Baldwin Road
> PO Box 761
> Shelter Island, NY 11964
> Email: orders@manning.com

Manning Publications Co. 20 Baldwin Road PO Box 761 Shelter Island, NY 11964	Development editor: Jeffrey Wajsberg Review editor: Radmila Ercegovac Production editor: Andy Marinkovich Copy editor: Keir Simpson Proofreader: Olga Milanko Technical proofreader: Joel Holmes Typesetter: Dennis Dalinnik Cover designer: Marija Tudor

ISBN: 9781633436886
Printed in the United States of America

This book is dedicated to
My friends and family, who lost me for more than a few nights
and weekends during the writing process
Co-workers who gave support and cover along the way
Colleagues and mentors who have taught and continue
to teach new things daily

—Nathan Kozyra

contents

I started developing software at age 12 and fell in love with the craft and art of programming. Looking back nearly 30 years, it's illuminating to see how far the industry has come and how broad it has become. A once-esoteric hobby is commonplace today. I've been writing code every chance I got ever since those early days and took that into undergraduate and graduate school and into the field. That I was able to take that excitement and make a career out of it is worth reflecting on periodically.

Although there are a lot of things about those early days I hold with a nostalgic love—the dedicated computer room, preinternet and early internet exploration and discovery—one thing I don't pine for is the programming languages of old. I cut my teeth on some fairly gnarly languages. Over those early years, I worked with various implementations of BASIC, C, Delphi, Perl, PHP, ASP, and Java but never felt truly comfortable with any of their designs or infrastructure. There was always something missing, some hiccup of design decisions that would bite me here and there (or often). In 2009, when Go was publicly announced, I gave it a shot without a lot of hope. I knew the pedigree of its designers but figured I was dealing with another complicated C alternative. Within a short period, I realized this was one of the cleanest and most enjoyable languages I'd ever worked with. It got out of my way. I got things done. I lobbied for using it for work and started building in Go almost immediately.

Although it's not the only tool in my toolbox these days, I still write Go every day. As amazing as it is, one underappreciated aspect of Go is how it jump-started zeal for creating new, modern languages that can use the power in the systems we have today and produce for the landscape of contemporary use cases. Since Go's arrival, we've seen Rust, Zig, Nim, Odin, Carbon, and others join the space, trying to solve the same problems in elegant ways. Although all of them have merits, Go still provides everything needed for simple, clean, garbage-collected compiled code.

If you're coming from another systems language, you'll appreciate the built-in tooling. The onboard package manager is simple and gets out of your way. The testing suite gives you everything you need to add tests and build into your pipeline. The code formatter `go fmt` means no more arguments about style or linting.

If you're coming in with some Go experience, I hope this book provides some tips and direction about getting things done with the language. We'll look at a lot of dissonant topics and hope to cover a lot of ground with small but demonstrative examples. More than anything, I hope you get some inspiration from this book to keep coding with Go and immersing in the Go community.

—Nathan Kozyra

acknowledgments

Writing a book (or even a book revision) takes a lot of blood, sweat, and tears, and a lot of people must come together to take the book from concept to print. I'd like to thank the people who helped this book come to fruition.

Time sacrifices from the author can affect a lot of people both related and unrelated, and I first want to thank my family and close friends, who worked around my obligations that took days and weekends away. Without their understanding, the book could never have been completed. Writing and revisions take more time than most authors anticipate, and I appreciate all the buffers those close to me provided to help me get to the finish line.

I received a similar cushion from my employer and co-workers, who knew the time commitment and gave me all the space and support I needed.

In writing this book, I got immeasurable support from the Manning team. In particular, I'd like to call out and thank my development editor, Jeffrey Wajsberg. Jeffrey was phenomenal along the way in calling out improvements in writing style, clarity, structure, and in some cases basic grammar. The scheduling, pacing, and writing would have been impossible without that guidance. The supporting team members at Manning never missed a beat, keeping this project moving along at a brisk but controlled pace.

To the book reviewers, I appreciate your attention to detail, finding small things at a technical level that might have slipped through the cracks otherwise. From small suggestions to idiomatic Go language improvements, the book greatly improved from their feedback. To all the reviewers: Adir Shemesh, Andreas Schroepfer, Anuj More,

Borko Djurkovic, Christopher Neeb, Clifford Thurber, Dan Sheikh, Diego Stamigni, Ernest Addae, Giuseppe Maxia, Jasmeet Singh, Jason Content, Jerome Meyer, Jim Amrhein, Joel Holmes, Jonathan Reeves, Keith Kim, Leonardo Taccari, Manzur, Michele Di Pede, Mihaela Barbu, Neeraj Shah, Nolan, Paul Snow, Pavel Anni, Peter Sellars, Ramanan N, Sachin Handiekar, Scott Ling, Sergio Britos Arevalo, Tom Howarth, Tony Holdroyd, and Zachary Manning, your suggestions helped make this book better.

Last, I'd like to show some love to the Go team at Google. In my 30-plus years of development both as a profession and as a hobby, I've never found a language that lets me just get things done like this one. Go is a legitimately fun language, and when I move to other languages I'm reminded of the simplicity and attention to tight, readable language design that's key to Go's core ethos. I hope the language keeps growing and you find working with Go as fun and as productive as I have.

—Nathan Kozyra

about this book

Go in Practice, Second Edition, is intended to be a high-level approach to getting comfortable with concepts above and beyond the basics of the language. Topics range from building concurrent systems with Go's goroutine approach to building performant web applications, all along learning about the tools that enable production-quality code. You'll learn about dealing with networking, file access, concurrency patterns, and using native communication protocols like TCP/REST, gRPC, and UDP. The book also emphasizes testing and error handling to empower the reader to build solid systems that hold up to real-world challenges.

Who should read this book?

This book is intended for intermediate Go developers and advanced developers in adjacent languages like Java, C/C++, C#, and Rust, among others. But developers from other languages just hoping to get their feet wet with Go should be able to follow along without too much trouble. Go is simple by design and has a low barrier to entry, which makes learning along the way more than manageable.

How this book is organized: A road map

This book has 13 chapters divided into four thematic parts.

The first part is an overview of the general structure, functionality, and tooling included in the Go suite.

- Chapter 1 makes sure the reader gets up and *Going* with the language. We compare Go to other comparable languages (both legacy and new), show how to lay out and build Go applications, and deal with dependencies.
- Chapter 2 looks at building command-line applications using flags, configuration, and environment variables. From the basics of command-line interface design, we'll dig into starting and gracefully stopping a web server.
- Chapter 3 digs into the core data structures in Go: structs and interfaces. We look at how to design custom abstract data types and use interfaces to guarantee compatibility with functions and methods. We also dig into the much-discussed, finally implemented generics features of Go.

The next part looks at the types of development fundamentals and tooling you'll need to ensure that your applications are ready for real-world users by focusing on error handling, testing, and performance improvements with concurrency.

- Chapter 4 discusses error handling approaches and dealing with panics. We'll cover various approaches to bubbling and wrapping errors, and compare panics to other methods of exiting a program.
- Chapter 5 explores concurrency, one of Go's primary selling points. We'll look at the model itself, demonstrating goroutines and channels for communication between concurrent goroutines.
- Chapter 6 jumps into Go's powerful testing functionality, showing how to benchmark and test your code. You use test tables to build easily readable and augmentable groups of tests and test suites to keep your code functioning through potential edge cases and regressions.
- Chapter 7 walks you through the basics of working with file systems and networking in Go. You'll learn how to access, read, and write files and glean insights from operating system-level file stats. We'll also build basic networking at a low level with both TCP and UDP.

The third part of this book puts the tools from the first two parts into practice in building a web service both as a server and as a client. You'll deal with handling requests and with delivering them as a consumer of other web services.

- Chapter 8 builds on the previous lessons and applies them to design a working HTTP server. Go has a robust standard library for building servers, and we'll build on that to create a working web server while demonstrating routing and dealing with HTTP requests and responses, including cookies and authentication.
- Chapter 9 extends basic web servers to something approaching a real-world web app. We'll look at Go's templating system to return responses using abstract templates for the web, email, and other text-based purposes.
- Chapter 10 deals with advanced topics related to web applications. You'll learn about creating standalone or adjacent static file servers, embedding data directly in your compiled binary, and working with POST data and file uploads.

- Chapter 11 looks at working with external services, wherein we work in a networking space as a client rather than exclusively as a server. You'll learn about designing APIs and dealing with external ones and their protocols. We'll also look at an alternative to REST, gRPC, and how it can be used to reinforce your code.

The final part looks at some more fine-grained and advanced use cases for Go as they relate to our previous chapters.

- Chapter 12 focuses on running and building your apps for cloud deployment. We first dig into using Go to help orchestrate your cloud service(s), dealing with networking and discoverability concerns that go along with such deployments, including monitoring. In addition, we look at alternatives for cloud communication like gRPC both as a server and as a consumer of APIs.
- Chapter 13 looks at some advanced and niche parts of the Go ecosystem. Going deeper on runtime reflection and the type system will help you build better libraries and more generalized code. We'll look at interoperability with C and more granular control of Go's garbage collection.

About the code

As you read the book, you'll encounter a bevy of code examples. Many of those are shown in their entirety and can be compiled without accompaniment. The fact that full source code could be included demonstrates the brevity and simplicity of Go's design! You'll also find code in text designated in this fixed-width font and style to demonstrate snippets that are referenced in preceding code or can be changed to affect the behavior of that code. Often, these blocks of code draw attention to code that warrants additional detail or explanation.

You can get executable snippets of code from the liveBook (online) version of this book at https://livebook.manning.com/book/go-in-practice-second-edition. You can find the complete and most up-to-date version of the code as a Git repository at https://github.com/nkozyra/go-in-practice and on the Manning website at www.manning.com.

liveBook discussion forum

Purchase of *Go in Practice, Second Edition*, includes free access to liveBook—Manning's online reading platform. Using liveBook's exclusive discussion features, you can attach comments to the book globally or to specific sections or paragraphs. It's a snap to make notes for yourself, ask and answer technical questions, and receive help from the authors and other users. To access the forum, go to https://livebook.manning.com/book/go-in-practice-second-edition/discussion. You can also learn more about Manning's forums and the rules of conduct at https://livebook.manning.com/discussion.

Manning's commitment to our readers is to provide a venue where meaningful dialogue between individual readers and between readers and authors can take place. It is not a commitment to any specific amount of participation on the part of the authors, whose contributions to the forum remain voluntary (and unpaid). We suggest you try asking the authors some challenging questions lest their interest stray! The forum and the archives of previous discussions will be accessible on the publisher's website as long as the book is in print.

Other online resources

Beyond this book and similar books, there are a few great resources for continued learning in Go.

- Reddit's Go subreddit at https://www.reddit.com/r/golang is a great place for both new and experienced Go developers.
- Stack Overflow remains a high-quality source to submit, assist, and review common questions and challenges using Go. See https://stackoverflow.com/questions/tagged/golang.
- Referenced heavily in this book, Go's internal documentation is comprehensive and easy to follow. The standard library reference provides quick access to the core platform's functionality. See https://pkg.go.dev/std.
- The authors highly recommend the Golang Weekly newsletter, which can surface cool projects written with Go and brings light to new and proposed changes to the language. Subscribe to it at https://golangweekly.com.

about the authors

NATHAN KOZYRA is a full-stack developer who has been building web and mobile applications for more than 30 years. An early adopter of the Go language, he's been actively developing with it since 2009. In addition to doing web/mobile work, he has an MS in Computer Science with a focus on machine learning and has been building machine learning solutions for more than a decade. In addition to Go, he works heavily with TypeScript and Rust and enjoys experimenting with new systems languages emerging in the space, like Odin and Zig.

MATT BUTCHER is an architect at Deis, where contributing to open source projects is his day job. He has written several books and dozens of articles. Matt holds a PhD in philosophy and teaches in the Computer Science department at Loyola University Chicago. Matt is passionate about building strong teams and developing elegant solutions to complex problems.

MATT FARINA is a Principal Engineer in the Advanced Technology Group at Hewlett Packard Enterprise. He is an author, speaker, and regular contributor to open source software who has been developing software for over a quarter century. He likes to solve problems for regular people by creating solutions using both the latest technology and the mundane that can be easily overlooked.

about the cover illustration

The figure on the cover of *Go in Practice, Second Edition* is captioned "Habit of the Wife of a Russian Peasant in 1768." The illustration is taken from Thomas Jefferys' *A Collection of the Dresses of Different Nations, Ancient and Modern*, published in London between 1757 and 1772. The title page states that these are hand-colored copperplate engravings, heightened with gum arabic.

In those days, it was easy to identify where people lived and what their trade or station in life was just by their dress. Manning celebrates the inventiveness and initiative of the computer business with book covers based on the rich diversity of regional culture centuries ago, brought back to life by pictures from collections such as this one.

Part 1

Background and fundamentals

This initial section of the book presents some background about Go and its built-in tooling and provides a foundation for building applications. In this section, we hope to build a foundation that will be useful for developing any project, including those later in the book.

In chapter 1, we start with an overview of Go and its landscape for those who are not familiar with it. Chapters 2 and 3 move to base components for a command-line application. Chapter 2 provides the foundation for building an application, including working with console applications and servers and handling configuration. Chapter 3 looks at core data structures and method calling by using structs and interfaces. As part of this discussion, we look at generic types and generic programming. Go resisted adding generic support for more than a decade, but its introduction allows you to streamline your code by generalizing some functions and methods without the need for overzealous runtime reflection.

Getting started with Go

1

This chapter covers

- Introducing Go
- Understanding where Go fits into the language landscape
- Getting up and running in Go

This chapter introduces the Go language and its features at a high level, providing the foundation for professional developers to use the language to address real-world problems on the job. In this chapter, you'll learn about Go and the toolchain that accompanies it, where Go fits into the landscape of languages, and how to install the language and get going quickly with your own application or module.

If you've been using Go for a while, some of this material will be a review, and you may find it beneficial to jump ahead. But in recent years, Go has changed quite a bit more than it did in its early days. The language remains tight and focused, but community feedback has led to some powerful new features, including support for generics.

1.1   *What is Go?*

Go, sometimes referred to as *golang*, is a statically typed and compiled open source programming language initially developed by Google. In 2007, Robert Griesemer, Rob Pike, and Ken Thompson attempted to create a language for modern systems programming that solved real-world problems they encountered while building large systems at scale. The language was publicly announced in November 2009 and quickly gained traction.

Instead of attempting to attain theoretical pureness, these designers engineered Go around real-world practical situations. It's inspired by the best languages that came before it, including C, Pascal, Java, and Python. The designers tried to take the best aspects of each language while reducing perceived complexity. The result is a powerful language that still feels lightweight. Go has a small syntactical footprint, an incredible toolset, and performance that places it in a sweet spot underserved by some of its modern counterparts.

Go isn't the typical statically typed and compiled language. Static typing has features that make it feel dynamic, and the compiled binaries have a runtime that includes garbage collection. The language's designers considered the types of projects that Google would need to use it for: large codebases operating at scale and being developed by large developer teams.

At its core, Go is a programming language defined by a specification that any compiler can implement. The default implementation is shipped via the go tool. But Go is more than a programming language. As figure 1.1 illustrates, multiple layers are built on top of the language.

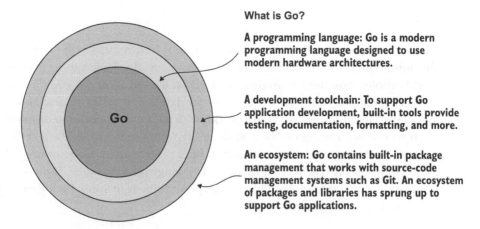

What is Go?

A programming language: Go is a modern programming language designed to use modern hardware architectures.

A development toolchain: To support Go application development, built-in tools provide testing, documentation, formatting, and more.

An ecosystem: Go contains built-in package management that works with source-code management systems such as Git. An ecosystem of packages and libraries has sprung up to support Go applications.

Figure 1.1   The layers of Go

Developing any application requires more than the programming language, including compilation, testing, documentation, and formatting. In many languages, support for any of these tasks is often left to third parties. But the go tool that's used to compile applications also provides functionality that supports these features, making it a full toolchain for application development. One of the most notable aspects of the toolchain is package management. Out of the box, the programming language Go and the go toolchain provide local and global dependency support. A built-in package system, along with a common toolchain for the essential elements of development, enabled an ecosystem to form around the language.

One of the defining characteristics of Go is its simplicity. When Griesemer, Pike, and Thompson designed the language, a feature didn't go in until all three agreed that it should be a feature of the language. This style of decision-making, along with the developers' years of experience, led to a simple but powerful language—simple enough to keep in your head yet powerful enough to write a wide variety of software.

This slow-and-steady approach to Go's design kept Go lean while allowing new features in after careful consensus. Type generics, for example—a feature common to languages such as C++ and Java—was held back in Go while the team publicly debated the merits and drawbacks of implementing it. The language's users and designers eventually decided that it was useful enough to add to the language without imposing any unnecessary complexity or code readability problems and without any backward-compatibility problems. We look at generics support in detail in chapter 3. An example of Go's simplicity philosophy is the variable syntax:

```
var i int = 2
```

Here, a variable is created as an integer and set to a value of 2. Because an initial value is given, you can shorten the syntax, enabling type assertion as follows:

```
var i = 2
```

When an initial value is provided, the compiler is smart enough to figure out the type. In this case, the compiler sees the value of 2 and knows that the type is an integer.

Go doesn't stop there. Do you need the var keyword? Go provides something called *short variable declarations*:

```
i := 2
```

This is a concise equivalent to the first variable statement. It's less than half the length of the first example, it's easy to read, and it happens because the compiler figures out the missing parts. This variable feels like lightweight runtime typing but has all the guardrails you'd find in any other statically typed compiled language. This kind of simplicity makes it easy to learn the basics of Go.

Although the core of the language is fairly simple, Go's built-in dependency management enables you to add missing elements of the standard library, which can be imported as third-party packages and incorporated into applications via the package management system.

1.2　Noteworthy aspects of Go

Because Go is designed around practical, real-world situations and development hurdles, it has several noteworthy features. These features, used together, provide the building blocks for Go applications.

1.2.1　Multiple return values

One of the first things you'll learn in Go is that functions and methods can accept *and* return multiple values. Most programming languages, even some newer than Go, support returning only a single value from a function. When you need to return multiple values, they're shoehorned into a tuple, hash, array, or other type, and that singular value is returned. Go is one of the few languages that natively supports multiple return values. This feature is used regularly, and you'll see it in virtually every part of Go and the libraries and applications written in it. Consider the following function, which returns two string names.

Listing 1.1　Multiple returns

```
package main

import (
    "fmt"
)

func getStrings() (string, string) {       A function with no input
    return "Foo", "Bar"                     parameters and two strings
}                                           defined for return by the
                                            function's signature

                                            Two strings, "Foo" and
                                            "Bar"," are returned.
func main() {
    n1, n2 := getStrings()                  The function's caller gets two
    fmt.Println(n1, n2)                     values and prints them.
    n3, _ := getStrings()
    fmt.Println(n3)                         A second caller accepts the
}                                           first return value, ignores the
                                            second, and prints the first.
```

> **TIP**　Imported packages used in this chapter, such as fmt, bufio and net, are part of the standard library. For details, including the APIs and how they work, see https://golang.org/pkg.

In this example, each return is defined in the function's signature after the arguments. In this case, the function accepts no input parameters and returns two string values. When return is called, it returns two strings to match the function's definition. When the getStrings function is called, you need a variable for each return to capture the value. But if you want to ignore one of the returned values, use _ instead of a variable name.

The most common way you'll see this in practice is in error return values. By convention, an error return value is the last variable. Seeing a, b, err := someFunc() will become extremely common, and it's a good idea to follow this pattern when returning an error (or `nil` value in the absence of error). We go into more detail on errors in chapter 4.

In addition to following this example, you can name your return values and work with these names the same way you do with variables. The names can be implicit to the return statement, saving a little boilerplate at the end of a method. To illustrate, let's rework the preceding example to use named return values, as shown in the next listing.

Listing 1.2   Named return values

```
package main

import (
    "fmt"
)

func getStrings() (first string, second string) {      ◁──┐ Returned values
    first = "Foo"                                              have names.
    second = "Bar"                        Values assigned to named return variables
    return                    ◁──┐
}                                  return is called with no values.

func main() {
    n1, n2 := getStrings()        ◁──┐ Variables are filled with values.
    fmt.Println(n1, n2)
```

As the `getStrings` function executes, the named return variables are available to have values assigned to them. When `return` is called without a return value, the current values for the return variable names are returned. This type of return is known as a *naked return*. For code calling the function, getting the response and using it works the same way as when not using names. This kind of flexibility lends itself to more concise, readable code, although this pattern is becoming less common as methods and functions become longer and it gets harder to follow the return through control flow.

1.2.2   A modern standard library

Modern applications have common themes, such as being networked and dealing with encryption. Instead of burdening you, the developer, with the task of hunting for common libraries, the Go standard library provides the most useful building blocks out of the box—networking, cryptography, serialization, math, and more. Let's look at a few elements in the standard library so you can get an idea of what's included.

> **NOTE**   The entire standard library is documented, with examples, at https://pkg.go.dev/std.

NETWORKING AND HTTP

A network application often needs to work both as a client that can connect to other networked devices and as a server that other applications can connect to (see the following listing). The Go standard library's net package makes this easy, whether you're working with HTTP or dealing directly with Transmission Control Protocol (TCP), User Datagram Protocol (UDP), or other common setups.

Listing 1.3   Read TCP status

```
package main

import (
    "bufio"
    "fmt"
    "log"
    "net"
)

func main() {
    conn, err := net.Dial("tcp", "golang.org:80")
    if err != nil {
        log.Fatal(err)
    }
    fmt.Fprintf(conn, "GET / HTTP/1.0\r\n\r\n")
    status, err := bufio.NewReader(conn).ReadString('\n')
    if err != nil {
        log.Fatal(err)
    }
    log.Println(status)
}
```

Connects over TCP to golang.org:80

Handles a TCP error if one occurs, ending execution

Sends a formatted string over the connection—in this case, a basic HTTP GET request line

Reads the response up until a newline (\n)

Prints the first response line

Handles any possible error reading from the connection

Connecting via TCP directly to a port is part of the net package, in which Go provides a common setup for different types of connections. The Dial function connects using the connection type and endpoint specified. In this case, it makes a TCP connection to golang.org on port 80. Over the connection, a GET request is constructed and sent, and the first line of the response is printed.

> **NOTE** In listing 1.3, we handle errors as they present themselves, and we call log.Fatal to provide helpful feedback and kill the process. There are a lot of ways to end execution with Go, and each method has its own purpose and merits. The log.Fatal has a formatted counterpart, and there's also os.Exit(STATUS_CODE) and panic(). We address these methods in depth in chapter 4.

The ability to listen on a port is similarly easy. Instead of calling out to an endpoint by using Dial, using the Listen function in the net package enables an application to listen on a port and respond to incoming connections.

To create a web server, Go provides the http package for both a client and a server (see the following code). The client is simple enough to use that it meets the needs of common use cases while being extensible enough for more complex cases.

Listing 1.4 HTTP GET

```go
package main

import (
    "io"
    "log"
    "net/http"
)

func main() {
    resp, err := http.Get("http://example.com/")
    if err != nil {
        log.Fatal("could not retrieve example.com", err)
    }
    defer resp.Body.Close()

    body, err := io.ReadAll(resp.Body)
    if err != nil {
        log.Fatal("could not read body", err)
    }
    log.Println(string(body))
}
```

Makes an HTTP GET request via the net/http package

Error handlers with additional handcrafted context

Defers closing a reader—in this case, the response

Prints the response as a string to standard out (or alternative logger)

Error handlers with additional handcrafted context

This example shows a more formal way to retrieve and print the body of a simple HTTP GET request. The HTTP client can go far beyond this example to deal with proxies, perform Transport Layer Security (TLS) handling, set headers and cookies, create client objects, and even swap out the Transport layer. Advanced TCP connections such as long-lived Websockets and server-sent events have both built-in standard library and third-party support. We look at those types of connections in chapter 8.

Note the defer keyword in listing 1.4. Any defer line is executed at the end of that code block—in this case, the main() function. In general, we do this as a cleanup method on any Reader, although in this example, there is no real negative effect. We'll talk more about this topic in chapter 4. For now, keep in mind that defer gets pushed onto the call stack, so the earlier you define it, the less likely it is that a subsequent panic will preclude its call.

Creating an HTTP server with Go is a common task. What Go provides in the standard library is powerful enough to operate at scale, easy to understand, and flexible enough to handle complex applications. Chapter 8 is dedicated to getting up and running with an HTTP server, including routing, cookie handling, and authentication. We'll tackle some of those complex use cases in that chapter.

HTML

If you're working with web servers, you're likely to work with HTML as well. The html and html/template packages provide a great start for generating web pages. Whereas the html package deals with escaping and unescaping HTML, the html/template package deals with creating reusable HTML templates, allowing you to substitute patterns for variables and control logic from the Go side. The security model for handling the data is documented, and helper functions are available for working with HTML, JavaScript, and more. The template system is extensible, making it an ideal base for more complicated functionality while providing good functionality to help anyone get started.

CRYPTOGRAPHY

Cryptography has become a common component of applications, whether for dealing with simple hashes or encrypting/decrypting sensitive information. Go provides common functionality including MD5 and Secure Hash Algorithm (SHA) hashing, TLS, Data Encryption Standard (DES), Triple Data Encryption Algorithm (TDEA), Advanced Encryption Standard (AES), Keyed-Hash Message Authentication Code (HMAC), and many others. Additionally, a cryptographically secure random number generator is available via `crypto/rand` in the standard library.

DATA ENCODING

When you share data between systems, the immediate concerns are format(s) and encoding. Did the data come in with Base64 encoding? Does JSON or XML data need to be turned into a local object? These situations are common in our modern networked world.

Go was designed with data encoding in mind. Internally, Go data is handled entirely as UTF-8, which should come as no surprise because the creators of UTF-8 also created Go. Not all data passed around between systems is in UTF-8, however, and you may need to deal with formats that add meaning to the text. To handle the translations and manipulations, Go has packages and interfaces, which provide features such as one that turns a JSON string into instantiated objects/structs, and the interfaces enable you to switch between encodings or add ways to work with encodings via external packages.

1.2.3 *Concurrency with goroutines and channels*

Computers with multiple processing cores have become the standard in computers of all forms, from servers to smartphones and even in embedded and microcontroller systems. Until fairly recently, most programming languages were designed with a single-core processor in mind, but Go was designed to work with multiple cores from the start.

Go has a feature called a *goroutine*, a function that can be run concurrently with the main program or other goroutines. Goroutines are managed by the Go runtime, where they're mapped and moved to the appropriate operating system thread and garbage-collected when no longer needed. When multiple processor cores are available, these goroutines can be run in parallel because various threads are running on different processing cores. But even in a single thread, Go handles context switching and concurrent orchestration for you.

From the developer's point of view, creating a goroutine is as easy as writing a function. Figure 1.2 illustrates how goroutines work. If you come from a language that takes an event-driven or async/await approach, this approach may seem different, but it can provide a lot of power for delivering and awaiting information going to and from concurrent operations.

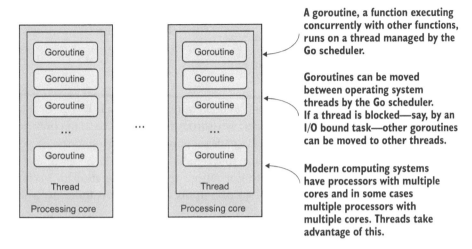

Figure 1.2 Goroutines running in threads distributed on the available processing cores

To further illustrate how goroutines work, let's look at a goroutine that counts from 0 to 4 while the main program prints `Hello World` concurrently, as shown in the following listing.

Listing 1.5 Concurrent output

```
0
1
Hello World
2
3
4
```

This printed output is a mix of two functions printing concurrently. The code that makes it happen is similar to normal procedural programming but with a small twist, as shown in the next listing.

Listing 1.6 Printing concurrently

```
package main

import (
    "fmt"
    "time"
)

func count() {
    for i := 0; i < 5; i++ {
        fmt.Println(i)
        time.Sleep(time.Millisecond * 5)
    }
}
```

Function to execute as goroutine

```
func main() {
    go count()
    time.Sleep(time.Millisecond * 20)              Starts goroutine
    fmt.Println("Hello World")
    time.Sleep(time.Millisecond * 10)
}
```

The count function is a normal function that counts from 0 to 4. To run count in parallel rather than in order, you use the go keyword, which causes main to continue executing immediately. Both count and main execute concurrently. Due to the time.Sleep() commands, you can see the execution in a reliable order.

Channels provide a way for two goroutines to communicate with each other or another process. By default, they block execution, allowing goroutines to synchronize. Figure 1.3 shows a simple example.

Step 1: A goroutine has an instance of a type.

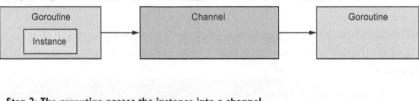

Step 2: The goroutine passes the instance into a channel.

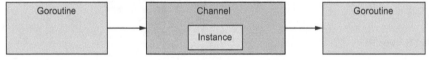

Step 3: The channel passes the instance into another goroutine.

Figure 1.3   Passing variables between goroutines via a channel

In this example, a variable is passed from one goroutine to another through a channel. This operation works even when goroutines are running in parallel on different processor cores. Although this example shows unidirectional information passing, channels can be one-directional or bidirectional, controlled by syntax that indicates the data direction: <- or ->. The following listing is a trivial example of taking advantage of a channel.

Listing 1.7   Using a channel

```
package main

import (
    "fmt"
    "time"
)

func printCount(c chan int) {
    num := 0
    for num >= 0 {
        num = <-c
        fmt.Print(num, " ")
    }
}

func main() {
    c := make(chan int)
    a := []int{8, 6, 7, 5, 3, 0, 9, -1}
    go printCount(c)
    for _, v := range a {
        c <- v
    }
    time.Sleep(time.Millisecond * 1)
    fmt.Println("End of main")
}
```

An int type channel is passed in.

Waits for value to come in

A channel is created.

Starts the goroutine

Passes ints into channel

main pauses before ending.

At the start of `main`, an integer-typed unbuffered channel `c` is created to send data and signals between goroutines. When `printCount` is started as a goroutine, the channel is passed in. As an argument to `printCount`, the channel needs to be identified as an integer channel parameter. In the `for` loop inside `printCount`, `num` waits for channel `c` to send in integers. Back in `main`, a slice of integers is iterated over, and the integers are passed into channel `c` one at a time. When each integer is passed into the channel on `main`, it's received in `num` within `printCount`. `printCount` continues until the `for` loop goes into another iteration and comes to the channel statement again, where it waits for another value to come in on the channel. When `main` is done iterating over the integers, it continues. When `main` is done executing, the entire program is done; therefore, you pause for a millisecond before exiting so that `printCount` can complete before `main` is done. Running this code produces the following listing.

Listing 1.8   Channel output

```
8 6 7 5 3 0 9 -1 End of main
```

Using channels and goroutines together provides functionality similar to that of lightweight threads and internal services that communicate over a type-defined API. You can use various techniques to chain or piece these together. If you think about channels as external listeners that can run concurrently with the rest of your code, you can mentally map how to keep concurrent and/or asynchronous processes running alongside your more linear code.

This book returns to goroutines and channels—two of Go's powerful concurrency concepts—several times. You'll see how they're used to write servers, handle message passing, and delay the execution of tasks. You'll also examine design patterns for working with goroutines and channels, and you'll learn how to use `WaitGroups` to maintain control flow with concurrency.

1.2.4   Go the toolchain: More than a language

Developing scalable, maintainable applications today requires using a bevy of supportive tools beyond the compiler. From the beginning, Go had this requirement in mind. Go is more than a language and compiler. The `go` executable is a toolchain that enables lightweight package management, testing, documentation generation, and more, in addition to enabling users to compile a Go codebase into an executable. Let's look at a few of the components in the toolchain.

PACKAGE MANAGEMENT

Many modern programming languages have package/dependency managers, but until recently, few built them directly into the language toolchain itself. Go does this with `go mod` (for *Go modules*), which is useful for two important reasons. The obvious reason is programmer productivity; the second reason is faster compile time. Package handling was designed with a compiler in mind and is one of the reasons why the compiler is so fast; dependency management is extremely efficient and eliminates some of the complicated header processing in C and C++. Go makes some tradeoffs to achieve this speed, but you'll appreciate the result.

The easiest way to ease into packages is to look at the standard library (see the following listing). This library is built on the package system.

Listing 1.9 Single package import

```
package main

import "fmt"                              ⟵——| The fmt package
                                             | is imported.
func main() {
    fmt.Println("Hello World!")           ⟵——| A function from
}                                            | fmt is used.
```

A package is imported by its name, which can take the form of a local module or a URL and works similarly to a namespace. In this case, `fmt` is the standard library format package. Everything in the package that can be referenced is available with the package name as the prefix. Here, you have `fmt.Println`:

```
import (
    "fmt"
    "net/http"
)
```

Package imports can be grouped in parentheses and should be in alphabetical order (Go has another tool that helps with this task: `go fmt`.) In this case, the `net/http` package is referenced with the `http.` prefix. The import system works with packages from outside the Go standard library, which are referenced like any other packages:

```
import (
    "fmt"
    "net/http"

    "golang.org/x/net/html"          ◁─────  External package
)                                            referenced by URL
```

Package names are unique strings and can be anything. By convention, nonstandard library packages come after standard library packages. Most IDEs that support `go fmt` or `go imports` take care of this task for you. In this case, our last dependency is identified by a URL to external packages, which enables Go to know this unique resource and to get it for us:

```
$ go get ./...
```

The `go get` command can accept a path, such as `golang.org/x/net/html`, to get an individual package. Or you can use `./...`, which walks through the codebase and gets any referenced external packages. The latter case is less common. Here, Go looks at the `import` statement, sees an external reference, gets the package, and makes it available in the current workspace.

Go can talk to version-control systems to get the packages. It can speak to Git when you have those systems installed in your local environment. In this case, Go retrieves the codebase from Git, checks out the latest commit from the default branch, and compiles it directly into your codebase. This process makes it easy for you to include private repositories but may require more configuration for deployment and containerization, as you'll see in chapter 12.

Starting a new project typically begins with using `go mod init [package name]` at the top level of your project. In most cases, you'll use a URL path to your repository as the package name, as in `go mod init github.com/[USERNAME]/[REPO]`. This creates a `go.mod` file that includes the target Go version and any third-party dependencies you might add via `go get`. If you change the target version or remove dependencies manually, `go mod tidy` will clean up the dependency tree and `go.mod` file for you. If you want to install a Go application in your `/bin` or equivalent, `go install [PACKAGE NAME]` will make a binary that you can call from the command line.

When you build a library, you can keep your file structure as files in the root directory or arbitrary subdirectories. When you build an executable, the convention is to nest the `main` and `init` functions within subdirectories of `./cmd`, as in `./cmd/host/main.go`. Go's test and build tools will complain if you have more than one `main` function in files in the same directory.

TESTING

Testing is a critical aspect of software development, and to proponents of test-driven development (TDD), it's the most important. Go provides a testing system that includes a package in the standard library, a command-line runner, code-coverage reporting, and race-condition detection. Creating and executing tests is fairly straightforward, as shown in the next listing.

Listing 1.10   Reverse `Hello World`

```go
package main

import (
    "bufio"
    "fmt"
    "log"
    "os"
    "strings"
)

func reverseName(name string) string {          // Makes a slice of bytes for each character
    reversed := make([]byte, 0)
    for i := len(name) - 1; i >= 0; i-- {       // Reverses through the string and appends characters to the slice
        reversed = append(reversed, name[i])
    }
    return string(reversed)                      // Returns the result as a string
}

func main() {
    fmt.Print("Enter your name: ")
    reader := bufio.NewReader(os.Stdin)          // Accepts a name from standard input into a reader
    name, err := reader.ReadString('\n')         // Makes a slice of bytes for each character
    if err != nil {
        log.Fatal("could not read from stdin", err)
    }
    name = strings.TrimSpace(name)               // Removes any leading or trailing space

    reversed := reverseName(name)                // Calls the reverseName method
    fmt.Println(reversed, ",olleH")              // Outputs the result
}
```

Starting with a variant form of a `Hello World` application, wherein you theoretically reverse user input, you have a function, `reverseName`, that can be tested. Go's naming convention for test files is that they end in `_test.go`. This suffix tells Go that the file is to be run when tests execute and excluded when the application is built, as shown in the next listing.

Listing 1.11   Reverse `Hello World` test

```go
package main

import (
    "log"
```

```
    "strings"
    "testing"
)

func TestName(t *testing.T) {
    name1 := reverseNameFixed(strings.TrimSpace("William"))
    expected1 := "mailliW"

    if !strings.EqualFold(name1, expected1) {
t.Errorf("Response from reverseName is unexpected
value. got [%s], expected [%s]", name1, expected1)
    }

    name2 := reverseNameFixed(strings.TrimSpace("Mister 🌍"))
    expected2 := "🌍 retsiM"
    log.Println(name2, expected2, len(name2), len(expected2))
    if !strings.EqualFold(name2, expected2) {
        t.Errorf("Response from reverseName is unexpected
        value. got [%s], expected [%s]", name2, expected2)     }
}
```

Although our reverse function looks generally correct, we introduced a subtle bug that may not be visible when testing by hand. When `go test` is run, it executes the function that begins with `Test`. In this case, `TestName` is executed, and a struct `t` is passed in to help with testing. It contains useful functionality such as reporting an error. If the name isn't correct, the test reports an error. Note that we used `strings.EqualFold` instead of a literal `==` equality check, which might provide some hint about the bug.

The output of `go test` shows the packages tested and how they fared, as shown in the following listing. To test the current package and the ones nested in subdirectories, you can use `go test ./...`.

Listing 1.12   Running `go test`

```
$ go test
--- FAIL: TestName (0.00s)
listing1_11_test.go:19: Respone from reverseName is unexpected value.
got [???? retsiM], expected [🌍retsiM]
```

The aforementioned subtlety is due to a multibyte, non-ASCII character, which should be better represented by a *rune*, an integer value that represents a Unicode code point. If we change our function to operate on a slice of runes, we fix this problem:

```
func reverseNameFixed(name string) string {
    reversed := make([]rune, 0)
    runes := []rune(name)
    for i := len(runes) - 1; i >= 0; i-- {
        reversed = append(reversed, runes[i])
    }
    return string(reversed)
}
```

With this problem addressed, we can run our test again.

Listing 1.13   Running `go test` **successfully**

```
$ go test
PASS
ok      chapter1. 0.249s
```

This kind of testing helps you identify regressions and common mistakes. Go itself uses these tools for its own language development. If you want something more opinionated, such as behavior-driven development or something in a framework from another language, you can use external packages that build on the built-in functionality. Tests in Go have the full power of the language, which includes third-party packages.

CODE COVERAGE

In addition to executing tests, the test system can generate code-coverage reports and provide a view of the coverage down to the statement level, as shown in listing 1.14. To see the code coverage from the tests, run the following command:

```
$ go test -cover
```

Adding the `-cover` flag to the `go test` command causes it to report code coverage alongside the other details about the tests.

Listing 1.14   Testing with code coverage

```
$ go test -cover
PASS
Coverage: 33.3% of statements
ok   go-in-practice/chapter1/hello          0.011s
```

Code coverage doesn't stop there. You can export coverage into files that other tools can use and use built-in tools to display those reports. Figure 1.4 shows a report displayed in a web browser that indicates which statements were executed in the tests.

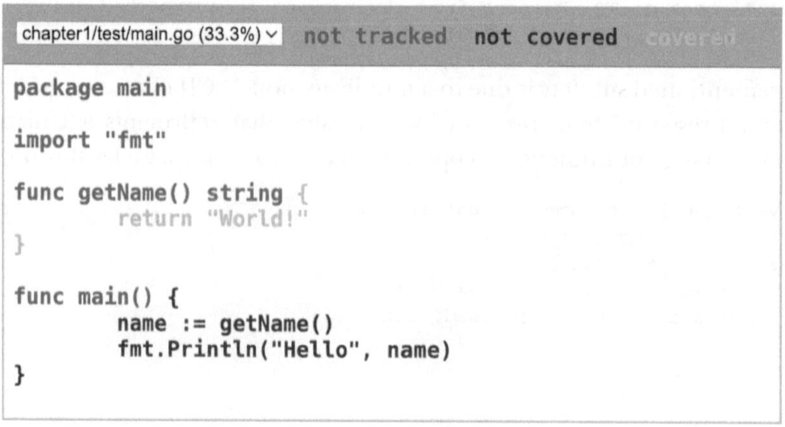

```
chapter1/test/main.go (33.3%) ⌄     not tracked   not covered   covered

package main

import "fmt"

func getName() string {
        return "World!"
}

func main() {
        name := getName()
        fmt.Println("Hello", name)
}
```

Figure 1.4   Code coverage displayed in a web browser

Often, test coverage reports provide details down to the line level. Most modern IDEs support Go's tooling, and in some cases, you can have more tactile control of running tests and formatting results inside the IDE itself. Multiple statements can be on the same line. You can see a simple example in `if` and `else` statements; Go displays which statements were executed and which don't have test coverage in the tests.

> **TIP** For more information about the `cover` tool, see the Go blog at https://go.dev/blog/cover.

Testing is a powerful feature of Go and flexible enough to design with your own approach. Note that listing 1.12 has more than one test case in a single test function. Chapter 6 looks at better options, including test tables.

FORMATTING

Should block indentations use tabs or spaces? Formatting and style questions are regularly discussed and debated when it comes to coding conventions. How much time would we save if these discussions didn't need to happen? With Go, we don't need to spend time debating formatting and other idioms.

Effective Go, available at https://go.dev/doc/effective_go, is a guide to writing idiomatic Go. It describes styles and conventions used throughout the Go community. Using these conventions makes it easier to read and interact with Go programs.

Go has a built-in tool that reformats code to meet many style guidelines. Running the `go fmt` command from the root of a package causes Go to go through each of the `.go` files in a package and rewrite them in the canonical style. The `go fmt` command can have a path to a package or `./...` (iterate over all subdirectories) appended to it. Most contemporary editors—such as Visual Studio Code, JetBrains' GoLand, and Sublime Text—have native or add-on support.

After you've tried `go fmt`, try the `goimports` command, which does formatting *and* adds or removes any missing/unused packages to prevent build problems. Go provides both tools for fine-grained control of code, but in most cases, `goimports` also does everything you need for formatting. To use it, you need to install `goimports` via `go get imports` or grab official extensions for your IDE.

1.3   Go in the vast language landscape

GitHub, the popular code-hosting service, holds projects in hundreds of languages. The TIOBE index, a listing of the most popular programming languages, indicates that those popular languages are capturing a diminishing percentage of the market. More languages have traction. With so many languages available, it's useful to know where Go fits in.

Go was designed to be a systems language. Although it's still a great, performant fit for systems, it's branched out to a lot of different use cases. But at its core, Go is still best for building services and system-level processes.

Being a systems-focused language narrows its focus. Although Go is useful where C or C++ has been used, for example, it's not a good language for embedded systems

largely because of memory management, although projects like TinyGo (https://tinygo
.org) exist to create a smaller footprint. Go has a runtime and a garbage-collection system that don't run well on embedded systems with limited resources, and although
there are ways to tweak them, Go shouldn't be the first arrow in your quiver if you
work on embedded systems.

Comparing Go with other popular programming languages can provide insight
into where it sits relative to those languages. Although we believe that Go is great for
some applications, this book isn't a debate about which programming languages to
use. Choosing the right languages requires taking into account more than the characteristics of those languages.

1.3.1 C and Go

Go came to life as an alternative to C, C++, and Java for developing applications internally. Because the original inspiration came from developing in C (and C is still one of
the most popular languages), it's helpful to examine the similarities and differences
between these languages.

Both languages compile into machine code for target operating system and architecture, but Go goes well beyond what C does, and in almost all cases, it builds much
faster than a nontrivial C project.

C + Go = cgo

Go provides support for binding C libraries to Go programs. Go provides a library of C
compatibility tools. This library eases the transition between, for example, C-style
strings and Go strings. Furthermore, the Go tools can build mixed C and Go programs.
Go also supports Simplified Wrapper and Interface Generator (SWIG) wrappers. You
can get a feel for the features by running `go help c` and `go doc cgo` to read a brief
overview. We look at these tools in more detail in chapter 13.

Go provides a runtime that includes features such as thread management and garbage
collection. When writing Go applications, you give up control of thread management
and work around interruptions for garbage collection as you would with other garbage-collected languages. In C, you manage threads and memory yourself, which
leads to common bugs with memory leaks, buffer overflows, and race conditions. The
application handles any threads and the corresponding work on them. Memory is
intentionally managed without a garbage collector. Although C standards have integrated some concurrency tools, unlike Go, C doesn't have standardized threading
across platforms.

C and its object-oriented derivatives such as C++ enable you to write a wide variety
of applications. High-performance embedded systems, large-scale cloud applications,
and complicated desktop applications can all be written in C. Go is useful as a system,
server, and cloud-platform language. Go applications have a sweet spot that provides
real productivity without the worry of memory management.

The Go runtime and toolchain provide a lot out of the box. This functionality enables Go applications to be written fairly quickly and with less tedious work than a comparable C counterpart. A Go application that takes advantage of all four cores in a server, for example, can use goroutines. The C version would need to start threads and manage the work moved between them in addition to the application code. The C++20 standard introduced coroutines, which work similarly to goroutines but with some less intuitive concepts, such as yielding versus a standard async/await or event-based system.

Compiling C applications can take a long time, especially when you're working with outside dependencies and need to compile them. Speedy compilation of applications in Go was a design goal, and Go applications compile faster—often by a large factor—than their C counterparts. When applications scale in size to the point that compiling can take minutes or hours, saving time in compiling can make a real difference in the productivity of your development. Compiling Go applications is fast enough that many applications and their dependent packages can compile in seconds or less.

1.3.2   *Rust, Zig, Nim, and Go*

The Go language turned out to be a catalyst for new, modern languages that aimed to be C replacements. First and most prominent on that list is Rust.

Whereas Go came from deep within the world of Google in 2009, Rust came from Mozilla in 2015 in an attempt to modernize aspects of the Firefox browser. Although the goals of Rust and Go largely overlap, Rust has skewed a little closer to being designed for operating systems and embedded software—areas Go doesn't focus on. To that point, the Linux kernel has started to incorporate Rust code into its toolchain.

Like Go, Rust has C-style syntax but with a bespoke borrow checker for memory management, which is more complex but provides more granular control for the lifetime(s) of variables and data. Performance is comparable, but Rust outperforms Go when more precise control of lifetime in memory management is beneficial. You won't worry too much about ownership and default immutability in Go.

Zig, which came a year after Rust, focuses on the same niche as Rust, but its coding style is a little more familiar to those who are familiar with C or C++. It also takes a C-like approach to garbage collection: it doesn't have any by default. Instead, it uses smart pointers to inject memory safety.

Another contender in this space is Nim, which eschews C-style syntax for a whitespace-delimited one (similar to Python). Nim has a lot of the same cross-compilation and C-integration goals as Zig, Rust, and Go, and all three languages have native Web-Assembly compilation options for building high-performance web tools.

All three languages are compelling for the same reasons that Go is, but Go is the most mature and has a nice mix of benefits and compromises that make getting started incredibly frictionless. Zig and Nim are newer, more in flux, and more likely to have backward-compatibility problems, whereas Go's team has fought hard for non-breaking changes.

1.3.3   Java and Go

Java, which is consistently one of the most popular and commonly used programming languages on the planet, is used for a wide variety of projects, ranging from server applications to mobile and Android applications to cross-platform desktop applications. Originally, Go was designed as a systems language. Although its use has expanded into areas such as web and mobile development, Go still isn't a language you can use to write a desktop application easily. It excels most when it's used as originally intended.

Given that Java is so popular and can be used for a wider variety of applications, why would anyone want to use Go instead? Although the basic syntax is similar, Java and Go are quite different. Go compiles to a single binary for an operating system. This binary contains the Go runtime, all the imported packages, and the entire application—everything needed to run the program. Java takes a different approach. With Java, you have a runtime installed in the operating system. Java applications are packaged into a file that can be run on any system with the runtime. The applications need to be executed in a compatible runtime version.

These differing approaches, depicted in figure 1.5, have practical implications. Deploying a Go application to a server generally entails deploying a single binary. Deploying a Java application requires installing and maintaining Java on the system along with deploying the application.

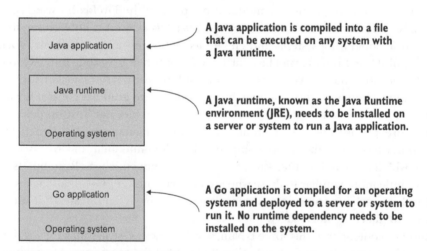

Figure 1.5   Java and Go running in an operating system

Another key difference between Java and Go has to do with how applications are executed. Go programs are compiled into a system binary and executed by the operating system. Java applications are executed in a virtual machine (VM) typically containing a just-in-time (JIT) compiler. A JIT can look at how the code is executing in context and optimize it accordingly.

This raises an important question: is code running a VM with a JIT faster than a compiled binary? The answer isn't straightforward because it depends on the JIT, the code being executed, and more. In tests comparing similar functionality side by side, no clear-cut winner emerges. There may be cases in which specific Java code executes faster in the VM than a compiled binary written in Go (and vice versa).

It's worth noting that Go includes options for garbage collection, which we'll touch on briefly in chapter 13. For the most part, you don't have to worry about how garbage collection works in Go; in most cases, it's unlikely to have any noticeable ill effect on runtime performance. But you can make these optimizations in some cases and even disable garbage collection by setting the environment variable `GOGC= "off"`. It should go without saying, but there are few reasons why you'd need to do that; exercise caution when experimenting with that option.

1.3.4 *Python, PHP, JavaScript, and Go*

Languages such as PHP, Python, and JavaScript (and its superset TypeScript) may seem out of place for comparisons, but as you use Go, you may find the language appropriate for quick scripting in cases when you might have used Python. Running with `go run` is so fast that compilation won't get in the way of changing and testing things quickly.

Python, JavaScript, and PHP are dynamically typed languages, whereas Go is a statically typed language with some dynamic features. Dynamic languages check type at runtime and even perform what appear to be type conversions on the fly. Statically typed languages do type checking based on static code analysis. Go can do some type switching without explicit coercion. Under some circumstances, variables of one type can be turned into variables of a different type, which may seem unorthodox for a statically typed language but is often useful, making code more concise and preventing casting or coercing variables. In TypeScript, the dynamic typing of JavaScript is replaced by better structure and type-checking.

Go has a built-in web server, illustrated in figure 1.6. Applications such as web browsers connect directly to a Go application, and the Go application manages the connection. This provides a lower level of control and interaction with applications that connect. The built-in Go web server handles connections concurrently, taking full advantage of the way the language works. In most production scenarios, applications built in JavaScript, Python, or PHP are proxied by a dedicated web server.

Although all three languages have some third-party alternatives, one reason why it's useful to put Python, JavaScript, and PHP behind a web server has to do with the way these languages handle threads and their concurrency models. The built-in Go web server takes advantage of goroutines to run connections concurrently. The Go runtime manages the goroutines across application threads, as you'll see in more detail in chapter 3. Whereas Python and PHP end up with separate processes for the different connections, Go shares an environment, allowing you to share resources where it makes sense to do so.

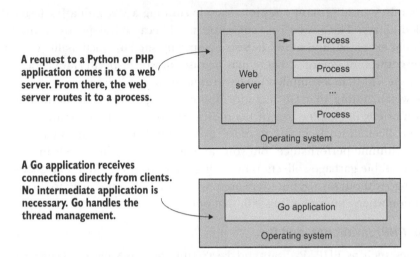

A request to a **Python or PHP** application comes in to a web server. From there, the web server routes it to a process.

A **Go application** receives connections directly from clients. No intermediate application is necessary. Go handles the thread management.

Figure 1.6   Python, PHP, and Go paths of a client request

Go and JavaScript, primarily through Node.js with TypeScript support, can fill a similar space but do so in different ways. Exploring how they fill the space differently highlights where Go fits in the space. With the rise of single-page applications, a swell of support rose for keeping backends and frontends in the same language. JavaScript via Node.js became a viable backend for running servers.

JavaScript has a single-threaded model. Although asynchronous I/O may use separate threads, the main program executes in a single thread. When code in the main thread takes a significant amount of time, it blocks other code from executing. JavaScript uses the event loop model and async/await model for internal context switching and a form of concurrency. Go uses a multithreaded model in which the runtime manages goroutines running concurrently on the different threads. The Go model, with multiple threads running across multiple cores, can take advantage of more of the available hardware than the single thread used in JavaScript.

As we mentioned earlier, Go has a built-in package-handling system. Languages such as Python, PHP, and JavaScript were not designed with one, and bolt-on options such as pip, composer, and npm came later. Being afterthoughts, these options left a lot to be desired; their design and central management have introduced some serious security exploits over the years.

1.4   *Getting up and running in Go*

You have a few options for getting into Go, depending on your level of commitment. The easiest way to get started with Go is to take the tour at https://go.dev/tour/welcome/1, which walks you through some of the language's main features. What separates the Go tour from typical tutorials is how the examples work. You can execute the examples right in your browser. If you want to change them and execute your changes, you can do that as well.

If you want to try executing simple Go applications, you can do that through the Go Playground at https://go.dev/play. The Go Playground enables the tour examples to be executable. Here, you can test code and share a link to it. The examples in this book that represent a program can be executed in the Playground. Another great option for exploring the core language is Go by Example (https://gobyexample.com).

1.4.1   Installing Go

Installing Go is fairly straightforward. Everything you need to know about getting and installing Go is documented at https://go.dev/doc/install, including the operating systems supported and the hardware architectures that can be targeted for these systems.

For Microsoft Windows and macOS, installers take care of installation, which is as easy as installing any other program. Users of Homebrew in macOS can install Go by using the command `brew install go`.

Installing Go in Linux includes a wider variety of options. You can install Go by using built-in package managers, such as `apt-get` and `yum`. The available version is usually an older one; newer versions are faster or contain new features. Through the Go install instructions, you can download the most recent version of Go, put it on your system, and add the Go executables to your path.

1.4.2   Working with Git and version control

To work with packages and external imports stored in version-control systems, Go expects these systems to be installed on the local system. Go doesn't reimplement any software configuration management tools; rather, it knows about them and takes advantage of them when they're installed.

Two of the dominant version-control systems that Go developers use for packages are Git and Mercurial (`hg`). Git is popular, used by numerous Google developers and the packages they release to GitHub. You need to have Git installed, but Go doesn't require a specific version. Any recent version should do.

1.4.3   Exploring the workspace

Go's module isolation means that you can create the root of your Go app anywhere you like. Your entire app should be self-contained, and no dependencies will conflict with other projects.

The one environment variable that you may need to set is `$GOPATH`. This variable points `go` to the base directory for the workspace. Source code, including both the code you're working on and any dependent code, can go in the root (for library code) and subdirectories such as `/src`. Although you'll do some management of this directory, the Go tools will help you manage external source-code repositories. As mentioned earlier, executable targets are usually nested below a top-level `cmd` directory. If you have multiple executables, it's common to have them in their own subdirectories, such as `./cmd/backend/main.go` and `./cmd/frontend/main.go`. Again, this practice is simply a convention; nothing will stop you from choosing another layout.

1.4.4   *Working with environment variables*

The two most common and most useful environment variables are `GOOS` and `GOARCH`, which specify the target operating system and CPU architecture, respectively. They're particularly useful when you're building binaries for systems other than your development machine. Chapter 12 talks about doing this in containers via Docker.

> **TIP**   To explore all available Go-specific environment variables, see https://mng.bz/mGyP.

1.4.5   *Using artificial intelligence tools with Go*

Although they're not related directly to the Go language, the rapid ascent of artificial intelligence (AI) tools like chatbots and other Large Language Models (LLMs) has enabled a period of near-exponential improvements in efficiency. This improvement applies to many fields and industries but especially to developers, who now use tools in their IDEs to seek help and generate code.

Periodically in this book, we'll touch on ways to harness AI tools to improve your Go development experience. Although Go is certainly technically capable of handling most machine-learning problems, we won't focus on that use case in this book. Rather, we'll explore ways to use prompt engineering and AI tools to do things like produce test cases, generate test data, and simulate user behavior to strengthen our application development and testing.

1.5   *Hello, Go*

In an obvious twist on the standard `Hello World` program, listing 1.15 shows a simple application that prints `Hello, my name is Inigo Montoya` through a web server. To begin, start in a directory where you want your application to live, and invoke `go mod init hellogo` to initialize a new application. The `hellogo` name is arbitrary but should be unique if you plan on sharing your code. Often, it refers to a unique URL to prevent conflicts, such as `github.com/[USERNAME]/[REPO]`. You'll see a `go.mod` file in your directory; this file contains module information and, optionally, dependencies. Now that you've initialized your project, create the following `main.go` file in that same directory.

> **TIP**   If you want to get a sense of the conventional layout of a larger project, move `main.go` into `cmd/example/`, and at the top layer, create a `hello.go` file containing your `Hello()` function. Note the case change; the function name is capitalized for public visibility.

Listing 1.15 `Hello World` web server

```
package main                                    ◁──  The main package is
                                                     used for applications.
import (
    "fmt"
    "net/http"                      Import needed packages
)

func hello(w http.ResponseWriter, r *http.Request) {          Handler for an
    fmt.Fprint(w, "Hello, my name is Inigo Montoya")          HTTP request
}

func main() {
    http.HandleFunc("/", hello)                     Main application
    http.ListenAndServe("localhost:4000", nil)      execution
}
```

This simple application has three parts. It opens with a package declaration. Where libraries are declared with a short name describing what they do, such as `net` or `crypto`, applications have the package `main`. To write strings and operate as a web server, the `fmt` and `http` packages are imported. Importing these packages makes them available in the code and in the compiled application.

The application execution begins with the `main` function, which has no arguments or returned values. Following the first line of `main`, the `http.HandleFunc` function is called, telling the web server to execute the function `hello` when the path / is matched. The `hello` function follows an interface for handlers. It receives an object for the HTTP request and response, followed by a call to `http.ListenAndServe` telling the web server to start up and listen on port `4000` of the domain `localhost`.

You can execute this application in two ways. In the next listing, you use `go run`, which compiles the application into a temp directory and executes it immediately.

Listing 1.16 Running `inigo.go`

```
$ go run inigo.go
```

The temporary file is cleaned up when the application finishes running. This is useful in developing new versions of applications that are tested regularly.

> **TIP** If you want to format your file(s) automatically, run `go fmt` or `goimports` in this directory. Per convention, you could move it into `./cmd/inigo/main.go`, but given that this project is a single-file project, keep it simple.

After the application starts, you can open a web browser and visit `http://localhost:4000` to view the response, shown in figure 1.7.

Figure 1.7 `Hello, my name is Inigo Montoya` **viewed in web browser**

Alternatively, you can build and run an application as shown in the following listing.

Listing 1.17   Building `inigo.go`

```
$ go build inigo.go
$ ./inigo
```

Here, the first step is building the application. Using `go build` without filenames builds the current directory. Using a filename (or set of filenames) or a wildcard pattern builds only the selection. From there, the built application must be executed. By convention, compiled binaries are created in the `bin` directory, but you can output the binary wherever you like. To choose your destination, use the `-o` flag, as in `go build -o bin/inigo inigo.go`.

Summary

- The Go philosophy of simplicity plus extensibility created a useful language and enabled an ecosystem to surround it.
- Go offers features that take advantage of modern hardware, such as goroutines that enable concurrent execution.
- The toolchain that accompanies the Go language—including testing, package management, formatting, and documentation—allows developers to build highly tested and safe applications.
- Go is a powerful, fast, general-purpose systems language, comparable to languages such as C, Java, JavaScript, Python, and PHP.

A solid foundation: Building a command-line application

This chapter covers

- Working with command-line flags, options, and arguments
- Passing configuration into an application
- Starting and gracefully stopping a web server
- Path routing for web and API servers

This chapter covers several foundational areas for developing command-line interface (CLI) applications. You'll learn about handling command-line options—sometimes called *flags* or *getopts*—in a way that's consistent with modern applications for Linux and other Portable Operating System Interface (POSIX) systems.

We'll follow up by looking at several ways to pass configuration into an application, including environment variables and various popular file formats used to store configuration. You'll also learn a bit about structs and interfaces; you'll see how to couple them tightly to maintain state for configuration. You'll look at Go's enum support and drawbacks as part of this topic.

From there, you'll move on to building and starting a simple server from the command line and learning best practices for starting and stopping it. Last, you'll learn

URL path-matching techniques for websites and servers, providing a Representational State Transfer (REST) API, which will give your server a bit more functionality.

2.1 Building CLI applications the Go way

Whether you're using a console application (system commands, the source-control management system Git, or an application such as the MySQL database, among many others), command-line arguments and flags are part of the application user interface. The Go standard library has built-in functionality for working with these arguments and flags, and it handles many of the hard parts and edge cases easily and elegantly.

> **Windowed applications**
>
> As a systems language, Go doesn't provide native support for building graphical user interface (GUI) applications like the ones you find in Microsoft Windows or macOS. There are libraries and frameworks that can create non-native GUI applications, but nothing is built into the standard library. Along with several QT or GTK bindings, you may find something similar to the popular JavaScript cross-platform framework Electron in Wails, which allows you to combine Go as a backend and web technologies (HTML, CSS, and JavaScript) as a frontend to make desktop applications. You can find out more at https://github.com/wailsapp/wails.

2.1.1 Command-line flags

Argument and flag handling in the Go standard library is based on Plan 9, which has a different style from the systems based on GNU/Linux and Berkeley Software Distribution (BSD), such as macOS and FreeBSD, that are wide used today. On Linux and BSD systems, for example, you can use the command `ls -la` to list all files in a directory. The command is `ls`, and the `-la` part of the command contains two flags, or options. The `l` flag tells `ls` to use the long form listing, and the `a` flag (for *all*) causes the list to include hidden files. The Go flag system won't let you combine multiple flags; instead, it sees one flag named `la`, partly because Go treats short command-line flags (`-la`) the same as long ones (`--la`).

GNU-style commands such as `ls` support long options (such as `--color`) that require two dashes to tell the program that the string `color` isn't five options (with a duplicate in this case), but one. Whether this style suits you boils down to preference.

This built-in flag system doesn't differentiate between short and long flags. A flag can be short or long, and each flag must be separate from the others. If you run `go help build`, for example, you'll see flags such as `-v`, `-race`, `-x`, and `-work`. For the same option, you'll see a single flag rather than a long or short name. To illustrate default flag behavior, the following listing shows a simple console application using the `flag` package.

Listing 2.1 `Hello World` **CLI using** `flag` **package**

```
$ flag_cli
Hello World!
$ flag_cli -name Buttercup
Hello Buttercup!
$ flag_cli -s -name Buttercup
Hola Buttercup!
$ flag_cli --spanish -name Buttercup
Hola Buttercup!
```

Each flag is separate from the rest and begins with - or --, which are used interchangeably. A method is available to define a flag with a short or a long name, but as you see in the next listing, it's not implicit.

Listing 2.2 `Hello World` **using command-line flags**

```
package main

import (
    "flag"          ◁——— Imports the standard
    "fmt"                 flag package
)
                                              Creates a new
                                              variable from
var name = flag.String("name", "World", "A name to say   a flag
hello to.")                              ◁———
var inSpanish bool
func init() {                            New variable
                                         to store flag
flag.BoolVar(&inSpanish, "spanish", false, "Use  value
Spanish language.")                      ◁———┘

flag.BoolVar(&inSpanish, "s", false, "Use Spanish    Sets variable to
language.")                              ◁———┘         the flag value
    flag.Parse()                         ◁——— Parses the flags,
}                                             placing values
                                              in variables
func main() {
    if inSpanish {
        fmt.Printf("Hola %s!\n", *name)  ◁——— Accesses name
    } else {                                  as a pointer
        fmt.Printf("Hello %s!\n", *name)
    }
}
```

Here you see two ways to define a flag. The first is to create from a flag a string typed variable with a default value of "World". In this example, you do this by using flag.String(). flag.String takes a flag name, default value, and description as arguments. The value of name is an address containing the value of the flag. To access this value, you need to access name as a pointer (as you would in a C-variant language).

The second method of handling a flag is the one that explicitly defines both a long and a short variant. Start by creating a normal variable of the same type as the flag.

This variable will be used to store the value of a flag. Then use one of the flag functions that places the value of a flag in an existing variable. In this case, `flag.BoolVar` is used twice, once for the long name and once for the shorthand version.

> **TIP** Flag functions exist for each basic data type, including `bool`, `string`, `int` (and unsigned and larger capacity variants), `byte`, `float32`, and `float64`. All these types follow a similar, predictable pattern. Both `flag.StringVar` and `flag.IntVar`, for example, try to assign an input argument to a variable of their respective types. To learn about them, see the `flag` package documentation at https://pkg.go.dev/flag.

Finally, to set the flag values in the variables, run `flag.Parse()`. The `flag` package provides an exit response with a default help response, but only if invalid or erroneous flags are passed to your application. In this case, what happens if you pass both `--spanish` and `-s`? They're Booleans, so including them without a value assignment will result in a `true` value. If you pass `--spanish=true` and `-s=false`, the value will be `false` because `flag.Parse()` runs through the flags in the order in which you declare them. This fact is important to keep in mind because you can allow one version of a flag to overwrite the others. We'll look at some alternatives in section 2.1.4.

Listing 2.3   Invoking built-in help descriptions

```
$ flag_cli --invalidFlag        ⟵    An invalid flag is passed
Usage of ./flag_cli:                 through the command line.
  -name string                  ⟵
        A name to say hello to. (default "World")    The usage help
  -s    Use Spanish language.                        text is returned
  -spanish                                           in this case.
        Use Spanish language.
```

This can also happen if you attempt to pass an incompatible type to your application, such as a number to the `-name` argument. Go won't attempt to coerce the value into the expected type, so passing a `float` when your application expects an `int` also triggers an early exit. One exception is a `time.Duration`, which is automatically typecast from an integer.

> **TIP** When you're working with `time.Duration` in mathematical operations, sometimes you'll have to cast an integer to a `time.Duration` manually by wrapping it with the `time.Duration`, as in `weekAgo := time.Now().Add(time.Duration(7 * 24) * time.Hour)`.

The `flag` package has two handy functions you can use to take more control of this messaging. The `PrintDefaults` function generates help text for flags. The line of help text for the preceding `name` option reads as follows:

```
-name string
    A name to say hello to. (default "World")
```

This feature is a nicety in Go that makes it easier to inform users how your program works and how they can interact with it.

Flags also have a `VisitAll` function that accepts a callback function as an argument. This function iterates over each of the flags executing the callback function on it and allows you to write your own help text for them. The following listing would display `-name: A name to say hello to. (Default: 'World')`.

Listing 2.4 Custom flag help text

```
flag.VisitAll(func(flag *flag.Flag) {
    format := "\t-%s: %s (Default: '%s')\n"
    fmt.Printf(format, flag.Name, flag.Usage, flag.DefValue)
})
```

You can also run through the entire list of passed arguments by calling `flag.Args()`, which skips flags passed with - or -- but shows other arguments given to your application as a slice of strings. These arguments aren't parsed and aren't subject to validation by `flag.Parse()`.

2.1.2 *Defining valid values via enums*

Let's detour briefly by expanding our example to support multiple languages. We'll do this to set the stage for demonstrating one of Go's less robust features and showing when and why to use it.

Suppose that you want to support English, Spanish, German, and French. In many strongly typed languages, you might reach for an enumeration (*enum*) as shown in the following listing.

Listing 2.5 Defining valid options in an enumeration

```
package main

import (
    "flag"
    "log"
)

var name = flag.String("name", "World", "A name to say hello to.")

type language = string          ⟵—— Defines a type alias to string

var userLanguage language       ⟵—— Our destination value

const (                         ⟵—— An enumeration of constants
    English language = "en"
    Spanish          = "sp"
    French           = "fr"
    German           = "de"
)
```

```
func init() {
    flag.StringVar(&userLanguage, "lang", "en", "language
    to use (en, sp, fr, de).")
    flag.Parse()
}
```

Assigns our variable's value via flag

```
func main() {
    switch(userLanguage) {
    case English:
        log.Printf("Hello %s!\n", *name)
    case Spanish:
        log.Printf("Hola %s!\n", *name)
    case French:
        log.Printf("Bonjour %s!\n", *name)
    case German:
        log.Printf("Hallo %s!\n", *name)
    }
}
```

A switch around our defined values, outputting our response by language

At the top, you declare an enum of languages. There is no enum keyword, which probably is helpful because enums don't necessarily work as you might expect. If you run this code and pass any valid language, you'll get the output you expect.

But if it's an enumeration, what happens if you pass --lang="xy"? Don't panic. There's no output because you've simply assigned input to a string type alias. This example highlights a possible shortcoming of enums compared with other languages: you can think of them as maps of constants to values. They offer little value here. Yes, you can have a default switch case or get a list of values from a map to return feedback to users, but this example mostly demonstrates a case in which Go doesn't do what you might expect of a language with true enum support. You're probably better off defining a slice or map of valid languages and checking for validity inside init().

Here's a quick example of validation. This code formalizes valid values in a slice and checks upon initialization:

```
validLanguages = []string{
    "en",
    "sp",
    "fr",
    "de",
}

func init() {
    flag.StringVar(&userLanguage, "lang", "en", "language
    to use (en, sp, fr, de).")
    flag.Parse()
    if slices.Contains(validLanguages, userLanguage) == false {
log.Fatalf("Invalid language %s. Please use one of %v",
userLanguage, validLanguages)
    }
}
```

2.1.3 *Slices, arrays, and maps*

Go has several approaches for lists/arrays/vectors and dictionaries. The standard library provides more data structure-like lists in its container packages, but for homogeneous collections, slices and arrays suffice for most use cases. Slices and arrays differ only in that slices have an unbounded length and arrays have a fixed length. The `flag.Args()` method returns a variable-length collection of strings and adds non-flagged, whitespace-delimited arguments to the slice.

For dictionary-like support, maps allow assignment via any type as a key and any type as a value. Support for generics also allows some flexibility on slice types, but you won't see built-in tuple-like heterogeneous support because slices need to satisfy the interfaces for ordering and comparability. You can build this yourself on top of the `interface{}` or any types. These are known as *empty interfaces* because they have no methods that must be satisfied. We'll talk more about this topic in chapter 3.

2.1.4 *Command-line frameworks*

Although the built-in `flag` package is useful and provides the basics, it doesn't provide flags in the manner that most of us have come to expect. The difference in user interaction between the style used in Plan 9 and the style in Linux- and BSD-based systems is enough to cause users to stop and think, often due to problems they encounter when trying to mix short flags, such as those used to execute a command like `ls -la`.

- *Problem*—Those of us who write for non-Windows systems will likely be working with a UNIX variant, and our users will expect UNIX-style flag processing. How do you write Go command-line tools that meet users' expectations? Ideally, you want to do this without writing one-off specialized flag processing.

  Processing flags certainly isn't the only important part of building a command-line application. Although Go developers learn as a matter of course how to begin with a `main` function and write a basic program, we often find ourselves writing the same set of features for each new command-line program. Fortunately, tools can provide a better entry point for creating command-line programs, and we'll look at one of them in this section.

- *Solution*—This common problem has been solved in a couple of ways. Some applications, such as the software container-management system Docker, have a subpackage containing code to handle Linux-style flags. In some cases, these are forks of the Go `flag` package to which the extra needs are added. But maintaining per-project implementations of argument parsing results in a lot of duplicated effort to solve the same generic problem repeatedly.

  A better approach is to lean on an existing command-line library. You can import several standalone packages into your own application. Many of these packages are based on the `flag` package provided by the standard library and have compatible or similar interfaces. Importing one of these packages and using it is faster than altering the `flag` package and maintaining the difference.

In advanced cases, you can parse a single argument for known tokens by using Go's built-in flag and parser tooling. Some third-party packages take this approach to building something a little different from Go's built-in `flag` package.

If you want something more opinionated and feature-rich for building a console application, frameworks are available to handle command routing, help text, subcommands, and shell autocompletion, in addition to flags. A popular framework used to build console-based applications is Cobra (https://github .com/spf13/cobra), which is used by Docker, Kubernetes, and many others. Another is cli (https://github.com/urfave/cli), which has been used by Docker and other projects such as the open source Platform as a Service (PaaS) project Cloud Foundry. You'll see how to implement the more robust Cobra framework in your command-line applications in the next section.

A SIMPLE CONSOLE APPLICATION

It's useful to look at a console application that executes a single action. You'll use this foundation to expand multiple commands and subcommands. Figure 2.1 shows the structure a single-action application can use from the command line.

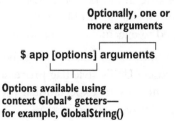

Optionally, one or more arguments

$ app [options] arguments

Options available using context Global* getters— for example, GlobalString()

Figure 2.1   Structure of a simple application

The following listing is a simple console application that displays `Hello World` or says `hello` to a name you choose.

Listing 2.6   Running `Hello World` in CLI with flags

```
$ hello_cli
Hello World!
$ hello_cli --name Inigo
Hello Inigo!
$ hello_cli -n Inigo
Hello Inigo!
$ hello_cli -help
NAME:
   hello_cli - Print hello world
USAGE:
   hello_cli [global options] command [command options] [arguments...]
VERSION:
   0.0.0
COMMANDS:
   help, h   Shows a list of commands or help for one command
```

```
GLOBAL OPTIONS:
   --name, -n 'World'      Who to say hello to.
   --help, -h              show help
   --version, -v           print the version
```

When you use Cobra, the application-specific code required to generate this application is only a dozen lines; it handles short and long flags, provides feedback for users, and more. You have to do a bit of a restructuring of the standard Go application by wrapping your `main`'s functionality as a `&cobra.Command`, which contains the logic necessary to add all the nice features that otherwise would require a lot of boilerplate.

Listing 2.7 Hello World! CLI: `hello_cli.go`

```go
package main

import (
    "fmt"

    "github.com/spf13/cobra"
)

var helloCommand *cobra.Command        ◁─── Creates a cobra.Command
                                            pointer, which wraps our
                                            app's functionality

func init() {
    helloCommand = &cobra.Command{      ◁─── Initializes our command,
        Use:   "hello",                      with details on usage
        Short: "Print hello world",
        Run:   sayHello,
    }
    helloCommand.Flags().StringP("name", "n", "World",    ◁─── Defines a flag
    "Who to say hello to.")                                    with long and short
    helloCommand.MarkFlagRequired("name")                 ◁─── version and help text
    helloCommand.Flags().StringP("language", "l", "en",        Marks the flag
    "Which language to say hello in.")                    ◁─── "name" as required
    }                                                     ◁─── Defines our language
                                                               flag but doesn't mark
func sayHello(cmd *cobra.Command, args []string) {             it as required
    name, _ := cmd.Flags().GetString("name")              ◁─── Extracts the name and
    greeting := "Hello"                                        language from Cobra
    language, _ := cmd.Flags().GetString("language")      ◁───
    switch language {                                     ◁─── Our language
    case "en":                                                 switch
        greeting = "Hello"
    case "es":
        greeting = "Hola"
    case "fr":
        greeting = "Bonjour"
    case "de":
        greeting = "Hallo"
    }
    fmt.Printf("%s %s!\n", greeting, name)
}

func main() {
    helloCommand.Execute()        ◁──── Executes our command
}
```

As you can see, a little more wrapping is happening here than in your straightforward code, but it's structurally similar. You use Cobra to define commands with a slice of arguments, which can be extracted within the function.

The basic setup for grabbing the arguments themselves is fairly ergonomic and similar to the standard library. These arguments aren't bound to a variable automatically, so we need to extract them to work with them within our target command.

`cli.go` enables you to have a default action when the application is run, including commands and nested subcommands. (The next section covers commands and subcommands.) Here, you set the `Action` property that handles the default action. The value of `Action` is a function that accepts `*cli.Context` as an argument and returns an error. This function contains the application code that should be run. In this case, it obtains the name to say hello to by using `c.GlobalString("name")` before printing `hello` to the name. If you want the returned error to cause the application to exit with a nonzero exit code, return an error of `cli.ExitError`, which you can create using the `cli.NewExitError` function.

The final step is running the application that you just set up. To do this, pass `os.Args` (the arguments passed into the application) into the `Run` method of the application.

> **TIP** Arguments are available to the `Action` function, having been passed to the `Run` initializer method. In this case, you can obtain a string slice of arguments by calling `c.Args`. The first argument would be `c.Args()[0]`.

COMMANDS AND SUBCOMMANDS

Applications built for the command line often have multiple context-specific conditional arguments, which we'll call commands and subcommands (figure 2.2). Think

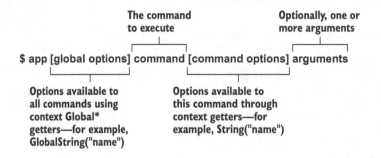

Figure 2.2   Usage structure of an application with commands and subcommands

of an application such as Git, in which we can run commands such as `git add`, `git commit`, and `git push origin/main`. This isn't uncommon, but using the wrong subcommand with a command can produce errors, as in `git add origin/main`.

To illustrate using commands, the following example is a simple calculator application that takes a command and two positional arguments.

Listing 2.8   A basic CLI calculator

```go
package main

import (
    "log"
    "strconv"

    "github.com/spf13/cobra"
)

func operation(op string, n1 string, n2 string) (float32, error) {
    num1, err := strconv.Atoi(n1)
    if err != nil {
        return 0, err
    }
    num2, err := strconv.Atoi(n2)
    if err != nil {
        return 0, err
    }
    fl1 := float32(num1)
    fl2 := float32(num2)
    switch op {
    case "add":
        return fl1 + fl2, nil
    case "sub":
        return fl1 - fl2, nil
    case "mul":
        return fl1 * fl2, nil
    case "div":
        return fl1 / fl2, nil
    }

    return 0, nil
}

var cmdAdd = &cobra.Command{
    Use:   "add",
    Short: "Add two numbers",
    Long:  "Add two numbers: add <number1> <number2>",
    Run: func(cmd *cobra.Command, args []string) {
        result, err := operation("add", args[0], args[1])
        if err != nil {
            log.Fatal(err)
        }
        log.Printf("result: %f\n", result)
    },
```

```go
    Args: cobra.ExactArgs(2),
}

var cmdSub = &cobra.Command{
    Use:   "sub",
    Short: "Subtract two numbers",
    Long:  "Subtract two numbers: sub <number1> <number2>",
    Run: func(cmd *cobra.Command, args []string) {
        result, err := operation("sub", args[0], args[1])
        if err != nil {
            log.Fatal(err)
        }
        log.Printf("result: %f\n", result)
    },
    Args: cobra.ExactArgs(2),
}

var cmdMul = &cobra.Command{
    Use:   "mul",
    Short: "Multiply two numbers",
    Long:  "Multiply two numbers: mul <number1> <number2>",
    Run: func(cmd *cobra.Command, args []string) {
        result, err := operation("mul", args[0], args[1])
        if err != nil {
            log.Fatal(err)
        }
        log.Printf("result: %f\n", result)
    },
    Args: cobra.ExactArgs(2),
}

var cmdDiv = &cobra.Command{
    Use:   "div",
    Short: "Divide two numbers",
    Long:  "Divide two numbers: div <number1> <number2>",
    Run: func(cmd *cobra.Command, args []string) {
        result, err := operation("div", args[0], args[1])
        if err != nil {
            log.Fatal(err)
        }
        log.Printf("result: %f\n", result)
    },
    Args: cobra.ExactArgs(2),
}

func main() {
var calculator = &cobra.Command{Use: "calculator", Short: "A simple
calculator"}
    calculator.AddCommand(cmdAdd)
    calculator.AddCommand(cmdSub)
    calculator.AddCommand(cmdMul)
    calculator.AddCommand(cmdDiv)
    calculator.Execute()
}
```

Although this calculator isn't robust by any measure—it accepts only two numbers and does no computation parsing—it shows some of Cobra's comfort features. We can add commands to commands, separate commands to route based on an initial argument, and requirements for the number of subcommands needed to route and process the command properly.

2.2 Handling configuration

A second foundational area that complements flag handling is persistent application configuration. Examples of this form of configuration include the files in the `etc` directory in some Linux installations and user-specific configuration dotfiles such as .gitconfig and .bashrc.

Passing configuration to an application is a common need. Virtually every nontrivial application, including console applications and servers, needs some form of persistent configuration. How can configuration information be easily passed to your applications and made available in them?

Whereas the preceding section talks about passing in more ephemeral configuration via command-line options, this section looks at passing in configuration via files—or, in the case of 12-factor apps, using environment variables. In this section, we will add support for common configuration formats, including JSON, YAML, and INI. Then we present the approach favored in the 12-factor pattern, which passes in configuration through environment variables.

Understanding 12-factor apps

This popular, widely used methodology for building web applications, Software as a Service (SaaS), and similar applications observes the following 12 factors:

- Use a single codebase, tracked in revision control, that can be deployed multiple times.
- Explicitly declare dependencies and isolate them from other applications.
- Store application configuration in the environment.
- Attach supporting services.
- Separate the build and run stages.
- Execute the application as one or more stateless processes.
- Export services via Transmission Control Protocol (TCP) port binding.
- Scale horizontally by adding processes.
- Maximize robust applications with fast startup and graceful shutdown.
- Keep development, staging, and production as similar as possible.
- Handle logs as event streams.
- Run admin tasks as separate processes.

You can find more details on these factors at https://12factor.net.

2.2.1   *Using configuration files*

Command-line arguments, like those covered earlier in this chapter, are good for many things and should be used for applications with functional variables in practical use. But when it comes to one-time configuration of a program installed in a particular environment, command-line arguments aren't the right fit. They need to be fed to the application repeatedly and are vulnerable to typos and mistakes. The most common solution is to store configuration data in a file that the program can load at startup. In the next few sections, you'll look at the three most popular configuration file formats and see how to work with them in Go:

- *Problem*—A program requires persistent configuration that may be too complex for command-line arguments.
- *Solution*—One of today's most popular configuration file formats is JavaScript Object Notation (JSON). The Go standard library provides built-in JSON parsing, unmarshaling, and marshaling.
- *Discussion*—Consider a JSON configuration file, `config.json`, with the following structure:

```
{
    "enabled": true,
    "path": "/usr/local"
}
```

The following listing demonstrates a JSON configuration parser.

Listing 2.9   Parsing a JSON configuration file: `json_config.go`

```
package main

import (
    "encoding/json"
    "fmt"
    "os"
)
type configuration struct {
    Enabled bool          A type capable of holding
    Path    string        the JSON values
}
func main() {
    file, err := os.Open("config.json")      Opens the
    if err != nil {                          configuration file
        panic(err)
    }
    defer file.Close()
    decoder := json.NewDecoder(file)          Parses the JSON into
    conf := configuration{}                   a variable with the
    err = decoder.Decode(&conf)               variables
    if err != nil {
        fmt.Println("Error:", err)
    }
```

```
        fmt.Println(conf.Path)
}
```

This method has only a few parts. First, a type or collection of types needs to be created via a struct representing the JSON file. The names and nesting must be defined and mapped to the structure in the JSON file. Because each field and property of this struct must be accessible to a package, each must begin with an uppercase letter, which effectively makes the properties public. Linters will warn you if you miss this requirement; otherwise, you may not notice when parts of your structure aren't unmarshaled properly. This is true not just of JSON unmarshaling but also of any struct that must share properties with another package. The main function begins by opening the configuration file and decoding the JSON file into an instance of the configuration struct. If no errors occur, the values from the JSON file will be accessible in the `conf` variable and can be used in your application.

> **NOTE** JSON parsing and handling have many features and nuances. Chapter 11, which covers working with JSON APIs, discusses JSON features in detail.

> **TIP** Notice that we shadow the variable `err` the second time we assign it to the `Decode()` method's return value. Error handling and bubbling in Go can be tricky for users who are comfortable with other patterns, and in some cases, you can ignore error return values by using the _ blank identifier. It's important to avoid getting into the habit of ignoring errors, though, and reassigning the `err` value or surrounding the code with { ... } block scoping is a good way to handle errors without much boilerplate. Chapter 4 talks more about error handling. Storing configuration in JSON is useful if you're familiar with JSON, if you use a distributed configuration store such as etcd, or if you want to stick with the Go standard library. JSON files can't contain comments, which is a common complaint when developers are creating configuration files or generating examples of them. It can also be a little brittle because its structure is so rigid. But you can use other options.

With the following two formats and techniques, you can use in-configuration comments to self-document the files better:

- *Solution*—YAML (a recursive acronym that means *YAML Ain't Markup Language*) is a human-readable data serialization format. YAML is easy to read, can contain comments, and is fairly easy to work with. Using YAML for application configuration is common and a method that we recommend and use. Although Go doesn't ship with a YAML processor, several third-party libraries are readily available. You'll look at one in this chapter.
- *Discussion*—Consider this simple YAML configuration file:

```
# A comment line
enabled: true
path: /usr/local
```

The following listing is an example of parsing and printing configuration from a
YAML file.

Listing 2.10   Parsing a YAML configuration file

```
package main

import (
    "fmt"

    "github.com/kylelemons/go-gypsy/yaml"          ◁──┤ Imports a third-party
)                                                       YAML parser

func main() {
    config, err := yaml.ReadFile("conf.yaml")      ◁──┤ Reads a YAML file
    if err != nil {                                     into a struct parser
            fmt.Println(err)
        return
    }
    var path string
    var enabled bool

    path, err = config.Get("path")
    if err != nil {
        fmt.Println("`path` flag not set in conf.yaml", err)
        return
    }

    enabled, err = config.GetBool("enabled")
    if err != nil {
        fmt.Println("`enabled` flag not set in conf.yaml", err)
        return
    }

    fmt.Println("path", path)                       ┤ Prints the values
    fmt.Println("enabled", enabled)                   from the YAML file

}
```

TIP We are again shadowing our error return value to avoid creating unnecessary variables, but notice that we're also returning early from `main` when an
unrecoverable error occurs. This pattern is useful for avoiding boilerplate
code, generating irrelevant errors, and dealing with `switch` and `if`/`else` logic.
We talk about error bubbling and handling, as well as the merits of early
returns, in chapter 4.

To work with YAML files and content, listing 2.10 imports the `github.com/kylelemons/`
`go-gypsy/yaml` package. This package, which we use and recommend, provides features that read YAML as a string or from a file, deal with different types, and turn configuration into YAML output.

Using the function `ReadFile`, the configuration file is read in and returns a `File`
struct from the `yaml` package. This struct provides access to the data in the YAML file.
Using the `Get` method, we can obtain the value of a string. For our second value,

`enabled`, we use the type-specific method `GetBool`, which coerces the type under the hood to a Boolean value. Other type-specific methods return their respective coercions and return types.

- *Solution*—INI, a format that's been widely used for decades, is another format that your Go applications can use. Although the Go developers didn't include a processor in the language, once again, libraries are readily available to meet your needs. Like YAML, INI has some readability advantages over JSON.
- *Discussion*—Consider the following INI file:

```
; A comment line
[Section]
enabled = true
path = /usr/local # another comment
```

In the following listing, this file is parsed, and you can see how to use the internal data.

Listing 2.11 Parsing an INI configuration file

```
package main

import (
    "fmt"
    "os"

    "github.com/go-ini/ini"              ← Includes third-party
                                           package to parse INI files
)
func main() {
    config, err := ini.Load("conf.ini")   ←
    if err != nil {
        fmt.Println(err)
        os.Exit(1)
    }                                                       Prints the
                                                            value of the
    fmt.Println(config.Section("Section").Key("path").String())  ← "path" setting
    enabled, err :=
    config.Section("Section").Key("enabled").Bool()       ←    Enables
    if err != nil {                                            parsing while
        fmt.Println(err)                                      checking for
        os.Exit(1)                                            the value's
    }                                                         existence
    fmt.Println(enabled)       ←   Prints the value of the
}                                  "enabled" setting
```

In this case, the third-party package `github.com/go-ini/ini` handles parsing the INI file into a data structure. This package provides a means to parse INI files and strings similar to JSON handling in the standard library.

Using the `config` value, the INI file's sections and respective values can be accessed via its getter function. In the case of string data types, we get either a set value or Go's default value for the type. We access the value `path` within the INI section `Section` as a string value.

When we attempt to read our Boolean value, though, we face a challenge. How do we know whether a value is explicitly `false` or simply falsey? In other words, does `false` mean that the value was set to `false` in the INI file or that it doesn't exist? This library provides a few methods for discerning the answer. In this case, we check for an error if the value doesn't exist; otherwise, we proceed as expected.

The `github.com/go-ini/ini` package has useful features, such as reading multiple INI files at the same time, providing default values for a type, and writing to INI files. For more information, see the package documentation at https://ini.unknwon.io.

> **TIP** You may notice that although you're again returning early from `main` if you encounter an unrecoverable problem, you're also returning an OS exit code. You can take multiple approaches to terminate a program early (such as `panic` or `log.Fatal`, as in chapter 1), and taking this one is useful when you want to distinguish between error codes and have them logged properly at the OS level.

2.2.2 Configuration via environment variables

The venerable configuration file certainly provides a great vehicle for passing configuration data to programs. But some emerging environments defy some of the assumptions we make about traditional configuration files. Sometimes, the one configuring the application doesn't have access to the filesystem at the level we assume. Some systems treat configuration files as part of the source codebase (and thus as static pieces of an executable), which removes some of the utility and flexibility of configuration files.

Nowhere is this trend clearer than in emerging PaaS cloud services. You usually deploy into these systems by pushing a source-code bundle to a control server (a `git push`, for example) into a continuous integration/continuous development (CI/CD) pipeline. But the only runtime configuration you get on such servers is done with environment variables, eschewing config files deployed with containers. Let's take a look at a technique for working in such an environment.

- *Problem*—Many PaaS systems don't provide a way to specify per-instance configuration files. Configuration opportunities are limited to a small number of environmental controls, such as environment variables. Containerized applications need these controls at build time. We'll look at containerization techniques in chapter 12.
- *Solution*—Today, 12-factor apps, commonly deployed to Heroku, Amazon Web Services' (AWS's) Elastic Container Service, and other cloud equivalents, are becoming more common. One factor of a 12-factor app is storing the configuration in the environment, which provides a way to have a different configuration for each environment in which an application runs.
- *Discussion*—Consider the environment variable `PORT`, containing the port a web server should listen to. The following listing retrieves this piece of configuration and uses it when starting a web server.

In the next listing, we show a common pattern for validating the existence of a critical environment variable and terminating if it doesn't exist.

> **Listing 2.12   Environment variable-based configuration**

```
package main

import (
    "fmt"
    "net/http"
    "os"
)

func main() {
    var port string
    if port = os.Getenv("PORT"); port == "" {
        panic("environment variable PORT has not been set!")
    }
    http.HandleFunc("/", homePage)
    http.ListenAndServe(":"+port, nil)
}

func homePage(res http.ResponseWriter, req *http.Request) {
    if req.URL.Path != "/" {
        http.NotFound(res, req)
        return
    }
    fmt.Fprint(res, "The homepage.")
}
```

Annotations:
- Retrieves the PORT from the environment
- Terminates if the environment variable isn't set
- Uses the specified port to start a web server

This example uses the `http` package from the standard library. You may remember it from the simple `Hello World` web server in listing 1.15. We cover web servers in the next section.

Retrieving configuration from the environment is fairly straightforward. From the `os` package, the `Getenv` function retrieves the value as a string. When no environment variable is found, an empty string is returned. In this case, we choose to terminate early by panicking if we haven't set the value, preventing unnecessary errors.

Because all environment variables are technically stored and retrieved as string values, you may need to convert the string to another type. In this instance, you can use the `strconv` package. If the PORT in this example needed to be an integer, for example, you could use the `ParseInt` function.

> **WARNING**   Be careful with the information in environment variables and the processes that can obtain that information. A third-party subprocess started by your application could have access to the environment variables, for example. It's also good practice to namespace your configuration variables to prevent conflicts. Instead of naming your target variable PORT, for example, you can call it MYAPP_PORT. When you're building containerized apps, a build stage will help you isolate these variables from the run stage. We look into this topic in depth in chapter 12.

2.3 Working with real-world web servers

Although the Go standard library provides a great foundation for building web servers, you may want to change some options and add some tolerances. Two common topics covered in this section are matching URL paths to callback functions (known as *routing*) and starting and stopping servers with an interest in gracefully shutting down.

Web servers are a core feature of the `http` package, which uses the `net` package as the foundation for handling TCP connections. Because web servers are a core part of the standard library and are in common use, we introduced simple web servers in chapter 1. This section moves beyond basic web servers to cover some practical gotchas in building applications.

> **NOTE** For more information on the `http` package, visit https://pkg.go.dev/net/http.

2.3.1 Starting up and shutting down a server

Using the `net` or `http` package, you can create a server, listen on a TCP port, and start responding to incoming connections and requests. But what happens when you want to shut down that server? What if you shut down the server while users are connected or before all the data (such as logs and user information) has been written to disk?

The commands used to start and stop a server in the operating system should be handled by an initialization daemon. Using `go run` in a codebase is handy during development; you can use it with some systems based on 12-factor apps, but this approach isn't typical or recommended. Starting an application manually is simple but isn't designed to integrate nicely with operations tools or to handle problems such as unexpected system restarts. Initialization daemons were designed for these tasks and perform them well.

Most operating systems have a default toolchain for initialization. The systemd tool (https://www.freedesktop.org/wiki/Software/systemd), for example, is common in Linux distributions such as Debian and Ubuntu. If systemd uses a script, you'll be able to use commands like those in the following listing.

Listing 2.13   Starting and stopping applications with upstart

```
$ systemctl start myapp.service        ⟵⎤ Starts the application myapp
$ systemctl stop myapp.service         ⟵⎤ Stops the running application myapp
```

A wide variety of initialization daemons is available. The daemons vary depending on your flavor of operating system, and numerous ones exist for various versions of Linux. You may be familiar with some of their names, including upstart, init, supervisor, and launchd. Because configuration scripts and commands vary widely among these systems, this book doesn't cover them. These tools are well documented, and many tutorials and examples are available.

NOTE We recommend that you don't run your applications as daemons; instead, use an initialization daemon to manage the execution of the application as well as rules for service health and automatic restarts. Some reverse-proxy web servers, such as NGINX, operate as daemons themselves. Although NGINX offers a ton of features, Go's built-in servers generally perform without an overarching web server. So unless and until you need those specific features, we recommend that you point a daemon directly to your service. Kubernetes and other cloud container orchestration tools work like daemons without running them as standalone processes on the OS level.

2.3.2 Graceful shutdowns using OS signals

When a server shuts down, you'll often want to stop receiving new requests, save any data to disk, and end existing open connections cleanly. The http package in the standard library shuts down immediately and doesn't provide an opportunity to handle any of these situations. In the worst cases, this situation results in lost or corrupted data:

- *Problem*—To prevent data loss and unexpected behavior, a server may need to do some cleanup on shutdown.
- *Solution*—To handle these, we can listen to OS-level signals and catch them in a context to ensure that we don't drop existing connections. By choosing a reasonable timeout, we can give existing connections a chance to complete before we close the server.
- *Discussion*—Chapter 5 digs deeper into concurrency. Here, we can combine our HTTP handlers with Go's goroutines and OS signals to be smarter about how we stop our servers. Don't worry too much about the details of the goroutine at this point; we'll get into the nitty-gritty in chapter 5.

To handle graceful shutdowns better, we can use a goroutine to manage a concurrent process. We can use that to listen to signals and do other concurrent work, but in this case, we'll arbitrarily stop our server with a timeout using the Shutdown() method. See the following listing.

> **Listing 2.14 More graceful shutdown using signals**

```
package main

import (
    "fmt"
    "net/http"
    "os"
    "os/signal"
    "time"
)

func main() {
    handleFunc := newHandler()          Gets instance of a
    server := &http.Server{             server and handler
```

```go
        Addr:    ":8080",
        Handler: handleFunc,
    }

    ch := make(chan os.Signal, 1)            Sets up a channel to listen
    signal.Notify(ch, os.Interrupt, os.Kill)  for specific signals

    go func() {
        server.ListenAndServe()          ◁──── Starts the web server
    }()

    time.Sleep(5 * time.Second)
    <-ch
    if err := server.Shutdown(nil); err != nil {   On signal, adds
        panic(err)                                  a 5-second delay
    }
}

type handler struct{}

func newHandler() *handler {
    return &handler{}
}

func (h *handler) ServeHTTP(res http.ResponseWriter,
req *http.Request) {
    query := req.URL.Query()                    ◁─┐  Our handler
    name := query.Get("name")
    if name == "" {
        name = "Inigo Montoya"
    }
    fmt.Fprint(res, "Hello, my name is ", name)
}
```

The main function begins by getting an instance of a handler function capable of responding to web requests. This handler is a simple Hello World response method. In its place, you could use a more complex handler for routing rules, such as a path or regular expression handler (listing 2.17).

To shut down gracefully, you need to know when it's appropriate to do so. The signal package provides a means to get signals from the operating system, including signals to interrupt or kill the application. The next step is setting up a concurrent channel that receives interrupt and kill signals from the operating system so that the code can react to them. ListenAndServe, like its counterpart in the http package, blocks execution. To monitor signals, a goroutine needs to run concurrently. The channel waits until it receives a signal. After a signal comes in, it sends a message to Shutdown on the server. This message tells the server to stop accepting new connections and shut down after all the current requests are completed. Calling ListenAndServe in the same manner as with the http package starts the server.

TIP The server waits only for request handlers to finish before exiting. If your code has separate goroutines that need to be waited on, they would have to happen separately, using your own implementation of `WaitGroup`.

This approach has several advantages:

- It allows current HTTP requests to complete rather than stopping them mid-request. Although not guaranteed through this code, you could extend it to wait until there are no active connections to allow your signal channel listener to shut down the server.
- It stops listening on the TCP port while completing the existing requests, opening the opportunity for another application to bind to the same port and start serving requests. If you're updating versions of an application, one version could shut down while completing its requests, and another version of the application could come online and start serving.
- It ensures that any in-flight data processing (such as form/file uploads, multi-statement database inserts, and file processing) is complete before the application exits.

One disadvantage exists under some conditions:

- In some cases, one version of an application wants to hand off exiting socket connections currently in use to another instance of the same application or another application. If you have long-running socket connections between a server and client applications, the shutdown will prevent this from ever happening.

2.3.3 Routing web requests

One of the fundamental tasks of any HTTP server is to receive a given request and map it to an internal function that can return a result to the client. This routing of a request to a handler is important; do it well, and you can build web services that are easy to maintain and flexible enough to fit future needs. This section presents various routing scenarios and solutions.

We start with simple scenarios and solutions, but we encourage you to plan ahead. The simple solution we talk about first is great for direct mappings but may not provide the flexibility that a contemporary web application needs. Starting with version 1.22, the Go `http` library provides more flexibility for handling advanced routing.

MATCHING PATHS TO CONTENT

Web applications and servers providing a REST API typically execute different functionality for different path and request method combinations. Figure 2.3 illustrates the path portion of the URL compared with the other components. In the `Hello World` example from chapter 1, listing 1.15 uses a single function to handle all possible paths. For a simple `Hello World` application, this approach works. But a single function doesn't handle multiple paths well and doesn't scale to real-world applications. This section covers multiple techniques for handling distinct paths and, in some

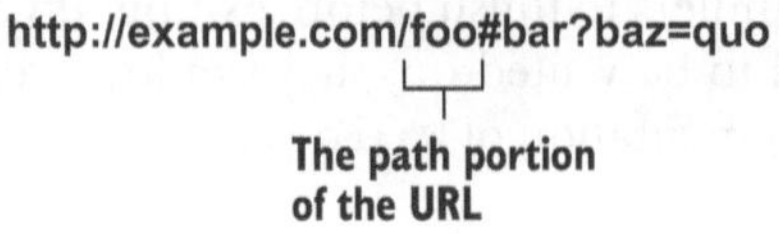

http://example.com/foo#bar?baz=quo

The path portion
of the URL

**Figure 2.3   The path portion of the URL
used in routing requests**

cases, different HTTP methods, such as GET, POST, PUT, and DELETE (sometimes referred
to as *verbs*).

- *Problem*—To route requests correctly, a web server needs to be able to parse the
  path portion of a URL quickly and efficiently and direct incoming requests to
  the proper response handler.
- *Solution (multiple handlers)*—To expand on the method used in listing 1.15, this
  technique uses a handler function for each path. This technique, presented in
  the guide Writing Web Applications (https://go.dev/doc/articles/wiki), uses a
  simple pattern that can be great for web apps with only a few simple paths. As
  you'll see in a moment, this technique has nuances that may make you consider
  it one of the most powerful techniques available.
- *Discussion*—Let's start with a simple program that uses multiple handlers,
  shown in the following listing.

In the next listing, we add a few more handlers and paths so we can direct the application's logic based on the request.

Listing 2.15   Multiple handler functions: `multiple_handlers.go`

```go
package main

import (
    "fmt"
    "net/http"
    "strings"
)

func main() {
    http.HandleFunc("/hello", helloHandler)
    http.HandleFunc("/goodbye/", goodbyeHandler)          // Registers URL
    http.HandleFunc("/", homePageHandler)                 // path handlers
    if err := http.ListenAndServe(":8080", nil); err != nil {
        panic(err)
    }                                   // Attempts to start the web server on
}                                       // port 8080 or quits if an error occurs
func helloHandler(res http.ResponseWriter, req *http.Request) {   // Handler function mapped to /hello
    query := req.URL.Query()
    name := query.Get("name")
    if name == "" {                     // Gets the name from
        name = "Inigo Montoya"          // the query string
    }
    fmt.Fprint(res, "Hello, my name is ", name)
}
```

```go
func goodbyeHandler(res http.ResponseWriter, req *http.Request) {
    path := req.URL.Path
    parts := strings.Split(path, "/")
    name := parts[2]
    if name == "" {
        name = "Inigo Montoya"
    }
    fmt.Fprint(res, "Goodbye ", name)
}
func homePageHandler(res http.ResponseWriter, req *http.Request) {
    if req.URL.Path != "/" {
        http.NotFound(res, req)
        return
    }
    fmt.Fprint(res, "The homepage.")
}
```

Looks in
the path
for a name

Handler
function for
/goodbye/

Checks the path to
decide whether the
page is the home
page or not found

Home and
not found
handler
function

NOTE Content collected from an end user should be sanitized before using it. That includes displaying the content back to a user because, in some cases, unsanitized user content injected into a response could deliver a malicious JavaScript payload. This functionality is part of the templating Go package covered in chapter 9.

Here, you use three handler functions for three paths or path parts. When a path is resolved, it tries to direct traffic from the most specific to the least specific. In this case, any path that isn't resolved before the / path resolves to this one.

The handler function `helloHandler` is mapped to the path `/hello`. As arguments, the handler functions receive an `http.ResponseWriter` and an `http.Request`. In this route, an optional name to say hello to can be in a query string with a key of `name`. The requested URL is a property on `http.Request` of the type `url.URL`. The `Query` method on the URL returns either the value for the key or an empty string if no value is available for the key. If the value is empty, it's set to `Inigo Montoya`.

TIP The `net/url` package, which contains the URL type, has many useful functions for working with URLs.

NOTE To differentiate among HTTP methods, check the value of `http.Request .Method`, which contains the method (`GET`, `POST`, and so on).

The `goodbye` function handles the path `/goodbye/`, including the case in which additional text is appended. In this case, a name can optionally be passed in through the path. A path of `/goodbye/Buttercup`, for example, sets the name to `Buttercup`. You split the URL by using the `strings` package to find the part of the path following `/goodbye/`.

The `homePage` function handles both the / path and any case in which a page isn't found. To decide whether to return a `404` (`page not found`) message or home page content, check the `http.Request.Path`. The `http` package contains a `NotFound` helper function that can be used to set the response HTTP code to `404` and send the text `404 page not found`.

TIP   The `http` package contains the `Error` function, which you can use to set the HTTP error code and respond with a message. The `NotFound` function takes advantage of this for the 404 case.

Using multiple function handlers is the core way to handle different functions alongside different paths. The pros of this method include the following:

- As the basic method in the `http` package, it's well documented and tested, and examples are right at hand. It requires no additional libraries or dependencies.
- The paths and their mappings to functions are easy to read and follow. Keep in mind that these functions can also be written inline, provided that they're small enough to maintain readability.

Additions to the `net/http` library in Go version 1.22 largely invalidated some concerns about earlier routing capabilities, including the following:

- Previously, there was no way to differentiate routes by HTTP method. When you create REST APIs, the verb (such as GET, POST, or DELETE) often requires significantly different functionality, which forces a lot of boilerplate code in addition to your handler deciding what to do with each respective method.
- Virtually every handler function needed to check for paths outside their bounds, returning a `Page Not Found` message. In listing 2.15, the handler `/goodbye/` receives paths prepended with `/goodbye`. Anything returned by any path is handled here, so if you want to return a `Page Not Found` message for the path `/goodbye/foo/bar/baz`, that task needs to be addressed inside each handler. Changes in precedence and URL variables after Go version 1.22 have expanded options in these handlers, which previously required a third-party routing/ muxing library.

Using multiple handlers is useful in simple cases. Because this approach doesn't require packages outside the `http` package, the external dependencies are kept to a minimum. If an application is going to move beyond simple use cases, one of the following techniques is likely to be a better fit, providing more advanced routing options.

HANDLING COMPLEX PATHS WITH WILDCARDS

The preceding technique is straightforward, but as you saw, it's decidedly inflexible in path naming. You must list every single specific path that you expect to see. For larger applications or for applications that follow the REST recommendations, you need a more flexible solution.

- *Problem*—Instead of specifying exact paths for each callback, an application may need to support wildcards or other URL patterns to respond accurately from the server.
- *Solution*—Go provides named variables in its routes as well as more specific precedence. These allow you to extract a variable from a path without needing deduplication logic inside your handlers.

▪ *Discussion*—The following listing builds a router that uses path matching to map URL paths and HTTP methods to a handler function.

The next listing shows how to use patterns inside HTTP requests to route as well as maintain a value for use within your handler.

Listing 2.16 Resolving URLs using `path` package

```
package main

import (
    "fmt"
    "net/http"
)

func main() {
    mux := http.NewServeMux()                              ◁── Creates a new multiplexer (mux)

    mux.HandleFunc("/hello", helloHandler)                   ┐
    mux.HandleFunc("GET /goodbye/", goodbyeHandler)          ├ Adds various endpoints to handle
    mux.HandleFunc("GET /goodbye/{name}", goodbyeHandler)    ┘

    if err := http.ListenAndServe(":8084", mux); err != nil {   ◁── Starts the server or panics if we cannot start it
        panic(err)
    }
}

func helloHandler(res http.ResponseWriter, req *http.Request) {
    query := req.URL.Query()
    name := query.Get("name")                         ┐ Takes the name variable from the query string, if available, or uses a default
    if name == "" {                                   ┤
        name = "Inigo Montoya"                        ┘
    }
    fmt.Fprint(res, "Hello, my name is ", name)
}

func goodbyeHandler(res http.ResponseWriter, req *http.Request) {
    name := req.PathValue("name")
    if name == "" {                           ┐ Accepts an optional path parameter; if available, uses that parameter as name . . .
        name = "Inigo Montoya"      ◁──       ┤
    }                                                  . . . otherwise, uses the default
    fmt.Fprint(res, "Goodbye ", name)    ◁──  Outputs the name as a response
}
```

Here, we've created a multiplexer (mux) that allows us to route requests properly. Note that in the second path, we include an optional HTTP method, which allows us to segment requests by method. This method is useful for following RESTful patterns.

The precedence of a router/multiplexer is often based on a few common patterns. Some patterns don't allow overlapping routes, so they would supercede our /goodbye/ endpoints. Other patterns go with last-in precedence. Another common pattern is longest-match-wins, which is what Go chose. In our example, without two endpoints, we'd have to do more advanced logic inside the handler to pull our request apart. Using the path value gives us quick access to that value.

The Go multiplexer handles more than just these patterns, and we'll dig a bit deeper into them in chapters 8 and 9. In some cases, however, you need more complex routing. Although it's not always advisable to do so due to performance optimizations that other libraries have made, let's walk through building our own simple muxer to allow routing via regular expressions. This use case is not necessarily common; it's more of a demonstration.

You should be aware of the pros and cons of path resolution when using a custom multiplexer over the built-in. Here are the pros of sticking with the standard `http` version:

- It's easy to get started with simple path matching.
- The `path` package is rock-steady, being part of Go's standard library.
- Performance will likely exceed that of using pattern matching such as regular expressions.

The cons have a common thread: the `path` package is generic to paths and not specific to URL paths. The cons are as follows:

- The wildcard capabilities of the `path` package are limited. A path of `foo/{bar}` will match `foo/bar` but not `foo/{bar}/baz`, for example. When `*` is used as a wildcard, it stops at the next `/`. To match `foo/bar/baz`, you'd need to look for a path like `foo/*/*`.
- Because this `path` package is generic rather than specific to URLs, some nice-to-have features are missing, including redirects on bare/path endings.

This method is useful for simple path scenarios with a few routes.

URL PATTERN MATCHING

For most REST-style apps, simple pattern matching with regular expressions is more than sufficient. But what if you want to do something fancy with your URLs? The `path` package isn't well suited to this purpose because it supports only simple POSIX-style pattern matching.

- *Problem*—Simple path-based matching isn't enough for an application that needs to treat a path more like a text string and less like a file path. This is particularly important for matching across a path separator (`/`).
- *Solution*—The built-in path package enables simple path-matching schemes, but sometimes, you need to match complex paths or have detailed control of the path. In those cases, you can use regular expressions to match your paths. You'll combine Go's built-in regular expressions with the HTTP handler and build a fast but flexible URL path matcher.
- *Discussion*—In the next listing, you walk through using paths and a resolver based on regular expressions.

The following listing shows another approach to routing that some of the frameworks employ to route based on regular expressions. It's not something that should be done trivially, as there are some downsides (including security), though we want to demonstrate how built-in routing can be extended to be more expressive.

Listing 2.17 Resolving URLs using regular expressions

```
package main

import (
    "fmt"
    "net/http"          Imports the regular
    "regexp"      ←     expression package
    "strings"
)
                                              Registers paths
func main() {                                  to functions
    rr := newPathResolver()
    rr.Add("GET /hello", helloHandler)
    rr.Add("(GET|HEAD) /goodbye(/?[A-Za-z0-9]*)?", goodbyeHandler)
    if err := http.ListenAndServe(":8080", rr); err != nil {
        panic(err)
    }
}
func newPathResolver() *regexResolver {
    return &regexResolver{
        handlers: make(map[string]http.HandlerFunc),
        cache:    make(map[string]*regexp.Regexp),
        cachedHandlers: make(map[string]http.HandlerFunc),
    }
}

                                         Stores compiled regular
type regexResolver struct {              expressions for reuse
    handlers map[string]http.HandlerFunc
    cache    map[string]*regexp.Regexp        ←    If no path matches, returns
    cachedHandlers map[string]http.HandlerFunc  ←  a Page Not Found error
}

func (r *regexResolver) Add(regex string, handler http.HandlerFunc) {
    r.handlers[regex] = handler
    cache, _ := regexp.Compile(regex)       Sets the method lookup key
    r.cache[regex] = cache                                         ←
}
func (r *regexResolver) ServeHTTP(res http.ResponseWriter, req *http.Request) {
    check := req.Method + " " + req.URL.Path                       ←

    if handlerFunc, ok := r.cachedHandlers[check]; ok {       ←   If in our cached
        handlerFunc(res, req)                                     handlers, skips
        return                                                    the loop . . .
    }

    for pattern, handlerFunc := range r.handlers {             . . . otherwise, finds a candidate
        if r.cache[pattern].MatchString(check) == true {       and sets as cache if it's found
            handlerFunc(res, req)
```

```
                r.cachedHandlers[check] = handlerFunc
                return
            }
    }                                    If no path matches, returns
}                                        a Page Not Found error
    http.NotFound(res, req)      ⟵
}
func helloHandler(res http.ResponseWriter, req *http.Request) {
    query := req.URL.Query()
    name := query.Get("name")
    if name == "" {
        name = "Inigo Montoya"
    }
    fmt.Fprint(res, "Hello, my name is ", name)
}
func goodbyeHandler(res http.ResponseWriter, req *http.Request) {
    path := req.URL.Path
    parts := strings.Split(path, "/")
    name := ""
    if len(parts) > 2 {
        name = parts[2]
    }
    if name == "" {
        name = "Inigo Montoya"
    }
    fmt.Fprint(res, "Goodbye ", name)
}
```

The layout of the regular expression-based path resolution (listing 2.17) is the same as the path-resolution example (listing 2.16). The differences lie in the format of the path patterns registered for a function and in the ServeHTTP method handling the resolution.

Paths are registered as regular expressions. The structure is the same as in the net/http example, with an HTTP method followed by the path, separated by a space. Whereas GET /hello showcases a simple path, a more complicated example is (GET|HEAD) /goodbye(/?[A-Za-z0-9]*)?. This more complicated example accepts either a GET or a HEAD HTTP method. The regular expression for the path accepts /goodbye, /goodbye/ (the trailing / matters), and /goodbye/ followed by letters and numbers. Keep in mind that the order of slices and maps isn't deterministic, so partial matches could be found before longer, more comprehensive ones.

In this case, ServeHTTP first generates our route as a lookup key. Then it checks whether we previously saw and resolved this key. If so, we avoid the inefficiency of the loop and return the handler; if not, the method iterates over the regular expressions looking for a match. When the first match is found, the method executes the handler function registered to that regular expression and set to cache our path lookup to its respective handler. If more than one regular expression matches an incoming path, the first one added is the first one checked and used.

NOTE   Compiled versions of the regular expressions are built and cached at the time they're added. Go provides a Match function in the regexp package that can check for matches. The first step of this function compiles the regular expression. When you compile and cache the regular expression, you don't need to recompile it each time the server handles a request.

Using regular-expression checking for paths provides a significant amount of power, allowing you to fine-tune the paths you want to match. This flexibility is paired with the complicated nature of regular expressions that may not be easy to read, and you'll likely want to have tests to make sure your regular expressions match the proper paths. Go also comes with a `path/filepath` package that can help you reduce complexity a bit by parsing a path, but it requires more high-level/generic routing to use.

By adding a layer of cache, we keep this method a bit more lightweight, but notice that we don't save our cache misses to a handler cache. Each approach has tradeoffs, but assuming a relatively small amount of paths, this prevents allocating growing memory for invalid routes, allowing us to avoid introducing a potential denial-of-service vector.

FASTER ROUTING (WITHOUT THE WORK)

One criticism of Go's built-in `http` package is that its routing and multiplexing (muxing) is basic. In the preceding sections, we showed you some straightforward ways of working with the `http` package, but depending on your needs, you may not be satisfied with the configurability, performance, or capabilities of the built-in HTTP server. Or you may want to avoid writing boilerplate routing code.

- *Problem*—The built-in `http` package isn't flexible enough or doesn't perform well in a particular use case.
- *Solution*—Routing URLs to functions is a frequent problem for web applications. Therefore, numerous packages have been built and tested and are commonly used to tackle the problem of routing. A widespread technique is to import an existing request router and use it within your application.

Popular solutions include the following:

- `github.com/julienschmidt/httprouter` is considered a fast routing package with a focus on using minimal memory and taking as little time as possible to handle routing. It has features such as using case-insensitive paths, cleaning up `/../` in a path, and dealing with an optional trailing `/`.
- `github.com/gorilla/mux` is part of the Gorilla web toolkit. This loose collection of packages provides components you can use in an application. The `mux` package provides a versatile set of criteria to perform matching against, including host, schemes, HTTP headers, and more. Gorilla was recently revived from deprecation and has a long history.
- `github.com/gin-gonic/gin` is a framework similar to Gorilla that focuses on performance, particularly in its zero-allocation router.

- `github.com/bmizerany/pat` provides a router inspired by the routing in Sinatra. The registered paths are easy to read and can contain named parameters such as `/user/:name`. It inspired packages such as `github.com/gorilla/pat`.

> **Sinatra web application library**
>
> Sinatra is an open source web application framework written in Ruby. This framework is used by numerous organizations and has inspired more than 50 frameworks in other languages, including several in Go.

Each package has a different feature set and API. Numerous other routing packages exist as well. With a little investigation, you can easily find a quality third-party package that meets your needs. Although improvements to the Go library have brought support for HTTP method-based routing and path variables, there's more complexity that some websites might benefit from. Some outperform Go's, which is important if you find yourself in the enviable position of needing that sort of scale.

Summary

- Command-line options can be handled in a comfortable and accessible manner, ranging from lightweight solutions to a simple framework for building console-based applications and utilities.
- You can retrieve configuration information from files and environment variables in different ways using various data formats.
- Starting and stopping a web server that works with ops tooling and graceful shutdowns will prevent a bad user experience or loss of data.
- You have several ways to resolve URL paths for an application and route to handler functions.

Structs, interfaces, and generics

This chapter covers

- Using structs to represent data and methods
- Comparing Go's structs and interfaces with object-oriented and functional programming patterns
- Creating interfaces to extend functionality of custom types
- Making code more flexible and reusable by implementing generic types

As we move toward more complex features and approaches in Go, including concurrency, let's first dig into some of the core building blocks of the language. We'll start by going into a little more depth on the nonprimitive data structure in Go. Custom structures, or *structs*, are the cornerstone of how we represent bespoke data and relationships between data. Go provides a system for building, extending, and manipulating data structs. In this chapter, we'll explore how structs, interfaces, and methods work together to empower you to design intuitive data structures and their methods and use them for data isolation/control and state management.

3.1   *Using structs to represent data*

In chapters 1 and 2, we built some basic command-line applications and a web server, using the custom data structures. In Go, structs are powerful language tools that represent rich data structures beyond primitives; you can use them to define the behaviors and data flow of your applications. Used thoughtfully, they keep your code readable and free of cruft and code duplication; they also accommodate encoding data with tags.

As we mentioned earlier, it took the Go language a long time—more than 10 years—to introduce the concept of generics. The reason was partially academic; the language's designers expressed a desire to keep Go lean and minimal without sacrificing functionality. Simplicity and readability have long been considered ideal traits of the language.

The other reason for delay was the potential cost in compile times. C++ specifically carries the weight of compile time in its design, although metaprogramming updates to that language are adding some flexibility.

With the introduction of generics in Go version 1.18, the way we treat our data structures and interfaces has changed a bit. We can generalize our types a bit more, knowing that functions and methods can accept more variation as input parameters. Using this new power, we can keep our code smaller without adding much mental overhead when we read the code.

In this chapter, you'll see how this works and what it adds to the Go language model in the way the syntax is implemented and the freedom it gives developers. We'll also add functionality to these data structures with methods. Then we'll look at how generics—a relatively new concept in Go—allow us to further generalize and simplify our code.

3.1.1   *Creating custom data structures*

At its core, a struct is a user-defined piece of data that can represent anything. In Go, structs generally are similar to C-style structs and have C interoperability (with some exceptions). You can think of them as generic object definitions from other languages or low-level classes in languages without custom complex type support. Here's a basic struct from chapter 2, which represents the configuration data available in a JSON file:

```
type configuration struct {
    Enabled bool
    Path    string
}
```

We can think of this struct as a collection of a data or an object analog in object-oriented languages. In an object-oriented pseudocode, it would look like this:

```
class configuration {
    public enabled boolean;
    public path string;
}
```

In language-agnostic pseudocode, we change the casing. Recall that uppercase attributes in Go structs are effectively public, whereas those that start with lowercase letters are inaccessible to any caller outside their package.

What we put in there—all basic types, complex types, slices, pointers, and so on—is up to us. If a thing can be represented in Go, it can be a struct field. We can also attach other custom types to a struct, which is known as composition or embedding. As we'll see in this chapter, we can use the empty interface or the any type to represent flexible type definitions. This is fairly straightforward, but how we use and operate on this data gives us many choices, as we'll see throughout this chapter.

One thing to note: although we've defined a reusable struct here, we can also create it inline in code or declare an anonymous struct like the one in the following listing.

> **Listing 3.1 A basic anonymous struct**

```
package main

import (
    "fmt"
)

func main() {
    animal := struct {          ← Creates an inline or
        name string                anonymous struct
        speak func() string
    } {
        name: "cat",
        speak: func() string {
            return "meow"
        },
    }

    fmt.Println(fmt.Sprintf("our animal's name is %s and it says %s",
        animal.name, animal.speak() ))     ←
}                                              Calls the speak function and
                                               formats it within a Sprintf string
```

Most of the time, you won't use an anonymous struct, but it's useful when you're dealing with pieces of data you need in only a single method or quickly packing/unpacking data to/from another source, particularly if you don't need all its fields. You'll use anonymous structs in chapter 6, which covers testing. Lightweight structs like this one make for easy, flexible test cases, and you'll use them to create test tables to test myriad conditions against a single method.

Even then, there's very little overhead to defining the struct inline. You usually take this approach when you're quickly marshaling data or encoding a structure in an arbitrary data format.

> **NOTE** We can initialize a new struct with the shorthand declaration as above or via the new keyword, which creates and returns a pointer reference to a zeroed value for that type. There's no real advantage to either approach, so

the choice comes down to preference. If you know the data you want to supply to the struct at creation time, the code is a little cleaner and easier to read when you define the struct with `value := struct{ … }` syntax.

3.1.2   *Functions inside structs*

Listing 3.1 supplied a function as a member of the `animal` struct. Functions are first-class citizens in Go, which means we can pass them and receive them as we would any other data type. Although we can pass functions to functions, callback functions are relatively rare in the wild, though not discouraged. Methods and functions as attributes (as in figure 3.1) are easier to follow and generally more ergonomic, but nothing prevents the use of a callback.

A function can be attached to a custom data type in two ways. The first is as a member, which we did earlier. The advantage is that it sits directly in the definition of the struct itself, alongside any other variables (in this case, `name`). But it lacks the ability to access the parent struct itself. What if we want to do something with the `name` value itself?

For this purpose, we use *methods*, which are functions that are bound to one or more specific types. Methods use the data type as a receiver, and we can create them for any type, including Go's built-in and primitive types.

- *Problem*—We want a function that belongs to a type or a member of that type and can access its properties without having to pass it as an input value. This approach is most useful when we want to modify the structure by reference or need access to more fields than are practical to pass as arguments to a function.
- *Solution*—Use methods, which take a receiver of a type and have access to its fields and other members.

Listing 3.2   Struct methods

```
package main

import (
    "fmt"
)

type Animal struct {          Defines our
    name string               custom type
}

func (a Animal) speak() string {      Defines a method with an
    switch a.name {                   Animal receiver type
    case "cat":
        return "meow"
    case "dog":
        return "woof"
    default:
        return "nondescript animal noise?"
```

```go
    }
}

func main() {
    a := Animal{
        name: "cat",
    }

    fmt.Println(a.speak())

    a.name = "dog"
    fmt.Println(a.speak())

    a.name = "llama"
    fmt.Println(a.speak())
}
```

Calls the speak method
on the data rather than
passing it as a value

This code is cleaner than the preceding example. We have a single `speak` function that returns a different animal noise depending on the receiver's animal name. If we give our method signature a pointer to our variable, `(a *Animal)`, we can mutate values along the way.

NOTE Visibility in Go is dictated by the case of the identifiers. In this case, `Animal` is public to other packages because its first letter is uppercase, but `animal` is not.

- *Discussion*—When to use methods versus functions depends on what you need to pass to a function. It's not ideal to pass around a lot of unnecessary data, so if you have functions that take a lot of input parameters, ask yourself whether using the receiver will reduce the amount of data being passed to and from functions.

  This approach not only reduces code but also allows you to control access to data more precisely. Passing entire structs to miscellaneous receiving functions makes its properties available for reference and potential mutation.

  Another reason to use a method with a receiver is to modify the data within your method. For this purpose, use a pointer receiver for the struct in the method.

TIP As mentioned in chapter 2, Go doesn't have an enum identifier, but enumerated types can be represented by named const values. If we want to constrain our input data in the preceding example, an enum wouldn't fundamentally change our pattern, though we might create a const of valid strings (`"cat"`, `"dog"`) and use the assignment to determine validity. Recall, however, that these values aren't enforced, so we'll have to check validity manually.

In the following listing, we'll use a pointer to the struct to enable mutations to the struct's properties.

Listing 3.3 A pointer receiver method

```
package main

import (
    "fmt"
)

type character struct {
    name string
}

func (ch *character) fixName() {
    ch.name = "Inigo Montoya"
}

func main() {
    ch := new(character)
    ch.name = "Prince Humperdinck"
    fmt.Println("my name is", ch.name)

    ch.fixName()
    fmt.Println("just kidding, my name is", ch.name)
}
```

Creates a character with a pointer via new

Calls the fixName method, which resets the name of the character

Shows the result of our change

Structs are high-level custom data types that can represent and contain any number of first-class data types, including primitives, slices, other structs, and channels, which we'll look at in chapter 4 as part of concurrency. We can use methods on top of structs to prevent unnecessary destructuring and redirection of the underlying data. We can also use methods to modify the struct's contents.

3.1.3 *Anonymous identifiers*

In the structs we've built so far, each field has a name, but a name is not required. Member fields can be anonymous or nameless, assuming that only one member of each type exists in the struct. To demonstrate, let's update our `Animal` struct:

```
type Animal struct {
    string
}
```

We can see that no name is defined for that particular string, which makes it an anonymous member of the struct. Then we can access the struct's value's slightly differently (by the unique type itself):

```
a := Animal{
    "cat",
}

func (a Animal) speak() {
    log.Println(a.string)
}
fmt.Println(a.speak())
```

```
a.string = "dog"
fmt.Println(a.speak())
```

TIP You need a trailing comma after each field of a struct when initializing. This practice is a good habit to get into for languages that support it, and it saves you time debugging parsing errors and copying/pasting data. Go enforces this convention, so you don't have a choice: if you don't follow it, the compiler will prevent you from running or building.

Instead of referencing the name of the field (in this case literally `name`), you reference the field's type. You can see why a struct with more than one unnamed member of a type is not permitted: the compiler wouldn't know which `int64` or string your code is working with.

NOTE If your field is named, you can't optionally access it by its type, even if it's the only member of that type in the struct.

3.1.4   *Tags in structs*

Struct tags are other aspects of structs that will become useful as you build code. *Tags* are annotations that allow you to append metadata to the field. You can use tags for anything you like, but they are used primarily as information on how the data should be encoded in various formats. You'll see this most commonly with XML and JSON encoding from the standard library. Tags are encapsulated by backticks and are expected to include key:value pairs separated by whitespace:

```
type Animal struct {
    name string `help:"the name or type of any animal, as long as it is a cat
    or dog"`
}
```

In this case, we added a little help metadata to our struct. If we want to, we can prevent our `Animal` from speaking unless it's a cat or dog and return the help message to the user:

```
func (a Animal) speak() string {
    switch a.name {
    case "cat":
        return "meow"
    case "dog":
        return "woof"
    default:
        if member, ok := reflect.TypeOf(a).FieldByName("name"); ok {
            return fmt.Sprintf("Invalid animal name: %s",
            member.Tag.Get("help"))
        }
        return "nondescript animal noise?"
    }
}
```

Getting this data requires use of Go's reflection package `reflect`, a powerful set of runtime analysis tools that help you understand how your code is structured and evaluated. When you successfully access a struct's field via `FieldByName`, you can access one or more of its tags—in this case, the `"help"` tag. You can use `reflect` coupled with an `any` type (or an empty interface, `interface{}`) to accept any data type in a field and examine its type within your methods.

> **TIP**   The `reflect` package (`pkg.go.dev/reflect`) has several helpful tools that help you peek into the details of a custom data type, including iterating through it and its tags. In practice, you'd likely return a string and possible error from the `speak` method, so you could represent this constraint as an error with a panic or early return with more helpful information for the user. Reflection comes at a cost at runtime and in code complexity, so it shouldn't be the first tool you reach for. It pops up somewhat frequently in analyzing JSON that has variable formats, such as a field that could be a string or a number.

3.1.5   *Encoding data in JSON format*

As briefly mentioned in chapter 2, the most common use of struct tags is to give a data format encoder information on how the data should be structured. We go into more detail on encoding various formats in chapters 9, 10, and 11. The following listing shows how we can take a struct and its data and design how we want our formatted and encoded JSON file to look.

> **Listing 3.4   Formatting data as JSON**

```
package main

import (
    "fmt"
    "encoding/json"
)

type Animal struct {                              ⟵  Creates our
    Name string `json:"animal_name"`                  Animal struct
    ScientificName string `json:"scientific_name"`
    Weight float32 `json:"animal_average_weight"`   Defines each field with a tag
}                                                   denoting how it should be
                                                    represented in JSON output
func main() {
    a := Animal{
        Name: "cat",
        ScientificName: "Felis catus",
        Weight: 10.5,
    }                           ⟵  Creates our Animal

    output, err := json.Marshal(a)
    if err != nil {
        panic("couldn't encode json")
    }
```

```
    fmt.Println(string(output))
}
```
⟵ **Outputs our JSON-encoded data as a readable string**

Running this code produces the following output:

```
go run union.go
{"animal_name":"cat","scientific_name":"Felis catus",
"animal_average_weight":10.5}
```

Notice first that we changed the `Animal` field(s) to have capitalized names. Remember that the case of a field, struct, or variable determines its public visibility. Uncapitalized names are not available for access from external packages or even files within the same package. In this case, the `encoding/json` functions would be unable to access the member fields if we didn't change them. The name of the struct itself doesn't need to be capitalized because it's passed by value.

Next, we added the tags with the `json:"name"` attribute. If we don't supply these tags, the field name will be used as is, and by convention, capitalized field names aren't used in JSON (though they're valid). We don't have to rename our fields, but doing so gives us more control of the output.

This pattern of tag use is the same for XML and other encoding types. Although help is the next most common use for this tag-based metadata, you can use it for whatever makes sense for your application. For data that's expected to be encoded in several formats, it's unusual to see JSON and XML tags next to each other. In section 3.2, we'll look at Go's struct design and how it compares to and dovetails with object-oriented and functional programming paradigms.

3.2   Contrasts with functional and object-oriented programming

When experienced developers first approach Go (or any other new language), they often start by asking about the structure and design of the language to get a sense of how to use it. Is it a classical object-oriented language like C++ or Java? Is it a pure functional language like Haskell or F#? Does it sit somewhere in between, such as Python or Rust?

Go is a multiparadigm language, which is a way of saying that it's in the in-between range. Languages in this space are not dogmatic; their designers borrowed bits and pieces of many paradigms and languages to develop something that works as a general-purpose language that is internally consistent.

Python, for example, is not a purely object-oriented language, but you can approach it as though it is one and use a lot of the same ideas. Rust is not a purely functional language, but you can approach it as though it is one. The same applies to each language. These languages are well suited to both imperative and declarative programming and don't prescribe the approach between functional and object-oriented other than by convention.

NOTE   Many languages are multiparadigm. A great many paradigms beyond functional and object-oriented exist, such as logical programming, meta-programming, and distributed programming.

In the purest sense, the Go language is not an object-oriented language. If you've come from C++ or Java, some of this is apparent in the lack of explicit inheritance or clear polymorphism. Much is due to syntactic sugar (or the lack thereof). A great deal of what you can do in a pure object-oriented language, you can also do via structs and interfaces in Go. The following listing uses basic Java code with the `Animal` example.

Listing 3.5   Inheritance in Java

```java
public class MyApp {
    public static void main(String[] args) {
        Animal a = new Animal();
        a.speak();

        Cat c = new Cat();
        c.speak();

        Dog d = new Dog();
        d.speak();

        Llama l = new Llama();
        l.speak();

    }
}

class Animal {
    void speak() {
        System.out.println("nondescript animal noise?");
    }
}

class Cat extends Animal {
    void speak() {
        System.out.println("meow");
    }
}

class Dog extends Animal {
    void speak() {
        System.out.println("woof");
    }
}

class Llama extends Animal { }
```

- *Problem*—We're comfortable with the concept of object-oriented programming (OOP) and the way it abstracts concepts, and we want to do something similar in our Go code.

- *Solution*—Use a combination of types to represent object-like data, interfaces to enforce precise requirements between data types, and methods to tie data manipulation to the data types we create. We take the same general ideas from a more traditional object-oriented language and apply it to our code using Go paradigms.

- *Discussion*—Here, we have a top-level class or object called `Animal`. `Cat` and `Dog` inherit and implement traits from the parent or superclass. This example is a logical, hierarchical way of looking at objects in the general sense and comes with useful guardrails that protect the objects from data skew and implementation errors. In this example, Java doesn't force an implementing class to honor all the methods in the abstract class `Animal`, which provides a fallback method as defined in the superclass. This is why the `Llama` implementation provides not a llama noise but the default `Animal` noise. Go has almost everything we need to achieve the same thing, but it's syntactically simpler and less overtly object-oriented in the academic sense.

The next listing shows something relatively close to an object-oriented approach using Go. It's not Java but conveys the same idea.

Listing 3.6 The same idea in Go

```go
package main

import (
    "fmt"
)

type Animal interface {          // Defines the signature of any Animal
    speak()
}

type Cat struct {}               // Defines the structs that implement Animal
func (c Cat) speak() {           // Implementations of our requisite speak() method
    fmt.Println("meow")
}

func NewCat() *Cat {             // Constructor methods return new objects.
    return &Cat{}
}

type Dog struct {}               // Defines the structs that implement Animal
func (d Dog) speak() {           // Implementations of our requisite speak() method
    fmt.Println("woof")
}

func NewDog() *Dog {             // Constructor methods return new objects.
    return &Dog{}
}

type Llama struct {}             // Defines the structs that implement Animal
```

```
func NewLlama() *Llama {          ◄──────  Constructor
    return &Llama{}                        methods return
}                                          new objects.

func main () {

    var a Animal

    c := NewCat()
    a = c
    a.speak()

    d := NewDog()
    a = d
    a.speak()

    l := NewLlama()
    a = l
}
```

This example breaks at compile time with the following error:

```
./animal.go:49:4: cannot use l (type *Llama) as type Animal in assignment:
    *Llama does not implement Animal (missing speak method)
```

The reason is that not every defined struct implements the interface. To make this code work, we need to ensure that the Llama struct implements speak():

```
type Llama struct {}
func (l Llama) speak() {
    fmt.Println("nondescript animal noise?")
}
```

Although this may seem like a limitation, it helps you think about some philosophical questions regarding your application. If your Llama doesn't speak, is it an Animal, and if it is, do all Animals speak? You may be familiar with the canonical example of this phrasing, which brought about the term *duck typing* ("If it walks like a duck and quacks like a duck, it must be a duck"). This helps you design the logic of your applications better and makes your interfaces more intuitive. You can also approximate some of the fallback mechanisms of a superclass; it just looks different in Go. OOP languages often implement similar interfaces as abstract classes, and it's fair to describe Go's as functioning similarly.

Here, we created the interface with the variable a and assigned it to our types that must implement the Animal signature. As we reassign a, the signature must be validated. When we give a Llama a speak() method, the interface is fulfilled, and the code runs without error.

Figure 3.1 attempts to visually demonstrate a subtle philosophical distinction between the direct inheritance and interface satisfaction.

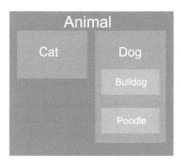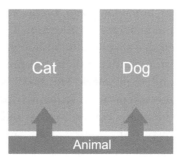

Figure 3.1 **(Left) Inheritance in languages like Java, with** `Poodle` **being a subset of** `Dog`**, which is a subset of** `Animal`**. (Right) Go's model showing the connections between independent types as defined by the interface** `Animal`**.**

An interface in Go is a generalization of a type that provides candidate method signatures. Although the interface itself doesn't contain its own data or the methods that a parent class might, it defines the type(s) of methods we must expect to be available to structs and other interfaces that implement its signature.

As in this example, you'll often use a `New()` style initializer to return your interface and possibly set specific values. This approach can be useful when you're building a module with some properties or fields you want to control more tightly, usually constrained by visibility.

For most of Go's early life, this was the extent of generic programming options in the language. Although some members of the Go team and its users believed that was enough, in version 1.18, official support for generic code with parameterized types was announced. We'll explore that topic in depth later in this chapter.

Although Go is not a textbook object-oriented language, it offers some of the same paradigms in less obvious and less rigid formats. There's no need to provide an explicit `extends` or `implements` keyword because Go handles this task implicitly. Either a type matches the contract of an interface or it doesn't, and you get an error, which is precisely what you saw when you added a `Llama` type that did not implement `speak()`. But you're free to extend any matching interface to include additional methods. `Dogs` can `woof()`, `Cats` can `meow()`, and so on.

This section shows an example of how Go can operate like and be used with the same mental models as an object-oriented language. To some extent, the same approach applies to functional language in this multiparadigm world. Functional languages tend to have stricter qualifying constraints applied to them, in large part because they're used primarily in academia and have a tighter bond with mathematics. Concepts such as pure functions and idempotence are about preventing any information outside the function from changing the result of an operation. There are good reasons for enforcing this kind of constraint, but if the language allows you to go around it, many diehards disqualify the language from being functional.

Go is *not* a functional language, but as with OOP, it can be used like one. Before the introduction of generics in Go version 1.18, you could fairly have argued that Go could not be used that way because although functions are first-class citizens (can be input or output, stored independent of definition), non-typed iterator methods could not be passed as function values. The result is that there was no opportunity to write generic code that could perform sequence operations on any given type.

All that said, idiomatic Go use is rarely inline with the aesthetic of functional programming. Although you can use Go similarly, Go wasn't designed for that purpose. Go's concurrency pattern was designed for passing state and retrieving state from other places. As in OOP, you can glean some patterns from the paradigm, but if you try to use it as you might an OOP or functional language, some approaches won't work or will be antithetical to idiomatic Go.

3.3   *Extending functionality with interfaces*

You saw in the last section how to use interfaces to define the valid method signature(s) of one or more custom types. But you can do a few more interesting things with them. In this section, you'll see how to apply constraints around your data structures. This approach allows you to create contracts that must be satisfied by distinct data types which share functionality.

First, although your `Cat`, `Dog`, and `Llama` types implement the `Animal` interface, this functionality is not restricted to custom types and structs. You can also use interfaces to build a sort of protogeneric functionality for built-in types.

- *Problem*—Your code needs to guarantee that certain structures satisfy interface patterns by having specific attributes and/or functions as part of their declaration.
- *Solution*—Use interfaces, which define these constraints and prevent your code from compiling if an incompatible type is assigned to one.

The following example defines an interface `Shuffleable` and applies it separately to strings and slices of other types.

> **Listing 3.7   Aliasing built-in types to guarantee valid methods**

```
package main

import (
    "encoding/json"
    "fmt"
    "math/rand"
    "strings"
    "time"
)

type Shuffleable interface {          ← Our interface that
    contents() string                      defines what can
    shuffle()                              be shuffled
}
```

```
type shuffleString string                          ←──┐  A type alias
                                                       │  for string
func (s *shuffleString) shuffle() {
    tmp := strings.Split(string(*s), "")
    rand.Shuffle(len(tmp), func(i, j int) {
        tmp[i], tmp[j] = tmp[j], tmp[i]
    })
    *s = shuffleString(strings.Join(tmp, ""))
}

func (s *shuffleString) contents() string {        ←──┐
    return string(*s)                                 │
}                                                     │

func NewShuffleString(init string) *shuffleString {  ←┤
    var s shuffleString = shuffleString(init)         │  Implementations
    return &s                                         │  that satisfy the
}                                ┌─ A type alias       │  Shuffleable
                                 │  for string         │  interface
type shuffleSlice []interface{}  ←──┘                  │

func (sl shuffleSlice) contents() string {         ←──┤
    data, _ := json.Marshal(sl)                       │
    return fmt.Sprintf("%v", string(data))            │
}                                                     │

func (sl shuffleSlice) shuffle() {                 ←──┘
    rand.Shuffle(len(sl), func(i, j int) {
        sl[i], sl[j] = sl[j], sl[i]
    })
}

func init() {
    rand.Seed(time.Now().UnixNano())
}

func main() {
    var myShuffle Shuffleable          ←──── Initializes a Shuffleable

    myShuffle = NewShuffleString("my name is inigo montoya")
    myShuffle.shuffle()
    fmt.Println(myShuffle.contents())        ←──┐
                                                │  Calls its methods
    myShuffle = &shuffleSlice{1, 2, 3, 4, 5}    │
    myShuffle.shuffle()                         │
    fmt.Println(myShuffle.contents())        ←──┘
}
```

If this example seems a bit convoluted, don't worry: it is! We can and will do better. But the general idea here is that we have a signature for built-in types that are aliased by shuffleString and shuffleSlice, both of which are Shuffleable and implement the shuffle() and contents() methods. Using a type alias allows us to add functionality to built-in (and external custom) types in this way:

```
type specialString string // a direct alias to string
type specialInt int8 | int16 | int32 | int64 // using unions to capture
    // multiple integer types
```

Our modest goal is to make both built-in types shuffle their contents and output a result. Why would we need to do this? The answer is that neither built-in type (string or slice) fulfills the interface's signature. By creating an alias type, we guarantee that we can treat both underlying types equally. Notice another interesting use of the interface in the declaration of shuffleSlice:

```
type shuffleSlice []interface{}
```

Here, we define it as a slice of interfaces but fill our initial value with integers. What gives? This slice is known as an *empty interface*, and because it has zero defined methods, it can and will apply to any type.

Sometimes, you'll see this as tantamount to an any type in other languages. The any keyword is a type alias for interface{}. You can use any and interface{} interchangeably, but a lot of legacy code keeps the empty interface{} type. The next section talks more about how to use these sorts of patterns. But keep in mind that in general, returning or accepting an interface means that either the caller or the method itself will likely need to do some work to determine the type being fed or returned (unless you're doing something trivial like logging its value). In practice, it's safer to return a single type from a function if you can to prevent complicated code and/or errors and reduce your testing footprint.

We can do more with interfaces, and we'll dig deeper into their value for testing and debugging in chapter 5. In section 3.4, we'll see how structs and interfaces work with generic programming, one of the new major features of Go.

3.4   *Simplifying code with generics*

As we've hinted before, generics have been a touchy subject in the Go community. For more than a decade, the developers of the Go language eschewed generic programming even while factions of the user base clamored for it. After all, generics can be powerful tools that eliminate the need to writing the same functionality multiple times throughout a codebase. The dev team, however, argued that Go provided the building blocks necessary to do generic programming without explicitly providing a variable input type declaration to functions.

> ### Go's original stance on generics
> Before version 1.18, this reasoning was stated in the Go FAQs (https://mng.bz/5gWz):
>
> "Generics are convenient but they come at a cost in complexity in the type system and run-time. We haven't yet found a design that gives value proportionate to the complexity, although we continue to think about it. Meanwhile, Go's built-in maps and

> slices, plus the ability to use the empty interface to construct containers (with explicit unboxing) mean in many cases it is possible to write code that does what generics would enable, if less smoothly."

We've seen in this chapter how true that last line is. We have a lot of flexibility in using built-in types and interfaces as a form of generic code, but this flexibility often comes with more boilerplate code and hardcoded logic. As mentioned earlier, the empty interface often does a lot of heavy lifting in place of a better generic model, but an empty interface doesn't ensure any guardrails around subsets of valid types as input to functions. For this reason, misusing `interface{}` can create more chances for runtime failures.

How do we best use the strength of generics in our code? To get started, let's refactor our `Animals` a bit. We'll abstract our `Animal` type into an interface that can apply to individual types of `Animal`. Recall that each earlier implementation required its own type-specific functions to satisfy the `Animal` constraint:

```
type Cat struct {}
func (c Cat) speak() {
    fmt.Println("meow")
}

type Dog struct {}
func (d Dog) speak() {
    fmt.Println("woof")
}
```

This code ends up being complicated if we want an interface and subsequently a function to apply to many different types. Our examples work fine for this purpose and are ideal for interfaces. But to demonstrate how generics can work, look at a different implementation.

Listing 3.8 A union type and a generic function parameter

```
package main

import (
    "fmt"
)

type Cat struct {
    wearsBow bool
}

type Dog struct {
    canFetch bool
}
```

```
type AnimalType interface {          ⊲──┤ Prints a formatted
    Cat | Dog                               string to stdout
}

type Animal[T AnimalType] struct {   ⊲──┤ Our interface representing
    value T                                 a union type
    AnimalNoise func() string
}                                                A struct that takes our
                                                 type and a function
func (a Animal[T]) Speak() {         ⊲──
    fmt.Println(fmt.Sprintf("we got a %T", a.value))   ⊲──┤ Prints a formatted
    fmt.Println(a.AnimalNoise())                              string to stdout
}

func main() {
    catAnimal := Animal[Cat]{ value: Cat{ }, AnimalNoise: func() string {
     return "meow!" }}
    dogAnimal := Animal[Dog]{ value: Dog{ }, AnimalNoise: func() string {
     return "woof!" }}

    catAnimal.Speak()
    dogAnimal.Speak()
}
```

This code demonstrates condensing multiple types into a function or method (as in this case). As we mentioned, our interface examples are perfectly fine for doing what we want, but some syntax and functionality are worth pointing out. There's no reason to create this generic in practice; it buys us nothing. We'll jump into a real-world case later in this chapter.

> **NOTE**   Our example uses the T identifier for type, but this can be any identifier you like. This convention comes largely from C++ templates and Java. Although the T is not universally used, many people stick with a single uppercase letter.

The first thing to note is that Dog and Cat are distinct types with no fundamental over-lap, but they're valid union types within the AnimalType interface. An Animal here gets what is called an *instantiation* with its type and has a method, Speak, that executes the supplied callback function.

Although this code doesn't need generics, we could rewrite it by removing the method on the Animal interface and have the Speak method take a typed parameter of AnimalType

```
func Speak[T AnimalType](a Animal[T]) {
    fmt.Println(fmt.Sprintf("we got a %T", a.value))
    fmt.Println(a.AnimalNoise())
}
```

which can infer the type (or not) on invocation:

```
Speak(catAnimal)
Speak[Cat](catAnimal)
```

NOTE The [Cat] type instantiation in our code is often unnecessary; the compiler can infer it.

Another minor thing worth noting is that we're dipping into reflection with this line:

```
fmt.Println(fmt.Sprintf("we got a %T", a.value))
```

The %T formatting verb uses reflection under the hood. You're doing this solely to output the data type the method gets. You may be tempted to use a switch statement inside a generic function to route logic, but doing this can be an antipattern. In theory, you can create a generic function that does pretty much anything you want it to on any type. You could take the input of a string and return an uppercase string or an input of a float and cube it, all from the same function. This would make for some confusing code because the logic and method naming would be muddled and unclear.

3.4.1 Using functions with generics

Overall, generics are more useful for related data types than ornate, custom types like the ones we're demonstrating. We can get by fine with the code we used earlier in this chapter. Better use is for maps or slices of data; the code used for access and manipulation is the same regardless of underlying type.

As an example, we'll try to replicate something like JavaScript's filter. Map, reduce, and filter are common functional patterns in other languages, and this example shows how we can take a functional approach to our Go code.

- *Problem*—As we build out functions that take generic types, we want to apply specific tests against items in an attempt to replicate functional filters and maps common in other languages.
- *Solution*—Create generic functions that loop through items in a slice and apply a test function against them to filter or manipulate individual member items.
- *Discussion*—In the following examples, our passed functions are specific to their type, but we can create functions that operate against multiple discrete types by extending the type with an interface and making sure that all types fulfill it.

Listing 3.9 Implementing a `filter` function

```
package main

import (
    "fmt"
    "unicode"
)

func filter[T any](items []T, fx func(T) bool) []T {      ◁─┐  A generic filter
    var filtered []T                                          function that takes
    for _, v := range items {                                 a slice of any type
        if fx(v) {                                            and a callback
            filtered = append(filtered, v)
        }
```

```
    }
    return filtered
}

func main() {
    strings := []string{"My", "name", "is", "Inigo", "Montoya"}

    strings = filter[string](strings, func(s string) bool {
        return unicode.IsUpper(rune(s[0]))
    })

    fmt.Println(strings)
}
```

The implementation of a slice that will be filtered with the supplied callback

```
go run generic.go
[My Inigo Montoya]
```

In this code, we have a generic `filter` function instantiated with a type that takes an array of any type and applies a callback method to each item in the list, returning a filtered list of only strings that start with a capital letter. This approach is extremely simple but also powerful. We could already do this with a slice of strings. With generics, we can use our `filter` function on a slice of any type we want.

Listing 3.10   Filtering a slice of integers

```
func main() {
    ints := []int{1,2,3,4,5,6,7,8,9,10,11,12,13,14,15}

    ints = filter[int](ints, func(i int) bool {
        if i % 3 == 0 {
            return true
        }
        return false
    })

    fmt.Println(ints)
}
```

Here, we're filtering our list of integers to those that can be divided by 3 without a remainder. We can see why generics work well for slices: no type-checking magic has to happen within them as long as we operate on the slice structure itself. Our generic code can also operate on a smaller subset of types.

Listing 3.11   A `filter` function with specific types

```
type Numeric interface {
    int8 | int16 | int32 | int64 | float32 | float64
}

func filterPositive[T Numeric](items []T) []T {
    var filtered []T
    for _, v := range items {
```

```
        if v > 0 {
            filtered = append(filtered, v)
        }
    }
    return filtered
}


func main() {
    ints := []int8{-4,-3,-2,-1,0,1,2,3,4,}
    ints = filterPositive[int8](ints)
        fmt.Println(ints)

    floats := []float32{-4.5,-3.5,-2.5,-1.5,0.5,1.5,2.5,3.5,4.5,}
    floats = filterPositive[float32](floats)
    fmt.Println(floats)
}
```

Here, we have a type constraint called `Numeric` that we use as valid type for instantiation in `filterPositive`. A slice of any of these types is valid input to the function.
This approach is tighter than duplicating code for different types or referring to
inputs as `[]interface{}` or any types.

> **NOTE** Go's generic functions don't allow you to access individual fields even
> if the candidate types share one or more fields. This design decision may
> change, but if you need to access internal fields and methods, generics may
> not be the right choice.

3.4.2 *Using constraints and type approximations*

In the preceding example, our function accepts a `Numeric` type. If we give it any members of that type constraint, it will happily accept our input. It accepts those types and
only those exact types. But what if we have a custom type?

```
type Smallint int8
```

See what happens when you run this type directly.

Listing 3.12 Exact types

```
package main

import (
    "fmt"
)

type Numeric interface {
    int8 | int16 | int32 | int64 | float32 | float64
}

type Smallint int8
```

```
func doubler[T Numeric](value T) T {
    return value * 2
}

func main() {
    var four Smallint = 4
    fmt.Println(doubler(four))
}
```

You get an error:

```
$ Smallint does not satisfy Numeric (possibly missing ~ for int8
in Numeric)
```

But `SmallInt` is an `int8`! It should work, but exact types means *exact* types. Even though the same underlying type is `int8`, it is still considered its own type and doesn't meet the criteria of our specified constraint. To allow underlying/inherited types to apply as well as exact types, we need to preface the types with a tilde:

```
type Numeric interface {
    ~int8 | int16 | int32 | int64 | float32 | float64
}
```

We'd need to repeat that process for each type to have the same logic apply to basic types such as `int16`, `int32`, and `int64`. But the tilde syntax tells the compiler that it applies to `int8` and any type that has `int8` as an underlying type. This is *type approximation.*

Laying out and switching against every possible variation on a type constraint, as in the `Numeric` interface, can get cumbersome, and it rarely deviates from what's expected. How often will a function need to accept `int8`, `int16`, and `int64` but not `int32`, for example? As we saw earlier, we'll almost always want our constraints to match the same underlying types. This case is where the `constraints` package comes in handy. This package contains the most commonly used constraints available, composed in various useful ways.

We can use `constraints.Signed` to get all signed integers, `constraints.Unsigned` for the unsigned variants, and `constraint.Integer` to get all underlying type integers, for example. The `constraints.Ordered` type encapsulates even more (including strings), but we know we're dealing with numbers, so we'll use `Integer` instead of the `Numeric` type to make the code even smaller.

Listing 3.13 **Using constraints for possible types**

```
import "pkg.go.dev/golang.org/x/exp/constraints"

type Smallint int8

func doubler[T constraints.Integer](value T) T {
    return value * T(2)
}
```

```
func main() {
    var four Smallint = 4
    fmt.Println(doubler(four))
}
```

> **TIP** Constraints are part of Golang's experimental package. You'll need to run `go get pkg.go.dev/golang.org/x/exp/constraints` to import it into your project.

We've explored the power and flexibility of Go's struct system and related ways to generalize and add functionality to our code. Seeing what kinds of data can be associated with a structure lets us design our application in a way that is instinctive and easy for another developer to reason about. Interfaces allow us to build guardrails around unique data types that have common functionality. Generics enable us to reduce or remove code duplication when we'd otherwise have to bind the same general algorithm in a function to multiple data types.

Summary

- Structs and interfaces comprise the building blocks of Go's data structure model.
- We can extend structs by adding functions as fields or members of a struct. We can go further by adding methods, which take a variable of a type as a receiver. This gives us access to other data within the data structure and allows us to modify the data via pointer receivers.
- Go is neither an object-oriented nor a functional programming language, but we can apply some concepts from both to our application designs. Structs, interfaces, and generics help us approximate these paradigms.
- Generics are a new feature of Go. They aren't necessary often, but when they operate on multiple similar types, they can prevent code duplication and make code more composable.

Part 2

Building robust applications

In the second part of this book, we'll take our fundamentals and start to put them into action, building the kind of Go applications that can stand up to real production stresses.

To kick things off, in chapter 4, we'll look at error handling. Go has a rather esoteric pattern for catching and bubbling errors, so we'll look at patterns that allow you to get comfortable with this without creating a nest of complexity.

In chapter 5, we dig into concurrency, one of Go's greatest strengths. You'll learn about goroutines and the Go approach to concurrency, message passing, and asynchronous communication.

Chapter 6 focuses on a critical, if often-overlooked, part of application development: code consistency, testing, and benchmarking. Getting confidence that the code you've written will work is the kind of foundation every developer needs.

In chapter 7, we'll learn how to interact with the filesystem and networking using Go. We'll get down to how Go can help you work with TCP/UDP at a lower level and how to deal with the filesystem using different approaches.

This part finalizes the foundations necessary to start building rock-solid applications for production, which we get into in part 3.

Handling errors and panics

This chapter covers

- Learning idiomatic error handling in Go
- Returning meaningful data with errors
- Adding custom error types the Go way
- Generating and working with panics
- Transforming panics into errors
- Working with panics on goroutines

As Robert Burns famously stated in his poem "To a Mouse," "The best laid schemes o' Mice an' Men/Gang aft agley." Our best plans often still go wrong. No other profession knows this truth as thoroughly as software development. This chapter focuses on handling situations when things go awry.

Go distinguishes between errors and panics—two types of bad things that can happen during program execution. An *error* indicates that a particular task couldn't be completed successfully. A *panic* indicates that a severe event occurred, probably as a result of a programmer error or unexpected environment state, and the program must exit as soon as possible. This chapter presents a thorough look at each category.

We start with errors. After briefly revisiting the error-handling idioms for Go, we dive into best practices. Errors can inform developers about something that has gone wrong, and if error handling is done right, they can also assist in recovering and moving on. Go's way of working with errors differs from the techniques used in languages such as Python, Java, and Ruby. It may at times feel repetitive to deal with errors one by one, but when you use idiomatic techniques, you can write robust code that isolates potential errors very clearly. Programs in Go typically "bubble up" errors to some receiver to be handled in one or more places in the call stack. This type of error propagation is unexpected to some people, but it ultimately yields to a single authority to handle underlying errors. That can be quite powerful when used thoughtfully.

The panic system in Go signals abnormal conditions that may threaten the integrity of a program. Our experience has been that it's used sporadically and often reactively to prevent invalid state mutation or unsatisfiable code branches, so our focus in this chapter is on making the most of the panic system, especially when it comes to recovering from a panic. You'll learn when to use panics, how (and whether) to recover from them, and how Go's error and panic mechanisms differ from those of other languages.

Although Go is occasionally criticized for having a repetitive error system, this chapter illustrates why this system is conducive to building better software with highly readable code. By keeping errors at the forefront of the developer's mind, Go fights against our own cognitive overconfidence bias. When we always keep error handling front and center, Go gets us used to the idea that we have to code defensively, regardless of how good we think we are.

4.1 Error handling

One Go style that often trips up newcomers is its approach to error handling. Many popular languages, including Python, Java, and JavaScript, approach exception handling by throwing and catching special exception objects. Others, like C, often use the return value for error handling and manage the mutated data through pointers.

In lieu of adding `try/catch`-style exception handlers, the Go creators used Go's ability to return multiple values. The most-used Go convention for issuing errors returns the error as the last value returned from a function, as shown in the following listing.

Listing 4.1   Returning an error

```
package main

import (
    "errors"          ⟵  The errors package for
    "strings"             producing custom
)                         errors via New

func Concat(parts ...string) (string, error) {   ⟵  Concat returns
    if len(parts) == 0 {                              a string and an
                                                      error.
```

```
                return "", errors.New("No strings supplied")
        }
        return strings.Join(parts, " "), nil
}
```

Returns an error if
nothing was passed in

Returns the new string
and nil (no error)

The Concat function takes any number of strings, concatenates them with a space separator, and returns the newly joined string. But if no strings are passed into the function, it returns a zero-value string and an error.

The declaration of the Concat function illustrates the typical pattern for returning errors. In idiomatic Go, the error is always the last return value. You may find, particularly in older Go code, that an error is returned in some position other than the last return value. This code likely originated before this convention was established in the Go community.

Variable-length arguments

As Concat illustrates, Go supports variable-length argument lists. By using the ... prefix before a type, you can tell Go that any number of arguments of that type are allowed. Go collapses these into a slice of that type. In listing 4.1, parts will be treated as a []string.

Because errors should always be the last value returned, error handling in Go follows a specific pattern. A function that returns an error is wrapped in an if/else statement that checks whether the error value is something other than nil, and handles it if so. The next listing shows a simple program that takes a list of arguments from the command line and concatenates them.

One thing you'll see in the example is that it returns the zero value of a string, or "". This shows why it's especially important to handle errors and avoid skipping them by using the blank identifier. As "" is a valid string, without error handling it's impossible to differentiate between an error (no parts supplied) or a valid input (one part input as a "), both of which return the same value.

Listing 4.2 Handling an error

```
func main() {
        args := os.Args[1:]
        if result, err := Concat(args...); err != nil {
                fmt.Printf("Error: %s\n", err)
        } else {
                fmt.Printf("Concatenated string: '%s'\n", r
                esult)
        }
}
```

Uses just the args after Args[0]
to bypass the program name

Runs Concat() to
return a result
and/or possible
error

Prints the result in
a nonerror case

If you were to run this code, you'd see output like this:

```
$ go run error_example.go hello world
Concatenated string: 'hello world'
```

If you didn't pass any arguments, you'd see the error message

```
$ go run error_example.go
Error: No strings supplied
```

Listing 4.2 shows how to use the `Concat` function you made already, and it illustrates a common Go idiom. As you no doubt recall, Go's `if` statement has an optional assignment clause before the expression. The intent is to provide a place to get ready for the evaluation but stay in the `if`/`else` scope.

> **TIP** Go lets you ignore return values using the underscore, or blank identifier, as in `result, _ := Concat()`. But even while you're building up your program, the best practice is not to do this for errors. If possible, handle errors whenever you might encounter them.

Listing 4.2 shows basic error handling in action. First, you run `Concat(args…)`, which expands the `args` array as though you called `Concat(arg[0], arg[1],…)`. You assign the two return values to `result` and `err`. Then, still on that line, you check to see whether `err` is not `nil`. If `err` is set to something, you know that an error occurred, so you print the error message. Both returned values are bound to the `if`/`else` scope and are not available afterward, so if you need the result later, it's better to break the function call outside that scope:

```
result, err := Concat(args...)
if err != nil {
    // handle err
}
// do something with result
```

This approach is the one we used most often in the preceding chapters, but there are times when handling it all in a discrete scope (as in listing 4.2) makes sense. This scoping illustrates why the two-clause `if` is a nice feature: it encourages good memory management practices and simultaneously prevents a pattern that can create debugging problems.

In listing 4.1, you saw the `Concat` function, and in listing 4.2, you saw how it's used. But you should look explicitly at a technique in this example.

4.1.1 *Nil best practices*

`nil`s are annoying for several reasons: they frequently cause bugs in a system, and we developers are often forced into the practice of checking values to protect against `nil`s.

In some parts of Go, `nil`s are used to indicate something specific. As you saw in the preceding code, any time an error return value is `nil`, you ought to construe that value to mean "There were no errors when this function executed." But in many other cases, the meaning of a `nil` is unclear. In perhaps the most annoying cases, `nil`s are treated as placeholders any time a developer doesn't feel like returning a value. That's where this technique comes in.

- *Problem*—Returning `nil` results along with errors isn't always the best practice. It puts more work on your library's users, provides little useful information, and makes recovery harder.
- *Solution*—When it makes sense to do so, avail yourself of Go's powerful multiple returns and send back not just an error but also a usable value.
- *Discussion*—This pattern is illustrated in the `Concat` function you saw previously. Let's take a second look, focusing on the line where an error is returned.

Listing 4.3   Returning useful data with an error

```
func Concat(parts ...string) (string, error) {
    if len(parts) == 0 {
            return "", errors.New("No strings supplied")      ⊲──┐ Returns both an
    }                                                            │ empty string and
    return strings.Join(parts, " "), nil                         │ an error
}
```

When an error occurs, both an empty string and an error message are returned. A savvy library user can use the preceding code without adding a lot of explicit error handling. In our contrived `Concat` case, returning an empty string makes sense. If you have no data to concatenate, but the return value's contract says you'll return a string, an empty string is the kind of thing that you would expect. Now you can see how not handling the error can introduce ambiguity.

This example also highlights the importance of error handling. Unlike languages like Rust, which conventionally return a result or error, our return types are set in stone. Unless we panic, we get a string as the first return value from `Concat()` even if an error has occurred. Checking that our string is empty is less useful than first checking whether our function returned an error.

> **TIP**   When you're creating errors, you can use Go's two useful assistive functions. The `errors.New` function from the `errors` package is great for creating simple new errors. The `fmt.Errorf` function in the `fmt` package gives you the option of using a formatting string on the error message as with `Printf` and `Sprintf`. Go developers use these two functions frequently.

By constructing `Concat` this way, you've done your library's users a favor. As mentioned earlier, nothing stops a user from ignoring the error, as in the following listing.

Listing 4.4   Ignoring returned errors

```
func main() {
    args := os.Args[1:]                                      ┐ Passes the
    result, _ := Concat(args...)                        ⊲────┘ values of batch
    fmt.Printf("Concatenated string: '%s'\n", result)
}
```

In this case, when you call `Concat`, you don't wrap it in an `if` statement to handle the error. Because `Concat` is written so that it returns a usable value even when an error occurs, and because the presence or absence of the error doesn't affect the task at hand, you can avoid having to do an extra error check. Instead of wrapping the code in an `if/else` block, you ignore the error and work with `result` as a string. If your function returns an error, it should mean something. You can see errorless examples like this in the standard library, such as `strings.Join` or `strings.Split`, which in an errorlike case still returns a value (`string` and slice of `string`, respectively).

When your context requires you to detect whether an error occurred and respond accordingly, this pattern facilitates that. You can still capture the error value and figure out what went wrong and why, so the pattern of returning both an error and a usable value makes it easier for users of your library to write the code that best fits their use case.

It's not always desirable or even possible to return non-`nil` values with every error. If no useful data can be constructed under a failure condition, returning `nil` may be preferable. The rule of thumb is that if a function can return a useful result when it errs, it should return one. But if it has nothing useful to return, it should send back `nil`.

Finally, it's important for you to make your code's behavior easy for other developers to understand. Go rightly emphasizes writing concise but useful comments atop every shared function. Documenting how your `Concat` function behaves should look something like the following listing.

Listing 4.5 Documenting returns under error conditions

```
// Concat concatenates a bunch of strings, separated by spaces.
// It returns an empty string and an error if no strings were passed in.
func Concat(parts ...string) (string, error) {
    //…
}
```

This brief comment follows the Go convention for commenting and makes clear what happens under normal operation as well as what happens under an error condition. If you're coming from a background that involves languages like Java and Python, the error system may at first seem primitive and repetitive. There are no special `try/catch` blocks that envelop large chunks of code and eject when an error occurs. Instead, convention suggests using `if/else` statements. Most errors that are returned are often of type `error`. Developers who are new to Go sometimes express concern that error handling seems clunky.

Such concerns vanish as developers get used to the Go way of doing things. Go's approach gives a developer a very granular view of errors. You see each error addressed in its own context. But we've noticed a surprising pattern with Go: whereas languages such as Java and Python favor developing specific error or exception types, Go developers rarely create specific error types. An error is an error, and any metadata returned with it is how we optionally explain what went wrong.

This is no doubt related to the fact that many Go core libraries use the error type as is. As Go developers see it, most errors have no special attributes that would be better conveyed by a specific error type. Consequently, returning a generic error is the simplest way to handle things. Take the `Concat` function, for example. Creating a `Concat-Error` type for that function has no compelling benefit. Instead, you use the built-in `errors` package to construct a new error message.

This simple error handling is often the best practice. But sometimes, it can be useful to create and use specific error types.

4.1.2   Custom error types

Go's error type is an interface that looks like the following listing.

> **Listing 4.6   The error interface**

```
type error interface {
    Error() string
}
```

Anything that has an `Error` function returning a string satisfies this interface's contract. Most of the time, Go developers are satisfied by working with errors as the error type. But in some cases, you may want your errors to contain more information than a simple string. In such cases, you may choose to create a custom error type or multiple custom types to allow the caller to handle them separately.

- *Problem*—Your function returns an error. Important details regarding this error might lead users of this function to code differently, depending on the details of the specific type of error you return.
- *Solution*—Create a type that implements the error interface but provides additional functionality.
- *Discussion*—Imagine that you're writing a file parser. When the parser encounters a syntax error, it generates an error. Along with having an error message, it's generally useful to have information about where in the file the error occurred. You could build such an error as shown in the following listing.

> **Listing 4.7   Parse error**

```
type ParseError struct {
    Message    string          The error message without
    Line, Char int             location information

}                              The location information
func (p *ParseError) Error() string {
    format := "%s oln Line %d, Char %d"           Implements the
    return fmt.Sprintf(format, p.Message, p.Line, p.Char)   Error interface
}
```

This new `ParseError` struct has three properties: `Message`, `Line`, and `Char`. You implement the `Error` function by formatting all three of those pieces of information into one string. But imagine that you want to return to the source of the parse error and display that entire line, perhaps with the trouble-causing character highlighted. The ParseError struct makes that easy to do.

This technique is great when you need to return additional information. But what if you need one function to return different kinds of errors?

4.1.3   Error variables

Sometimes, you have a function that performs a complex task and may break in a couple of different but meaningful ways. The previous technique showed one way of implementing the error interface, but that method may be a little heavy-handed if each error doesn't also need additional information. Let's look at another idiomatic use of Go errors.

- *Problem*—A single complex function may encounter more than one kind of error. It's useful to show users which kind of error was returned so that the ensuing applications can appropriately handle each error case.
- *Solution*—One convention that's considered good practice in Go (although not in certain other languages) is to create package-scoped error variables that can be returned whenever a certain error occurs. These are also known as *sentinel errors*—those that have meaning in a specific context or scenario. The best example of this in the Go standard library comes in the io package, which contains errors such as io.EOF and io.ErrNoProgress.
- *Discussion*—Before diving into the details of using error variables, let's consider the problem and one fairly simple approach that leaves a little room to add more specificity to our errors. The problem you'd like to solve is being able to tell the difference between two errors. The next listing builds a small program that simulates sending a simple message to a receiver.

Listing 4.8   Handling two different errors

```
package main

import (
    "errors"
    "fmt"
    "math/rand"
    "time"
)
const MAX_TIMEOUTS = 5
var ErrTimeout = errors.New("The request timed out")        ◁─┘  The timeout error instance
var ErrRejected = errors.New("The request was rejected")    ◁───  The rejection error instance

func init() {
    rand.Seed(time.Now().UnixNano())                        ◁───  Seeds our random number generator
}

func main() {
    response, err := SendRequest("Hello")                   ◁───  Calls the stubbed-out SendRequest function
```

```
    if errors.Is(err, ErrTimeout) {
        timeouts := 0
        for err == errors.Is(err, ErrTimeout) {
            timeouts++
            fmt.Println("Timeout. Retrying.")
            if timeouts == MAX_TIMEOUTS {
                panic("too many timeouts!")
            }
            response, err = SendRequest("Hello")
        }
    }

    if err != nil {
        fmt.Println(err)
    } else {
        fmt.Println(response)
    }
}
func SendRequest(req string) (string, error) {
    switch rand.Intn(3) % 3 {
    case 0:
        return "Success", nil
    case 1:
        return "", ErrRejected
    default:
        return "", ErrTimeout
    }
}
```

Handles the timeout condition with retries and a maximum retry with panic mechanism

Handles any other error as a failure

If there's no error, prints the result

Defines a function that superficially behaves like a message sender

Randomly generates a response

Handles the timeout condition with retries

Instead of sending a message, randomly generates behavior

This listing exemplifies using variables as fixed errors. The code is designed to simulate the basics of a sending function. But instead of sending anything anywhere, the SendRequest function randomly generates a response. The response could be a success, or it could be one of our two errors: ErrTimeout or ErrRejected.

NOTE In our init() method, we call rand.Seed() with a unique value. The init() function in a main package is called before the main() function, as in C.

Not so random

One interesting detail of listing 4.8 is the randomizer. Random-number generators (RNGs) need a seed, and using a unique seed is required to guarantee a pseudorandom number. Any RNG with a seed is deterministic and not truly random. This is perfect for this use case but should not be used for anything related to security; for this, look to the crypto package. If you set this to a fixed integer, you will see its nonrandom nature. Starting with Go version 1.20, the seed is autogenerated at runtime, so this is not strictly needed.

Running the preceding program will result in the output like the following:

```
$ go run two_errors.go
Timeout. Retrying.
The request was rejected
```

Because we're randomizing our responses, we might also get a success. Run it a few times to see what kinds of behaviors you can generate and how this makes for a nice form of fuzz testing. Some requests to `SendRequest` will return a timeout error, and some will return a generic rejection. Our timeout errors are retried up to `MAX_TIMEOUTS` times until its caller receives a success. It's common to see patterns like this in network servers.

Software developers working in a language such as Java or Python would be likely to implement `ErrTimeout` and `ErrRejected` as classes and then throw new instances of each class. The `try/catch` pattern used by many languages is built for dealing with error information encapsulated in error types. But as you've seen previously, Go doesn't provide a `try/catch` block. You could use type matching (especially with a type `switch` statement) to provide the same functionality, but that's not the Go way. Instead, idiomatic Go uses a method that's both more efficient and simpler: create errors as package-scoped variables and reference those variables.

You can see in the preceding code that handling error variables is as simple as checking for equality. If the error is a timeout, you can retry sending the message repeatedly. But when the error is a rejection, you stop processing. As before, returning a `nil` indicates that no error occurs, and you handle that case accordingly. With a pattern like this, the same error variables are used repeatedly. This is efficient because errors are instantiated only once. It's also conceptually simple. As long as your error doesn't have special properties, you can create variables and work with them as such.

4.2   *Wrapping errors*

In listing 4.8, we were able to define our own custom errors that could be evaluated for error "type" elsewhere in the code. This is helpful but on its own is somewhat limiting: if we want to annotate (or *wrap*) an error with more detail, we won't be able to evaluate the same way. Consider the following example.

Listing 4.9   Wrapping an error

```
package main

import (
    "errors"
    "fmt"
    "log"
)

var ErrTimeout = errors.New("The request timed out")    ◁─── Declaration of
                                                             our error type,
                                                             as in listing 4.8
func SendRequest(req string) (string, error) {
    return "", fmt.Errorf("we got an error: %w ", ErrT
```

```
     imeout)              ◄───┐  Wrapping our custom
}                             │  error in an annotation
func main() {
    if _, err := SendRequest("Hello "); err != nil {
        if err == ErrTimeout {                              Testing against
            log.Println("we got a timeout error")           our custom
        } else {                                  ◄───┘     error or . . .
            log.Println("we got some other error")  ◄───┐
        }                                               │  . . . any other
    }                                                   │  error
}
```

In this case, despite its being an instance of our custom `ErrTimeout`, running this will display the test in the `else` clause. To discern the true error, we can unwrap it using the `errors.Unwrap` method, like so:

```
if errors.Unwrap(err) == ErrTimeout {
    log.Println("we got a timeout error")
} else {
    log.Println("we got some other error")
}
```

This will return the response we expect by unwrapping the outer error and giving us the underlying error. This is helpful if you only wrap an error once, but consider the number of levels you could accumulate with functions that pass errors back up the chain. Go provides a helper method that does the recursive unwrapping for you and lets you know if an error is ultimately a specific type. In the preceding case, we could change our check to

```
if errors.Is(err, ErrTimeout) {
    log.Println("we got a timeout error")
} else {
    log.Println("we got some other error")
}
```

Here, even if we wrapped our initial error three times or more, the code would return `true` for `ErrTimeout`. For all practical purposes, you'll want to call `Is()` rather than `Unwrap`ping manually. `Unwrap` can return `nil`, leading to a lot of extra code that can be avoided by cutting to the chase and finding out what an error . . . well, *is*.

NOTE You may have noticed the formatting verb `%w`, and it's important to know that this verb (for *wrap*) is critical for enabling `Unwrap`.

In general, errors are a way of relaying significant problems with an application, its environment, or input(s). There are times, however, when those problems are such that the app must be stopped or some inner process must be bypassed. That could be because future processing is impossible or because it would leave some aspect of the application in an invalid state. This is where the panic concept comes in.

4.3   The panic system

In addition to the preceding error handling, Go provides a way of indicating that something is very wrong: the panic system. As the name indicates, a *panic* tells you that something has errored in a way that the application may not be able to recover from. It should be used sparingly and intelligently. In this section, we explain how and when panics should be used, and along the way, we tell you about some of our own failures.

4.3.1   Differentiating panics from errors

The first thing to understand about panics is how they differ conceptually from errors. An error indicates that an event occurred that might violate expectations about what should have happened. A panic, by contrast, indicates that something has gone wrong in such a way that the system (or the immediate subsystem) can't continue to function. If you think about a program as a series of steps that depend on one another and if one goes wrong, the others cannot continue, that's when and where a panic is best implemented. At the top level, a panic (or `log.Panic()`) will also give you stack traces, so even if you haven't created discrete error types, you can see what went wrong and where.

Go assumes that errors will be handled by you, the programmer. If an error occurs and you ignore it, Go doesn't do anything on your behalf. If you ignore it, there's a possibility that unexpected state will be fed to successive steps in your application. Not so with panics. When a panic occurs, Go unwinds the stack, looking for handlers for that panic. If no handler is found, Go eventually unwinds all the way to the top of the function stack and stops the program. An unhandled panic will kill your application. The following listing illustrates this difference.

Listing 4.10   Error and panic

```go
package main

import (
    "errors"
    "fmt"
)

var ErrDivideByZero = errors.New("Can't divide by zero")
func main() {
    fmt.Println("Divide 1 by 0")
    _, err := precheckDivide(1, 0)          // First, you divide using the
    if err != nil {                          // precheckDivide function,
        fmt.Printf("Error: %s\n", err)       // which returns an error.
    }
    fmt.Println("Divide 2 by 0")            // Then you run a similar division
    divide(2, 0)                             // with the divide function.
}
func precheckDivide(a, b int) (int, error) {     // The precheckDivide
    if b == 0 {                                  // function returns an
        return 0, ErrDivideByZero                // error if the divisor is 0.
    }
    return divide(a, b), nil
}
```

```
func divide(a, b int) int {
    return a / b
}
```

← The regular divide function wraps the division operator with no checks.

Here, you define two functions. The `divide` function performs a basic division operation. But it doesn't account for division by 0, a common undefined arithmetic behavior in programming languages. By contrast, the `precheckDivide` function explicitly checks the divisor and returns an error if the divisor is 0. You're interested in seeing how Go behaves under these two conditions, so in `main`, you test first with the `precheck-Divide` function and then with the plain old `divide` function. Running this program provides this output:

```
go run zero_divider.go
Divide 1 by 0
Error: Can't divide by zero
Divide 2 by 0
panic: runtime error: integer divide by zero
[signal 0x8 code=0x7 addr=0x22d8 pc=0x22d8]
goroutine 1 [running]:
main.main()
    /Users/mbutcher/Code/go-in-practice/chapter4/zero_divider.go:18 +0x2d8
```

The first division using `precheckDivide` returns an error, and the second division causes a panic because you never checked the divisor. Conceptually speaking, the reasons are important:

- When you checked the value before dividing, you never introduced the situation where the program was asked to do something it couldn't.
- When you divided, you caused the system to encounter a state that it couldn't handle. This is when a panic should occur.

Practically speaking, errors are things that we developers ought to expect to go wrong. After all, they're documented in the code. You can glance at the definition of `pre-checkDivide` and see an error condition that you need to handle when you call the function. Although an error might represent something outside the norm, we can't say that they're *unexpected*.

Panics, on the other hand, are unexpected. They occur when a constraint or limitation is unpredictably surpassed. When it comes to declaring a panic in your code, the general rule of thumb is don't panic unless there's no clear way to handle the condition within the present context. When possible, return errors instead.

4.3.2   *Working with panics*

Go developers have expectations about how to panic correctly, though those expectations aren't always laid out clearly. Before diving into the proper handling of panics, we'll look at a technique that all Go developers should know when it comes to issuing panics.

The definition of Go's panic function can be expressed like this: `panic(inter-face{})`. When you call `panic`, you can give it almost anything as an argument. Should you so desire, you can call `panic(nil)`, as shown in the following listing.

Listing 4.11 Panic with `nil`

```
package main

func main() {
    panic(nil)       ◁─── Panic about nothing!
}
```

When you run this program, Go captures your panic just fine:

```
$ go run proper_panic.go
panic: nil
goroutine 1 [running]:
main.main()
      /chapter4/proper_panic.go:4 +0x32
```

This error isn't particularly useful. Instead, you could panic with a string: `panic("Oops, I did it again.")`. Now when you run the code, you get this:

```
$ go run proper_panic.go
panic: Oops, I did it again.
goroutine 1 [running]:
main.main()
      /chapter4/proper_panic.go:4 +0x64
```

This seems better. At least you have some helpful information. But is this the right thing to do?

- *Problem*—When you raise a panic, what should you pass into the function? Are there ways of panicking that are useful or idiomatic?
- *Solution*—The best thing to pass to a panic is an error. Use the error type to make it easy for a recovery function to capture it and make decisions based on its error type.
- *Discussion*—With a signature that accepts `interface{}`, it's not obvious what you're supposed to pass into a panic. You could give it the object that caused the panic. As you've seen, you could give it a string, a `nil`, or an error.

The best thing to pass a panic (under normal circumstances, at least) is something that fulfills the error interface. There are two good reasons for this. The first is that it's intuitive. What sort of thing would cause a panic? An error. It's reasonable to assume that developers will expect this. The second reason is that it eases handling of a panic. In a moment, you'll look at recovering from panics. You'll see how to take a panic, handle the dire part, and use the panic's content as a plain old error. The next listing shows the idiomatic way to issue a panic.

Listing 4.12 A proper panic

```
package main

import "errors"

func main() {
    panic(errors.New("Something bad happened."))
}
```

Calls panic and passes it an error

With this method, it's still easy to print the panic message with print formatters: `fmt.Printf("Error: %s", thePanic)`. It's just as easy to send the panic back through the error system. That's why it's idiomatic to pass an error to a panic.

> **Thinking outside the panic box**
>
> Although we've just claimed that the best thing to send a panic is an error, there's a reason why panics don't require error types: the panic system is defined to be flexible. In some ways, this is analogous to the way that Java allows Throwables that aren't necessarily exceptions. A Go panic is one way to unwind the stack.

Very often, a `panic()` can be a recipient of the bubbling up of errors. Consider a `main()` function that calls `Initialize()` error, which calls `StartServer()` error. If the server cannot be started, it returns an error, which bubbles it up to `Initialize` and subsequently bubbles to main, which panics.

Now that you have a firm understanding of how to raise panics, you can turn to the other half of the problem: recovery.

4.3.3 Recovering from panics

Any discussion of panics would be incomplete without a discussion of recovering from panics. Panic recovery in Go depends on a feature of the language called *deferred functions*. Go can guarantee the execution of a function at the moment its parent function returns. This happens whether the reason for the parent function's return is a return statement, the end of the function block, or a panic. The next listing helps explain.

Listing 4.13 Simple defer

```
package main

import "fmt"

func main() {
    defer goodbye()
    fmt.Println("Hello world.")
}
func goodbye() {
    fmt.Println("Goodbye")
}
```

Defers execution of goodbye

Prints a line. This happens before goodbye.

Without the `defer` statement, this program would print `Goodbye` followed by `Hello world`. But `defer` modifies the order of execution. It defers executing `goodbye` until the rest of `main` has executed. Right as the `main` function completes, the deferred `goodbye` function is run. The output of the program is

```
$ go run simple_defer.go
Hello world.
Goodbye
```

The `defer` statement is a great way to close files or sockets when you're finished, free up resources such as database handles, or handle panics. Listing 4.12 showed the appropriate strategy for emitting a panic. Now you can take what you know about `defer` and concentrate on recovering from panics.

4.3.4 *Capturing panics with defer*

Capturing a panic in a deferred function is standard practice in Go. We cover it here for two reasons: this discussion is a building block for another technique, and it provides the opportunity to take a step from the pattern into the mechanics so you can see what's happening instead of viewing panics as a formula to be followed.

- *Problem*—A function your application calls is panicking, and as a result, your program is crashing.
- *Solution*—Use a deferred function and call `recover` to find out what happened and handle the panic.

  The left side of figure 4.1 illustrates how an unhandled panic will crash your program. The right side illustrates how the `recover` function can stop the function stack from unwinding and allow the program to continue running.

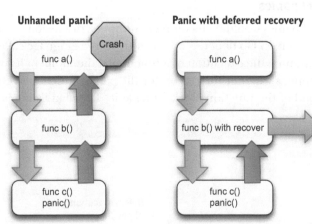

Figure 4.1   Recovering from a panic

- *Discussion*—Go provides a way of capturing information from a panic and, in so doing, stopping the panic from unwinding the function stack further. The `recover` function retrieves the data.

The next listing is a small example that shows both emitting and handling a panic.

Listing 4.14 Recovering from a panic

```go
package main

import (
    "errors"
    "fmt"
)
func main() {
    defer func() {
        if err := recover(); err != nil {
            fmt.Printf("Trapped panic: %s (%T)
\n", err, err)
        }
    }()
    yikes()
}
func yikes() {
    panic(errors.New("Something bad happened."))
}
```

Provides a deferred closure to handle panic recovery

Calls a function that panics

Emits a panic with an error for a body

This program illustrates what's probably the most common pattern for panic recovery. To catch the panic that `yikes` raises, you write a deferred anonymous function that checks for a panic and recovers if it finds one. We call this a *closure function*, which is executed at the end of the function's scope by calling it directly with a trailing `()`.

> **NOTE** Closures can be used for a lot of other things. They can be stored to variables and repeatedly called while maintaining internal state. We'll see them quite a bit when we talk about concurrency in chapter 5.

In Go, when you defer a closure, you're defining a function and then marking it to be called (in this case, with an empty argument list). The general form is `defer func(){ /* body */ }()`. Note that although it looks like it's defined and called at once, Go's runtime won't call the function until it's appropriate for a deferred function to execute. In a moment, you'll see how the separation between defining the closure and then executing it later affects the scope of the closure in a useful way. This could be written as a separate function and called via `defer someFunction()`, of course, but it's helpful to see the control flow with the code inline.

The `recover` function in Go returns a value (`interface{}`) if a panic has been raised, but in all other cases, it returns `nil`. The value returned is whatever value was passed into the panic. Running the preceding code returns

```
$ go run recover_panic.go
Trapped panic: Something bad happened. (*errors.errorString)
```

Notice that because you add the `%T` to the formatting string, you also get information about the type of `err`, which is the error type created by `errors.New`. You may recognize that formatting verb from our discussion of generics in chapter 3.

Now you can take things one step further and look at how to use this closure/recover combination to recover from a panic. Closures inherit the scope of their parent. Deferred closures, like the preceding one, inherit whatever is in scope before they're declared. The following listing works fine.

Listing 4.15   Scope for deferred closures

```
package main

import "fmt"

func main() {                        Defines the variable
    var msg string          ⟵        outside the closure
    defer func() {
            fmt.Println(msg)    ⟵    Prints the variable in
    }()                              the deferred closure
    msg = "Hello world"     ⟵    Sets the value of the variable
}
```

Because `msg` is defined before the closure, the closure may reference it. As expected, the value of the message will reflect whatever the state of `msg` is when the deferred function executes. The preceding code prints `Hello world`.

But even though `defer` is executed after the rest of the function, a closure doesn't have access to variables that are declared after the closure is declared. The closure is evaluated in order but not executed until the function returns. For that reason, the following listing causes a compile error.

Listing 4.16   `msg` out of scope

```
package main

import "fmt"
                                     Prints a variable
func main() {
    defer func() {
            fmt.Println(msg)    ⟵    Declares and sets the variable.
    }()                              Compiles will fail because the
    msg := "Hello world"    ⟵    declaration is after the function.
}
```

Because `msg` isn't declared before the deferred function, when the code is evaluated, `msg` is undefined.

Bringing together the details, you can take one final step in this technique. Let's look at a slightly more sophisticated use of a deferred function. This one handles a panic and cleans up before returning. It's a good representative sample of how to use deferred functions and recover in practice.

Imagine that you're writing a piece of code that preprocesses a CSV file, removing empty lines from the beginning. For the sake of boiling this code down to an example, `RemoveEmptyLines` isn't fully implemented. Instead, it always returns a panic. With this bad behavior, we can illustrate how to recover from a panic, close the problematic file, and then return an error, as shown in the following listing.

Listing 4.17 Cleanup

```
package main

import (
    "errors"
    "fmt"
    "io"
    "os"
)

func main() {
    var file io.ReadCloser
    file, err := OpenCSV("data.csv")
    if err != nil {
        fmt.Printf("Error: %s", err)
        return
    }
    defer file.Close()
    // Do something with file.
}
func OpenCSV(filename string) (file *os.File, err error) {
    defer func() {
        if r := recover(); r != nil {
            file.Close()
            err = r.(error)
        }
    }()
    file, err = os.Open(filename)
    if err != nil {
        fmt.Printf("Failed to open file\n")
        return file, err
    }
    RemoveEmptyLines(file)
    return file, err
}
func RemoveEmptyLines(f *os.File) {
    panic(errors.New("failed parse"))
}
```

Runs OpenCSV and handles any errors. This implementation always returns an error.

Uses a deferred function to ensure that a file gets closed

Normally, you'd do more with the file here.

OpenCSV opens and preprocesses your file. Note the named return values.

The main deferred error handling happens here.

Opens the data file and handles any errors (such as file not found)

Runs our intentionally broken RemoveEmptyLines function

Instead of stripping empty lines, you always fail here.

Again, the problem in the preceding code is that your RemoveEmptyLines function always panics. If you were to implement this function, it would check to see whether the leading lines of the file were empty, and if they were, it would advance the reader past those lines.

Listing 4.17 uses deferred functions in two places. In the main function, you use a deferred function to ensure that your file is closed. This is considered good practice when you're working with files, network connections, database handles, and other resources that need to be closed to prevent side effects or leaks. It's a great way to perform cleanup on any resources that need to be handled if the program terminates abruptly. The second deferred function appears inside the OpenCSV function. This deferred function is designed to do three things:

- Trap any panics.
- Make sure that if a panic occurs, the file is closed. This is considered good practice even though in this context, it may be redundant.
- Get the error from the panic and pass it back by using the regular error-handling mechanism.

One detail of the declaration of OpenCSV is worth mentioning: we label the return values in the function declaration. That makes it possible to refer to the file and err variables inside the closure and ensures that when err is set to the panic's error, the correct value is returned.

As we've shown, defer is a powerful and useful way of dealing with panics, as well as reliably cleaning up. As we close out this technique, here are a few useful guidelines for working with deferred functions:

- Put deferred functions as close to the top of a function declaration as possible.
- Deferred functions don't have to be inline functions and often are called on methods of data structures.
- Simple declarations such as foo := 1 are often placed before deferred functions.
- More-complex variables are declared before deferred functions (var myFile io.Reader) but not initialized until after.
- Although it's possible to declare multiple deferred functions inside a function, avoid this if possible. If you choose to have multiple deferred functions, keep in mind that the order of execution will be the reverse of the order in which they were declared.
- Best practices suggest closing files, network connections, and other similar resources inside a defer clause. This ensures that even when errors or panics occur, system resources will be freed.

In the next section, you'll take one more step in handling panics and learn how to reliably prevent panics on goroutines from halting a program.

4.3.5   *Handling panics on goroutines*

So far, we haven't talked much about one of Go's most powerful features: concurrency. You start goroutines by using the go keyword. If you have a function called run, you can start it as a goroutine like this: go run. To quote the Go Programming Language Specification, the go statement "starts the execution of a function call as an independent concurrent thread of control, or *goroutine*, within the same address space" (https://go.dev/ref/spec#Go_statements). More simply, you can think of it as running a function on its own lightweight thread.

> ### Goroutines under the hood
> The implementation of goroutines is a little more sophisticated than just running a function on its own thread. The Go Concurrency Wiki page (https://github.com/golang/go/wiki/LearnConcurrency) provides a big list of articles that dive into various aspects of Go's CSP-based concurrency model.

To illustrate this idea, imagine that you have a simple server. The server functions as follows:

1 The `main` function runs `start` to start a new server.
2 The `start` function processes configuration data and then runs the `listen` function.
3 The `listen` function opens a network port and listens for new requests. When it gets a request, instead of handling the request itself, it calls `go handle`, passing any necessary information to the `handle` function.
4 The `handle` function processes the request and then calls `response`.
5 The `response` function sends data back to the client and terminates the connection.

The `listen` function uses goroutines to handle multiple client connections at the same time. As it receives requests, it can push the workload to any number of handle functions, each running in its own space. Variations of this powerful pattern are used frequently in Go server applications. In fact, the simple HTTP servers we built in chapters 1 and 2 used the `http` package, which uses goroutines in its `ServeHTTP` method to route requests. Figure 4.2 illustrates this application and its function stacks when you use goroutines.

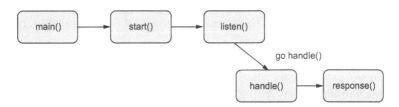

Figure 4.2   A simple server

Each row represents a function stack, and each call to `go` starts a new function stack. Whenever `listen` receives a new request, a new function stack is created for the ensuing `handle` instance. Whenever `handle` finishes (such as when `response` returns), that spawned goroutine is cleaned up.

Goroutines are powerful and elegant. Because they're both simple to write and cheap to use (they incur little overhead on your program), Go developers use them frequently. But in one specific and unfortunately common situation, the combination of goroutines and panics can result in a program crash.

When handling a panic, the Go runtime unwinds the function stack until a `recover` occurs. But if it gets to the top of a function stack and `recover` is never called, the program dies. Recall figure 4.2, which showed how a goroutine gets its own function call stack. What happens when a panic occurs on that goroutine? Take a look at figure 4.3.

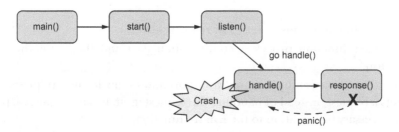

Figure 4.3 Crash on a goroutine

Imagine that during a request, the `response` function encounters an unforeseen fatal error and panics. As a good server developer, you've added all kinds of error-handling logic to `listen`. But if you haven't added anything to `handle`, the program will crash. Why? When a panic is unhandled at the top of a function stack, it causes Go to terminate in an error state. A panic on a goroutine can't jump to the call stack of the function that initiated the goroutine. There's no path for a panic to go from `handle` to `listen` in this example because goroutines are effectively fire-and-forget from the caller's perspective. This is the problem our current technique focuses on.

- *Problem*—If a panic on a goroutine goes unhandled on that goroutine's call stack, it crashes the entire program. Sometimes, this is acceptable, but often, the desired behavior is recovery.
- *Solution*—Simply stated, `handle` panics on any goroutine that might panic. Our solution will make it easier to design servers that handle panics without relying on panic handling in every single handle function.
- *Discussion*—The interesting thing about this particular problem is that although it's trivially easy to solve, the solution is repetitive. The burden of implementing it is often pushed to developers outside your control. First, you'll look at a basic implementation of the code outlined in figure 4.3. Then you'll explore the trivial solution and discover how Go's idioms make this solution troublesome. Finally, you'll see a pattern for solving it more conveniently.

The next listing shows a basic implementation of the kind of server illustrated in figure 4.3. It functions as a basic echo server. When you run it, you can connect to it on port 1026 and send a plain line of text. The remote server will echo that text back to you.

Listing 4.18   An echo server

```go
package main

import (
    "bufio"
    "fmt"
    "net"
)

func main() {
    listen()
}

func listen() {
    listener, err := net.Listen("tcp", ":1026")
    if err != nil {
        fmt.Println("Failed to open port on 1026")
        return
    }
    for {
        conn, err := listener.Accept()
        if err != nil {
            fmt.Println("Error accepting connection")
            continue
        }
        go handle(conn)
    }
}

func handle(conn net.Conn) {
    reader := bufio.NewReader(conn)
    data, err := reader.ReadBytes('\n')
    if err != nil {
        fmt.Println("Failed to read from socket.")
        conn.Close()
    }
    response(data, conn)
}

func response(data []byte, conn net.Conn) {
    defer func() {
        conn.Close()
    }()
    conn.Write(data)
}
```

Starts a new server listening on port 1026

Listens for new client connections and handles any connection errors

When a connection is accepted, passes it to the handle function

Tries to read a line of data from the connection

If you fail to read a line, prints an error and closes the connection

When you get a line of text, passes it to response

Writes the data back out to the socket, echoing it to the client, then closes the connection

If you ran this code, it would start a server. Then you could interact with the server like this:

```
$ telnet localhost 1026
Trying ::1...
Connected to localhost.
```

```
Escape character is '^]'.
test
test
Connection closed by foreign host.
```

When you type test (indicated in bold in the preceding code), the server echoes back that same text and then closes the connection.

This simple server works by listening for new client connections on port 1026. Each time a new connection comes in, the server starts a new goroutine that runs the handle function. Because each request is handled on a separate goroutine, this server can effectively handle numerous concurrent connections.

The handle function reads a line of text (raw bytes) and then passes that line and the connection to the response function. The response function echoes the text back to the client and closes the connection.

This isn't exactly an ideal server, but it illustrates the basics. It also shows some pitfalls. Imagine that response could panic. Suppose that you replace the preceding code with the following listing to simulate that case.

Listing 4.19 Panic in the response

```
func response(data []byte, conn net.Conn) {
    panic(errors.New("Failure in response!"))        ◄─┤  Instead of doing something
}                                                          useful, simulates a panic
```

It might immediately stand out to you that even though the connection is never closed in this situation, things are more worrisome: this panic will crash the server. Servers shouldn't be so fragile that they crash when one particular request fails. Adding recovery handling to the listen function seems like a natural move, but that won't help because the goroutine is operating on a separate function stack.

From here, let's refactor our first pass at a server and make it fault-tolerant. This time, you'll add the panic handling in the handle function. The following listing presents only the handle and response functions; the rest of the code is the same as listing 4.18.

Listing 4.20 Handling panics on a goroutine

```
func handle(conn net.Conn) {
    defer func() {
        if err := recover(); err != nil {
            fmt.Printf("Fatal error: %s", err)
        }
        conn.Close()
    }()
    reader := bufio.NewReader(conn)
    data, err := reader.ReadBytes('\n')
    if err != nil {
        fmt.Println("Failed to read from socket.")
    }
```

The deferred function handles the panic and makes sure that in all cases the connection is closed.

```
        response(data, conn)
}
func response(data []byte, conn net.Conn) {
    conn.Write(data)
    panic(errors.New("Pretend I'm a real error"))
}
```

> **Again, you issue a panic to simulate a failure.**

Your new `handle` function includes a deferred function that uses `recover` to see whether a panic has occurred. This stops the panic from propagating up the stack. Notice that you've also slightly improved the connection management: you use `defer` to ensure that in all cases, no matter what happens, the connection is closed when `handle` is done. With this new revision, the server no longer crashes when `response` panics.

So far, so good. But you can take this example another step with the Go `handler` server idiom. It's common in Go to create a server library that provides a flexible method of handling responses. The `net/http.Server` library is a fantastic example of this. As shown in listing 1.15, creating an HTTP server in Go is as simple as giving the HTTP system a `handler` function and starting a server (see the following listing).

Listing 4.21 A small HTTP server

```
package main

import (
    "errors"
    "net/http"
)

func main() {
    http.HandleFunc("GET /", handler)
    if err := http.ListenAndServe(":8080", nil); err
    != nil {
        panic("could not start server", err)
    }
}
```

> **Gives the HTTP system a handler function**

> **Starts up a server**

All the logic for starting and managing a server is within the `net/http` package. But the package leaves it up to you, the developer, to tell it how to handle a request. In the preceding code, you have an opportunity to pass in a handler function. This is any function that satisfies the following type:

```
type HandlerFunc func(ResponseWriter, *Request)
```

Upon receiving a request, the server does much the same as you did in the earlier echo server architecture: starts a goroutine and executes the handler function on that thread. What do you suppose would happen if you wrote a handler that panics? See the next listing.

Listing 4.22 A panicky handler

```
func handler(res http.ResponseWriter, req *http.Request) {
    panic(errors.New("Fake panic!"))
}
```

If you run the server with that code, you'll find that the server dumps the panic information to the console, but the server keeps running:

```
2015/04/08 07:57:31 http: panic serving [::1]:51178: Fake panic!
Goroutine 5 [running]:
net/http.func·011()
    /usr/local/Cellar/go/libexec/src/net/http/server.go:1130 +0xbb
main.handler(0x494fd0, 0xc208044000, 0xc208032410)
    /chapter4/http_server.go:13 +0xdd
net/http.HandlerFunc.ServeHTTP(0x3191e0, 0x494fd0, 0xc208044000,
0xc208032410)
...
```

But your handler function didn't do anything to handle the panic! That safety net is provided by the library in `ServeHTTP`, which uses a panic recovery pattern to keep the error message for display but allow the application to remain running. With this in mind, if you were to take the echo service and turn it into a well-behaving library, you'd slightly modify your architecture so that panics were handled inside the library.

When we began working with Go in earnest, we wrote a trivial little library (now part of `github.com/Masterminds/cookoo`) to protect us from accidentally unhandled panics on goroutines. The following listing shows a simplified version of that library.

Listing 4.23 Panics in goroutines

```
package safely

import (
    "log"
)

type GoDoer func()                      ← GoDoer is a simple
func Go(todo GoDoer) {                     parameterless function.
    go func() {                          ← safely.Go runs a function as a
        defer func() {                     goroutine and handles any panics.
            if err := recover(); err != nil {   ← First, you run an
                log.Printf("Panic in safely        anonymous function.
                .Go: %s", err)
            }                            The anonymous function
        }()                              handles panics, following
        todo()                           the usual pattern of
    }()                                  deferring a recovery.
}
```

The function calls
the GoDoer that
was passed in.

This simple library provides panic handling, so you don't have to remember to do it on your own. The next listing shows an example of `safely.go` in action.

Listing 4.24   Using `safely` to trap panics

```
package main

import (
    "errors"
    "time"

    "github.com/Masterminds/cookoo/safely"     ← Imports the
)                                                 safely package

func message() {                               ← Defines a callback that
    println("Inside goroutine")                  matches the GoDoer type
    panic(errors.New("Oops!"))
}

func main() {                                  ← Instead of a go message,
    safely.Go(message)                            you use this.
    println("Outside goroutine")
    time.Sleep(1000)                           ← Make sure that the goroutine has
}                                                 a chance to execute before the
                                                  program exits.
```

In this example, you define a simple function that satisfies the `GoDoer` type (it has no parameters and no return value). Then, when you call `safely.go(message)`, it executes your `message` function in a new goroutine but with the added benefit of trapping any panics. Because `message` does panic, running this program provides the following output:

```
$ go run safely_example.go
Outside goroutine
Inside goroutine
2015/04/08 08:28:00 Panic in safely.Go: Oops!
```

Instead of the panic's stopping the program execution, `safely.go` traps and logs the panic message.

Closures help here
Instead of using a named function such as `message`, you could use a closure. A closure allows you to access variables that are in scope; you can use it to sidestep the fact that `GoDoer` doesn't accept any parameters. But if you do this, beware of race conditions and other concurrency problems! Go itself comes with a helpful `-race` flag that can be appended to `go run` or `go build`. If you're writing concurrent code, this is a great tool for catching any potential race conditions.

This library may not suit your exact needs, but it illustrates a good practice: construct libraries so that a panic on a goroutine doesn't have the surprising or unintended result of halting your program.

Go's provision of both an error-handling system and a runtime panic system is elegant. But as you've seen in this section, panics tend to arise in surprising situations. If you forget to plan for them, you can find yourself mired in difficult debugging situations. That's why we've spent so much time discussing remedial techniques here—and why we suggest preventative no-brainer techniques like `safely.go` instead of relying on developers to remember to do the right thing.

Summary

- Error handling is not glamorous, but understanding Go's patterns for error handling helps prevent unexpected failures.
- Creating and using error variables lets us handle error cases properly.
- Adding custom error types gives a user more information and additional options to decide what to do next.
- Knowing when to use panics versus errors keeps our application resilient to recoverable errors and safer when those errors are not recoverable.
- Goroutines introduce some edge cases when it comes to panicking, and understanding how to react to a panic within a goroutine can prevent deadlocks or crashes in an application.

Concurrency in Go 5

This chapter covers

- Viewing Go's concurrency model
- Using goroutines for concurrent processing and communication
- Locking data and awaiting responses
- Using channels for intercoroutine communication
- Strategically closing channels

This chapter presents Go's approach to and implementation of concurrency. Unlike many recent procedural and object-oriented languages, Go doesn't provide a threading model for concurrency. Instead, it uses the concept of event-style goroutines and channels for communication between them. Concurrency is cheap (resource-wise) and much easier to manage than traditional thread pools. This chapter first focuses on goroutines, which are functions capable of running concurrently. Then it dives into channels, Go's mechanism for handling communicating between goroutines. We'll also look at mutexes, which are synchronization primitives that enable locking of resources as a way of enforcing consistency in concurrent systems.

5.1   *Understanding Go's concurrency model*

Roughly speaking, concurrency is a program's ability to do multiple things at the same time. In practice, when we talk about concurrent programs, we mean programs that have two or more tasks that run independently, at about the same time, but remain part of the same program.

Popular programming languages such as Java and Python implement concurrency by using OS threads or a lightweight version known as green threads. Both rely on the virtual machine to treat subprocesses like threads and handle the context switching between them. Go takes a different route. Following a model proposed by the renowned computer scientist Tony Hoare, Go uses the concurrency model called *Communicating Sequential Processes* (CSP). This chapter covers the practical aspects of working with Go's concurrency model, though we suggest reading a little about the theory behind CSP and Go at go.dev.

> **A look at concurrency patterns**
>
> Go's Rob Pike has done a retrospective on the design of Go and on the concurrency patterns that influenced Go's goroutine approach. You can see the presentation at https://www.youtube.com/watch?v=yE5Tpp2BSGw or look at the slides at https://mng.bz/6eNy.

Two concepts make Go's concurrency model work:

- *Goroutines*—A *goroutine* is a function that runs independently of the function that started it. Sometimes, Go developers explain a goroutine as a function that runs as though it were on its own thread.
- *Channels*—A *channel* is a pipeline for sending and receiving data. Think of it as a socket that runs inside your program and accepts and/or sends signals. Channels provide a way for one goroutine to send structured data to another. This is the main data stream for allowing goroutines to communicate with their caller and other goroutines.

The techniques in this chapter use goroutines and channels. We won't spend time on the theory or underpinnings of the goroutine and channel systems but will stick to practical use of these two concepts.

Go's approach to concurrency is intuitive enough that you'll frequently see it used in libraries and tools. This chapter introduces several concurrency topics, with emphasis on how Go's model differs from that of other popular languages. It also focuses on best practices. Goroutines and channels are among the few places in the Go language where programmers can introduce memory leaks and concurrency can open a door for race conditions. You can remedy these situations by following certain patterns, which we'll introduce in this chapter.

5.2 Working with goroutines

When it comes to syntax, a goroutine is any function that's called after the keyword go. Almost any function could in theory be called as a goroutine, though there are plenty of functions you probably wouldn't want to call as goroutines. One of the most frequent uses of goroutines is to run a function in the background while not blocking your program to do something else as it goes on. As an example, let's write a short program that echoes back any text you type in, but only for 30 seconds, as shown in the next listing. After that, it exits on its own.

Listing 5.1 Using a goroutine to run a task

```
package main

import (
    "fmt"
    "io"
    "os"
    "time"
)

func main() {
    fmt.Println("Type anything below for up to 30 seconds")
    go echo(os.Stdin, os.Stdout)
    time.Sleep(30 * time.Second)
    fmt.Println("Timed out.")
    os.Exit(0)
}

func echo(in io.Reader, out io.Writer) {
    io.Copy(out, in)
}
```

Calls the function echo as a goroutine, yielding control back to main

Sleeps for 30 seconds

Prints out a message saying we've timed out

Exits the program, stopping the goroutine

The echo function is a normal function.

io.Copy copies data to an os.Writer from an os.Reader.

This program uses a goroutine to run the echoing behavior in the background while a timer runs in the foreground. If you were to run the program and type in some text, the output would look something like this:

```
$ go run echoback.go
Type anything below for up to 30 seconds
Hello.
Hello.
My name is Inigo Montoya
My name is Inigo Montoya
You killed my father
You killed my father
Prepare to die
Prepare to die
Timed out.
```

Here's how the program works. Each line you type is displayed by the shell as you type it, and echoed back by the program as soon as it reads the line (in other words, when you press Enter, creating a newline). It continues this concurrent `echo` loop while `main` sleeps for 30 seconds. As you can see in the example, there's nothing special about the `echo` function, but when you call it with the keyword `go`, it's executed as a goroutine. The `main` function fires the goroutine; then control flow is ceded to `main`.

The `main` function starts the goroutine and waits for 30 seconds. When the `main` function exits, it terminates the main goroutine, which effectively halts the program. The `time.Sleep` call here is critical because even if a goroutine is doing work, the end of the `main` function effectively ends the program, as goroutines are asynchronous and `main` comprises the ultimate lifetime of the application.

In practice, something like this is suited for Go's `context` package, which wraps a lot of helpful abstractions around concurrency, in this case deadlines and timeouts. Specifically, `context.WithDeadline()` can handle what we wrote from scratch in listing 5.1. This exercise gets us comfortable with the flow and potential quirks of concurrency.

5.2.1 *Waiting for goroutines*

Sometimes, you'll want to start multiple goroutines but not continue working until those goroutines have completed their respective jobs. In Go, wait groups provide a simple and intuitive way to achieve this by explicitly defining the number of expected calls to their `Done` method.

- *Problem*—One goroutine needs to start one or more other goroutines and then wait for them to finish. In this practical example, you'll focus on a more specific problem: you want to compress multiple files as fast as possible and then display a summary.
- *Solution*—Run individual tasks inside goroutines. Use `sync.WaitGroup` to signal the outer process that the goroutines are done and that it can safely continue. Figure 5.1 illustrates this general design: several workers are started, and work is delegated to the workers. One process delegates the tasks to the workers and then waits for them to complete.

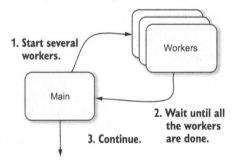

Figure 5.1 **Start multiple workers and wait for completion.**

- *Discussion*—Go's standard library provides several useful tools for working with synchronization. One that frequently comes in handy is `sync.WaitGroup`, a tool for telling a process to wait until one or more goroutines complete, specified by a numeric count.

Let's begin with a simple tool that compresses an arbitrary number of individual files. In the following listing, you'll use the built-in Gzip compression library (compress/gzip) to compress each file.

Listing 5.2 Simple Gzip compression tool

```go
package main

import (
    "compress/gzip"
    "io"
    "os"
)

func main() {
    for _, file := range os.Args[1:] {        Collects a list of files
        compress(file)                         passed in on the
    }.                                         command line
}

func compress(filename string) error {
    in, err := os.Open(filename)              Opens the source
    if err != nil {                           file for reading
        return err
    }
    defer in.Close()                          Opens a destination file, with
    out, err := os.Create(filename + ".gz")   the .gz extension added to
    if err != nil {                           the source file's name
        return err
    }
    defer out.Close()                         The gzip.Writer compresses
    gzout := gzip.NewWriter(out)              data and then writes it to the
    _, err = io.Copy(gzout, in)               underlying file.
    gzout.Close()
    return err                                The io.Copy function does
}                                             all the copying for you.
```

This tool takes a list of files on the command line and compresses each of them creating a file with the same name as the original but with .gz appended as an extension. Suppose that you have a directory that looks like this:

```
$ ls -1 exampledata
example1.txt
example2.txt
example3.txt
```

You have three text files in your `exampledata` directory. Using your tool, you can compress them:

```
$ go run simple_gz.go exampledata/*
$ ls -1 exampledata
example1.txt
example1.txt.gz
example2.txt
example2.txt.gz
example3.txt
example3.txt.gz
```

In that example run, you can see that your `simple_gz.go` program created a Gzipped version of each file.

But let's talk about performance. As written, the preceding program employs no concurrent file compression. It's unlikely that this program is going to make good use of available disk I/O bandwidth either. Although the code runs fine, it's nowhere near as fast as it could be, and because each file can be compressed individually, it's conceptually simple to break out your single thread of execution into something concurrent or parallelized rather than linear.

You can rewrite a program like this to compress each file in its own goroutine. Although this would be a suboptimal solution for compressing thousands of files (you'd probably overwhelm the I/O capacity of the system), it works well for dealing with a few hundred files or fewer.

Here's the trick: you want to compress a bunch of files in parallel but have the parent goroutine (`main`) wait around until all the workers are done. You can easily accomplish this with a wait group. In listing 5.3, you modify the code so that you don't change the `compress` function at all. This is a better design because it creates a good division of labor and doesn't require your worker function (`compress`) to use a wait group in cases where files need to be compressed serially.

Listing 5.3   Compressing files in parallel with a wait group

```go
package main

import (
    "compress/gzip"
    "fmt"
    "io"
    "os"
    "sync"
)

func main() {
    var wg sync.WaitGroup
    for i, file := range os.Args[1:] {
        wg.Add(1)
        go func(filename string) {
            compress(filename)
            wg.Done()
        }(file)
    }
```

A WaitGroup is declared but doesn't need to be initialized.

For every file you add, you tell the wait group that you're waiting for one more compress operation.

This function calls compress and then notifies the wait group that it's done.

Because you're calling a goroutine in a for loop, you need to pass your parameter into the closure.

```
    wg.Wait()
    fmt.Printf("Compressed %d files\n", len(os.Args[1:]))
}

func compress(filename string) error {
    // Unchanged from above
}
```

> The outer goroutine (main) waits until all the compressing goroutines have called wg.Done.

In this revised compression tool, you've changed the `main` function in significant ways. First, you've added a wait group to capture the number of goroutines that must register as done before the wait group is satisfied and the program can continue.

A *wait group* is a message-passing facility that signals a waiting goroutine when it's safe to proceed. To use it, you tell the wait group when you want it to wait for something, and you signal it again when that thing is done. In this case, for each iteration in the for loop, we add another goroutine to the wait group's count. A wait group doesn't need to know more about the things it's waiting for other than the number of things it's waiting for and when each thing is done. You increment the first with `wg.Add,` and as your task completes, you signal this with `wg.Done`. The `wg.Wait` function blocks until all tasks that were added have completed. Figure 5.2 illustrates the process.

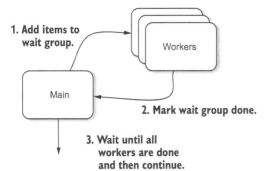

Figure 5.2 Wait groups in action

In theory, you could add the entire queue based on the length of the arguments, but what happens if one fails in the loop? The `Wait()` method is blocking, so it will wait in perpetuity. It's safer to explicitly add each item to the wait group as you fire the goroutine.

For this reason, you also call `wg.Done` inside a goroutine, which keeps all your initialization and satisfaction of a goroutine code close together. When the `Done()` call is deferred, you reduce the chances that a `WaitGroup` will hang if something goes wrong in the interim. That goroutine accepts a filename and then runs your `compress` function on it. Notice that you've done something that at first blush appears redundant. Instead of closing over `file` inside the closure, you pass the file into the program as `filename`. You do this for a reason related to the Go scheduler.

As you saw earlier in the chapter, declaring a goroutine doesn't result in its immediate execution. If your loop runs five times, you'll have five goroutines scheduled but possibly none executed, and on each of those five iterations, the value of `file` will change. By the time the goroutines execute, they may all have the same (fifth) version of the `file` string. That isn't what you want. You want each to be scheduled with that iteration's value of `file`, so you pass it as a function parameter, which ensures that the value of `file` is passed to each goroutine as it's scheduled.

Although this might at first seem an esoteric problem, it's not uncommon. Any time a loop executes goroutines, you need to be extra careful that the variables the goroutine uses aren't changed by the loop and that data is copied for use with that goroutine to prevent it from being stale or overwritten.

5.2.2 *Locking with a mutex*

Any time two or more goroutines are working with the same piece of data, and that data may change, you have the potential for a race condition. In a *race condition*, two things are "racing" to read or write the same piece of information. Problems arise when both are working with the same data at approximately the same time. One goroutine may be only partway through modifying a value when another goroutine tries to use it, and that situation can have unintended consequences. If you can't trust the data your program is working with, data integrity problems come into play very quickly. Mutations that happen out of expected order can lead to outright errors.

- *Problem*—Multiple processes and/or goroutines need to access or modify the same piece of data.
- *Solution*—One simple way to avoid this situation is for each goroutine to place a lock on a resource it's using and unlock the resource when it's done. When all other goroutines see the lock, they wait until the lock is removed before attempting to use and lock that resource themselves. Use `sync.Mutex` to lock and unlock the object.
- *Discussion*—The built-in `sync` package provides a `sync.Locker` interface as well as a couple of lock implementations. These provide essential locking behavior.

The following listing is an example of a program with a race condition. This simple program reads any number of files and tallies the number of occurrences for each word it finds. At the end of its execution, it prints a list of words that appear more than once.

Listing 5.4   Word counter with race condition

```
package main

import (
        "bufio"
        "fmt"
        "os"
        "strings"
        "sync"
)
```

```
func main() {
    var wg sync.WaitGroup
    w := newWords()
    if len(os.Args) < 2 {
        fmt.Println("no files provided")
        os.Exit(1)
    }
    for _, f := range os.Args[1:] {
        wg.Add(1)
        go func(file string) {
            if err := tallyWords(file, w); err
            != nil {
                fmt.Println(err.Error())
            }
            wg.Done()
        }(f)
    }
    wg.Wait()
    fmt.Println("Words that appear more than once:")
    for word, count := range w.found {
        if count > 1 {
            fmt.Printf("%s: %d\n", word, count)
        }
    }
}

type words struct {
    found map[string]int
}
func newWords() *words {
    return &words{found: map[string]int{}}
}

func (w *words) add(word string) {
    count, ok := w.found[word]
    if !ok {
        w.found[word] = 1
        return
    }
    w.found[word] = count + 1
}
func tallyWords(filename string, dict *words) error {
    file, err := os.Open(filename)
    if err != nil {
        return err
    }
    defer file.Close()
    scanner := bufio.NewScanner(file)
    scanner.Split(bufio.ScanWords)
    for scanner.Scan() {
        word := strings.ToLower(scanner.Text())
        dict.add(word)
    }
    return scanner.Err()
}
```

Again, you'll use a wait group to keep track of a group of goroutines.

The main loop uses the pattern in technique 12.

At the end of the program, you'll print what you found.

You track words in a struct. You could use the underlying map directly, but using a struct here makes the next refactor easier.

Creates a new words instance

Tracks the number of times you've seen this word

If the word isn't already tracked, add it; otherwise, increment the count.

Open a file, parse its contents, and count the words that appear. The Copy function does all the copying for you.

Scanner is a useful tool for parsing files like this.

The main function loops over all the files you supply on the command line, generating statistics for each as it goes. When you run the preceding code, you expect that the tool will read text files and print a list of the words that it finds. Let's try it on a single file:

```
$ go run race.go 1.txt
Words that appear more than once:
had: 2
down: 2
the: 5
have: 2
that: 3
would: 3
...
```

That's what you'd expect the output to look like. If you pass in more than one file-name, the tool will process each file in its own goroutine. Let's try that:

```
$ go run race.go *.txt
fatal error: concurrent map writes
goroutine 8 [running]:
runtime.throw(0x115890, 0xd)
      /usr/local/go/src/runtime/panic.go:527 +0x90 fp=0x82029cbf0
      sp=0x82029cbd8
runtime.evacuate(0xca600, 0x8202142d0, 0x16)
      /usr/local/go/src/runtime/hashmap.go:825 +0x3b0 fp=0x82029ccb0
      sp=0x82029cbf0
runtime.growWork(0xca600, 0x8202142d0, 0x31)
      /usr/local/go/src/runtime/hashmap.go:795 +0x8a fp=0x82029ccd0
      sp=0x82029ccb0
runtime.mapassign1(0xca600, 0x8202142d0, 0x82029ce70, 0x82029cdb0)
      /usr/local/go/src/runtime/hashmap.go:433 +0x175 fp=0x82029cd78
      sp=0x82029ccd0
...
```

At least some of the time, this will fail. Why? The error gives a hint: concurrent map writes. If you rerun the command with the --race flag, you'll get an even better idea:

```
go run --race race.go *.txt
==================
WARNING: DATA RACE
Read by goroutine 8:
  runtime.mapaccess2_faststr()
      /chapter5/hashmap_fast.go:281 +0x0
  main.tallyWords()
      /chapter5/race/race.go:62 +0x3ed
  main.main.func1()
      /chapter5/race/race.go:18 +0x66
Previous write by goroutine 6:
  runtime.mapassign1()
      /chapter5/hashmap.go:411 +0x0
  main.tallyWords()
      /chapter5/race/race.go:62 +0x48a
  main.main.func1()
      /chapter5/race/race.go:18 +0x66
```

```
Goroutine 8 (running) created at:
  main.main()
      /chapter5/race/race.go:22 +0x238
Goroutine 6 (running) created at:
  main.main()
      /chapter5/race/race.go:22 +0x238
==================
```

The call to words.add has a problem. Multiple goroutines are accessing the same bit of memory, the words.found map, at the same time (note the bold lines). This causes a race condition while multiple goroutines attempt to modify the map.

> **Go includes built-in race detection**
>
> Many of the Go tools, including go run and go test, accept a --race flag, which enables race detection. Race detection substantially slows execution, but it's useful for detecting race conditions during the development cycle. Including this into your code review or continuous integration workflow is a great way to catch these before they become a real-world problem in more distributed systems.

If you look at the original program, you can quickly find the problem. If add is called by multiple goroutines at around the same time, multiple simultaneous operations may occur on the same map. This is a recipe for corrupting the map, and if left unchecked, it leads to unexpected or incorrect results.

One simple solution is to lock the map before you modify it and unlock it afterward. You can accomplish this with a few changes to the code, as shown in the next listing.

Listing 5.5 Word counter with locks

```
package main

import (
    // Same as before...
    "sync"
)

func main() {
    var wg sync.WaitGroup
    w := newWords()
    if len(os.Args) < 2 {
        fmt.Println("no files provided")
        os.Exit(1)
    }
    for _, f := range os.Args[1:] {
            wg.Add(1)
            go func(file string) {
                    if err := tallyWords(file, w); err != nil {
                            fmt.Println(err.Error())
                    }
```

```
                    wg.Done()
            }(f)
    }
    wg.Wait()
    fmt.Println("Words that appear more than once:")
    w.Lock()
    defer w.Unlock()
    for word, count := range w.found {
            if count > 1 {
                    fmt.Printf("%s: %d\n", word, count)
            }
    }
}

type words struct {
    sync.Mutex
    found map[string]int
}

func newWords() *words {
    return &words{found: map[string]int{}}
}

func (w *words) add(word string) {
    w.Lock()
    defer w.Unlock()
    count, ok := w.found[word]
    if !ok {
            w.found[word] = 1
            return
    }
    w.found[word] = count + 1
}

func tallyWords(filename string, dict *words) error {
    // Unchanged from before
}
```

> **Locks and unlocks the map when you are done iterating. Strictly speaking, this isn't necessary because you know that this section won't happen until all files are processed.**

> **The words struct now inherits the mutex lock.**

> **Locks the object, modifies the map, and then unlocks the object**

In this revised version, the `words` struct declares an anonymous field referencing `sync.Mutex`, basically granting the `words.Lock` and `words.Unlock` methods. This is a common way of exposing a lock on a struct. (You used these methods when looping over the words at the end of `main`.)

Now, inside the `add` method, you lock the object, modify the map, and then unlock the object. When multiple goroutines enter the `add` method, the first will get the lock, and the others will wait until the lock is released. This will prevent multiple goroutines from modifying the map at the same time.

It's important to note that locks work only when all access to the data is managed by the same lock. If some data is accessed with locks and others without, a race condition can still occur.

Sometimes, it's useful to allow multiple read operations on a piece of data but allow only one write (and no reads) during a write operation. The `sync.RWMutex` provides this functionality. When using an `RWMutex`, you can use `RLock` to lock but allow nonexclusive reads and `RUnlock` to release the lock. It's effectively a drop-in replacement for `Lock` and `Unlock`. The `sync` package has several other useful tools that simplify coordination across goroutines. But let's turn our attention to another core concept in Go's concurrency model: channels.

5.3 Working with channels

Channels provide a way to send data in the form of messages from one goroutine to another. This section covers several ways of using channels to accomplish common tasks and solve common problems in concurrent code.

The easiest way to understand channels is to compare them to network sockets. Two applications can connect over a network socket. Depending on how these applications were written, network traffic can flow in a single direction or bidirectionally. Sometimes, network connections are short-lived, and sometimes, they stick around for a long time. Smart applications may even use multiple network connections, each sending and receiving different kinds of data. Just about any data can be sent over a network socket, but there's a drawback: that data must be marshaled into raw bytes.

Go channels work like sockets between goroutines within a single application, pipes that can share information asynchronously. Like network sockets, they can be unidirectional or bidirectional. Channels can be short-lived or long-lived. It's common to use more than one channel in an app, having different channels send different kinds of data. But unlike network connections, channels are typed and can send structured data. There's generally no need to marshal data onto a channel, as Go is managing all the communication itself. Let's dive into channels by refactoring an earlier code sample to use channels.

5.3.1 Using channels

Go developers are fond of pointing out that channels are communication tools. They enable one goroutine to communicate information to another goroutine. Sometimes, the best way to solve concurrency problems in Go is to communicate more information, which often translates into using more channels.

- *Problem*—You want to use channels to send data from one goroutine to another and be able to interrupt that process to exit if and when needed.
- *Solution*—Use `select` and multiple channels. It's a common practice in Go to use channels to signal when something is done or ready to close.
- *Discussion*—To introduce channels, let's revisit the first code example in this chapter. That program echoed user input for 30 seconds. It accomplished this by using a goroutine to echo the information and used a `time.Sleep` call to wait in our `main` function before ending the program. Let's rewrite that program to use channels in addition to goroutines.

We're not looking to add new functionality or even vastly improve the initial example, but we're taking a different approach to solving the same problem with a new concept. In doing so, you'll see several idiomatic uses of channels.

Before looking at the code in listing 5.6, consider the following concepts that come into play here:

- Channels are initialized with `make`, just like maps and slices.
- The arrow operator (`<-`) is used both to signify the direction of a channel (`out chan<- []byte`) and to send or receive data over a channel (`buf := <-echo`). Without this operator, a channel is bidirectional.
- The `select` statement can watch multiple channels (zero or more). Until something happens, it'll wait (or execute a `default` statement, if supplied). When a channel has an event, the `select` statement will execute that event. You'll see more on channels later in this chapter.

Listing 5.6   Using channels

```
package main

import (
    "fmt"
    "os"
    "time"
)

func main() {
    echo := make(chan []byte)
    go readStdin(echo)
    for {
        select {
        case buf := <-echo:
            os.Stdout.Write(buf)
        case <- time.After(30 * time.Second):
            break
        }
    }
}

func readStdin(out chan<- []byte) {
    for {
        data := make([]byte, 1024)
        l, _ := os.Stdin.Read(data)
        if l > 0 {
            out <- data
        }
    }
}
```

Makes a new channel for passing bytes from Stdin to Stdout. Because you haven't specified a size, this channel can hold only one message at a time.

Starts a goroutine to read Stdin and passes it to our new channel for communicating

Uses a select statement to pass data from Stdin to Stdout when received, or to shut down when the time-out event occurs

Takes a write-only channel (chan<-) and sends any received input to that channel

Reads from time.After, which resets every 30 seconds each time a message is received

Copies some data from Stdin into data. Note that File.Read will block until it receives data.

Sends the buffered data over the channel

Running the preceding code results in the following:

```
$ go run echoredux.go
test 1
test 1
test 2
test 2
```

```
test 3
test 3
Timed out
```

As you saw with the previous implementation, if you type `test 1`, that text is echoed back. After 30 seconds of inactivity, the program halts.

Rewriting the echo example introduced new concepts regarding channels. The first channel in the preceding code is created by the `time` package. The `time.After` function builds a channel that will send a message (a `time.Time`) when the given duration has elapsed. Calling `time.After(30 * time.Second)` returns a `<-chan time.Time` (receive-only channel that receives `time.Time` objects) that, after 30 seconds, will receive a message. Thus, practically speaking, the two methods of pausing in the following listing are operationally equivalent. If we move this to a variable declaration above the `select` statement, we can create a full program time-out channel.

> **Listing 5.7   Pausing with `Sleep` and `After`**

```
package main

import (
    "time"
)

func main() {
    time.Sleep(5 * time.Second)        ◁──┐  Blocks for 5 seconds
    sleep := time.After(5 * time.Second)     Creates a channel that will get
    <-sleep                                  notified in 5 seconds and then
}                                            blocks until that channel
                                             receives a notification
```

Some functions (as in this example, `time.After`) create and initialize channels for you. But to create a new channel, you can use the built-in `make` function.

Channels are bidirectional by default. But as you saw in the preceding example, you can specify a direction for the channel when passing it into a function (or during any other assignment). The `readStdin` function can only write to the `out` channel. Any attempt to read from it will result in a compile-time error. Generally, it's considered good programming practice to indicate in a function signature whether the function receives or sends on a channel.

The last important facet of this program is `select`. A `select` statement is syntactically similar to a `switch` statement. It can take any number of `case` statements, as well as a single optional `default` statement.

The `select` statement checks each `case` condition to see whether any of them has a send or receive operation that needs to be performed. If exactly one of the `case` statements can send or receive, `select` will execute that case. If more than one can send or receive, `select` randomly picks one. If none of the `case` statements can send or receive, `select` falls through to a default (if specified). If no default is specified, `select` blocks until one of the `case` statements can send or receive.

In this example, `select` is waiting to receive on two channels. If a message comes over the echo channel, the string that's sent is stored in `buf` (`buf := <-echo`) and then written to standard output. This illustrates that a receive operation can assign the received value to a variable.

But the second `case` that your `select` is waiting for is a message on the `done` channel. Because you don't particularly care about the contents of the message, you don't assign the received value to a variable. The underlying data can be treated as a truthy Boolean. You just read it off the channel, and the `select` discards the value (`<-done`).

> **TIP** If you have a single goroutine to listen to, you can skip the `for/select` loop and instead `range` over the channel itself, particularly on buffered channels. This is less common in practice when multiple channels are being orchestrated, but some linting tools recommend eschewing the `select` loop when dealing with just a single channel.

There's no `default` value on your `select`, so it'll block until a message is received on `<-echo` or a message is received on `<-done`. When the message is received, `select` will run the `case` block and then return control. You've wrapped your `select` in a conditionless `for` loop, so the `select` will be run infinitely until the `<-done` channel receives a message and the program exits.

One thing we didn't cover in this technique is closing channels when you're done with them. In our example app, the program is too short-lived to require this, and you rely on the runtime to clean up after you. In the next technique, you'll look at a strategy for closing channels.

5.3.2   *Closing channels*

In Go, developers rely on the memory manager to clean up after themselves. When a variable drops out of scope, the associated memory is scrubbed. But you have to be careful when working with goroutines and channels. What happens if you have a sender and receiver goroutine and the sender finishes sending data? Are the receiver and channel automatically cleaned up? Nope. The memory manager will only clean up values that it can ensure won't be used again, and in our example, an open channel and a goroutine can't be safely cleaned.

Imagine for a moment that this code was part of a larger program and that the function `main` was a regular function called repeatedly throughout the lifetime of the app. Each time it's called, it creates a new channel and a new goroutine. But the channel is never closed, and the goroutine never returns. That program would leak both channels and goroutines.

A question arises: how can you correctly and safely clean up when you're using goroutines and channels? Failing to clean up can cause memory leaks or channel/goroutine leaks, where unneeded goroutines and channels consume system resources but do nothing.

- *Problem*—You don't want leftover channels and goroutines to consume resources and cause leaky applications. You want to safely close channels and exit goroutines.
- *Solution*—The straightforward answer to the question "How do I avoid leaking channels and goroutines?" is "Close your channels and return from your goroutines." Although that answer is correct, it's also incomplete. Closing channels the wrong way will cause your program to panic or leak goroutines.

   The predominant method for avoiding unsafe channel closing is to use additional channels to notify goroutines when it's safe to close a channel.
- *Discussion*—You can use a few idiomatic techniques for safely shutting down channels.

Let's start, though, with a negative example, shown in the following listing. Beginning with the general idea of the program from listing 5.6, let's construct a program that incorrectly manages its channel.

Listing 5.8 Improper channel close

```
package main

import (
    "fmt"
    "time"
)

func main() {
    msg := make(chan string)
    until := time.After(5 * time.Second)
    go send(msg)
    for {
            select {
            case m := <-msg:
                    fmt.Println(m)
            case <-until:
                    close(msg)
                    time.Sleep(500 * time.Millisecond)
                    return
            }
    }
}

func send(ch chan string) {
    for {
            ch <- "hello"
            time.Sleep(500 * time.Millisecond)
    }
}
```

Starts a send goroutine with a sending channel

Loops over a select that watches for messages from send or for a time-out

If a message arrives from send, prints it

When the time-out occurs, shuts things down. You pause to ensure that you see the failure before the main goroutine exits.

Sends "Hello" to the channel every half-second

This example code is contrived to illustrate a problem that's more likely to occur in a server or another long-running program. You'd expect this program to print 10 or so hello strings and then exit. But if you run it, you get this:

```
$ go run bad.go
hello
hello
hello
hello
hello
hello
hello
hello
hello
hello
panic: send on closed channel
goroutine 20 [running]:
main.send(0x82024c060)
        /chapter5/closing/bad.go:28 +0x4c
created by main.main
        /chapter5/closing/bad.go:12 +0x90
goroutine 1 [sleep]:
time.Sleep(0x1dcd6500)
        /usr/local/go/src/runtime/time.go:59 +0xf9
main.main()
        /chapter5/closing/bad.go:20 +0x24f
exit status 2
```

At the end, the program panics because main closes the msg channel while send is still sending messages to it. An attempted send on a closed channel panics. In Go, the close function should be closed only by a sender, and in general, it should be done with some protective guards around it.

What happens if you close the channel from the sender? No panic happens, but something interesting does. Take a look at the quick example in the next listing.

Listing 5.9   Close channel from sender

```
package main

import (
    "log"
    "time"
)

func main() {
    ch := make(chan bool)
    timeout := time.After(600 * time.Millisecond)
    go send(ch) //
    for { //
        select {
        case m, ok := <-ch: //
            if !ok { //
                log.Println("Channel closed.")
                return
            }
            log.Println("Got message:", m)
```

Loops over a select with two channels and a default

If you get a message over your main channel, prints something

If that message consists of a closed channel, outputs message

```
        case <-timeout: //
            log.Println("Time out")
            return
        default: //
            log.Println("*yawn*")
            time.Sleep(100 * time.Millisecond)
        }
    }
}

func send(ch chan bool) { //
    time.Sleep(120 * time.Millisecond)
    ch <- true
    close(ch)
    log.Println("Sent and closed")
}
```

⟵ If a time-out occurs, terminates the program

⟵ By default, sleeps for a bit. This makes the example easier to work with.

⟵ Sends a single message over the channel and then closes the channel

After running this code, you'd expect that the `main` loop would do the following: hit the default clause a couple of times, get a single message from `send`, and then hit the default clause a few more times before the time-out happens and the program exits. Instead, you'll see this:

```
$ go run sendclose.go
*yawn*
*yawn*
*yawn*
*yawn*
Got message.
Got message.
Sent and closed
*yawn*
Sent and closed
*yawn*
Got message.
Got message.
Got message.
Got message.
… #thousands more
Time out
```

This occurs because a closed channel always returns the channel's zero value, so `send` sends one `true` value and then closes the channel. Each time the `select` examines `ch` after `ch` is closed, it'll receive a `false` value (the `nil` value on a `bool` channel).

You could work around this problem. For example, you could break out of the `for/select` loop as soon as you see `false` on `ch`. Sometimes, that's necessary. But the better solution is to explicitly indicate that you're finished with the channel and then close it.

The best way to rewrite listing 5.8 is to use one additional channel to indicate that you're done with the channel. This gives both sides the opportunity to cleanly handle the closing of the channel, as shown in the next listing.

Listing 5.10   Using a close channel

```go
package main

import (
    "log"
    "time"
)

func main() {
    msg := make(chan string) //
    done := make(chan bool)  //
    go send(msg, done) //
    for {
        select {
        case m := <-msg: //
            log.Println(m)
        case <-time.After(5 * time.Second): //
            done <- true
            return
        }
    }
}

func send(ch chan<- string, done <-chan bool) {
    for {
        select {
        case <-done: //
            log.Println("Done")
            close(ch)
            return
        default:
            ch <- "hello"
            time.Sleep(500 * time.Millisecond) //
        }
    }
}
```

Creates a channel
for messages

Adds a Boolean channel
that indicates when
you're finished

Passes two channels
into send

Outputs messages
as they're received

When you time-out,
lets send know the
process is done

When done has
a message, shuts
things down

ch is a receiving
channel, and done is
a sending channel.

When done has
a message, shuts
things down

This example demonstrates a pattern that you'll observe frequently in Go: using a channel (often called done) to send a signal between goroutines. In this pattern, you usually have one goroutine whose primary task is to receive messages and another whose job is to send messages. If the receiver hits a stopping condition, it must let the sender know. You can also extend this pattern to other types of messages that you may want to organize away from your normal data pipeline channels, like logging.

In listing 5.10, the main function is the one that knows when to stop processing. But it's also the receiver. As you saw before, the receiver shouldn't ever close a channel. Instead, it sends a message on the done channel indicating that it's done with its work. Now the send function knows—when it receives a message on done—that it can (and should) close the channel and return.

> **Don't overuse channels**
>
> Channels are fantastic tools for communicating between goroutines. They're simple to use, as you'll see, and make concurrent programming much easier than the threading models of other popular languages.
>
> But be wary of overuse. Channels carry overhead and affect performance. They introduce complexity into a program. Most important, channels are the single biggest source of memory management problems in Go programs. As with any tool, use channels when the need arises, but resist the temptation to polish your new hammer and then go looking for nails.

5.3.3 *Locking with buffered channels*

So far, you've looked at channels that contain one value at a time and are created like this: `make(chan TYPE)`. This is called an *unbuffered channel*. If such a channel has received a value and is then sent another one before the channel can be read, the second send operation will block. Moreover, the sender will block until the channel is read.

Sometimes, you'll want to alter those blocking behaviors. You can do so by creating buffered channels.

- *Problem*—In a particularly sensitive portion of code, you need to lock certain resources. Given the frequent use of channels in your code, you'd like to do this with channels instead of the `sync` package.
- *Solution*—Use a channel with a buffer size of 1, and share the channel among the goroutines you want to synchronize.
- *Discussion*—Listing 5.4 introduced `sync.Locker` and `sync.Mutex` for locking sensitive areas of code. The `sync` package is part of Go's core and thus is well tested and maintained. But sometimes (especially in code that already uses channels), it's desirable to implement locks with channels instead of the mutex. Often, this is a stylistic preference: it's prudent to keep your code as uniform as possible. It also provides a performance advantage by enabling locks per buffer rather than the item itself.

When talking about using a channel as a lock, you want this kind of behavior:

1. A function acquires a lock by sending a message on a channel.
2. The function proceeds to do its sensitive operations.
3. The function releases the lock by reading the message back off the channel.
4. Any function that tries to acquire the lock before it's been released will pause when it tries to acquire the lock.

You couldn't implement this scenario with an unbuffered channel. The first step in this process would cause the function to block because an unbuffered channel blocks on send. In other words, the sender waits until something receives the message it puts on the channel.

But one of the features of a buffered channel is that it doesn't block on send provided that buffer space still exists. A sender can send a message into the buffer and then move on. But if a buffer is full, the sender will block until there's room in the buffer for it to write its message.

This is exactly the behavior you want in a lock. You create a channel with only one empty buffer space. One function can send a message, do its thing, and then read the message off the buffer (thus unlocking it). The next listing shows a simple implementation.

Listing 5.11   Simple locking with channels

```
package main

import (
    "log"
    "time"
)

func main() {
    lock := make(chan bool, 1) //
    for i := 1; i < 7; i++ { //
        go worker(i, lock) //
    }
    time.Sleep(10 * time.Second)
}

func worker(id int, lock chan bool) {
    log.Printf("%d wants the lock\n", id)
    lock <- true //
    log.Printf("%d has the lock\n", id) //
    <-lock //
    log.Printf("%d is releasing the lock\n", id)
}
```

Creates a buffered channel with one space

Starts up to six goroutines sharing the locking channel

A worker acquires the lock by sending it a message. The first worker to hit this gets the one space and thus owns the lock. The rest will block.

The space between the lock <- true and the <- lock is "locked" by this goroutine.

Releases the lock by reading a value, which opens that one space on the buffer again so that the next worker can lock it

This pattern is simple: there's one step to lock and one to unlock. If you run this program, the output will look like this:

```
$ go run lock.go
2 wants the lock
1 wants the lock
2 has the lock
5 wants the lock
6 wants the lock
4 wants the lock
3 wants the lock
2 is releasing the lock
1 has the lock
1 is releasing the lock
5 has the lock
```

```
5 is releasing the lock
6 has the lock
6 is releasing the lock
3 has the lock
3 is releasing the lock
4 has the lock
4 is releasing the lock
```

In this output, you can see how your six goroutines acquire and release the lock. Within the first few milliseconds of starting the program, all six goroutines have tried to get the lock. But only goroutine 2 gets it. A few hundred milliseconds later, 2 releases the lock and 1 gets it. The lock trading continues until the last goroutine (4) acquires and releases the lock. (Note that in this code, you can rely on the memory manager to clean up the locking channel. After all references to the channel are gone, it'll clean up the channel for you.)

This example shows a method for multiple cooperating concurrent operations to work on a single piece of data while avoiding race conditions using a different approach from mutexes, which were used earlier in this chapter, in listing 5.5.

Listing 5.11 illustrates one advantage of using buffered queues: preventing send operations from blocking while there's room in the queue. Specifying a queue length also allows you to specify just how much buffering you want to do. You might be able to imagine needing a lock that can be claimed by up to two goroutines, and you could accomplish this with a channel of length 2. Buffered queues are also employed for constructing message queues and pipelines. They are not replacements for mutexes; they operate in a similar space.

Summary

- Go's CSP-based model gives us the framework for how Go approaches concurrency.
- Goroutines provide the primitive mechanism for creating and managing concurrent functions.
- Using the `sync` package for waiting and locking allows us to protect data integrity when multiple concurrent operations are attempting to work with it.
- Channels provide a system for sending and receiving data between goroutines and their callers.
- Closing channels properly is important to prevent memory leaks, and we saw the idiomatic way to use dedicated `done` channels to signal that another channel should be closed.

Formatting, testing, debugging, and benchmarking

This chapter covers

- Creating well-formatted and readable code with updated dependencies
- Making resilient and structured logs for your application
- Creating unit tests and building strategies for designing test suites
- Analyzing your code's performance and finding bottlenecks and problems

Go provides several tools out of the box that help keep your code clean, performant, and up to date. As you have experienced by now, the go tool lets you build and run your packages, but it also provides some incredibly useful functionality that can help make working code rock-solid and production-ready. To get to this point, code typically should have good testing, both for performance and functionality (unit testing). We can use all of Go's tooling to do this without the need for third-party software.

In this chapter, we'll dig into linting our code, keeping imports up to date, following best-practice logging strategies, and testing and benchmarking our code. We'll also look at features some common integrated development environments

(IDEs) can provide to push us even further toward battle-tested apps and reduce errors in production.

> **Go's other tools**
>
> In this chapter, we'll talk about `benchmark`, `cover`, `fmt`, `test`, and `vet`, but Go has additional static analysis tools that are worth exploring as you progress on your journey toward expertise. See https://pkg.go.dev/golang.org/x/tools.

6.1 Keeping your code and projects clean

Some of Go's built-in tooling helps you build and ship your code, but few other languages come with a batteries-included suite to keep your code clean and well-formatted. If you've ever had contentious code style discussions for other languages, this approach should come as a breath of fresh air. Go users have plenty to debate, but you'll rarely see a pull request for a Go project that includes any notes about style or layout guidelines.

6.1.1 Keeping code well formatted

We touched on `go fmt` in chapter 1, and we hope you've been using it to keep your code neatly organized and laid out in Go's heavily opinionated style. If you haven't been doing this by default or haven't added it as part of your normal coding workflow, do so now. There's little debate on the coding styles of idiomatic Go, so if you plan to share your code with others, this is practically a requirement. We'll look at ways to add this tool and similar Go tools to your IDE's workflow later in this chapter, but for now, familiarize yourself with the `fmt` tool and its output.

The `go fmt` tool can catch small, subtle things that might make their way into your code. Extraneous whitespace, for example, can be removed from within code blocks on formatting. Choices that may be more personal or stylistic, like extra newlines, are left to the user's discretion.

It's worth noting that `go fmt` is itself an alias to a distinct tool called `gofmt`. The full `gofmt` gives you some additional options that can give you more insight into the types of changes it might make. Although you can always use version control systems like git to review and undo formatting decisions, `gofmt` also accepts a `-d` flag to show the diff without committing the change to your code. Let's look at a particularly badly formatted block of code and what the `fmt` tool suggests via its diff.

Listing 6.1 Formatting some badly formatted code

```
package main

import "fmt"
import "os"
```

```
func main() {
        fmt.Println(  "checking for environment variable CLEANUP")          ←
                                                                            ┐ Extraneous
                                                                            │ space
        if envvar := os.GetEnv("CLEANUP"); envvar != "" {
            fmt.Println(" did not find it, value is:"
            ,    envvar);                                    ←┐ Unnecessary
        }                                                     │ semicolon

}
```

Here's the same code, linted via `gofmt --d myfile.go`:

```
-- myfile.go.orig
+++ myfile.go
@@ -1,16 +1,13 @@
-
-
 package main

 import "fmt"
 import "os"

-
 func main() {
-    fmt.Println(  "checking for environment variable                    ┐ Space
CLEANUP")                                                             ←  │ removed
-
-        if envvar := os.GetEnv("CLEANUP"); envvar != "" {             ┐ Semicolon
-            fmt.Println(" did not find it, value is:", envvar);    ←  │ removed
-        }
+    fmt.Println("checking for environment variable                     ┐ Space
CLEANUP")                                                            ←  │ removed
+
+        if envvar := os.GetEnv("CLEANUP"); envvar != "" {
            fmt.Println(" did not find it, value is:", env          ┐ Semicolon
            var)                                                 ←  │ removed
+    }

}
```

All the extra spaces are cleaned up, and unnecessary semicolons are removed. Code indents are all tabs per the Go spec and everything will align the same for any user of Go who uses fmt as part of their workflow. Note that some choices are left up to the developer, like the independent import lines and some newlines, but not extraneous ones between imports and between functions.

Having style dictated to you by the language may feel foreign, but it's incredibly useful for eliminating stylistic debates that happen in other languages. As Go cocreator Rob Pike put it at Gopherfest 2015: "gofmt's style is no one's favorite, yet gofmt is everyone's favorite." Not having to think about formatting, linting, and style is refreshing when it comes to producing clean code at a good pace.

> **Using go imports**
>
> As we briefly touched on in chapter 1, `go fmt` is a great tool that can be supplanted by go imports, a separate tool from the Go language team that wraps `gofmt` and also automatically brings in any third-party dependencies you may have forgotten to include in your code. It also removes any packages you happened to leave in your code that are unused, which helps prevent compiler errors due to refactors or leftover code.
>
> To install: `go install golang.org/x/tools/cmd/goimports@latest`. To use: `goimports [FILE_PATTERN].go`.

Adding `gofmt` or `goimports` to your workflow is generally easy in the most common IDEs. For Intellij's Goland, choose Preferences > Tools > File Watchers. Then you can add `goimports` on saving any `.go` file. Language support for IDEs is provided by gopls, another part of the toolset intended exclusively for use by any Language Server Protocol-enabled IDE (figure 6.1).

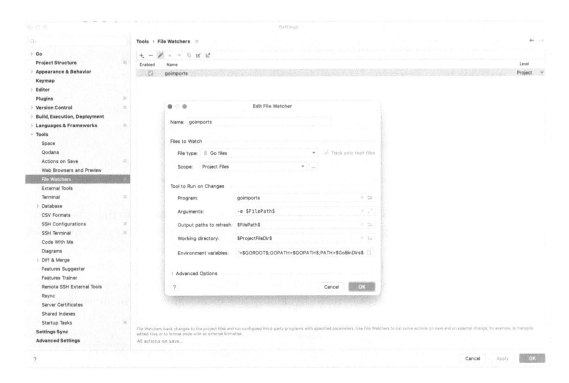

Figure 6.1 Adding `goimports` to Goland

For Visual Studio Code (VS Code), choose Settings > Text Editor > Formatting. Enable Format on Save, and you'll get the same functionality (figure 6.2).

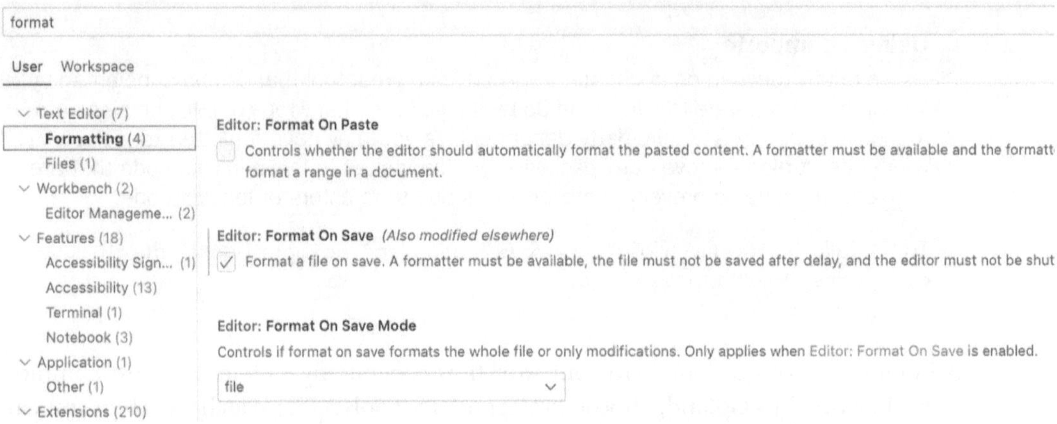

Figure 6.2   **Adding Format on Save to VS Code**

6.1.2   *Catching common errors with go vet*

In addition to go `fmt/gofmt`, the Go toolset comes with an application that can analyze your code a bit to find other mistakes or inefficiencies. This tool, `go vet`, can catch things that will compile in your code but do unexpected things like not marshaling code because a value is passed instead of a pointer, malformed tests, channels that need to be buffered, and `printf` commands that use the wrong verbs.

The tool can do a lot for you but is also susceptible to false positives. For this reason, it may not be the kind of tool you run every day on your code but can be very useful for sanity checks before building and distributing your code.

You can run any of the checks independently, so mistakes that may not apply to your code can be skipped. Alternately, you can set the `vet` tool free on your codebase with `go tool vet yourcode.go`.

Let's look at two examples of somewhat insidious coding mistakes that can be hard to catch because they won't always be triggered. The first deals with contexts, which are used in Go to manage share state across the application and associated signals. They provide deadlines, timeouts, and cancellation callbacks to control their lifetimes. You'll find these most frequently in concurrent code and in servers particularly. Because contexts are kept in memory, failing to cancel will lead to memory leaks that are otherwise hard to identify.

In the following listing, we wrap an HTTP server's handlers with a context to allow us to share some configuration data without needing a global variable. This is generally the preface for some kind of web server middleware that we're not building yet, so it's not a real-world example per se. But as we'll build some actual middleware in chapter 8, you'll see this pattern extended in the book.

Listing 6.2 Leaking context

```
package main

import (
    "context"
    "fmt"
    "net/http"
)

type config struct {
    HomepageDescription string
    Pageviews           int64
}

func main() {
    c := config{
        HomepageDescription: "my 1997-style personal web site",
        Pageviews:           0,
    }
    ctx, _ := context.WithCancel(context.Background())
    ctx = context.WithValue(ctx, "webConfig", c)

    http.HandleFunc("/home", homeHandler(ctx))
    http.HandleFunc("/guestbook", guestbookHandler(ctx))
    http.ListenAndServe(":8081", nil)
}

func homeHandler(ctx context.Context) http.HandlerFunc {
    myValue := ctx.Value("webConfig").(config) #D
    return func(w http.ResponseWriter, r *http.Request) {
        fmt.Fprintln(w, fmt.Sprintf("welcome to %s",
    myValue.HomepageDescription))
    }
}

func guestbookHandler(ctx context.Context) http.HandlerFunc {
    myValue := ctx.Value("webConfig").(config) #D
    return func(w http.ResponseWriter, r *http.Request) {
        myValue.Pageviews++
        fmt.Fprintln(w, fmt.Sprintf("welcome to my guestbook. hit counter
    since se
rver restart: %v", myValue.Pageviews))    }
}
```

> Creates a configuration

> Creates a context

> Applies our config as a value to the context

> Reads our context as a config type

We're doing a few new things here. First, instead of defining a `handlerFunc` for each route, we have a wrapper method that is called for each request and returns a `handler-Func`. In this we access the value from our context, perform type assertion to our config type, and use that shared configuration data. This isn't the only or ideal way of passing shared state, but it gives us an opportunity to have a leaky context. We have a cancellable background context, but we're ignoring the cancellation here:

```
ctx, _ := context.WithCancel(context.Background())
```

If we run go vet in our program's directory, we'll see

```
$ ./context_noclose.go:19:7: the cancel function returned by context.WithC
```

cancel should be called, not discarded, to avoid a context leak. The next listing can be especially annoying when you're dealing with encoding data, which (as you recall from chapter 3) requires the use of public attributes to work properly.

Listing 6.3   Unmarshaled JSON output

```go
package main

import (
    "encoding/json"
    "fmt"
)

type user struct {
    username  string `json:"username"`      Our struct has two
    Email     string `json:"email"`         nonexported/private fields.
    firstName string
}

func main() {

    m := user{
        username: "manning_go",
        Email:    "email@example.com",
        firstName: "Joe",
    }

    out, err := json.Marshal(m)            We are able
    if err != nil {                        to run Marshal
        panic("could not marshal")         without an error.
    }

    fmt.Println(string(out))

}
```

go vet catches this:

```
$ ./vet_marshal.go:9:2: struct field username has json tag but is not exported
```

Here, go vet gives us helpful information about why our JSON file is not coming out as we expected. You may have noticed that it didn't complain about the field first-Name, which is explained in the error message itself. There's no JSON tag, so it does not consider this a problem. Running go vet can save a few frustrating minutes here and there, so it's worth running this periodically to catch minor errors or putting it directly into your toolchain.

6.1.3 *Keeping dependencies updated*

One last note that can sometimes be forgotten about is `go mod`'s functions. We've already touched on `go mod init` and how that establishes our dependency file in `go.mod`. But what happens when we need to update a version or pick a specific one?

If you need a version of a library that is not the latest, you can simply specify a tag, which is a semantic versioning tag, such as 0.1.1. To do this, at any time after the `go mod init`, you can `go get http://[yourpackage]/here@0.1.1`. Assuming that tag exists in the specified repository, you will get that exact version.

For simply updating all dependencies, you need two commands: `go get -u` and `go mod tidy`. The `u` flag stands for *update*, and `go mod tidy` re-walks your dependency graph to ensure that all packages are compatible and satisfied. If you want to update only a single dependency, `go get -u http://[yourpackage]/here` will do this. Keep in mind it will possibly need to update transitive dependencies, so if you want to see the result, the `go mod graph` command will display your versions and their own dependencies.

> **NOTE** The `go get` tool also accepts a `-t` flag, which considers packages that may be needed for testing.

6.2 *Logging*

Before we dive into testing, there's one prerequisite to strong debugging and code analysis that will help us find information about our programs faster: logging. This is another rather unusual inclusion in a language's standard library. Most languages are hands-off and let developers handle how to format and save data, and indeed, it's also possible to build bespoke logging solutions in Go. But the language designers knew the importance of good logging, and so we have a host of nice tools around this.

If we're going to dig into our applications to find problems, it will be critical to persist our data beyond the console. In this section, we'll implement logging to file and memory and talk about strategies for working with init systems like systemd, systemctl, and Supervisor.

The log package in the standard library provides out of the box simple logging that follows similar interfaces to the `fmt` package's print methods. In fact, by replacing a lot of our previous `fmt.Println` calls with `log.Println`, we get formatted log output to stdout, as shown in the next listing.

Listing 6.4 Basic logging

```
package main

import (
    "fmt"
    "log"
)
```

```
func main() {
    fmt.Println("This is fmt package output")
    log.Println("This is log package output")
}
```

When we run with this simple change, the difference is clear in the output:

```
$ go run logging2.go
This is fmt package output
2023/08/29 15:52:24 This is log package output
```

The authors of this book have found it advantageous to reach for `log` before `fmt` when sending any messages to console, even if the log will never be persisted. Having better detail around the messages we may need to read can only be a good thing when trying to figure out where something went wrong or when data was mutated in an unexpected order.

The output is nice, but what if we want to specify how our message looks? The `Set-Flags` option can take flags in a union to handle the most common needs, as shown in the next listing.

Listing 6.5   Custom log output

```
package main

import (
    "log"
)

func main() {
    log.SetFlags(log.Ltime)            ←    Shows time as
    log.Println("Only show the time")       a log prefix

    log.SetFlags(log.Llongfile)        ←    Shows the filename
    log.Println("Show the full filename")   with full path

    log.SetFlags(log.LUTC | log.Lshortfile)   ←   Shows only the
    log.Println("Display in UTC and use a short filename")   filename
}
```

Running this gives us a few style outputs:

```
$ go run logging_formats.go
09:46:29 Only show the time
/usr/go/code/logging/logging_formats.go:12: Show the full filename
logging_formats.go:15: Display in UTC and use a short filename
```

Mixing and matching the flags will get most of the common formats you could want. You can see some runtime introspection details, like line numbers and filenames. In addition, you can create a custom logger with even more flexibility by implementing a `Writer` interface. In the next example, we get a little more creative with our output.

Listing 6.6 Colorful, detailed logs

```go
package main

import (
    "fmt"
    "log"
    "runtime"
    "strings"
    "time"
)

type myLogger struct{}

func (l myLogger) Write(msg []byte) (int, error) {
    pc := make([]uintptr, 50)
    n := runtime.Callers(0, pc)
    pc = pc[:n]
    frames := runtime.CallersFrames(pc)
    caller := ""

    frameCount := 0
    for {
        frameCount++
        fr, hasMore := frames.Next()

        if hasMore {
            caller = fr.Function
        } else {
            break
        }
    }

    output := fmt.Sprintf("%s%s - %s%s (called from %
    s%s)", "\033[32m", time.Now().Format("2006/01/02
    3:04:05 pm"), "\033[0m", strings.TrimSpace(string
    (msg)), "\033[35m", caller)
    return fmt.Println(output)
}

func main() {
    myLog := new(myLogger)
    log.SetFlags(0)
    log.SetOutput(myLog)
    go concurrentLog()
    for i := 0; i < 10; i++ {
        log.Println(fmt.Sprintf("run #%d", i+1))
        time.Sleep(1 * time.Second)
    }
}
```

Annotations:
- Leans on the runtime package to find our caller
- Assigns the caller's function
- Outputs our custom format with the caller and color codes
- Unsets any other log flags

```
func concurrentLog() {
    for i := 0; i < 2; i++ {
        log.Println(fmt.Sprintf("concurrent run #%d", i+1))
        time.Sleep(5 * time.Second)
    }
}
```

In this example, we've added TTY color via ASCII escape codes, chosen our own time-stamp format, and captured the calling function for our log. For terminals that support colors, it highlights some information that might make it easier to parse by eye (figure 6.3).

```
2023/08/30 4:03:08 pm – run #1 (called from runtime.main)
2023/08/30 4:03:08 pm – concurrent run #1 (called from main.concurrentLog)
2023/08/30 4:03:09 pm – run #2 (called from runtime.main)
2023/08/30 4:03:10 pm – run #3 (called from runtime.main)
2023/08/30 4:03:11 pm – run #4 (called from runtime.main)
2023/08/30 4:03:12 pm – run #5 (called from runtime.main)
2023/08/30 4:03:13 pm – concurrent run #2 (called from main.concurrentLog)
2023/08/30 4:03:13 pm – run #6 (called from runtime.main)
2023/08/30 4:03:14 pm – run #7 (called from runtime.main)
2023/08/30 4:03:15 pm – run #8 (called from runtime.main)
2023/08/30 4:03:16 pm – run #9 (called from runtime.main)
2023/08/30 4:03:17 pm – run #10 (called from runtime.main)
```

Figure 6.3 **Our pretty output**

Note that SetFlags is set to 0. This tells logging that we're controlling the output and don't need any of its built-in log adornments. The log is a bit flashy and bespoke but gives you an idea of the kind of flexibility you have when it comes to generating your own preferred style of log. In most cases, Go's built-in formatter will work fine, and if you plan on distributing your software to the masses, it's a good idea to stick to known formats like RFC 5424.

> **NOTE** The Internet Engineering Task Force maintains standards for logging. Details on the most common format, 5424, are at https://datatracker.ietf.org/doc/html/rfc5424.

> **TIP** Although there's nothing wrong with adding support for color, not all terminals support color codes and will be plagued by escape-sequence noise if you force it on users, not to mention that it will be represented literally in any saved files! If you do decide to support color, make it optional via a command-line flag, ideally as an opt-in.

For the most part, only two pieces of information in a log entry are generated for you automatically: information about when the event happened and information about where it happened. With the date and time information, you can set the precision of the timestamp:

- `Ldate` controls print the date.
- `Ltime` prints the timestamp.
- `Lmicrosends` adds microsecond precision to the time, which automatically results in the time being printed even if `Ltime` isn't set.
- `LstdFlags` turns on both `Ldate` and `Ltime`.

Then a pair of flags deals with the location information:

- `Llongfile` shows a full file path and then the line number: `/foo/bar/baz.go:123`.
- `Lshortifle` shows just the filename and the line number: `baz.go:123`.

Although you can combine flags with a Boolean `OR`, some combinations are obviously incompatible—namely, `Llongfile` and `Lshortfile`.

6.2.1 Logging data to different outputs

So far, we're just logging to the screen. But we want to keep and revisit these logs later, so let's explore ways to persist our logs.

The first and most common way is to persist to a file. We used the `SetOutput` method from listing 6.4 and listing 6.5 to generate output to screen, but because it operates on any `Writer`, we can point a file to this output.

> **TIP** The 12-factor pattern recommends keeping logs as a stream of events, such as logging to stdout. You may find logging to a file (or memory) useful, which is why we look at the options here, but using shell redirection or daemons to handle the logging is generally a better approach. The simplest shell redirection can be achieved by running `go run [file].go &> file.log`. Try that on our colorful log example to see the possible problems with not using options for disabling/enabling color.

A logger can be any `Writer`, which as you recall is any type that satisfies by implementing a `Write` method taking in bytes and returning a number of bytes written and an optional error. Go has a several built-in `Writer` types, including the file handlers. This means if we want to write to file, we can use a file as a drop-in replacement!

- *Problem*—We need to persist our log output without relying on shell redirection or third-party daemon software. Ideally, this would be accessible via a filesystem and/or in memory.
- *Solution*—Use any writer type that implements the `Write` method, including `os.File`, as an output option for the logging library.
- *Discussion*—By creating our own custom types (which we explored in depth in chapter 3), we're able to manipulate the format and storage of our logging any way we please. Logs can be directed to the multiple places at the same time and laid out exactly how we want them to look.

In the next listing, we look at the most basic logging approach beyond straight to standard out: saving our logs to a file.

Listing 6.7   A simple file logger

```go
package main

import (
    "log"
    "os"
)

func main() {                                        // Creates or
    file, err := os.OpenFile("logging.log",          // opens a file for
os.O_RDWR|os.O_CREATE, 0755)                          // read and write
    if err != nil {
        panic("could not open log file")             // Sets the output
    }                                                // for logging
    log.SetOutput(file)
    log.SetFlags(log.LUTC | log.Lshortfile)          // Sets UTC time and
    log.Println("Display in UTC and use a short filename")  // short filename for
}                                                    // entry prefix
```

In this case, we set our output `Writer` to be the `File` handler returned from `OpenFile`, but `SetOutput` will take any writer, so wrapping another destination in a `Write` handler is trivial. Another good way to test this is to store logs in an in-memory key-value store like Redis for more ephemeral information.

6.2.2   *Going deeper with structured logging*

Although the standard log package offers more than enough to get going tracking important events in your code, the Go development team heard calls for more powerful logging out of the standard library and in Go version 1.21 introduced structured logging.

Structured logging is not radically different from standard logging, but it introduces an extra annotation to distinguish between default log messages and log levels like info and error. Also, as the name implies, it enables structured file formats, which have become increasingly useful as log analysis tools have risen in popularity. Recall that we talked about format variants and standards. Isn't it nice not to have to worry about parsing the data itself? Many applications that read structured logs take in JSON, preventing this problem. All this comes together to give you more power to find important needles in the haystack of your logs.

- *Problem*—Plaintext logging introduces ambiguity in formats and in message types. Structural logging provides both better readability and parseability with consistent formats and more room for contextual detail. For these reasons, it can be employed by automation tools.
- *Solution*—Replace the standard library log with the new slog structured logging library, which will give you the ability to decorate logs with log level messages and automatically allow marshaling log data into well-known formats.
- *Discussion*—Could we do all this with the standard log library? Of course, but it would require reinventing the wheel for each project or using a third-party

library. People expect logs to be parseable, searchable, and easy to iterate. Structured logging is ideal for this.

In the following listing, we'll generate a set of responses to explore the log levels and see the output of a structured log entry.

Listing 6.8 Log levels

```
package main

import (
    "log/slog"
)

func main() {
    slog.Info("this is default logging")
    slog.Warn("keep an eye on this, it might be an issue")
    slog.Error("oh no, an error happened here!")
    slog.Debug("this is good while developing ...")
}
```

When we run this, we'll see that our output has a little more detail than we got previously:

```
$ go run structured_logging.go
2023/08/31 11:37:30 INFO this is default logging
2023/08/31 11:37:30 WARN keep an eye on this, it might be an issue
2023/08/31 11:37:30 ERROR oh no, an error happened here!
```

What's more interesting is that we lost our `slog.Debug` message. That's what makes this package even more powerful: we can control exactly what kind of messaging we want to see in our logs. It's very common to want debug messages to be visible only to local or staging environments. We can specify our level by creating our own custom logger, as we did with standard logging. While we're at it, we can have our messages formatted in JSON.

Listing 6.9 Structured logging in JSON

```
package main

import (
    "log/slog"
    "os"
)

func main() {
    file, err := os.OpenFile("structured.log",          ◁─┐ Creates a file
os.O_RDWR|os.O_CREATE, 0755)                               │ to use as a log
    if err != nil {                                        │ destination
        panic("could not open log file for writing")
    }
    logger := slog.New(slog.NewJSONHandler(file,         ◁─┐ Sets the file and
&slog.HandlerOptions{                                      │ the log level
```

```
        Level: slog.LevelDebug,
    }))

    slog.SetDefault(logger)
    slog.Info("this is default logging")
    slog.Warn("keep an eye on this, it might be an issue")
    slog.Error("oh no, an error happened here!")
    slog.Debug("this is good while developing ...")
    slog.Info(
        "this is a more complex message",
        slog.String("accepted_values","key/value pairs with
        specific types for marshalling"),
        slog.Int("an int:", 30),
        slog.Group("grouped_info",
            slog.String("you_can","do this too"),
        ),
    )
}
```

An example of embedded messaging

A couple of new concepts are included in this listing. First, we've created our own custom logger as we did with the standard log library. We set the HandlerOptions to have a logging level of debug, which means none of our Debug messages will be swallowed.

But look at that last Info line to see how we can quickly build up bigger JSON structures without having to build and marshal custom structs. The slog package allows you to specify types and group logs into hierarchical groups without having to canonize it all in a struct with JSON tags. That's a really good way to speed up turning messages into JSON.

One last thing worth mentioning: if you look at the output, you'll notice that the file is not a valid JSON file at all! Rather, it's a stream of JSON messages, known as json-streaming or JSONS. In this case it's newline-separated, but there are other variants. As it's intended to be a streaming format, it's supported by a lot of logging and analytics platforms.

> **TIP**   If you're looking for a simple way to deal with JSON and JSONS output, the authors strongly recommend the jq tool, which enables extremely powerful and fast querying tools for using these formats. To install and learn more, see https://jqlang.github.io/jq.

6.2.3   *Accessing and capturing stack traces*

Many languages provide access to the call stack. A *stack trace* (or *stack dump*) provides a human-readable list of the functions being used at the time the stack is captured. Imagine a program in which main calls foo, which then calls bar. The bar function dumps a stack trace. The trace would be three calls deep, showing that bar is the current function, called by foo, which is in turn called by main.

Stack traces can give developers critical insight into what's happening in the system. They're useful for logging and debugging. Go makes it possible to access the stack trace at any given point in program execution.

- *Problem*—You want to fetch a stack trace at a critical point in the application.
- *Solution*—Use the `runtime` package, which has several tools.
- *Description*—Generating stack dumps in Go isn't a particularly difficult exercise when you know how to do it, but how to get one seems to be a commonly asked question. If all you need is a trace for debugging, you can easily send one to standard output by using the `runtime/debug` function `PrintStack`, as the next listing shows.

Listing 6.10 Print stack to standard output

```go
package main

import (
    "runtime/debug"
)
func main() {                      ◁─┐
    foo()
}                                    │  Defines a few
func foo() {                       ◁─┤  functions so you have
    bar()                            │  something to trace
}                                    │
func bar() {                       ◁─┘
    debug.PrintStack()             ◁──┐ Prints the trace
}
```

Running the code prints a stack trace like this:

```
$ go run trace.go
/chapter6/stack/trace.go:20 (0x205b)
    bar: debug.PrintStack()
/chapter6/stack/trace.go:13 (0x203b)
    foo: bar()
/chapter6/stack/trace.go:9 (0x201b)
    main: foo()
/usr/local/Cellar/go/1.22/libexec/src/runtime/proc.go:63 (0x12983)
    main: main_main()
/usr/local/Cellar/go/1.22/libexec/src/runtime/asm_amd64.s:2232 (0x37711)
    goexit:
```

This can be helpful for simple debugging cases. But if you want to capture the trace to send it somewhere else, you need to do something slightly more sophisticated. You can use the `runtime` package's `Stack` function, shown in the next listing.

Listing 6.11 Using the `Stack` function

```go
package main
import (
    "fmt"
    "runtime"
)
func main() {
    foo()
```

```
}
func foo() {
     bar()
}
func bar() {
     buf := make([]byte, 1024)
     runtime.Stack(buf, false)
     fmt.Printf("Trace:\n %s\n", buf)
}
```

Makes a buffer

Writes the stack into the buffer

Prints the results

In this example, you send the stack to stdout, but you could just as easily log or store it. Running this code produces output like this:

```
$ go run trace.go
Trace:
 goroutine 1 [running]:
main.bar()
        /Users/mbutcher/Code/go-in-practice/chapter5/stack/trace.go:18 +0x7a
main.foo()
        /Users/mbutcher/Code/go-in-practice/chapter5/stack/trace.go:13 +0x1b
main.main()
```

You may notice that this version is shorter than the other. The lower-level system calls are left out of `Stack`'s data. We have a few quick things to point out about this code:

- With `Stack`, you must supply a presized buffer. But there's no convenient way to determine how big the buffer needs to be to capture all the output. (In some cases, the output is so big that you might not want to capture it all.) You need to decide ahead of time how much space you'd like to allocate.
- `Stack` takes two arguments. The second is a Boolean flag, which is set to `false` in this example. Setting it to `true` will cause `Stack` to also print out stacks for all running goroutines. This can be tremendously useful when debugging concurrency problems, but it substantially increases the amount of output. The trace of the preceding code, for example, runs an entire printed page.

If all of this isn't sufficient, you can use the `runtime` package's `Caller`, `Callers`, and `CallersFrames` functions, as we did earlier in this chapter to get programmatic access to the details of the call stack. Although it's quite a bit of work to retrieve and format the data, these functions give you the flexibility to discover the details of a particular call stack. The `runtime` and -`runtime/debug` packages contain numerous other functions for analyzing memory use, goroutines, threading, and other aspects of your program's resource use.

6.3   *Unit testing in Go*

As a broad topic, testing is an enormous area of the application development process. There's distinct testing for behavior, accessibility, integration, and more. This section will focus on unit testing and Go's built-in tooling for enabling tests within your code.

6.3.1   Creating a test suit with table-driven tests

Outside a few conventions to facilitate finding tests and test files, Go is not very opinionated on how you use the testing package. You can write individual test functions for different scenarios, generate random data for fuzz testing or use static data, have a full test fail with any unit failure, or continue with the tests.

One best practice that is recommended for tests is building your unit tests as table-driven, which effectively means a slice of input(s) and condition(s) necessary to feed a function and evaluate its output. This allows you to stack any number of testing scenarios on top of one another and, in a loop, try each one against the specified function. The table part refers to this layout, which is generally easy to read. There's no magic here, but keeping this as one test per function makes it much easier to maintain a set of unit tests, and it's not uncommon to have a separate file for each corresponding `.go` file or even function.

Let's put this in practice by generating a simple coding exercise function for Fizz Buzz, which as many developers know works like this:

1   The function receives an integer.
2   It increments from 1 to that number.
3   It allocates an array of strings.
4   For each number in the sequence, it tests as follows:

    a   If the number is evenly divisible by 3 and 5, add `FizzBuzz` to the array.
    b   Otherwise, if the number is divisible by 3, add `Fizz` to the array.
    c   Otherwise, if the number is divisible only by 5, add `Buzz` to the array.
    d   Otherwise, add the number itself as a string to the array.

5   It returns a string array or joined string.

The next listing shows a basic implementation for Fizz Buzz, which we'll use to build an initial unit test.

Listing 6.12   Basic Fizz Buzz

```
package main

import (
    "fmt"
    "strings"
    "strconv"
)

func main() {
    var input string
    fmt.Println("Enter a number for fizzbuzz")
    fmt.Scanln(&input)

    numInput, err := strconv.ParseInt(input, 10, 16)
    if err != nil {
```

Takes in user input as string to be converted to integer

```
        panic("that's not a number!")
    }

    result := fizzbuzz(numInput)        ◄─── Invokes the function
    fmt.Println("result:", result)
}

func fizzbuzz(n int64) string {
    var fizzbuzzes []string
    for i := int64(0); i < n; i++ {        ◄─┐  Our Fizz Buzz
        v := ""                              │  algorithm
        isThree := i % 3 == 0
        isFive := i % 5 == 0
        if isThree && isFive {
            v = "Fizz Buzz"
        } else if isThree {
            v = "Fizz"
        } else if isFive {
            v = "Buzz "
        } else {
            v = fmt.Sprintf("%d", i)
        }
        fizzbuzzes = append(fizzbuzzes, v)
    }


    return strings.Join(fizzbuzzes, " ")
}
```

If we run this manually and evaluate its output, things might seem to operate normally, at least from the eyeball test:

```
Enter a number for fizzbuzz
11
result: Fizz Buzz 1 2 Fizz 4 Buzz  Fizz 7 8 Fizz Buzz
```

The 3 is `Fizz`, the 5 is `Buzz`, and so on. But we know this isn't comprehensive, and testing like this is prone to error. So let's make some unit tests in a test table. To start, we'll want a slice of structs that represents the input and expected output of our tests. In this case, that's very simple: we'll feed our function `fizzbuzz` a 64-bit integer and get back a string. As a first step, we'll grab the example output from Wikipedia's entry on a typical round of Fizz Buzz:

> *1, 2, Fizz, 4, Buzz, Fizz, 7, 8, Fizz, Buzz, 11, Fizz, 13, 14, Fizz Buzz, 16, 17, Fizz, 19, Buzz, Fizz, 22, 23, Fizz, Buzz, 26, Fizz, 28, 29, Fizz Buzz, 31, 32, Fizz, 34, Buzz, Fizz,*
> *. . .*

In this case, it looks like we can stop at 36 to test. So we'll set up our first test in the table as follows:

```
    tests := []struct {
        input int64
```

```
        expected string
    } {
        {37, "1, 2, Fizz, 4, Buzz, Fizz, 7, 8, Fizz, Buzz, 11, Fizz, 13, 14, Fizz
Buzz, 16, 17, Fizz, 19, Buzz, Fizz, 22, 23, Fizz, Buzz, 26, Fizz, 28, 29,
Fizz Buzz, 31, 32, Fizz, 34, Buzz, Fizz"},    }
```

We have only one, but it's enough to get started. We need to import the testing library and prefix our test functions with `Test`. By convention, this is `TestFunctionName` or `Test_FunctionName`. Let's look at our entire test file comprising a single unit test in the next listing.

Listing 6.13   A test of Fizz Buzz

```
package main

import (
    "testing"
)

func Test_FizzBuzz(t *testing.T) {          ◄─┐  The structure of our
    tests := []struct {                       │  tests with input and
        input int64                           │  expected output
        expected string
    } {
        {37, "1, 2, Fizz, 4, Buzz, Fizz, 7, 8, Fizz, Buzz, 11, Fizz, 13, 14, Fizz
Buzz, 16, 17, Fizz, 19, Buzz, Fizz, 22, 23, Fizz, Buzz, 26, Fizz, 28, 29,
 Fizz Buzz, 31, 32, Fizz, 34, Buzz, Fizz"},    }
    for i := range tests {                   ◄──── Runs each test
        test := tests[i]
        res := fizzbuzz(test.input)
        if res != test.expected {
            t.Fatalf("\ngot \n%s \nexpected \n%s", res
            , test.expected)                 ◄─┐  An unrecoverable
        }                                      │  failure if any test fails
    }
}
```

We can run this with `go test` or `go test [TARGET_FILE]`, or via our IDE, and when we execute the suite as in the following listing.

Listing 6.14   Our test output

```
$ go test
--- FAIL: Test_FizzBuzz (0.00s)
    tabletests_test.go:20:
        got
        FizzBuzz 1 2 Fizz 4 Buzz  Fizz 7 8 Fizz Buzz  11 Fizz 13 14 FizzBu
        zz 16 17 Fizz 19 Buzz  Fizz 22 23 Fizz Buzz  26 Fizz 28 29 FizzBuz
        z 31 32 Fizz 34 Buzz  Fizz
        expected
        1, 2, Fizz, 4, Buzz, Fizz, 7, 8, Fizz, Buzz, 11, Fizz, 13, 14, Fiz
        z Buzz, 16, 17, Fizz, 19, Buzz, Fizz, 22, 23, Fizz, Buzz, 26, Fizz
        , 28, 29, Fizz Buzz, 31, 32, Fizz, 34, Buzz, Fizz
```

```
FAIL
exit status 1
FAIL    tabletests    0.112s
```

We see an error immediately. Throwing a fatal error is not necessary, as an error like that would exist only if no subsequent tests could succeed or if we have tests that build on previous tests. But because we have one test, let's get the output as succinctly as possible with the first failing test.

We have two errors in our code. First, we start our loop with a 0 index, which is not what we expect per the example from Wikipedia, which begins at 1. Similarly, we aren't inclusive of our target number in the loop, so this is an off-by-one error, one of the most common programming mistakes. We also had an extra space after the ifFive Buzz output, and finally, we joined our strings by space but didn't include the comma. After we fix those small mistakes and rerun, we get a much happier test:

```
$ go test
PASS
ok      tabletests    0.102s
```

Augmenting these tests with more values becomes pretty simple. We just add more cases to the slice of tests:

```
{
        {37, "1, 2, Fizz, 4, Buzz, Fizz, 7, 8, Fizz, Buzz, 11, Fizz, 13,
 14, Fizz Buzz, 16, 17, Fizz, 19, Buzz, Fizz, 22, 23, Fizz, Buzz, 26, Fizz,
 28, 29, Fizz Buzz, 31, 32, Fizz, 34, Buzz, Fizz, 37"},
        {5, "1, 2, Fizz, 4, Buzz"},
        {12, "1, 2, Fizz, 4, Buzz, Fizz, 7, 8, Fizz, Buzz, 11, Fizz"},
    }
```

In this case, adding more tests is fruitless because the largest possible input will include every subset of integer, but if you imagine a function that also includes a starting integer offset, you could find more value in this approach. But the slice above is a test table—a collection of testable scenarios you can use to make sure your functions return what you expect.

6.3.2 *Fuzzing test input*

The preceding tests work well enough because the programmer knows what output should be given a specific input. But there are only so many variants you can test against, and this approach leans exclusively on a developer's ability to generate test cases from a mental model.

For something like FizzBuzz, this is generally reliable. There aren't too many wild edge cases that can happen with our code. But wouldn't it be nice if we could generate test cases from thin air? After all, we won't know for certain what will be generated in a real-world scenario. As the saying goes, you don't know what you don't know.

Fuzz testing is a strategy for preparing for and mitigating the unknown. It allows input to functions to be fuzzed or generated/modified to find unexpected edge cases.

> ### The value of fuzz testing
>
> Fuzz testing is particularly good as a security measure against potentially malicious input. Although a developer shouldn't rely upon it, fuzz testing can generate text intended for exploiting vulnerabilities, like especially long input, input with special characters, and input with special meaning (as in SQL injection).
>
> By generating random input, we have a better chance of replicating the kind of behavior a malicious user might employ to find exploits. When things break due to some but not all user input, it's a strong indication that there is an exploitable problem.

As you might guess, a problem with fuzz-testing test cases is that you can't give an expected answer. In these cases, we're looking for things that introduce errors or unexpected formats in return.

In the following listing, we'll give the fuzz tester an easy path to failure. We've created a function that produced some score for a short word or sentence. In it, we take each character in a string, get its character code (or rune) value, and add it to a summed result.

Listing 6.15   A function to sum a string's characters

```go
package main

import (
    "fmt"
    "strings"
)

func summedRuneCodes(input string) int16 {
    value := 0
    inRunes := strings.Map(func(r rune) rune {      // Converts a string slice to a rune slice
        return r
    }, input)

    for r := range inRunes {
        value += int(inRunes[r])                     // Gets the ascii value
    }

    return int16(value)
}

func main() {
    var testString = "i am a test string"
    output := summedRuneCodes(testString)
    fmt.Println(output)
}
```

This is a very brittle algorithm. We're assuming that our value will always fit in an `int16`, but substitute `int32` or `int64`, and the same problem exists, just at a larger scale. If our input string translates to a number outside `int16`'s range, we'll get an overflow. Similar type problems exist with floating numbers and precision and have been the source of errors since computers started dealing with them.

In our test cases, we don't encounter this because we don't consider very long strings. This is one of the problems with hand-generating test cases. (We'll come back to that in a sidebar shortly.) We tried our best but didn't break the code, as shown in the following listing.

Listing 6.16   Best-effort test cases

```
func TestSummedRuneCodes(t *testing.T) {
    tests := []struct {
        name string
        input string
        expected int16
    } {
        { "test 1", "i am trying things", 1729 },
        { "test 2", "doing my best to find a way to break this!", 3772 },
        { "test 3", "even adding emojis or unicode doesn't break it, I'm
        sure I'm fine 🌍", 6065 },
    }

    t.Run("my rune sum tests", func(t *testing.T) {
        for k := range tests {
            test := tests[k]
            t.Run(test.name, func(t *testing.T) {
                if got := summedRuneCodes(test.input); got != test.expected {
                    t.Errorf("expected %d, got %d", test.expected, got)
                }
            })
        }
    })
}
```

We could add dozens more tests and still miss the edge cases. This is where fuzz testing comes in. We can make a single assumption about the return value of our function and find problems we couldn't generate by hand.

In this case, we might logically assume that we'll *always* get a number greater than or equal to 0, which is the empty string case. Fuzz testing will catch this quickly. To do this, we can add to our test file a `Fuzz` function, as shown in the following listing.

Listing 6.17   Letting fuzz testing find errors for us

```
func FuzzSummedRuneCodes(f *testing.F) {
    tests := []string{"i am trying things", "doing my best to find a way to
    break this!", "even adding emojis or unicode doesn't break it, I'm sure
    I'm fine 🌍"}
```

```
    for t := range tests {
        f.Add(tests[t])
    }
    f.Fuzz(func(t *testing.T, seed string) {
        got := summedRuneCodes(seed)
        if got < 0 {
            t.Errorf("how did this happen? somehow we got %d from string
            %s", got, seed)4        }
    })
}
```

The big difference is that we can't know what to expect from this output, so we look for a more general failure case. To run with fuzzing, we can use `go test --fuzz=Fuzz`. On your first pass, you should see a failure like in figure 6.4.

```
fuzz: elapsed: 0s, gathering baseline coverage: 0/3 completed
fuzz: elapsed: 0s, gathering baseline coverage: 3/3 completed, now fuzzing with 8 workers
fuzz: minimizing 2117-byte failing input file
fuzz: elapsed: 1s, minimizing
--- FAIL: FuzzSummedRuneCodes (0.57s)
    --- FAIL: FuzzSummedRuneCodes (0.00s)
        fuzzy_test.go:38: how did this happen? somehow we got -32661 from string xacxaxxXa
00A0Z0A0000x00XA00y0a00x00YB0x020a000000x0X00000000x0xZ2000C7c0X0XX00A0000x0000X0X00000A0X

    Failing input written to testdata/fuzz/FuzzSummedRuneCodes/9eee599ff3d2736e
    To re-run:
    go test -run=FuzzSummedRuneCodes/9eee599ff3d2736e
FAIL
exit status 1
FAIL    fuzzy   0.731s
```

Figure 6.4 Fuzz testing to the rescue

This is exactly what we're looking for! Would we have come up with that random, noisy string for testing? Maybe, but probably not. We let Go throw spaghetti at the wall, and it found an error for us.

Generating test cases with Large Language Models

As we've talked about using AI and other Large Language Models (LLMs) to help you code, testing is another area that can benefit greatly from this tech. If you give the expected output of a function and a number and format of test cases, AI can often produce something more varied and much faster than a developer could.

In the case of Fizz Buzz, we can reliably get test cases in some format from ChatGPT and variants and likely in Go's struct style if we work on our prompt engineering.

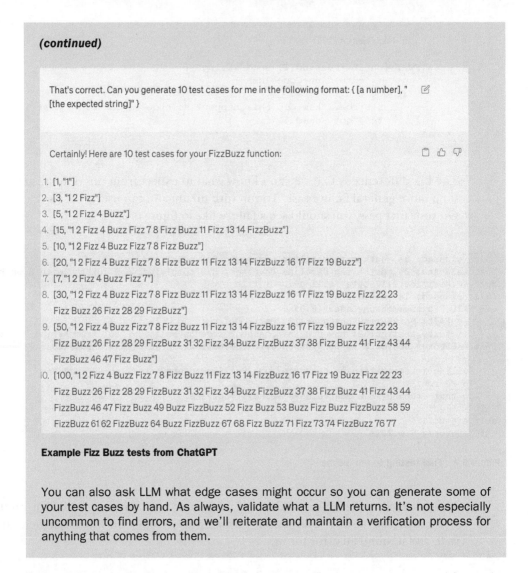

(continued)

That's correct. Can you generate 10 test cases for me in the following format: { [a number], " [the expected string]" }

Certainly! Here are 10 test cases for your FizzBuzz function:

1. [1, "1"]
2. [3, "1 2 Fizz"]
3. [5, "1 2 Fizz 4 Buzz"]
4. [15, "1 2 Fizz 4 Buzz Fizz 7 8 Fizz Buzz 11 Fizz 13 14 FizzBuzz"]
5. [10, "1 2 Fizz 4 Buzz Fizz 7 8 Fizz Buzz"]
6. [20, "1 2 Fizz 4 Buzz Fizz 7 8 Fizz Buzz 11 Fizz 13 14 FizzBuzz 16 17 Fizz 19 Buzz"]
7. [7, "1 2 Fizz 4 Buzz Fizz 7"]
8. [30, "1 2 Fizz 4 Buzz Fizz 7 8 Fizz Buzz 11 Fizz 13 14 FizzBuzz 16 17 Fizz 19 Buzz Fizz 22 23 Fizz Buzz 26 Fizz 28 29 FizzBuzz"]
9. [50, "1 2 Fizz 4 Buzz Fizz 7 8 Fizz Buzz 11 Fizz 13 14 FizzBuzz 16 17 Fizz 19 Buzz Fizz 22 23 Fizz Buzz 26 Fizz 28 29 FizzBuzz 31 32 Fizz 34 Buzz FizzBuzz 37 38 Fizz Buzz 41 Fizz 43 44 FizzBuzz 46 47 Fizz Buzz"]
10. [100, "1 2 Fizz 4 Buzz Fizz 7 8 Fizz Buzz 11 Fizz 13 14 FizzBuzz 16 17 Fizz 19 Buzz Fizz 22 23 Fizz Buzz 26 Fizz 28 29 FizzBuzz 31 32 Fizz 34 Buzz FizzBuzz 37 38 Fizz Buzz 41 Fizz 43 44 FizzBuzz 46 47 Fizz Buzz 49 Buzz FizzBuzz 52 Fizz Buzz 53 Buzz Fizz Buzz FizzBuzz 58 59 FizzBuzz 61 62 FizzBuzz 64 Buzz FizzBuzz 67 68 Fizz Buzz 71 Fizz 73 74 FizzBuzz 76 77"]

Example Fizz Buzz tests from ChatGPT

You can also ask LLM what edge cases might occur so you can generate some of your test cases by hand. As always, validate what a LLM returns. It's not especially uncommon to find errors, and we'll reiterate and maintain a verification process for anything that comes from them.

One item of note on the last test: although our overflow errors can occur with any size int and Go will do nothing to stop us, some packages can help us detect these in advance. A quick way of doing this in our example, however, is to cast to the next larger integer type and check equality against the original. Of course, we can use an unsigned `uint16` as a return value.

6.3.3   *Annotating tests with names*

In listing 6.16, you may have noticed that we added a name to our test cases. A nice way of getting this test output formatted a little better is to use the `Run` method, which treats each test as a named subtest. Then you can have a large test case and smaller independent subtests within. Let's wrap our previous test table execution with this and look at the output, shown in the following listing.

> **Listing 6.18   Giving our tests better formatting and names**

```
tests := []struct {
    name string         ⟵—— Adds a name to our case
    input int64
    expected string
} {
    {"fizz buzz test1", 37, "1, 2, Fizz, 4, Buzz, Fizz, 7, 8, Fizz, Bu
    zz, 11, Fizz, 13, 14, Fizz Buzz, 16, 17, Fizz, 19, Buzz, Fizz, 22,
     23, Fizz, Buzz, 26, Fizz, 28, 29, Fizz Buzz, 31, 32, Fizz, 34,
     Buzz, Fizz, 37"},
    {"fizz buzz test2", 5, "1, 2, Fizz, 4, Buzz"},
    {"fizz buzz test3", 12, "1, 2, Fizz, 4, Buzz, Fizz, 7, 8, Fizz, Bu
    zz, 11, Fizz"},
}
for i := range tests {
    test := tests[i]

    t.Run(test.name, func(t *testing.T) {      ⟵—— Wraps subtests in t.Run
        res := fizzbuzz(test.input)
        if res != test.expected {
        t.Fatalf("\ngot \n%s \nexpected \n%s", res, test.expected)
    }
    })
}
```

Running it in verbose mode gives us a nicely decorated test run:

```
% go test -v
=== RUN    Test_FizzBuzzSubTest
=== RUN    Test_FizzBuzzSubTest/fizz_buzz_test1
=== RUN    Test_FizzBuzzSubTest/fizz_buzz_test2
=== RUN    Test_FizzBuzzSubTest/fizz_buzz_test3
--- PASS: Test_FizzBuzzSubTest (0.00s)
    --- PASS: Test_FizzBuzzSubTest/fizz_buzz_test1 (0.00s)
    --- PASS: Test_FizzBuzzSubTest/fizz_buzz_test2 (0.00s)
    --- PASS: Test_FizzBuzzSubTest/fizz_buzz_test3 (0.00s)
PASS
ok      subtests    0.129s
```

We can see individually named tests as part of the path of our full test run. In many cases, instead of `fizz buzz test 1`, we can have more declarative names like `should generate [some result]`. The reason is primarily IDE support, which can break out the names separately. IntelliJ's GoLand and VS Code have support for this when you run tests directly in the IDE.

6.3.4   *Checking test coverage with go cover*

Having tests is critical, and in our example cases, we have one function and one corresponding unit test. Most serious codebases have hundreds if not thousands of independent functions. How to choose *what* to test is almost a science itself, but finding out *how much* you're testing is something you can do simply with the cover option. The following listing is a trivial example that does nothing but return a few integers.

> **Listing 6.19   An app with three dummy functions**

```
package main

func main() {}

func foo() int {
    return 1
}

func bar() int {
    return 2
}

func baz() int {
    return 3
}
```

The corresponding test code is

```
package main

import (
    "testing"
)

func TestFoo(t *testing.T) {
    t.Run("testing foo", func(t *testing.T) {
        foo()
    })
}

func TestBar(t *testing.T) {
    t.Run("testing foo", func(t *testing.T) {
        bar()
    })
}
```

Then run go test -v -cover:

```
=== RUN    TestFoo
=== RUN    TestFoo/testing_foo
--- PASS: TestFoo (0.00s)
    --- PASS: TestFoo/testing_foo (0.00s)
=== RUN    TestBar
```

```
=== RUN    TestBar/testing_foo
--- PASS: TestBar (0.00s)
    --- PASS: TestBar/testing_foo (0.00s)
PASS
coverage: 66.7% of statements
ok       covertest    0.320s
```

The coverage shows you how much of your application's functions and implementations are covered by test cases. This is great and enough to give you a sense of what function has a test and what might not. But you can take this further with the `coverprofile` option, which allows you to save to a formatted output file and display in a browser (or other tools) to better visualize what you have in tests.

In this case, we used `go test -v -cover -coverprofile mycover.out` to generate the output and `go tool cover -html mycover.out` to display it. A browser window should open automatically (figure 6.5).

Figure 6.5   Our test coverage in the browser

Seeing it laid out like this makes it a lot easier to conceptualize your code and its test coverage. You may not be shooting for 100% test coverage (and there are arguments that you should not), but this is a great way to see in a single view what kind of testing is in place for your application. Your IDE of choice will probably provide similar test visualizations, but it's often easier to mentally separate your testing, and Go provides something out of the box that helps you see when and where you might be missing test coverage.

6.3.5   *Wait, where is my debugger?*

The go-to debugging tool of choice for many software developers is (surprise!) the debugger. This magnificent tool executes your code and walks you through each step of the way at whatever pace you desire.

Before we dive headlong into the discussion, there's one thing worth noting. Despite the plethora of developer-oriented features in Go, it doesn't yet have a fully functional debugger. The core team has focused on other things, and the closest thing to an official Go debugger is the GNU Debugger (GDB) plugin. You can use the venerable old GDB to do some debugging, but it's not as reliable as many developers desire.

> **TIP**   If you'd like to get GDB configured for debugging Go, the golang website has a great introduction (https://go.dev/doc/gdb).

But in the rare case where the standard distribution of Go lacks strong tools, the Go community has stepped in and provided a strong debugging tool. Delve (https://github .com/go-delve/delve) is a Go debugger under active development. You can build and use Delve yourself, but it's also become a standard in many IDE's Go implementations. It's built directly into the VS Code Go language extension, for example.

6.4   *Benchmarking and performance tuning*

Having dipped into testing and debugging, let's go a little deeper into some good code-quality practices in Go. One last nice feature of testing we want to touch on here is the benchmarking option, which comes in handy any time you have a function that's doing something (potentially) algorithmically complex. To demonstrate, the following listing uses Bubble Sort, one of the least efficient sorting algorithms.

Listing 6.20   Bubble Sort

```go
package main

import (
    "fmt"
)

func main() {
    sorted := bubbleSort([]int{20, 19, 3, 75, 1, 7, 4, 17})
    fmt.Println(sorted)
}

func bubbleSort(in []int) []int {        ⟵  Bubble Sort loops repeatedly through
    sorted := false                          an array and transposes blocks of two
    for !sorted {                            entries if they're out of order.
        sorted = true
        for i := 1; i < len(in); i++ {
            if in[i-1] > in[i] {
                in[i-1], in[i] = in[i], in[i-1]
                sorted = false
            }
```

```
        }
    }
    return in
}
```

Although we already know this is not a particularly efficient sorting algorithm, we should quantify it. We just need to add a benchmark to a corresponding `_test.go` file. To do this, we'll add some setup and a helper function. In the next listing, we'll do runs with random integer slices of 10, 100, 1000, 10000, and 100000 lengths. Keep in mind that there is overhead to generating the random numbers, but it will pale in comparison to the algorithmic problem here. For each, we'll run the benchmark function.

Listing 6.21 A benchmark suite for Bubble Sort

```
package main

import (
    "math/rand"
    "testing"
    "time"
)

func runBenchmark(arr []int, runs int) {          The invocation
    for i := 0; i < runs; i++ {                   of our Bubble
        bubbleSort(arr)                           Sort function
    }
}
                                                  A function that
func generateRandoms(num int) []int {             produces a slice of
    out := make([]int, num)                       random integers
    for k := range out {
        out[k] = rand.Intn(num-1) + 1
    }
    return out
}
                                                  The first benchmark,
func BenchmarkBubbleSort10(b *testing.B) {        with 10 entries to
    runBenchmark(generateRandoms(10), b.N)        the slice
}

func BenchmarkBubbleSort100(b *testing.B) {
    runBenchmark(generateRandoms(100), b.N)
}

func BenchmarkBubbleSort1000(b *testing.B) {
    runBenchmark(generateRandoms(1000), b.N)
}

func BenchmarkBubbleSort10000(b *testing.B) {
    runBenchmark(generateRandoms(10000), b.N)
}
```

```
func BenchmarkBubbleSort100000(b *testing.B) {
    runBenchmark(generateRandoms(100000), b.N)
}
```

To run benchmarks, use the `go test` tool, but pass it `–bench PATTERN`, where `PATTERN` is a regular expression that matches the benchmarking functions you want to run. The dot (`.`) tells the benchmarker to run all the benchmarks. To run just our smallest benchmark, it could be `-bench=BenchmarkBubbleSort10$`. With our full suite, however, we can see exactly how inefficient our sorting is:

```
BenchmarkBubbleSort10-8              248036485              4.703 ns/op
BenchmarkBubbleSort100-8             36479984               33.06 ns/op
BenchmarkBubbleSort1000-8            3704248                323.5 ns/op
BenchmarkBubbleSort10000-8          288595                 3517 ns/op
BenchmarkBubbleSort100000-8              1         13268521541 ns/o
```

Our last benchmark completed only once compared to nearly 250 million times for the 10-entry version. We can adjust the benchmark's minimum time to run with the `-benchtime` setting, which is 5 seconds by default. Increasing this (in our case to `10s`) will give us more data and make the benchmark take longer. For algorithms that may make a lot of memory allocations, pass the `-benchmem` flag to get that data as well.

> **TIP**   Go's experimental package also offers benchstat, which allows you to go deeper by doing A/B tests against your benchmarking and keeping statistical analysis over multiple runs. You can learn more about this at https://pkg.go .dev/golang.org/x/perf/cmd/benchstat.

In the next few chapters, we'll dig deeper into working with filesystems and networking, working our way to building production-quality HTTP servers.

Summary

- Go brings us a suite of tools for keeping our code clean, well-formatted, and up to date.
- Logging tools let developers produce custom or standard log entries and can enable structured logs or handcrafted ones.
- Testing is a first-class citizen of the Go toolchain, and unit tests are simple to add and run.
- In addition to basic unit tests, the test tool empowers us to do fuzz testing to generate test cases we might not consider.
- Taking testing a step further, we can run benchmarks against our functions to see how efficient and resource-intensive they are at scale.

File access and basic networking

7

This chapter covers

- Handling the manipulation of files locally or on a network
- Networking with Transmission Control Protocol (TCP) and User Datagram Protocol (UDP)
- Applying basic bidirectional networking to a web chat app using websockets
- Using unidirectional networking to send messages from a server to a persistent client connection

Go was initially designed as a systems language but quickly became more general-purpose prior to the first release. By that point, its concurrency focus put it in a unique position in the language landscape and made it especially viable and popular for servers and networking. In this chapter and chapters 8 through 11, we'll cover how Go fits in the web landscape, including some niche use cases.

In chapter 6, we worked with log files, which let us touch the filesystem a little bit via a proxy in Go's log package. But we didn't look too deeply into the file access methods that Go uses under the hood to create, read, and manipulate files.

Some of the prerequisites for this include being able to open and use data from our filesystem. We'll look at opening, reading, and writing to files. Next, we'll go a little low-level by working with UDP and TCP connections outside the standard library net/http package. Finally, we'll build some small web applications that work with persistent network connections to provide more real-time functionality.

7.1 Dealing with files

In chapter 6, we looked at logging to various destinations. One of the most common destinations for logs is the filesystem, so as part of that process, we had to create and write to one or more files. Using the filesystem is a near-universal task when building any application, but it's especially useful as we work toward building a web server in the next few chapters. From reading and writing templates to caching to handling uploads and downloads, large-scale web applications touch filesystems a lot. So before we get into the networking side, let's go through some basics when it comes to using files in our application. We'll also combine the networking side with the filesystem side when we build a basic network filesystem (NFS) to read files from another server.

7.1.1 Reading files

Although it may seem a relatively intuitive task, Go provides different ways to open and read a file using only the standard library, each with its own sets of caveats and gotchas. We've seen a bit of the io.Writer interface in play, and several of these methods use the io.Reader interface under the hood.

The first approach is os.ReadFile, which returns a byte slice and a possible error given a file location. This is the most straightforward approach if you want the entire contents of a file. The caveat to this method is that an unexpected end of file (EOF) during the read won't be detected, causing your program to crash. Given that this is a hard thing to trigger, if you need the contents of a file, this is the easiest method, but if you need to handle an unexpected EOF, you can also handle the ErrUnexpectedEOF separately. In the following listing, we'll open a file and output its contents as a string to standard output.

Listing 7.1   Outputting contents of a file

```
package main

import (
    "log"
    "os"
)

func main() {
    data, err := os.ReadFile("myfile.txt")      ← Attempts to open myfile.txt
    if err != nil {
        panic(err)
    }
```

```
    log.Println(string(data))        ⟵┐   Casts to a string and
}                                        └  outputs to stdout
```

Because this method reads the entire file, one thing to consider is that `ReadFile` will preallocate space in the byte slice (`[]byte`) for the file, even if an error occurs accessing the first byte. This can be a memory concern when dealing with especially large files. Handling larger files takes some coordination because especially large files can outsize the memory or even disk available to us.

`ReadFile` does a lot of the magic for us, but if we want more control, `os.Open` gives us the chance to get information about our file and process it sequentially ourselves. You may remember our JSON-streaming (JSONS) format log files from chapter 6, which look something like this:

```
{"time":"2023-08-31T12:09:23.32325-04:00","level":"INFO","msg":"this is
default logging"}
{"time":"2023-08-31T12:09:23.32354-04:00","level":"WARN","msg":"keep an eye
 on this, it might be an issue"}
{"time":"2023-08-31T12:09:23.323548-04:00","level":"ERROR","msg":"oh no, an
error happened here!"}
{"time":"2023-08-31T12:09:23.323551-04:00","level":"DEBUG","msg":"this is
good while developing ..."}
{"time":"2023-08-31T12:09:23.323555-04:00","level":"INFO","msg":"this is a
 more complex message","accepted_values":"key/value pairs with specific types
 for marshalling","an int:":30,"grouped_info":{"you_can":"do this too"}}
```

In this case, each entry is newline-separated rather than a larger, singular, valid JSON file. Any time we have data that can be streamed or processed in pieces, it's a good idea to chunk our data as appropriate and handle the blocks individually. Although we could read the entire file into memory and split into lines, that can be very inefficient and will likely start to affect performance as input grows. Instead, we can compartmentalize this process. First, let's open the file, returning a file descriptor, as shown in the following listing.

Listing 7.2 **More details from our file**

```
package main

import (
    "fmt"
    "log"
    "os"
)

func main() {
    file, err := os.Open("structured.log")
    if err != nil {
        panic(err)
    }                                         Gets metadata
    defer file.Close()                        about our
    info, err := file.Stat()        ⟵┘       opened file
```

```
    if err != nil {
        panic(err)
    }
    log.Println(fmt.Sprintf("File: name is %s, mode is        ┐ Displays some of the
        %v, size is %d. Is directory: %v", info.Name(),        │ most commonly used
        info.Mode(), info.Size(), info.IsDir()))      ◄────────┘ attributes
}
```

What we're doing here is getting and displaying some information about the file itself. But we can use that to guide our approach. If the file is small, we can likely handle it in memory without too much concern. But if it's especially big, we can do something smarter about it. In our JSONS example, we know we can process this file line by line and expect each line to be valid. Although we could also use a buffer to chunk the data, that would require some parsing of JSON to know when to stop appending buffered data. Consider the following amendment to our code from listing 7.2.

Listing 7.3   Finding JSON needles in a haystack

```
    lineJSON := make(map[string]interface{})    ◄───┐ Creates our most basic concept
    var bChunk []byte                               │ of JSON, an attribute assigned
    for {                                           │ to any valid JSON type
        b := make([]byte, 2)
        _, err := file.Read(b)

        if err != nil {
            break
        }                                          ┐ Adds data to our
                                                   │ chunk 2 bytes at
        bChunk = append(bChunk, b[0:]...)     ◄────┘ a time

        if err := json.Unmarshal(bChunk, &lineJSON);
        err == nil {                                ◄──┐ Attempts to validate the data
            log.Println(lineJSON)                      │ as it arrives, resetting our
            bChunk = []byte{}                          │ byte array if it succeeds
        }
    }
```

In this rough approach, we take in up to 2 bytes—the minimum valid JSON being []
or {}—at a time until we find valid JSON, at which point we start again until a file read-error (or EOF) occurs. This is brittle and falls apart if there's malformed JSON, as it will continue to append bytes until valid JSON is encountered. In this case, we're safe taking 2 bytes at a time because at worst it will include a newline, but in other scenarios, we might overshoot our valid file format. It also isn't accounting for 4-byte Unicode characters, although in this example it won't break the functionality. But for these reasons and more, a real parser would be used if this were the general approach we took.

> **Clearing maps**
>
> In listing 7.3, you can see that we reassign our byte slice with `[]byte{}`. Starting with Go 1.21, `clear` has been added as a built-in function for use on slices and maps. In a map, this deletes all entries, but in a slice, it sets each element to its type's zero value. If we used this here, we'd reset each entry to the null byte, which would leave us with invalid JSON after the first iteration. Hence, we reassign the variable. The clear function is still a very useful feature and can be used to quickly empty an existing set. For more about how `clear` works, see https://go.dev/ref/spec#Clear.

Because in our JSONS example we know that our files will be newline-delimited records, we can eschew the weight of a full parser and introduce our final common method for reading a file: `bufio.ScanLines`. The `bufio` package wraps `Readers` and `Writers` that add some buffered functionality for streaming. This is particularly useful for looking at each line, which could be used for JSONS as well as CSV and other line-delimited formats. In this case, a single invalid JSON entry can be ignored, and we can continue on with the file.

- *Problem*—We'd like to open files and process them in a streaming format to avoid scalability problems.
- *Solution*—We'll use buffered I/O with the `bufio` package, which wraps our `Readers` and `Writers`, allowing us to process text content in a more efficient, streaming way.
- *Discussion*—There's a lot we can do beyond this if we want to optimize further Problems such as these can be parallelized easily, assuming that we have some sort of central process for managing which processors get what lines to process. In addition, in a multithreaded environment, making this a concurrent job can be faster (but not always).

In the following listing, we read the contents of our generated structured log file in JSONS format and use streaming to process the file more efficiently.

Listing 7.4 Using `bufio` to read line by line

```go
package main

import (
    "bufio"
    "encoding/json"
    "log"
    "os"
)

func main() {
    file, err := os.Open("structured.log")
    if err != nil {
```

```
        panic(err)
    }
    defer file.Close()

    scan := bufio.NewScanner(file)
    scan.Split(bufio.ScanLines)
    lineJSON := make(map[string]interface{})
    for scan.Scan() {
        if err := json.Unmarshal([]byte(scan.Text()), &lineJSON); err != n
        il {
            log.Println(err)
        } else {
            log.Println(lineJSON["level"])
        }
    }
}
```

We initiate our scanner, which is a type that keeps track of where we are in the file and accepts a splitting function.

We split by the function bufio.ScanLines.

Iterates through the file line by line

This solution is already a better way to break our problem into smaller parts. As pointed out, this can be further optimized when dealing with especially large files, as parts of the file can be distributed to different processes and/or servers.

7.1.2 Writing to files

Creating and writing to files generally follows the same patterns as reading. You can write from memory or stream to a target file incrementally. A simple file write includes a few steps, as shown in this listing.

Listing 7.5 Creating and writing to a file

```
package main

import (
    "os"
)

func main() {
    file, err := os.Create("test.txt")
    if err != nil {
        panic(err)
    }
    defer file.Close()

    file.WriteString("test")
}
```

Attempts to create a file and gets its handler if successful

Remember that the file handler needs to be closed.

Writes a string directly to the file

There's very little to this: the Create function returns a file handler to a newly created file or an existing one. Then the WriteString method of a Writer interface sends the string contents directly to the file.

But we seem to have the same problem we had with our reader. We need a string (or bytes) in memory to write to a file. What if we want to stream content into our write the same way we streamed content from our read?

Luckily, the `io` package has `Copy`, which uses a buffer to read from any `Reader` and copy bytes in that buffer size to any `Writer`. This is a neat and tidy way to sidestep having to write a buffer to walk through both source and destination. In the next listing, we'll use the `Copy` method to facilitate buffer-based reads and writes.

Listing 7.6 Copying buffered data from `Reader` to `Writer`

```
package main

import (
    "io"
    "os"
)

func main() {
    src, err := os.Open("test.txt")           ◁── Opens our source
    if err != nil {                                file and gets its
        panic(err)                                 contents
    }
    defer src.Close()

    dest, err := os.Create("test2.txt")
    if err != nil {
        panic(err)
    }
    defer dest.Close()
                                              Copies bytes to a destination,
                                              ignoring the first returned
    _, err = io.Copy(dest, src)           ◁── value, bytes written
    if err != nil {
        panic(err)
    }

}
```

This skips a lot of the boilerplate we had to deal with to stream a read properly. We'll now move into networking, returning to our logs to send data across custom TCP and UDP servers.

7.2 Basic networking via TCP

Outside niche protocols, most of the networking you'll do in Go or any language in a modern application will be TCP-based. It is, of course, the largest part of the TCP/IP protocols and application layers, and comprises most of the networking you'll encounter when building web applications.

To build a basic TCP server, we'll continue with our logs from section 7.1 and from chapter 6, this time sending data over the network instead of logging directly to standard out, disk, or memory. Keep in mind, though, that we can use the techniques in this section to write any custom server that can benefit from the built-in handshaking, error detection, and reconnection features that TCP brings.

7.2.1   *Logging to a network resource*

The logging code we wrote in chapter 6 used a simple file as a destination for the log message. But these days, many of the applications we write—especially servers—run in the cloud inside Docker images, virtual machines, or other resources that have only ephemeral storage. Furthermore, we often run servers in clusters, where it's desirable to aggregate the logs of all servers onto one logging service. With that in mind, let's use a network resource as a destination for delivering files—in this case, log files.

Many popular logging services, including Logstash (https://www.elastic.co/logstash) and Heka (http://hekad.readthedocs.org/en/v0.9.2), aggregate logs. These services typically expose a port to which you can connect and stream log messages. This style of logging has been popularized in the influential 12-factor app paradigm (https://12factor.net). As you may recall from chapter 2, the 11th factor of the 12 is "Treat logs as event streams." As simple as all that sounds, some surprises can arise when you're sending log messages as streams.

- *Problem*—Streaming logs to a network service is error-prone, but you don't want to lose log messages if you can avoid it.
- *Solution*—By using Go's channels and some buffering, you can vastly improve reliability.
- *Discussion*—Before you can get going on the code, you need something that can simulate a log server. Although existing services such as Logstash and Heka are available, you'll avail yourself of a simple UNIX tool called Netcat (nc). Netcat ships standard on most UNIX and Linux flavors, including macOS. A Windows version is also available.

You want to start a simple TCP server that accepts simple text messages and writes them to the console. This is a simple Netcat command:

```
nc -lk 1902
```

Now you have a listener (-l) listening continuously (-k) on port 1902. (Some versions of Netcat may need the -p flag.) This little command will do a fine job of simulating a log server. You can get some code running by adapting one log example from chapter 6 to write to a network socket, as shown in the following listing.

Listing 7.7   Network log client

```
package main

import (
    "log"
    "net"
)

func main() {                                          Connects to
    conn, err := net.Dial("tcp", "localhost:1902")     the log server
    if err != nil {
```

```
        panic("Failed to connect to localhost:1902")
    }
    defer conn.Close()                               ←
    f := log.Ldate | log.Lshortfile                  ←
    logger := log.New(conn, "example ", f)           ←
    logger.Println("This is a regular message.")
    logger.Panicln("This is a panic.")               ←
}
```

Makes sure you clean up by closing the connection, even on panic

Logs a message and then panics. Don't use Fatalln here.

Sets a bitwise value for the log options

Sends log messages to the network connection

Surprisingly, little needs to be changed to write to a network connection instead of to a file. Go's network library is convenient and simple. You create a new TCP connection with net.Dial, connecting it to the port you opened with Netcat. It's always recommended to close a network connection in a defer block. If nothing else, when a panic occurs (as it will in this demo code), the network buffer will be flushed on close, and you're less likely to lose critical log messages telling you why the code panicked.

As in chapter 6, you use the log package to log to the remote server. Using the logging package here gives you a few advantages:

- You get a timestamp for free, and when logging to a network server, it's always a good idea to log the host time and not rely solely on the log server's timestamp. This helps you reconstruct a record of events even if the log messages are delayed on their way to the log server.
- As you can see by comparing examples from chapter 6 to listing 7.7, when you stick with the logging system, it's trivially easy to swap out the underlying log storage mechanism. Recall that to do so, we only had to swap one Writer interface with any other type that also implemented the Write method. Having the destination as a configurable option is great for testing and running developer environments.

Did you notice that we also changed log.Fatalln to a log.Panicln in this example? There's a simple reason for this. The log.Fatal* functions have an unfortunate side effect: the deferred function isn't called. Why not? log.Fatal* calls os.Exit, which immediately terminates the program without unwinding the function stack. We covered this topic in chapter 6. Because the deferred function is skipped, your network connection is never properly flushed and closed. Panics, on the other hand, are easier to capture. In reality, production code for anything but simple command-line clients should avoid using fatal errors. As you saw in chapter 6, there are specific cases in which you should call a panic, such as when an error in the state of your system makes it impossible for any future processing to succeed. With all this in mind, when you execute the preceding code, your nc instance should receive some log messages:

```
$ nc -lk 1902
example 2015/05/27 log_client.go:23: This is a regular message.
example 2015/05/27 log_client.go:24: This is a panic.
```

These messages made their way from the example client to the simple server you're running on nc. You have a nice, simple network logging utility. But you may also have a problem in the form of a culprit commonly known as *back pressure*.

7.2.2   *Handling back pressure in network logging*

In the previous technique, you saw how to log messages to a network server. Logging to a network offers compelling advantages:

- Logs from many services can be aggregated to one central location.
- In the cloud, servers with only ephemeral storage can still have logs preserved.
- Security and auditability are improved.
- You can tune log servers and app servers differently.

But there's one major drawback to sending your log messages to a remote logging server: you're dependent on the network. When latency from requests exceeds the ability of the server to process and return them, we observe the problem known as back pressure. Back pressure can exist in any system that accepts and processes data, but it's particularly evident in systems that also use the network and/or (as in our case) the filesystem, where file reads are always faster than file writes. By using this technique, you'll see how to deal with network-based problems in logging.

- *Problem*—Network log services are prone to connection failures and back pressure. This leads to lost log messages and sometimes even service failures.
- *Solution*—Build a more resilient logger that buffers data.
- *Discussion*—You're likely to run into two major networking problems:
  - The logger's network connection drops (either because the network is down or because the remote logger is down).
  - The connection over which the logs are sent slows down.

  The first problem is familiar to us all and is clearly a problem to be addressed. The second is a little less obvious.

Listing 7.7 detailed a rough sequence of events. Let's trace it at a high level, as shown in figure 7.1. (The network mechanics are a little more complicated, but you don't need to know them to understand the situation.)

Your application opens a TCP connection, sends messages, and then closes the connection. But something you don't see in your code is the response from the logger because things are going on at the TCP layer that don't bubble up into the application code.

Specifically, when a message is sent as a TCP/IP packet, the receiver is obligated to respond to the packet by acknowledging (Ack) that the message was received. It's possible and even likely that one log message may become more than one packet sent across the network. Suppose that a log message is split into two separate packets. The remote logger would receive the first part and send an ACK. Then the client would send the second half, to which the logger would also send an ACK. With this

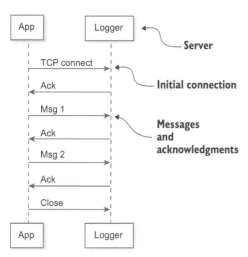

Figure 7.1 Sending messages over TCP, with a sequence of commands between a client (App) and server (Logger). First we connect; then an acknowledgement (Ack) is sent to the connection as well as to each message.

system, the client gains some assurance that the data it sent was indeed received by the remote host.

7.3 Basic networking with UDP

Our example with a TCP server is all well and good until the remote host slows down. Imagine a log server that's receiving thousands of messages from many clients at once. With all that data coming in, the server may slow down if there isn't enough throughput. But while it slows, the volume of logs behind it doesn't diminish and will in fact build up like floodwater behind a dam. With TCP, the log server must send an Ack for each new message that comes in. When it delays sending the Ack, the client sits waiting. The client must slow down too, as its resources are tied up waiting for log messages to send. This is our back pressure scenario.

One solution to the back-pressure problem is to switch from TCP to UDP. By doing this, you get rid of connection overhead at the protocol level. Most significantly, the application doesn't need to wait for Ack messages from the log server. Figure 7.2 illustrates this method.

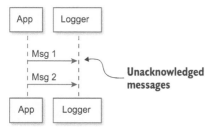

Figure 7.2 UDP log messages, showing the relative simplicity compared to TCP. Messages receive no Ack from the server.

UDP requires no network connection maintenance. The client sends information to the server whenever it's ready. Altering the Go code from listing 7.7 is simple, as you can see in the next listing.

Listing 7.8   UDP-based logging

```
package main

import (
    "log"
    "net"
    "time"
)

func main() {
    timeout := 30 * time.Second
    conn, err := net.DialTimeout("udp",
    "localhost:1902", timeout)
    if err != nil {
            panic("Failed to connect to localhost:1902")
    }
    defer    conn.Close()
    f := log.Ldate | log.Lshortfile
    logger := log.New(conn, "example ", f)
    logger.Println("This is a regular message.")
    logger.Panicln("This is a panic.")
}
```

Adds an explicit timeout ◁

Dials a UDP connection instead of a TCP one ◁

The changes to the code are minimal. Instead of using the regular `net.Dial`, this code has `net.DialTimeout`, which adds a nicety to the regular `net.Dial` call: it specifies how long it will wait for the connection before giving up. You set this to 30 seconds. With TCP, the timeout includes time to send the message and receive the `Ack`. But with UDP, you set the timeout largely for just how long it takes your app to resolve the address and send the message. Setting a timeout gives you a little bit of a safety net when the network isn't functioning as expected.

To run the preceding code, you also need to restart your `nc` server as a UDP server: `nc -luk 1902`. Using UDP for logging has some distinct advantages:

- The app is resistant to back pressure and log server outages. If the log server hiccups, it may lose some UDP packets, but the client won't be affected.
- Sending logs is faster even without back pressure.
- The code is simple.

But this route also has some major disadvantages. Depending on your needs, these drawbacks may indicate that this is the wrong route for you:

- Log messages can get lost easily. UDP doesn't equip you to know whether a message was received correctly.
- Log messages can be received out of order. Large log messages may be packetized and then get jumbled in transition. Adding a timestamp to the message (as you've done) can help with this but not totally resolve it.

- Sending the remote server lots of UDP messages may overwhelm the remote server because it can't manage its connections and slow down the data intake. Although your app may be immune to back pressure, your log server may be worse off.

Based on our own experiences, UDP-based logging has a time and a place. It's quick and efficient. If you can predict with relative accuracy how much work your log server needs to do, this method provides a useful and simple path to network logging.

But a few cases might definitively tilt your decision away from UDP logging. You may not want to use UDP logging when you can't accurately predict how much logging data will go from the app server to the log server or when losing occasional log messages is unacceptable.

TCP logging is prone to back pressure, but UDP logging won't guarantee data accuracy. It's a conundrum that we're used to dealing with from image encoding. Do you want precise images at the expense of large file sizes (GIF, PNG), or compact images that lose some data (JPEG)? With logging, you may need to make a similar choice. This isn't to say that nothing can be done to make things better. Back-pressure stress can be delayed by creating a large buffer for logs to be stored temporarily in case of network saturation, for example.

7.4 Websockets and server-sent events

Creating web servers in Go is a straightforward Application-layer-level task that we'll explore in depth in chapters 8 through 10. As the web has evolved, more apps and websites are using real-time and bidirectional persistent connections to deliver data more efficiently. Although client polling is still relatively common, inefficiencies in the HTTP/TCP layer can add a lot of overhead and delays to data transmission that could be otherwise delivered in real time.

Starting with chapter 8, we'll begin building out a robust web server using standard HTTP servers. But before we do, let's look at two ways to implement persistent connections in our apps: websockets and server-sent events.

7.4.1 Implementing websockets for real-time chat

Websockets are a unique feature of the TCP/IP web stack that solve a common problem in the post-Web 2.0 world: keeping connections active and distributing messages bidirectionally across that connection. Managing state in an inherently stateless protocol has led to a lot of extra work in the history of the web. Each request is its own independent entity, and that leads to a lot of repetition of intents and history to go along with it. Consider a series of REST calls, which must reassert identity and queries while modifying small bits of a request like a page or cursor. Websockets were introduced to reduce some of this repetition in certain use cases by keeping the client and server connected via a single TCP connection; although they're not specifically a replacement for REST, they can be used for some interesting real-time, lightweight, communication purposes.

- *Problem*—Using traditional HTTP methods and approaches to message passing has a lot of overhead and relies on timed polling approaches, leading to applications that feel stale and aren't updated immediately.
- *Solution*—Employ websockets, a protocol that keeps connections active and can be used to distribute incoming messages to multiple clients as they arrive.
- *Discussion*—Websockets are a very targeted approach to very specific problems. You may not need websockets most of the time, but when you need instantaneous responses multiplexed to many users, it's the best tool in the toolbox.

NOTE   As the docs themselves indicate, the built-in `websockets` package in the x sub repository may lack some more advanced features that exist in third-party packages. For a smaller example, though, we'll stick with the (almost) standard library. You can find recommendations for those on the main package page: https://pkg.go.dev/golang.org/x/net/websocket.

The primary change you'll make to a normal HTTP server is to use a `websocket.Handler` wrapper, which manages the handshake and upgrade from an HTTP connection to a websocket. In the next listing, we'll create a simple chat service that enables multiple clients to join and distributes messages to them as they come in from other clients.

Listing 7.9   **A chat application using websockets**

```
package main

import (
    "encoding/json"
    "fmt"
    "log"
    "math/rand"
    "net/http"

    "golang.org/x/net/websocket"
)

var chars =
    []rune("0123456789abcdefghijklmnopqrstuvwxyzABCDEFGHIJKLMNOPQRSTUVWXYZ")
var clients map[string]*websocket.Conn          ◁──── List of characters
                                                       to use to create
func init() {                                          our random IDs
    clients = make(map[string]*websocket.Conn)
}

func generateId() string {          ◁──┤ Random ID
    r := make([]rune, 16)                generation script
    for i := range r {
        r[i] = chars[rand.Intn(len(chars))]
    }
    return string(r)
}
```

```
func chatHandler(w http.ResponseWriter,
r *http.Request) {
    fmt.Fprintf(w, `
    <!DOCTYPE html>
        <html>
        <head>
            <title>Let's Chat</title>
            <style>
            #chat {
                max-width: 400px;
                margin: auto;
                font-family: system-ui, sans-serif;
            }
            .message {
                padding: 1rem 0.25rem;
                border: 1px solid black;
                margin-bottom: 0.5rem;
            }
            </style>
        </head>
        <body>
            <div id="chat">
            <h1>Chat</h1>
            <div id="messages"></div>
            <input id="message" autofocus type="text"
            placeholder="Enter message ..." />
            <div>
                <p>Chat members:</p>
                <ul id="chat-members"></ul>
            </div>
        </div>
        <script>
            const text = document.getElementById('message');
            const messages = document.getElementById('messages');
            const members = document.getElementById('chat-members');
            const ws = new WebSocket('ws://localhost:8081/ws');
            ws.onmessage = e => {
                const msg = JSON.parse(e.data);
                if (msg.message_type == 'joinleave') {
                    members.innerHTML = '';
                    msg.chat_members.forEach(member => {
                        const li = document.createElement('li');
                        li.innerHTML = member;
                        members.appendChild(li);
                    });
                    return;
                }
                if (msg.message_type === 'message') {
                    const message = document.createElement('div');
                    message.classList.add('message');
                    message.innerHTML = msg.sender_id + " said: " +
                    msg.message;
                    messages.appendChild(message);
                    return;
                }
```

Our main publicly facing web page for chat, outputting HTML and JavaScript

```
                    }
                    document.getElementById('message').addEventListener('keyup',
                    e => {
                        if (e.key == 'Enter') {
                            ws.send(e.target.value);
                            message.value = '';
                        }
                    });
            </script>
            </body>
            </html>
        `)
}

type servermsg struct {
    MessageType string   `json:"message_type"`
    Message     string   `json:"message,omitempty"`
    Id          string   `json:"id,omitempty"`
    SenderId    string   `json:"sender_id,omitempty"`
    ChatMembers []string `json:"chat_members"`
}
```

A function that returns all the current chat members in a slice

```
func compileChatMembers() []string {
    var chatMembers []string
    for k, _ := range clients {
        chatMembers = append(chatMembers, k)
    }
    return chatMembers
}
```

A global broadcast function that sends a message to all users

```
func sendToClients(msg servermsg) error {
    msgJSON, err := json.Marshal(msg)
    if err != nil {
        return err
    }
    for k := range clients {
        if err := websocket.Message.Send(clients[k], string(msgJSON));
        err != nil {
            return err
        }
    }
    return nil
}
```

Disconnection functionality, removing a user by ID

```
func disconnectClient(id string) error {
    delete(clients, id)
    if err := sendToClients(servermsg{
        MessageType: "joinleave",
        Message:     "",
        Id:          id,
        SenderId:    "",
        ChatMembers: compileChatMembers(),
    }); err != nil {
        return err
    }
```

```
    return nil
}
func ws(ws *websocket.Conn) {
    id := generateId()
    clients[id] = ws

    join := servermsg{
        MessageType: "joinleave",
        Message:     "",
        Id:          id,
        SenderId:    "",
        ChatMembers: compileChatMembers(),
    }

    sendToClients(join)

    for {
        var incoming string
        if err := websocket.Message.Receive(ws,
        &incoming); err != nil {
            if err := disconnectClient(id); err != nil {
                log.Println(err)
            }
            break
        }
        if err := sendToClients(servermsg{
            MessageType: "message",
            Message:     incoming,
            Id:          "",
            SenderId:    id,
            ChatMembers: compileChatMembers(),
        }); err != nil {
            if err := disconnectClient(id); err != nil {
                log.Println(err)
            }
            break
        }
    }
}

func main() {

    http.HandleFunc("/chat", chatHandler)
    http.Handle("/ws", websocket.Handler(ws))
    if err := http.ListenAndServe(":8081", nil); err != nil {
        panic(err)
    }
}
```

The primary handler function for the websocket

An event loop that listens for messages

If we cannot receive from a websocket, the likeliest possibility is they've disconnected, so we remove them from the clients.

Similarly, if we can't send, we'll remove them from the clients.

A wrapper function around our handler

If this looks like a lot, keep in mind it's a working multiuser chat application for both client and server side in fewer than 200 lines of code that allows users to join, broadcast messages, and update a list of active users when they join and leave.

In this case, we've put the string value representation of the template directly in the code, but we have other options, including embedding data directly in our compiled binary. We'll look at that in more detail in chapter 10.

> **Keeping secure**
> Just as HTTP has a TLS/HTTPS encrypted secure protocol, so do websockets, which can be upgraded via an initial HTTPS endpoint. On your local machine, without a secure certificate, we use the `ws://` scheme, but just as we would use HTTPS in production, we'd use `wss://`.

The general idea of this chat app should be easy to map mentally to the idea of joining and using a chat application. When a new client joins, they are assigned a random string ID and get a join message with that and a list of members in chat. In our JavaScript, we show the current users. The random ID here could be anything—sequential, a unique name provided by the user—but we're using it to keep track of the connection if and when we need to broadcast the fact that said user has left (figure 7.3).

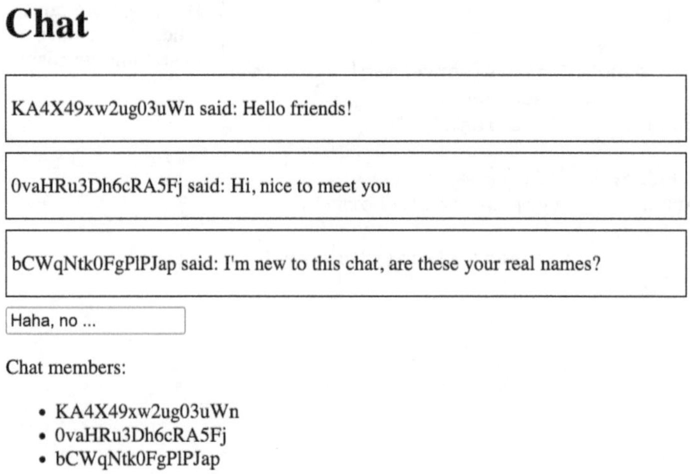

Chat

KA4X49xw2ug03uWn said: Hello friends!

0vaHRu3Dh6cRA5Fj said: Hi, nice to meet you

bCWqNtk0FgPlPJap said: I'm new to this chat, are these your real names?

Haha, no ...

Chat members:

- KA4X49xw2ug03uWn
- 0vaHRu3Dh6cRA5Fj
- bCWqNtk0FgPlPJap

Figure 7.3   Some comments from our chat application, showing messages coming through with a list of active members, updated in real time

Any message that comes in will be distributed to all active clients. When we receive an error on `Message.Send` or `Message.Receive`, we'll remove the client from the list and broadcast a `joinleave` message to all active clients. This acts as a trigger to update the list of members on the page itself.

Building something like this with traditional HTTP via REST or similar mechanism would be a much more daunting and inefficient endeavor and unlikely to feel as responsive as this fairly simple example. By using websockets, we avoid all the overhead associated with non-persistent connections.

There's a lot missing here that we'd expect from a fully featured chat app, but it gives us the basics needed to chat with other users. Additional features such as setting a client's name and back-filling messages on join would be relatively simple to bolt on top of this. It's also not reentrant, which brings up an important distinction between websockets and HTTP: no headers, including cookies, get sent with a request. This means reestablishing identity needs to be done through other means.

> **JSON Web Tokens**
>
> Although session IDs could be one option to append to requests, a more secure method is to use JSON Web Tokens (JWTs), which are signed to mitigate the risk of session hijacking. JWTs come with their own risks—primarily invalidation—but in general are a better idea for identity, particularly over a protocol like websockets.

When using websockets, it's important to keep a few things in mind:

- *Connection logic can be hard to maintain on both the server and client side.* If a server closes a connection, the client may not know about it, and when it finds out, reconnect logic has to be built into the frontend. Because websockets are stateful, they will have to reestablish themselves in some cases using the same logic and processes they used to connect in the first place.
- *There aren't true polyfills for older browsers that don't support them.* Those that do exist generally rearchitect as standard HTTP requests/responses.

7.4.2 Server-sent events

Although web sockets are great for real-time bidirectional communication, there are some caveats and problems that come along with them, and they're not always the right tool for the job of keepalive messaging. For a chat application, we need both client(s) and server to be able to maintain state, but what if we want to send notifications one-way, from server to client only? This is where server-sent events (SSE, or `EventSource` in JavaScript) come into play. A SSE is, like websockets, a long-lived HTTP connection but one that allows communication only from the server to the client. It is a lightweight connection that requires less connection maintenance from the client side.

- *Problem*—We don't need bidirectional communication but still want to send events to our clients periodically in real time without the need for polling or separate, successive requests.
- *Solution*—Using the networking basics we've already explored, we can modify our HTTP/TCP server to deliver SSEs in response to an event or update. This allows our server to communicate directly with a client within a persistent connection.

- *Discussion*—This approach is relatively novel and still not widely used but has a lot of practical application on the web. It's ideal for things like notifications, such as when someone responds to a social media post. In our example case, we'll create a simple web app that updates clients when a file on the server has been modified.

This is a great example of unidirectional communication, the kind you might see in any collaboration tool where a server is a central source of truth. These system messages are sent, naturally, from the system rather than individual clients themselves. To make this work, we'll use a third-party package, `fsnotify`, which lets us watch for file changes in a goroutine. Inside that goroutine, we'll monitor for changes in our filesystem and send them directly to our client. In the following listing, we create a web service that watches a directory for file changes and updates the frontend of that site via SSEs.

Listing 7.10   A file-change notification website

```go
package main

import (
    "context"
    "encoding/json"
    "fmt"
    "log"
    "net/http"
    "os"

    "github.com/fsnotify/fsnotify"
)

var directory string
var watcher *fsnotify.Watcher

type FileUpdateInfo struct {          // The structure of
    Name      string `json:"name"`    //  our message
    Op        string `json:"operation"`
    SizeBytes int    `json:"size"`
}

func init() {
    if osdir := os.Getenv("SSE_DIRECTORY"); osdir == "" {
        panic("SSE_DIRECTORY environment variable not set")
    } else {
        directory = osdir
    }
}

func main() {
    var err error
    watcher, err = fsnotify.NewWatcher()   // Initializes our
    if err != nil {                        //  file watcher
        log.Fatal(err)
    }
```

```
    defer watcher.Close()
    watcher.Add(directory)

    http.HandleFunc("/sse", sseHandler)
    http.HandleFunc("/files", filesHandler)
    http.ListenAndServe(":8080", nil)
}

func sseHandler(w http.ResponseWriter, r *http.Request) {
    flusher, ok := w.(http.Flusher)
    if !ok {
        http.Error(w, "byte streams not supported by your client",
        http.StatusInternalServerError)
        return
    }
    w.Header().Set("Content-Type", "text/event-stream")

    changes := make(chan FileUpdateInfo)
    go fileListener(r.Context(), changes)
    for change := range changes {
        changeJSON, err := json.Marshal(change)
        if err != nil {
            log.Println(err)
            continue
        }
        response := fmt.Sprintf("event:
        file-update\ndata: %s\n\n", changeJSON)
        fmt.Fprint(w, response)
        flusher.Flush()
    }
}

func filesHandler(w http.ResponseWriter, r *http.Request) {
    fmt.Fprint(w, `<!DOCTYPE html>
<html>
<head><title>File changes</title></head>
<style>
    body > div {
        margin: auto;
        max-width: 800px;
    }
    .message {
        padding: 1rem;
        background-color: grey;
        margin-bottom: 0.5rem;
    }
    .message.create {
        background-color: palegreen;
    }
    .message.remove {
        background-color: tomato;
    }
</style>
<body>
    <div>
```

A Flusher, which we use to send byte streams but also determine whether the client is compatible

Sets the proper header to tell the browser to keep listening for messages

Starting a goroutine that listens for file changes

Sending our formatted payload

```
            <h1>File changes</h1>
            <div id="files"></div>
        </div>
        <script>
            const sse = new EventSource('/sse');
            const files = document.getElementById('files');
            const createMessage = (message) => {
                const div = document.createElement('div');
                div.classList.add('message');
                div.classList.add(message.operation.toLowerCase());
                div.innerText = message.operation + ':' + message.name + ' ('
                + message.size + ' bytes)';
                return div;
            }
            sse.onmessage = (e) => {
                alert(e.data);
            }
            sse.addEventListener('file-update', (e) => {
                console.log(e, e.data);
                files.prepend(createMessage(JSON.parse(e.data)));

            });
        </script>
</body>
</html>`)                  ◁———┤ Full HTML payload with
}                              │ JavaScript to listen to SSEs


func fileListener(ctx context.Context, changes chan<- FileUpdateInfo) {
    for {
        select {
        case <-ctx.Done():
            return
        case event, ok := <-watcher.Events:
            if !ok {
                break
            }
            size := 0
            if stat, err := os.Stat(event.Name); err == nil {
                size = int(stat.Size())
            }
            changes <- FileUpdateInfo{event.Name,
            event.Op.String(), size}         ◁——┐ Sending any file
        }                                       │ listener events
    }                                           │ through our channel
}
```

You'll note that in our `init` function, we need to set an environment variable, SSE_DI-RECTORY. After doing so and running, we can visit `localhost:8080/files` and then create, append, or delete files within our specified folder. As we do so, we'll see our various changes in the page itself in chronological order (figure 7.4).

When changes come in, we see them stack on top of one another. As noted, there's no bidirectional communication, and we don't need it. Clients are simply receivers of

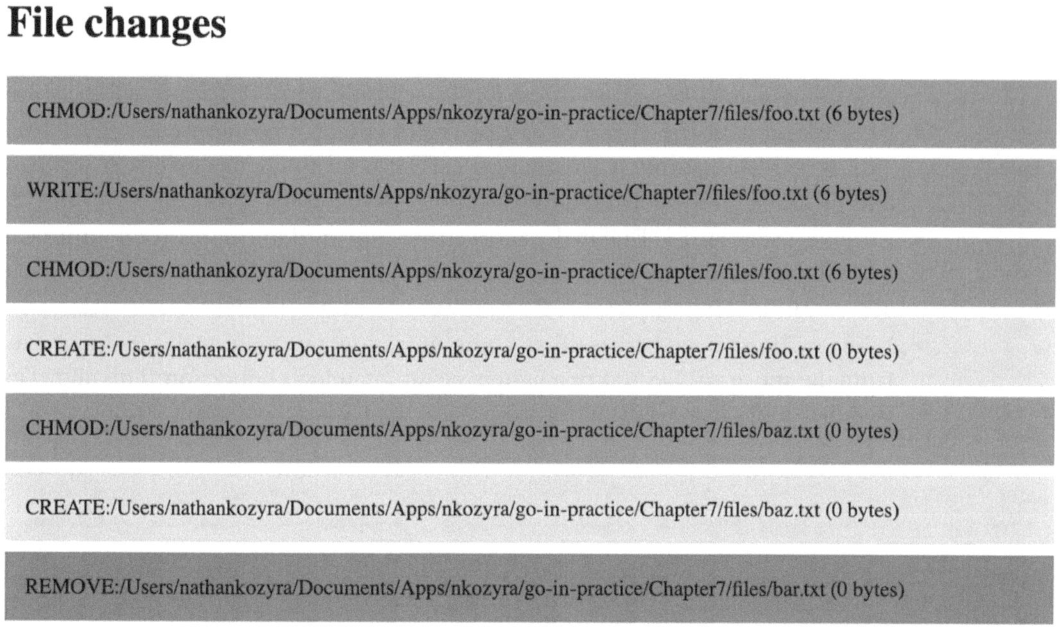

File changes

CHMOD:/Users/nathankozyra/Documents/Apps/nkozyra/go-in-practice/Chapter7/files/foo.txt (6 bytes)

WRITE:/Users/nathankozyra/Documents/Apps/nkozyra/go-in-practice/Chapter7/files/foo.txt (6 bytes)

CHMOD:/Users/nathankozyra/Documents/Apps/nkozyra/go-in-practice/Chapter7/files/foo.txt (6 bytes)

CREATE:/Users/nathankozyra/Documents/Apps/nkozyra/go-in-practice/Chapter7/files/foo.txt (0 bytes)

CHMOD:/Users/nathankozyra/Documents/Apps/nkozyra/go-in-practice/Chapter7/files/baz.txt (0 bytes)

CREATE:/Users/nathankozyra/Documents/Apps/nkozyra/go-in-practice/Chapter7/files/baz.txt (0 bytes)

REMOVE:/Users/nathankozyra/Documents/Apps/nkozyra/go-in-practice/Chapter7/files/bar.txt (0 bytes)

Figure 7.4 File changes happening in real time. Changes that result in a file remaining with content will show the byte length.

information. The two technologies can be combined in robust apps that have different use cases for the flow of information, of course.

> **TIP** The Flusher interface is our hint that a client likely does not support buffered data streams, in which case we return that message and say goodbye. This is a bit of a brute-force approach to determining compatibility, but gives us a high probability that the client's browser does not support event streams.

As with websockets, there are some downsides to SSEs. There's a per-browser limit on the number of open connections to a distinct domain. This means if you have an app that uses SSEs, you can hit that limit if you open multiple EventSources in your app. Worse, it applies across all windows and tabs, so if a user opens your site more than their browser's limit (generally 2 to 10 EventSource connections per domain), they will be met with errors.

There are ways to work around these limitations, the most common of which is ensuring that you're using HTTP/2. But the risk of these browser limitations might be risky enough that you should keep them in mind whenever you're planning on implementing SSEs in your app and build in some contingency plans.

Summary

- Go offers lightweight methods for reading and writing files but also makes it easy to manage either with more robust streaming, buffered approaches.
- Networking is at the core of Go's powerful concurrency approach. UDP and TCP servers are simple to create and can be used to create servers, store logs, and facilitate multiplexed communication among users.
- Although standard HTTP is the most straightforward and most used approach to TCP, we have tools like `websockets` to build longer-lived connections that allow multiplexing requests and responses to myriad clients.
- When we don't need bidirectional communication, we can use SSEs to direct data from the server to client(s) in a lighter-weight, stateless connection. This allows us to build things like notifications simply and with low network overhead.

Part 3

Building web applications end to end

In this part, we'll explore the key concepts needed to build production-grade web services using Go. From API responses to templates, to sending and receiving data in various formats and protocols, we'll flesh out the requisites for a full web app.

Along the way, we'll look at routing—basic and advanced, authentication, static file service, form handling, and everything in between.

In chapter 8, we'll create a backend for a web server, learning how to deal with HTTP requests and routing. We'll extend our server by touching Go's templating system so we can create safe, formatted responses for both the web and other destinations. In chapter 9, we put that all together and build a front-to-back web application; then we dig into more advanced functionality for our applications by supporting file uploads and POST data and dealing with HTTP header data.

In addition to building our own services, we need to understand how to interface with other web services, which is critical for data pipelines and extract, transform, load (ETL) processes and for proxying third-party services and their various protocols. We'll touch on REST, JSON, and remote procedure call (RPC) as data-transfer options and explore how to best design our own clients and servers to interact with such services.

By the end of this part, you will be able to both build a full-featured web application and interface with external web services.

Building
an HTTP server

8

This chapter covers

- Using built-in routing via HTTP verbs and path variables
- Hardening a web server with timeout options
- Using middleware and context to prevent code duplication
- Understanding the basics of accepting header, cookie, and form data
- Processing other types of request data
- Reducing code duplication through middleware

In the previous chapters, we examined some critical building blocks necessary for designing production-ready applications. We looked at testing and debugging, concurrency, and (in chapter 7) networking and file access. We'll build on the networking aspect in this chapter as we work toward building web applications that can hold up to real-world requirements and traffic. We begin by going over the basics of routing and move on to multiplexers and routers so we can better match the endpoints we want and create responses from the right handlers. We'll also build middleware to capture common tasks that might otherwise create code duplication or spaghetti logic in our web handlers.

Although Go's `http` package in the standard library is simple by design, and though the tools provided can get us high-performance web servers out of the box, it's also created with the kind of building-block style that encourages extending it. Creating an HTTP server is a matter of a few lines of Go, but building one that handles real-world scenarios requires the developer to do some planning and careful construction of these building blocks.

Frameworks: build vs. buy

Like most languages, Go has a lot of third-party frameworks that bring additional bells and whistles together in one package. You may find one that meets your needs exactly, but keep in mind that these often come with a lot more than you may need and can introduce latency or unexpected security problems. The authors of this book have found that Go gives you enough in the standard library to get going very easily, so go to frameworks only if they give you something you can't easily build yourself.

8.1 Routing requests and accepting data

Although we've done some basic web servers in previous chapters, in particular chapter 1 and chapter 7, we haven't yet dug into any complex topics needed to build a production-quality server. A full-formed web application has a lot of moving parts that can require a wide array of data processing. A lot of this is abstracted by the libraries we use—in this case, Go's standard library `http` package. But the details of how an app works require building on these abstractions. We need to know what a client is requesting and in what context. Are they creating content or reading it? Should the requests be authenticated? If so, how? These are the types of details that dictate how the app will work. A lot of these questions need to be answered even before the logic of a response can be executed.

First things first. We need to know how to send and receive data in the proper format(s), how to route requests to the right handler, and how to use header information to express and understand the intent of the request.

Router, multiplexer, or muxer?

Although we'll use the words *multiplexer* (or *muxer*) and *router* throughout the chapter, it's worth noting that aside from subtle differences, they are synonymous. For the purposes of this book, a router can be thought of as something that takes an exact matching pattern and pairs it with a handler function. This is not a hard and fast definition, and you may see the reverse described in the wild.

First, we'll look at how to route requests in a way that lets us have overlapping endpoints and route them based on HTTP method. In section 8.2, we'll refine this simple approach a bit.

8.1.1 Routing via HTTP verbs

When we get a request from a client or user, we first have to decide what to do with that request. This is almost always done via a combination of the path and request type; it's the responsibility of a router. In anything but the simplest web application, we'll have multiple routes to handle. As we've seen in previous chapters, matching an endpoint and pairing it with a route is trivial in Go's `http` package. It's as simple as this:

```
http.HandleFunc("/home", func(w http.ResponseWriter, r *http.Request) {
    fmt.Fprint(w, "Welcome to my homepage")
})
```

Supplying any function that matches the `HandlerFunc` interface signature will work here. But what if we were setting up a REST-style API, wherein the HTTP verb dictates the logic? Consider a simple comments section on a web page, such as a blog post. We use GET to retrieve comments, and typically, we'd use POST to create them. In this case, we may want to use the `/comments` endpoint for both and let the HTTP method determine the logic and expected response.

> **To CRUD or not to CRUD**
>
> In the early days of REST adoption, a strict adherence to a Create Read Update Delete (CRUD) architecture was popular to the point of near dogma. Although it does map well to the standard HTTP methods, keep in mind that applications often get so complicated that it's worth unbinding yourself from this approach. In addition, some client software may not have robust support for necessary methods like OPTIONS, PUT, PATCH, and DELETE, and some clients may take an incorrect approach on which methods should be cached.
>
> Like most things, CRUD is not a one-size-fits-all approach, and the goals should determine the architecture, not the other way around.

- *Problem*—We want to use the same endpoint to create data and read data. Out of the box, Go's router will match the shortest possible path, regardless of supplied request data, including header and HTTP method.
- *Solution*—We'll show two approaches. The first is the simplest option, which is to include the method directly in the path pattern itself. We'll also write a wrapper handler that can route the requests manually, which gives you additional control over routing depending on different request attributes.
- *Discussion*—The second approach has drawbacks, such as that it's not reusable and requires each collection of possible routes to have a handler that wraps all the possible HTTP methods. But if you have a single shared path that has multiple response branches per route, this will do this job.

Accepting a request to the same path and contextualizing it through the request's verb requires adding some decoration or a method prefix to the path, which we show in the following listing, allowing Go to restrict requests by HTTP method.

Listing 8.1   Using built-in method routing

```go
package main

import (
    "net/http"
)

func getComments(w http.ResponseWriter,
r *http.Request) {
    w.Write([]byte("here you'll get the comments"))
}

func postComments(w http.ResponseWriter,
r *http.Request) {
    w.Write([]byte("thank you for posting a comment"))
}

func main() {
    http.HandleFunc("GET /comments", getComments)
    http.HandleFunc("POST /comments", postComments)
    if err := http.ListenAndServe(":8000", nil); err != nil {
        panic(err)
    }
}
```

Our handler function for GET requests ⟵

Our handler function for POST requests ⟵

Routes GET requests to our getComments handler ⟵

Routes POST requests to our postComments handler ⟵

We can put this into practice by allowing users to view and post comments by adding handlers that allow users to view comments via GET and create them via POST, appending to an in-memory slice of comments, as in the next listing.

Listing 8.2   Using the same route with different HTTP verbs

```go
package main

import (
    "fmt"
    "io/ioutil"
    "net/http"
    "time"
)

type comment struct {
    text       string
    dateString string
}

var comments []comment
```

The shape of our initial comment data structure ⟵

```
func getComments(w http.ResponseWriter,
r *http.Request) {                                    ◄──┐  Our destination
    commentBody := ""                                      │  handler functions
    for i := range comments {
        commentBody += fmt.Sprintf("%s (%s)\n", comments[i].text,
        comments[i].dateString)
    }
    fmt.Fprintln(w, fmt.Sprintf("Comments: \n%s", commentBody))
}

func postComments(w http.ResponseWriter,
r *http.Request) {                                    ◄──┐  Our destination
    commentText, err := ioutil.ReadAll(r.Body)            │  handler functions
    if err != nil {
        w.WriteHeader(http.StatusInternalServerError)
        return
    }
    comments = append(comments, comment{text: string(commentText),
    dateString: time.Now().Format(time.RFC3339)})
    w.WriteHeader(http.StatusOK)
}

func main() {

    http.HandleFunc("GET /comments", getComments)
    http.HandleFunc("POST /comments", postComments)

    if err := http.ListenAndServe(":8004", nil); err != nil {
        panic(err)
    }
}
```

We can try this out in practice by triggering both routes through the browser and/or cURL. With a cURL command, you can include a comment via your POST body and create a new entry:

```
curl -X POST http://localhost:8004/comments -d "I'm new here"
```

Visit the same URL in your browser or via GET (figure 8.1).

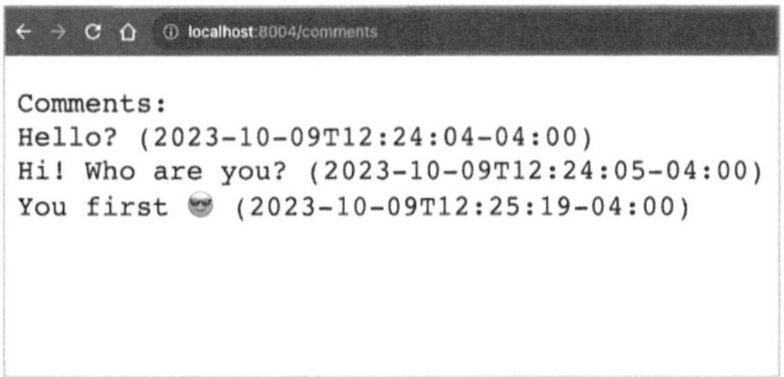

```
←  →  C  ⌂  ⓘ localhost:8004/comments

Comments:
Hello? (2023-10-09T12:24:04-04:00)
Hi! Who are you? (2023-10-09T12:24:05-04:00)
You first 😈 (2023-10-09T12:25:19-04:00)
```

Figure 8.1 Our comments via GET, displayed in chronological order

Requests to the /comments endpoint with anything other than GET or POST will return a 405 Method Not Allowed response. It's worth noting that you're not restricted to standard HTTP methods. The following is valid and will route properly but is obviously nothing more than a curiosity:

```
http.HandleFunc("FOOBAR /comments", fooBarHandler)
```

The logic behind method-based subrouting isn't particularly difficult to replicate manually. There aren't many use cases for this, but consider an upsert endpoint in response to POST commands. Although most databases can handle partial updates like this, consider the pattern in the next listing.

Listing 8.3 Manual method-based routing with additional logic

```
package main

import (
    "encoding/json"
    "io"
    "net/http"
)

type comment struct {
    ID int `json:"id,omitempty"`
    Comment string `json:"comment,omitempty"`
}

func upsertHandler(w http.ResponseWriter, r *http.Request) {
    if r.Method == http.MethodPost {                              ◁─┐ Checks whether
        postBody, err := io.ReadAll(r.Body)                          we get a more
        if err != nil {                                              generic POST
            w.WriteHeader(http.StatusBadRequest)                     request
            return
        }
        var postComment comment
        if err := json.Unmarshal(postBody, &postComment); err != nil {
            w.WriteHeader(http.StatusInternalServerError)
            return
        }                                              ┌─ If a POST request, ensures
        if postComment.ID == 0 {                       │  that an ID is supplied; if not,
            // createCommentHandler(w, r)              ─┤  creates a comment
        } else {                                       │
            // upsertCommentHandler(w, r)              ◁─┐ If an ID is supplied, routes
        }                                                │ to an update handler
    }
    if r.Method == http.MethodPut || r.Method == http.MethodPatch {
        // upsertCommentHandler(w, r)              ◁─┐
    }                                                │ If PUT or PATCH, goes
}                                                    │ straight to an update
                                                     │ handler
```

```
func main() {
    http.HandleFunc("/comments/upsert", upsertHandler)     ◁─── Routes to an
    if err := http.ListenAndServe(":8000", nil); err != nil {        intermediate
        panic("could not start server")                              endpoint against
    }                                                                all methods
}
```

Doing this supplies a little more tolerance for user error in the case that supplied data is not expressed as we might expect. This at minimum handles some implementation cases we might encounter. As we expand on this, we can make the code generally easier to follow without having to implement such a subrouter for each top-level path.

TIP A great tool for interacting with APIs directly from your browser is Postman, which is available as an extension for Google Chrome at https://mng .bz/PdXw.

In some cases, it's helpful to provide some additional metadata with error responses. In a RESTful architecture, the OPTIONS method is used to show what valid HTTP methods can be called against an endpoint. Adding these can be cumbersome and is a great use-case for self-documenting APIs or getting Large Language Models (LLMs) to produce such an endpoint Although StatusMethodNotAllowed should be self-explanatory, there's little harm in returning some textual error message on other statuses, if applicable.

NOTE The REST architectural design is more than just HTTP verbs, and it's worth reading (or reviewing) the original proposal from Roy Fielding's dissertation, as the approach is still well used in the web world more than 20 years later. See https://mng.bz/JY6o.

8.1.2 More control over our server

So far, we've launched our server via http.ListenAndServe, but we can add more fine-grained control over how the server operates. The following listing provides more customization.

Listing 8.4 Server control

```
package main

import (
    "fmt"
    "net/http"
    "time"
)

func timeoutHandler(w http.ResponseWriter, r *http.Request) {
    time.Sleep(3 * time.Second)                           ◁─── Passes our
    w.Write([]byte("you should never see me"))                 handler to our
}                                                              custom server
```

```
func main() {
    muxer := http.NewServeMux()                              ◄──┐  Defines an http.Handler for
    muxer.HandleFunc("GET /timeout", timeoutHandler)            │  our multiplexing/routing

    server := http.Server{                                   ◄──┐  Defines a custom
        Addr:         ":8000",                                  │  http.Server with options
        ReadTimeout:  1 * time.Second,                          │  Provides specific timeouts,
        WriteTimeout: 2 * time.Second,                          │  including one for writing a response
        Handler:      muxer,                                 ◄──┐  Passes our handler to our custom server
    }
    if err := server.ListenAndServe(); err != nil {                              ◄──┐
        panic(fmt.Sprintf("could not start server: %s", err.Error()))              ──┐│
    }                                                                               ││
}                                                          Listens and serves on our server
```

If you visit the /timeout URL via curl http://localhost:8000, you'll get an empty
200 response. The WriteTimeout parameter for our Server just sets a context deadline for the handler to respond. Because our Sleep() is longer than that timeout, the
context deadline is exceeded. ReadTimeout will return a 503 error, however. Go provides a wrapper called http.TimeoutHandler that can take care of these basics for you,
like so:

```
Handler:      http.TimeoutHandler(muxer, 2*time.Second, "request
took too long"),
```

This will return 503 errors for any request that exceeds that deadline. The http
.Server struct also includes timeout options for headers and idle connections, as well
as TLS and logging options.

You can also handle timeouts individually at the handler level by using the http
.Request's context, via r.Context. Contexts can be used for any function that might
need to control or knowledge of the life cycle of a function call.

Contexts can also be used for some state management; the http.Request context
already carries information about the web request (query parameters, URL, path, and
so on), so you will use it regularly in web projects. But a simple WithContext wrapper
allows you to append values to the context, as shown in the next listing.

Listing 8.5   Sharing state via context

```
package main

import (
    "context"
    "fmt"
    "net/http"
    "regexp"                                                        ┐  Regular
)                                                                   │  expression to
                                                                    │  test for valid
var validAgent = regexp.MustCompile(`(?i)(chrome|firefox)`)   ◄──┘  browsers
```

```
func uaMiddleware(next http.HandlerFunc) http.HandlerFunc {

return func(w http.ResponseWriter, r *http.Request) {
        userAgent := r.UserAgent()
        if !validAgent.MatchString(userAgent) {
            w.WriteHeader(http.StatusBadRequest)
            return
        }
        ctx := context.WithValue(r.Context(), "agent", userAgent)
        r = r.WithContext(ctx)
        next(w, r)
    }
}
```

Returns a function that has access to our standard handler variables

Tests the user agent

Adds context to our original http.Request

Calls the passed handler with our updated http.Request

```
func uaStatusHandler(w http.ResponseWriter, r *http.Request) {
    ua := r.Context().Value("agent").(string)
    fmt.Fprint(w, fmt.Sprintf("congratulations, you
    are using: %s", ua))
}
```

Extracts the value from context

Prints the success to the response

```
func main() {
    http.HandleFunc("GET /withcontext",
    uaMiddleware(uaStatusHandler))
    if err := http.ListenAndServe(":8000", nil); err != nil {
        panic("could not start server")
    }
}
```

Wraps our handler with middleware

This does nothing more than prevent or allow requests depending on whether their user agent matches a pattern. What's noteworthy is that this is reusable, and you can wrap other handlers in the same logic. It's often used for authentication for this reason: you can wrap any request that must be authenticated with a session test or read another request attribute, such as a user agent. If we just need to share values across multiple requests, we can try another technique, wherein we allow some top-level struct values with handlers. See the next listing.

Listing 8.6   Sharing state via struct

```
package main

import (
    "context"
    "encoding/json"
    "fmt"
    "log"
    "net/http"
    "os"

    "github.com/jackc/pgx/v5"
)
```

```
type serverControl struct {          ◄───    A top-level struct that
    db *pgx.Conn                             will hold our database
}                                            connection

func main() {
    var sc serverControl              ◄───    Invokes serverControl for
    {                                         use in the lifetime of main()
        var err error
        sc.db, err = pgx.Connect(context.Background(),          Connects to
         "postgres://localhost:5432")                    ◄───   PostgreSQL
        if err != nil {
            fmt.Fprintf(os.Stderr, "Unable to connect to database: %v\n",
            err)
            os.Exit(1)
        }                                                          Uses a method of
    }                                                              serverControl,
                                                                   making its
    http.HandleFunc("GET /database",                              properties
    sc.databaseHandler)                                    ◄───   accessible
    if err := http.ListenAndServe(":8000", nil); err != nil {
        log.Fatal(err)
    }
}

type comment struct {
    UserID  int     `json:"userID"`
    Comment string `json:"comment"`
}

func (sc serverControl) databaseHandler(w http.ResponseWriter,
r *http.Request) {
    var comments []comment
    rows, err := sc.db.Query(`select user_id, comment
    from comments limit $1`, 5)                            ◄───
    defer rows.Close()                                            Queries the
    if err != nil {                                               database from
        w.WriteHeader(http.StatusInternalServerError)             serverControl's
        return                                                    connection
    }
    for rows.Next {
        var c comment
        if err := rows.Scan(&c.UserID, &c.Comment); err != nil {
            w.WriteHeader(http.StatusInternalServerError)
            return
        }
        comments = append(comments, c)
    }

    output, err := json.Marshal(comments)
    if err != nil {

    }
    w.Header().Set("Content-type", "application/json")
    w.Write(output)
}
```

In this example, we've invoked a PostgreSQL database and wrapped a handler to provide access to it within the handler. Here, we're using Go's built-in `database/sql` package and a third-party driver for PostgreSQL, `pgx`. These values can be passed down the chain as in this example and accessed from anywhere along the way. You cannot mutate a value up the chain, however. Often, that's desirable, but there's another common way to share mutable data: making our handlers methods on a known structure. The risk is that any handler can change or close the database connection, breaking subsequent requests.

8.2 Routing path values

In the previous examples, we were able to allow users to create and read a list of comments. If we wanted to provide a quick method to see individual comments, we could of course rely on a query parameter. But it's become fairly common for identifiers—numerical, slug, or UUID—to be included directly in the path of the URL.

In our middleware examples, you can probably imagine an easy way to parse the request URL and extract the `id` using `path.Split` or regular expressions, but Go has provided a simpler option since version 1.22 with `PathValue` from a request. See the next listing.

Listing 8.7   Extracting information from request path

```go
func getComment(w http.ResponseWriter, r *http.Request) {        // Extracts the value at the handler
    commentID, err := strconv.Atoi(r.PathValue("id"))
    if err != nil {                                              // If the value isn't an integer, returns an error
        w.WriteHeader(http.StatusInternalServerError)
        return
    }
    if commentID == 0 || len(comments) < commentID {            // If the ID is not valid, returns 404 . . .
        w.WriteHeader(http.StatusNotFound)
        return
    }
    fmt.Fprintf(w, "Comment %d: %s", commentID,                 // . . . otherwise, prints the comment to the browser
    comments[commentID-1].text)
}

func main() {
    http.HandleFunc("GET /comments", getComments)
    http.HandleFunc("GET /comments/{id}", getComment)           // Includes the path value in the route pattern
    http.HandleFunc("POST /comments", postComments)

    if err := http.ListenAndServe(":8000", nil); err != nil {
        panic(err)
    }
}
```

You may recall that Go's path matching typically operates on the longest matching path; this changes a bit when you introduce path variables. Here, Go focuses on the specificity of the path, such that `/comments/{id}` will win over `/comments/longerpathvalue`. If we go to our endpoint, we'll get a 404 error if the comment ID or index doesn't match the text of our intended comment (figure 8.2).

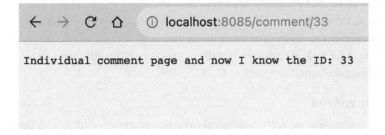

Figure 8.2   Retrieving a value from a path variable

Nothing is preventing you from invoking multiple handlers via `http.NewServeMux` and using those as routers for individual paths. Each can be passed individually to a path pattern and subroute from under that. `/users/new` and `comments/new` can be defined as follows:

```
usersRouter := http.NewServeMux()
commentsRouter := http.NewServeMux()

usersRouter.HandleFunc("/new", func(w http.ResponseWriter,
r *http.Request) {
    w.Write([]byte("New user form"))
})

commentsRouter.HandleFunc("/new", func(w http.ResponseWriter,
r *http.Request) {
    w.Write([]byte("New comment form"))
})

mainRouter := http.NewServeMux()
mainRouter.Handle("/users/", http.StripPrefix("/users", usersRouter))
mainRouter.Handle("/comments/", http.StripPrefix("/comments",
 commentsRouter))
if err := http.ListenAndServe(":8085", mainRouter); err != nil {
    panic(err)
}
```

This is just one pattern, and if you look at other web frameworks in Go, you'll see a different approach for each. Some frameworks have separate methods for adding routes, such as `muxer.Post()` and `muxer.Get()`; others jam the method into the handler registration as we have. You'll find other opinions, such as using predefined values as we did for `:id` versus allowing regular expressions directly. In simple cases, simply extending `ServeMux` should be your first choice, and in that case, it's worth looking at some common frameworks to see which approaches you like most:

- *Chi*—Takes an iterative approach to middleware, allowing you to group sections and add middleware to those groups as needed (https://github.com/go-chi/chi)
- *httprouter*—Fast and powerful, but with some opinionated approaches such as accepting only exact path matches (https://github.com/julienschmidt/httprouter)
- *Gin*—Builds on httprouter and was inspired by Sinatra, a classic Ruby framework from the early Web 2.0 days (https://github.com/gin-gonic/gin)

8.2.1 *Accepting POST data and query parameters*

Now that we have different requests coming toward the same endpoint properly routed, let's look at how to deal with the most common data that comes with each type of request. For GET requests, we're most likely to use query parameters to declare any options that come with that request. With POST, the requests body will generally encompass this. Although technically, the data will look the same, this approach mitigates errors with accidental replay and caching. But these are more conventions than strict technical requirements. In the next listing, we'll process query parameters to allow basic searching of comments against both a username and the text of the comment itself.

Listing 8.8 Using query parameters

```
package main

import (
    "fmt"
    "net/http"
    "regexp"
    "time"
)

type comment struct {
    text      string
    username  string
    timestamp time.Time
}

var comments = []comment{ //                           A prebaked list
    {text: "first!", username: "Bill", timestamp: makeTime("2023-09-01T00:
    00:00Z")},
    {text: "darn, I _just_ missed it", username: "Jill", timestamp:
    makeTime("2023-09-01T00:00:20Z")},

{text: "😌 maybe next time", username: "Bill", timestamp:
makeTime("2023-09-01T00:01:00Z")},
    {text: "ah, I see I'm late to the show, hello everyone", username:
    "Phil", timestamp: makeTime("2023-09-01T00:01:05Z")},
}

func makeTime(val string) time.Time {
    t, err := time.Parse(time.RFC3339, val)
```

```
        if err != nil {
            panic(err)
        }
        return t
    }

func commentsHandler(w http.ResponseWriter,                  Our comments
r *http.Request) {                                           display handler
    params := r.URL.Query()
                                                             Checks to see whether
    if username := params.Get("username"); username !=       the username is
    "" {                                                     provided in the URL
        filteredComments := []comment{}
        for k := range comments {
            if comments[k].username == username {
                filteredComments = append(filteredComments, comments[k])
            }
        }
        comments = filteredComments                          If search is provided,
    }                                                        filters our results
                                                             down to those that
    if search := params.Get("search"); search != "" { //     match the text of the
        filteredComments := []comment{}                      comment using a
        re := regexp.MustCompile(search)                     regular expression
        for k := range comments {
            if re.MatchString(comments[k].text) {
                filteredComments = append(filteredComments, comments[k])
            }
        }
        comments = filteredComments
    }                                                        Adds the matching
                                                             comments to a
    commentString := ""                                      string slice
    for k := range comments { //
        commentString += fmt.Sprintf("%s (%s) @ %s\n", comments[k].text,
        comments[k].username, comments[k].timestamp.Format("2006-01-02
    15:04:05"))
    }
    fmt.Fprint(w, commentString)
}
                                                             Our single path
                                                             router and listener
func main() { //
    http.HandleFunc("/comments", commentsHandler)
    if err := http.ListenAndServe(":8000", nil); err != nil {
        panic(err)
    }
}
```

By accepting query parameters, we're filtering what we display through an exact username match and/or a simple regular expression across the comment text. In both
parameters, username and query, we check whether the value is empty. Though the
Values type in the url package has a Has method to check whether a value is set, this will
be true even if the value is an empty string, so a check against that is the better choice.

NOTE Although we're allowing a regular expression to be passed directly by a user via the URL, this is not a safe practice because regular expressions can be vulnerable to denial of service attacks. Although Go's implementation states "guaranteed to run in time linear in the size of the input," which could allow mitigation, in general it's still advisable to never let users send regular expressions directly to the server for parsing.

8.2.2 Processing form data

In the comments handlers in listing 8.2, you enabled the same path to fork to a read operation and a write operation. We could read comments from our browser, but we'd need to use cURL or some other HTTP library to create them. If we want to add data to this collection of comments from the same web application, as with a comment box on a blog, we can create a simple form with a POST method to send relevant data along. *Form data* is nothing more than the request body, generally for POST, PUT, and PATCH methods. To create a form, we'll need to call ParseForm, which marshals the data into a url.Values struct and provides some nice helper methods—in our case, to check for posted form fields. In the next listing, we add a form to the web page, and our POST handler will process the form data into key-value pairs that we can use to append comment data to our slice.

Listing 8.9 Posting form data

```go
package main

import (
    "fmt"
    "net/http"
    "time"
)

type comment struct {          ←── Slightly modified
    username   string               comment data
    text       string               type
    dateString string
}

var comments []comment

func commentsHandler(w http.ResponseWriter,
r *http.Request) {
    body := `                  ←── HTML with a form
        <html>                      for submitting
            <head>                  comments
                <!-- style and metadata -->
            </head>
        <body>`
    commentBody := ""
    for i := range comments {
        commentBody += fmt.Sprintf("<div class='comment'>%s (%s) - @%s</div
        >", comments[i].text, comments[i].dateString, comments[i].username)
    }
```

```
    body += fmt.Sprintf(`
        <h1>Comments</h1>
        %s
        <form method="POST" action="/comments">
            <div><input type="text" placeholder="Username" name="username"
            /></div>
            <textarea placeholder="Comment text" name="comment"></textarea>
            <div><input type="submit" value="Submit" /></div>
        </form>
        </body>
        </html>
    `, commentBody)
    w.Write([]byte(body))
}

func postHandler(w http.ResponseWriter, r *http.Request) {        ◁——  ParseForm to
    r.ParseForm()                                                       marshal data into
                                                                        a url.Values struct
    username := r.Form.Get("username")                            |    Gets values
    commentText := r.Form.Get("comment")                          |    from the form
    comments = append(comments, comment{username: user
    name, text: commentText, dateString:
    time.Now().Format(time.RFC3339)})                        ◁——  Adds the comment
                                                                  to our slice
    http.Redirect(w, r, "/comments", http.StatusFound)
}

func main() {
    http.HandleFunc("GET /comments", commentsHandler)
    http.HandleFunc("POST /comments", postHandler)
    if err := http.ListenAndServe(":8085", nil); err != nil {
        panic(err)
    }
}
```

Note that we're expecting `Form.Get` to have a value and not checking it with a `Has` test. This would be useful if someone submitted an invalid form either by accident or with malice. To check for this, we could simply add a check before reading the data:

```
if !r.Form.Has("username") || !r.Form.Has("comment") {
    w.WriteHeader(http.StatusBadRequest)
    return
}
```

This might give the user better detail. In the case of malice, however, it might provide more information to allow an attacker to get more detail about the underlying handler and what data it accepts and expects.

We'll talk more about mitigating potentially malicious payloads including form requests and Cross-Site Request Forgeries in chapter 10. *This example is not intended to be safe.* After all, we're displaying user input unsanitized, which can allow for cross-site scripting attacks. Go's built-in templating in the `html/template` package can mitigate this for you and carries with it escape user input.

TIP   As mentioned with the regular expression parsing in the last example, never trust user input unsanitized. By this, we mean that any input from a user should be run through some cleaning process before it touches any other system. Some of the most critical and common security flaws come from passing along raw data to some other process. You can see a list of OWASP's most common flaws at https://owasp.org/www-project-top-ten. We'll talk about mitigation strategies in chapters 9 and 10.

If we visit our site via the browser, we'll see something similar to what we saw before but with our data delivered via an HTML form (figure 8.3).

Comments

Hello? Is this thing on? (2023-10-29T19:56:29-04:00) - @Nathan

I'm here, what's up? (2023-10-29T19:56:46-04:00) - @guest

Nathan

Not much, just checking into the comment section

Submit

Figure 8.3   A form that allows users to post to our comments section

Now you should know how to get data from web requests and generally route them as you need based on path, method, query parameters, and more. In addition to query-based data, we can process POST body data at a basic level and evaluate individual POST parameters in our target handler.

We've used these skills to generate data input for our users and process comment data, but there are a great many applications for handling POST/PATCH/PUT/DELETE data, particularly for common uses like API design.

> **Best way to write**
>
> You may have noticed that the last example wrote to the `ResponseWriter` in a different way from before. If there's a double edge to having interfaces like this, there's not always a clear-cut way to know which `Writer` to use. We've used `w.Write([]byte)` and `fmt.Fprint(w, []byte)`, but there are any number of ways to do the same thing, including other `io` `Writer`s. The `w.Write()` approach is most common, but all ultimately do the same thing, so find the one you like and be consistent.

8.2.3   *Reading and writing cookies and other header data*

Recall that HTTP is a stateless protocol, so we may need some method for keeping state across requests, typically done via cookies. Generally, cookies keep information that is ephemeral and can easily be re-created, so in the next listing, we'll track the username from request to request, setting it only if it doesn't exist on the first request.

Listing 8.10   Setting a cookie

```
func postHandler(w http.ResponseWriter, r *http.Request) {
    r.ParseForm()

    username := r.Form.Get("username")
    usernameCookie, err := r.Cookie("username")
    if err == nil {
        username = usernameCookie.Value
    }

    commentText := r.Form.Get("comment")
    comments = append(comments, comment{username: username, text:
    commentText, dateString: time.Now().Format(time.RFC3339)})

    http.SetCookie(w, &http.Cookie{Name: "username", Value: username,
    Expires: time.Now().Add(24 * time.Hour)})

    http.Redirect(w, r, "/comments", http.StatusFound)
}
```

Using this cookie going forward is easy enough. If we find a username cookie and it matches a comment's username, we'll replace the username with the text `"You"`, as shown in the next listing.

Listing 8.11   Reading and using the cookie value

```
func commentsHandler(w http.ResponseWriter, r *http.Request) {

    username := ""
    usernameCookie, err := r.Cookie("username")    ◀── Retrieves the
    if err == nil {                                     cookie value
        username = usernameCookie.Value
    }
```

```
body := `
    <html>
        <head>
            <title>Comments</title>
            <style type="text/css">
                body {
                    width: 500px;
                    margin: 0 auto;
                }
                h1 {
                    margin: 0;
                    padding: 0;
                }
                div {
                    padding: 20px 0;
                }
                textarea, input[type="text"] {
                    width: 100%;
                }
                textarea {
                    height: 200px;
                }
                .comment {
                    padding: 10px;
                    border: 1px solid #ddd;
                    margin-bottom: 4px;
                }
            </style>
        </head>
    <body>`
commentBody := ""
for i := range comments {
    displayName := comments[i].username
    if username != "" && displayName == username {        ◁─┐ Tests against the
        displayName = "You"                                    comment value
    }                                                          to alternately
    commentBody += fmt.Sprintf("<div class='comment'>%s (%s) - @%s</div   display "You"
    >", comments[i].text, comments[i].dateString, displayName)
}
```

Obviously, we have no guard against multiple users selecting the same username, but this demonstrates a way to retain and reuse a value. Even if we didn't have a persistent backing store, we could use a map to determine whether a username was in use and reject or append some additional disambiguation string.

Our example isn't the end of the use of cookies, as those pesky popups on seemingly every website prove. Cookies serve as a simple way of persisting state from request to request in a stateless protocol. Use them any time you want to retrieve stateful data from a user. In the next section, we'll look at a more secure way of using cookies for identity (figure 8.4).

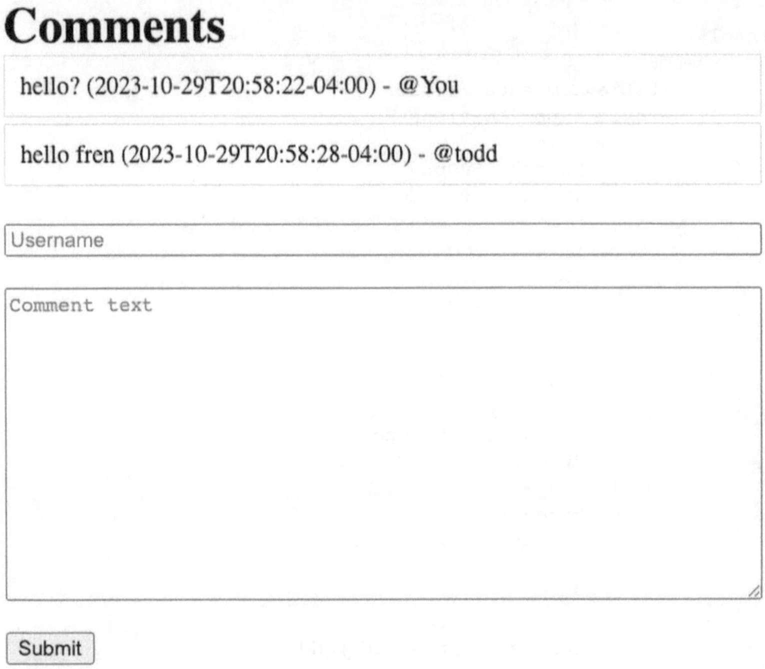

Comments

hello? (2023-10-29T20:58:22-04:00) - @You

hello fren (2023-10-29T20:58:28-04:00) - @todd

Username

Comment text

Submit

Figure 8.4   Using cookie values to indicate a user's comments. The cookie value keeps track of a username, and we rewrite that to "You" if the same user views this page again.

Templates vs. formatted text

So far, we've been writing output directly to our `ResponseWriter`, often with a formatter like `Fprintf`. Go has a very strong templating system for generating all sorts of data, but its HTML templates are a particularly nice feature with baked-in logic, template includes, and variables. We'll dig more into those templates in chapter 9.

8.2.4   *Processing JSON Web Tokens*

In the preceding example, we use cookies to store a text value, but frequently, they're used to keep session identifiers, which are stored in a database or some other session store on the backend. These are used to determine the user and their respective metadata. Cookies for sessions have some downsides. They're susceptible to session hijacking attacks if they're exposed as cleartext, and they usually require a per-request backend response, such as a database lookup.

One alternative to cookies for something like session handling is JSON Web Tokens (JWTs). Unlike cookie values or session IDs, JWTs are intended to safely contain identification within the value itself. The primary benefits are better privacy for the value across the wire and less traffic and resource allocation to databases and session stores. Unlike a session cookie, in listing 8.11 we kept track of a user's identity—in this case, a username—via cookie. Although that's lightweight and requires no server-side validation, it can be easily spoofed by the client. After all, it's just a cleartext cookie value. JWTs operate somewhat similarly but have safety features that mitigate the potential for spoofing.

At their core, JWTs are stores of public/private key encrypted information stored in JSON format that include details on the encryption and a payload with claims, which typically include identifying information like email and name.

Authenticating securely

With anything related to security, particularly identity and authentication, we recommend using mature, vetted libraries rather than rolling your own. Even though JWT itself is not especially complicated, mistakes in implementation can lead to account takeovers or worse. The website https://jwt.io provides a fantastic breakdown of the libraries on a per-language basis, including the subset of features that are included (or not) and GitHub stars with each: https://jwt.io/libraries?language=Go.

The next listing shows one simple implementation using one of the most popular libraries, jwt-go (https://github.com/golang-jwt/jwt). The most important things to note are the way that keys are decrypted and the types of claims that can be included.

Listing 8.12 Creating and validating JWTs

```
package main

import (
    "log"
    "time"

    jwt "github.com/golang-jwt/jwt/v5"
)

var SIGNING_KEY = []byte("this-value-should-be-secret"
)

type claim struct {
    jwt.RegisteredClaims
}

func generateClaim() (string, error) {
    claims := claim{
        jwt.RegisteredClaims{
            ExpiresAt: jwt.NewNumericDate(time.Now().Add(time.Hour)),
            IssuedAt:  jwt.NewNumericDate(time.Now()),
            NotBefore: jwt.NewNumericDate(time.Now()),
            Subject:   "nobody@example.com",
        },
    }
```

Our private key. Public and private keys are often pulled from a .pem file.

A wrapper around our claims section

```
    token := jwt.NewWithClaims(jwt.SigningMethodHS256, claims)      ┐ Generates the
    ss, err := token.SignedString(SIGNING_KEY)                      │ token from our
    if err != nil {                                                 │ claims and
        return "", err                                              │ signing key
    }
    return ss, nil
}

func main() {
    if signed, err := generateClaim(); err != nil {
        panic(err)
    } else {
        token, err := jwt.Parse(signed, func(token *jwt.Token)
        (interface{}, error) {
            return SIGNING_KEY, nil
        })                                   ←┤ Parses the
        if err != nil {                        │ token itself
            panic(err)
        }
        if validatedClaims, ok :=
        token.Claims.(jwt.MapClaims); ok && token.Valid {    ←┐ Validates the
            log.Println(validatedClaims["sub"])                │ claims and
        } else {                                               │ returns a map
            panic("error getting claims")                      │ of values
        }
    }
}
```

To force this to break with an invalid signature, simply change SIGNING_KEY in the validation portion to any other byte slice. You can see that this is a much easier way of dealing with identity because the client is simply returning a set of claims that are ostensibly protected via encryption. In general, this may not be useful for small projects, although you'll encounter it if you use a third-party single-sign-on identity provider such as Auth0.

> **The cons of JWTs**
>
> We've outlined some of the benefits of JWTs, but possible drawbacks include difficulty invalidating a value via revocation. Unlike with a value stored in a database, the only way to invalidate it is to check such a service with each request, which negates one of the benefits. The JWT spec is at https://datatracker.ietf.org/doc/html/rfc7519.

8.3   Generating errors and basic authentication

Although we've been creating responses throughout, our error responses have been limited, and it's important to highlight that HTTP response codes are one of the most lightweight ways to consume error data. Although JWTs are a nice way to maintain identity without a lot of work on the backend, we also have a much older technology that's pretty lightweight as well: basic authentication. We can lean on basic authentication

with our original comments app to return proper errors when a user is not authenticated, as shown in the following listing.

Listing 8.13 **Generating responses against basic authentication**

```
package main

import (
    "fmt"
    "io/ioutil"
    "log"
    "net/http"
    "time"
)

type comment struct {
    username   string
    text       string
    dateString string
}

var comments []comment

var validUsers = map[string]string{
    "bill": "abc123",
}

func login(username, password string) bool {
    if validPassword, ok := validUsers[username]; ok {
        return validPassword == password
    }
    return false
}

func main() {
    http.HandleFunc("GET /comments", getComments)
    http.HandleFunc("POST /comments", postComments)


    if err := http.ListenAndServe(":8000", nil); err != nil {
        panic(err)
    }
}

func postComments(w http.ResponseWriter, r *http.Request) {
    username, password, auth := r.BasicAuth()

    if !auth || !login(username, password) {
        w.WriteHeader(http.StatusUnauthorized)
        return
    }
```

A hardcoded map
of username to
password

Our login method
to test against
that map

Derives username
and password
from BasicAuth
from a POST

Returns a 403
error on failure

```
    commentText, err := ioutil.ReadAll(r.Body)
    if err != nil {
        w.WriteHeader(http.StatusInternalServerError)
        return
    }
    comments = append(comments, comment{username: username, text:
    string(commentText), dateString: time.Now().Format(time.RFC3339)})
    w.WriteHeader(http.StatusOK)
}

func getComments(w http.ResponseWriter, r *http.Request) {
    commentBody := ""
    for i := range comments {
        commentBody += fmt.Sprintf("%s (%s) - @%s\n", comments[i].text,
        comments[i].dateString, comments[i].username)
    }
    fmt.Fprintln(w, fmt.Sprintf("Comments: \n%s", commentBody))
}
```

Our list of users will come from a different source than the source code itself, ideally well encrypted in a one-way fashion, but this gets the general idea across. We'll dig into pulling data from a database and doing some basic username/password valida- tion in chapters 9 and 10. But by sending an invalid request, as with cURL in this example,

```
curl -X POST -i http://localhost:8085/comments -d "This will never succeed"
    -u "bill:abc124"
```

we can trigger the proper error code. Other than 200 OK responses, it's important to send error status codes and return early whenever possible.

> **TIP** Go's HTTP response codes are constants tied to their numerical value (in other words, `StatusNotFound` = 404), but it's useful to use the variable names whenever possible to increase code readability. Other developers may not immediately remember that 425 is `Too Early`, 510 is `Not Extended`, and 418 is `Teapot`.

Muxers and middleware: build vs. buy

Earlier in this chapter we recommended caution when evaluating frameworks in Go. Some very powerful ones are batteries-included: they have great muxers, built-in mid- dleware, and so on. But you might not need all that and end up with a bigger footprint than necessary.

Muxers and multiplexers have a smaller footprint and can save a lot of hand-coded, bespoke work. A lot of the frameworks have individual muxer libraries that can be used on their own, including stalwarts like Gorilla's mux (https://github.com/gorilla/mux), which was once deprecated but has since found a new set of core maintainers.

Summary

- Go's standard library routing is basic enough to get started with, but if you need more complicated logic, the language provides everything you need to extend and create more ornate routing.
- Nontrivial web applications need to access myriad data sources from requests, from form data to query parameters to header and cookie information. Go makes this easy and supports everything needed out of the box. Third-party libraries support alternatives to things like cookies and sessions such as JWTs.
- Middleware lets us reduce code duplication by wrapping HTTP handlers with preceding logic; using the decorator pattern allows us to wrap multiple times and supply additional data and/or short-circuit the chain.
- Returning error information when a request is invalid or a response cannot be handled is critical, particularly with client-correctable problems like authentication errors.

HTML and email template patterns

This chapter covers

- Adding functionality inside templates
- Nesting templates
- Using template inheritance
- Rendering objects to HTML
- Using email templates

When you're programmatically creating text or HTML responses in many programming environments, you need to seek out the right library to handle producing the HTML to return. In previous chapters, we've often output formatted strings directly to a writer. But in the real world, this is hard to maintain, leads to a lot of work, and is more prone to error. It's trivial to introduce cross-site scripting (XSS) problems, for example, by not accounting for user input properly. In most languages, developers would reach for a third-party templating library. Go handles this a little differently. In the standard library, Go provides template handling for both text and HTML. The HTML handling, including security for untrusted data, is built on top of the text template engine to add HTML-aware intelligence.

Although the standard library enables you to work with HTML templates, it stops short of being overly opinionated. Instead, it provides a foundation along

220

with the ability to extend and combine templates. You could nest templates or have a template inherit from another one, for example. This simple and extensible design allows you to use many common template patterns.

In this chapter, you'll learn how to extend the functionality inside HTML templates and techniques for using templates together. Along the way, we offer tips, including some related to performance, that can speed up applications. You'll learn where you can parse a template that can save overall processing time; then you'll learn how to use text templates when you send email messages.

9.1 Working with HTML templates

The `html` and `html/template` packages in the standard library provide the foundation for working with HTML, including the ability to work with variables and functions in the templates. The `html/template` package is built on the `text/template` package, which provides general text template handling. HTML, being text, can of course use the text handling, but the advantage of the `html/template` package over the `text/template` package for HTML is the context-aware intelligence that saves developers work.

> **NOTE** In previous chapters, we've written responses directly to the `Writer` via `fmt` or the `Write` method. While we're exploring templates, it's worth noting that in some cases, this lightweight `Write` approach is still worth using and carries less overhead.

In the next few sections, we'll look at patterns that will be helpful in using and extending the template packages for your own applications.

9.1.1 Standard library HTML package overview

Before you look at those patterns, you need to see how the packages in the standard library work. Whereas the `html` package provides only a couple of functions to escape and unescape strings for HTML, the `html/template` package provides a good foundation for working with structured templates that are intended to be parsed. Let's look at a basic HTML template in the first listing.

Listing 9.1 A simple HTML template

```
<!DOCTYPE HTML>
<html>
  <head>
    <meta charset="utf-8">
    <title>{{.Title}}</title>          Title based on
  </head>                              Title property
  <body>
    <h1>{{.Title}}</h1>               The title and content
    <p>{{.Content}}</p>               being displayed
  </body>
</html>
```

This listing illustrates the basics of a template. Aside from the actions (also called *directives*), which are enclosed in double curly brackets, the template looks like a normal HTML file. Here, the directives are to print a value passed into the template, such as printing the passed-in title. But actions can represent more than just values for display, as we'll see while exploring logic in templates. The next step is calling this template from code and passing it the values to fill in for {{.Title}} and {{.Content}}, as shown in the next listing.

Listing 9.2 Using a simple HTML template

```
package main

import (
    "html/template"          ◁─── Uses html instead of
    "net/http"                     text template package
)

type Page struct {
    Title, Content string
}
func displayPage(w http.ResponseWriter, r *http.Request) {
    p := &Page{                          Data object to pass to
        Title:   "An Example",           template containing
        Content: "Have fun stormin' da castle.",   properties to print
    }
    t := template.Must(template.ParseFiles("templates
    /simple.html"))          ◁─── Parses a template
    t.Execute(w, p)          ◁───     for later use
}                                 Writes to HTTP output
func main() {                     using template and
    http.HandleFunc("/", displayPage)   dataset
    http.ListenAndServe(":8080", nil)
}              Serves the output via
               simple web server
```

This simple application takes some data and displays it via a simple web server, using the template from listing 9.1. The html/template package is used here instead of the text/template package because it's context-aware and handles some operations for you.

Being context-aware is more than knowing that these are HTML templates. The package understands what's happening inside the templates. Take the following template snippet:

```
<a href="/user?id={{.Id}}">{{.Content}}</a>
```

The html/template package expands this intelligently. For escaping purposes, it adds context-appropriate functionality. The preceding snippet is automatically expanded to look like this:

```
<a href="/user?id={{.Id | urlquery}}">{{.Content | html}}</a>
```

The variables (in this case, `.Id` and `.Content`) are piped through appropriate functions to escape their content before turning it into the final output. Escaping turns characters that could be seen as markup and that alter the page structure or meaning into references that display properly but don't alter the structure or meaning. If you were using the `text/template` package, you would need to add the escaping yourself.

The context-aware escaping is built around a security model in which template developers are considered trusted and user data, injected via variables, is considered untrusted and should be escaped. If an application user input the string `<script>alert('busted pwned')</script>`, and you displayed that string through the HTML template system, it would be escaped, and the HTML escaped text `&lt;script&gt;alert(&#39;busted pwned&#39;)&lt;/script&gt;` would be rendered in the template. This is safe to display to users and prevents a potential XSS vulnerability.

When you want a variable to be rendered as is without being escaped, you can use the `HTML` type in the `html/template` package. Keep in mind that at this point, it is your responsibility to ensure that the content is safe enough to display unescaped. In chapter 10, we'll look at ways we may need to output unescaped content, such as to create tokens to prevent cross-site request forgeries.

Variables aren't the only things that can go into a template. We can also natively loop through things and create nested `if/else` conditions called *pipelines* in the Go templating language. The following simple example outputs a slice of a custom data structure to a template.

Listing 9.3 Making slices/arrays available for templates

```go
package main

import (
    "html/template"
    "log"
    "net/http"
)

type comment struct { //
    Username string
    Text     string
}

type Page struct {
    Title, Content string
    Comments       []comment //
}

var t = template.New("templates")

func routeComments(w http.ResponseWriter, r *http.Request) {
    p := &Page{
        Title:    "An Example",
        Content: "Have fun stormin' da castle.",
        Comments: []comment{
```

Our Page, with a slice of comments now added to the structure

```
                 {Username: "Bill", Text: "Looks like a good example."},
                 {Username: "Jill", Text: "I really enjoyed this article."},
                 {Username: "Phil", Text: "I don't like to
                    read."},
             }, //                                         ←  Some boilerplate
         }                                                    comments
         if err := t.ExecuteTemplate(w, "list.html", p);
         err != nil { //                                   ←  Executes our
             log.Println(err)                                 primary template
             w.WriteHeader(http.StatusInternalServerError)
         }
    }

    func init() {                                             Parses a
        _, err := t.ParseGlob("templates/*.html") //      ←  directory of
        if err != nil {                                       templates
            log.Fatal("Error loading templates:" + err.Error())
        }
    }

    func main() {
        http.HandleFunc("/comments", routeComments)
        if err := http.ListenAndServe(":8085", nil); err != nil {
            panic(err)
        }
    }
```

In the Go code, we're simply adding a `routeComments` handler that carries some boilerplate content, including some hardcoded comments. Unlike with the other string values, we can't format these cleanly in the template/output by using the `{{.Comments}}` variable. Although such a formatted string could be constructed as an HTML string, we can use these slices in an iterator, using the built-in `range` keyword in the template parser as shown in the following listing.

Listing 9.4 A template for iterating

```html
<!DOCTYPE HTML>
<html>

<head>
  <meta charset="utf-8">
  <title>{{.Title}}</title>
  <style type="text/css">
    body {
      max-width: 400px;
    }

    .comment {
      padding: 1rem;
      border: 1px solid black;
      margin-bottom: 0.25rem;
    }
  </style>
</head>
```

```
<body>
  <h1>{{.Title}}</h1>
  <p>{{.Content}}</p>
  {{ range .Comments }}
  <div class="comment">
    {{.Text}} #B
    <div>by {{.Username}}</div>
  </div>
  {{ end }}
</body>

</html>
```

The range keyword
to iterate our
comments ←

Individual comment
properties ←

In figure 9.1, you see the output as a frontend user adds comments, displayed via the template in listing 9.4.

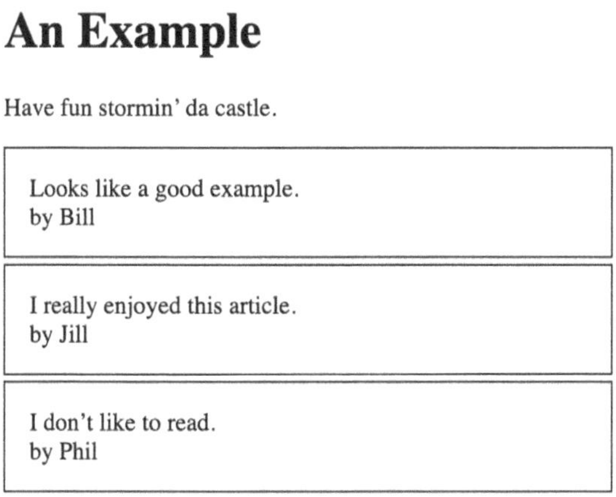

An Example

Have fun stormin' da castle.

Looks like a good example. by Bill

I really enjoyed this article. by Jill

I don't like to read. by Phil

Figure 9.1   Our comments, displayed through a `range` **iterator template keyword**

Keep in mind that within a range, you're effectively block-scoped to what's available to the `.Comments` slice. If you want to move up and access the `{{.Title}}` value, preface the action with a `$` to get to the scope above (in this case, global scope), such as `{{$.Title}}`. If you're iterating a slice of values rather than structures/objects, using the `{{.}}` notation will retrieve that value.

In addition to loops and pipelines, the following four techniques look at ways to extend the built-in template system, allowing you to use common template patterns.

9.1.2   Adding functionality inside templates

In addition to just outputting values, you can call functions and methods directly from the templates themselves. As you just saw, the intelligence in the HTML templates adds escaping functions in the right place for you. These functions are where complex functionality is handled in the templates. Out of the box, the template packages provide fewer than 20 functions, and several support this intelligence.

Consider one of the built-in functions, `sprintf`, whose implementation is provided by `printf` inside a template. The following code shows the syntax for its use inside a template:

```
{{"output" | printf "%q"}}
```

The snippet takes the string `output` and passes it into `printf` by using the format string `%q`. The output is the quoted string `output`. This pipe style may take a little getting used to because it's not equivalent to function calling in Go itself, and it's worth chaining these to see how they work together, especially as they relate to values as parameters.

Although templates provide quite a few features, you often need to extend them with your own functionality. The need to add features isn't uncommon or uncalled for. We've often seen the need to display a date and time in an easy-to-read format. Although you can certainly do this by hand for each respective date value in the source code, you could also easily implement it as part of the template system. This kind of code reuse helps us keep consistent output in our templates and is ideal for things like formatting for the display side without having to carry multiple values for a single variable.

- *Problem*—The built-in functions in the templates don't provide all the functionality you need to build a mature web application.
- *Solution*—Just as Go makes functions available in templates (such as `fmt.Sprintf` being available in templates as `printf`), make your own functions available to the templating system, extending it as you see fit.
- *Discussion*—You can display information in templates in various ways. Although the way data is generated should be kept in the application logic, the way it's formatted and displayed should happen cleanly in a template. Presenting date and time information is a good example. In an application, the time information should be stored in a type, such as `time.Time`. When displayed to users, it could be displayed in myriad ways.

Go actions, the data and commands enclosed in double curly brackets, can have commands that act on the data. These commands can be chained into pipelines separated by a |. This is the same idea as using pipes from a UNIX-based command-line interface (CLI). Go provides an API to add commands to the set available to a template. The limited commands that come out of the box need not be the only ones available to your templates. The following listing gives a template the capability to display formatted dates.

Listing 9.5   Adding template functions

```
package main

import (
    "html/template"
    "net/http"
```

```
     "time"
)
var tpl = `<!DOCTYPE HTML>
<html>
  <head>
    <meta charset="utf-8">
    <title>Date Example</title>
  </head>
  <body>
      <p>{{.Date | dateFormat "Jan 2, 2006"}}</p>
  </body>
</html>`
var funcMap = template.FuncMap{
    "dateFormat": dateFormat,
}
func dateFormat(layout string, d time.Time) string {
    return d.Format(layout)
}
func serveTemplate(res http.ResponseWriter, req *http.Request) {
    t := template.New("date")
    t.Funcs(funcMap)
    t.Parse(tpl)
    data := struct{ Date time.Time }{
            Date: time.Now(),
    }
    t.Execute(res, data)
}
func main() {
    http.HandleFunc("/", serveTemplate)
    http.ListenAndServe(":8080", nil)
}
```

An HTML template as a string

Pipes Date through the dateFormat command

Maps Go functions to template functions

Function to convert a time to a formatted string

Creates a new template.Template instance

Passes additional functions in map into template engine

Parses the template string into the template engine

Creates a dataset to pass into template to display

Sends template with data to output response

Serves the template and dataset using a web server

Rather than referencing an external file, this HTML template is stored as a string in a variable. Inside the template, the data in Date is passed through the template function dateFormat with a specified format string before becoming part of the output. It's important to know that the piping mechanism passes the output from one item in the pipeline into the next item in the pipeline as the last argument.

Because dateFormat isn't one of the core template functions, it needs to be made available to the template. Making custom functions available in templates requires two steps. First, a map needs to be created in which names to be used inside the template are mapped to functions in Go. Here, the function dateFormat is mapped to the name dateFormat. Although the same name is used for both the Go function and name available inside the template, that doesn't have to be the case. Their names can be different for templates, but for mental mapping, it makes some sense to keep them the same.

When a new `template.Template` instance is created, the function map (here named `funcMap`) needs to be passed into `Funcs` to make the new function mapping available to templates. After this happens, templates can use the functions. Before using the template, the final step is to parse the template into `template.Template`.

From here, the template instance is used normally. The data structure is defined in this case by an anonymous `struct`, with the data to pass in as a key-value mapping. The data structure is passed into `Execute` along with the `io.Writer` to output the rendered template. In this case, when `dateFormat` is encountered in the template, the format of `Jan 2, 2006` is passed in, followed by the `time.Time` instance. The instance of `time.Time` is converted to a string following this format.

> **NOTE** The date and time used in format strings need to be specific, as detailed in the package documentation at http://golang.org/pkg/time/#Time.Format.

If you're going to apply the same function set to numerous templates, you can use a Go function to create your templates and add your template functions each time:

```
func parseTemplateString(name, tpl string) *template.Template {
    t := template.New(name)
    t.Funcs(funcMap)
    t = template.Must(t.Parse(tpl))
    return t
}
```

This function could be repeatedly used to create a new template object from a template string with your custom template functions included. In listing 9.5, this could be used inside the `serveTemplate` function instead of parsing the template and adding the template functions there. Using a Go function to configure your templates for you could be done with files as well.

9.1.3   *Limiting template parsing*

Parsing templates that were originally in text into type instances is a bit of work for a Go application. Parsing a template turns a string of characters into an object model with a variety of nodes and node types that Go knows how to use. The parser in the `text/template/parser` package sits behind functions in the template packages such as `Parse` and `ParseFiles`. Unless you work directly with the parser, which isn't recommended, it's easy to miss all the work going on behind the functions you use.

Methods such as the following technique allow you to avoid extra work by using a parser that can speed up your application. Go applications, as servers that respond to multiple requests, can generate many responses to requests from many different clients. If the application must parse a template for each response, a lot of duplicate work is going on. If you can eliminate some of that work at response time, you can speed up your application's performance.

- *Problem*—You want to avoid repeatedly parsing the same template while an application is running.

- *Solution*—Parse the template, store the ready-to-use template in a variable, and repeatedly use the same template each time you need to generate the output.
- *Discussion*—Instead of parsing the template in the `http` handler function, which means parsing the template whenever the handler function runs, you can move the parsing out of the handler. Then you can repeatedly execute the template against different datasets without parsing it each time. The following listing is a modified version of listing 9.2 that caches the parsed template.

Listing 9.6 Caching a parsed template

```
package main

import (
    "html/template"
    "net/http"
)

var t = template.Must(template.ParseFiles("templates/simple.html"))
type Page struct {
    Title, Content string
}

func displayPage(w http.ResponseWriter, r *http.Request) {
    p := &Page{
            Title:   "An Example",
            Content: "Have fun stormin' da castle.",
    }
    t.Execute(w, p)
}

func main() {
    http.HandleFunc("/", displayPage)
    http.ListenAndServe(":8080", nil)
}
```

Parses the template when the package is initialized

Executes the template in the http handler function

Instead of parsing the template in the handler function, as listing 9.2 does, the template is parsed once when the package is initialized. When the `http` handler function is executed, the template is executed normally.

As the benchmark test examples from chapter 5 showed, parsing a template and reusing the parsed template is faster than parsing each time. This is a subtle, simple way to speed up application responses.

If you need to parse a full directory of templates instead of referencing them individually, you can use the `ParseGlob` method to read and parse multiple files in a directory ala `template.ParseGlob("templates/*.html")`.

9.1.4 When template execution breaks

All software has the potential to fail. Template execution is no exception. When template execution fails, an error is returned. But in some cases, template execution can fail, and partial output is displayed to the end user. In other words, the template parsing halts but returns data until it hits the error.

When templates are executed, the output is written as it walks through the template. If a function is called, causing an error midway through the template, an error will be returned and execution will stop. But the part of the template before the error would already be displayed to end users.

- *Problem*—When an error happens while executing a template, you want to catch the error before anything is displayed to the user. Instead of displaying the partially broken pages, display something more appropriate, such as an error page.
- *Solution*—Write the output of the template to a buffer. If no errors occur, write the output of the buffer to end users; otherwise, handle the error.
- *Discussion*—Templates should be fairly unintelligent. They display data, and functions can be used to format the data. Any errors in the data should be handled before templates are used with the data, and the functions called within the templates should be for display and basic logic purposes. This keeps the separation of concerns in place and limits failures when templates are executed.

  Streaming these responses can be useful. When you execute a template to a response writer, end users start to receive the page more quickly. When you buffer a response, there's a delay in end users receiving it. End users expect native desktop performance out of web applications, and streaming responses helps achieve that. When possible, write to output.

  But at times, the optimal case doesn't work out. If executing templates carries a potential for errors, you can write the output of the template to a buffer. If errors occur, they can be handled before displaying anything to the end users. The following listing builds on listing 9.6 to introduce a buffered output.

Listing 9.7   Buffering a template response

```go
package main

import (
    "bytes"
    "fmt"
    "html/template"
    "io"
    "net/http"
)

var t *template.Template
func init() {
    t = template.Must(template.ParseFiles("./templates/simple.html"))
}
type Page struct {
    Title, Content string
}
func displayPage(w http.ResponseWriter, r *http.Request) {
    p := &Page{
```

```
            Title:    "An Example",
            Content: "Have fun stormin' da castle.",
    }
    var b bytes.Buffer                          Creates a buffer to store the
    err := t.Execute(&b, p)                     output of the executed template
    if err != nil {
        fmt.Fprint(w, "A error occured.")       Handles any errors from
        return                                  template execution
    }
    b.WriteTo(w)                        ◁────   Copies the buffered
}                                               output to the
func main() {                                   response writer
    http.HandleFunc("/", displayPage)
    http.ListenAndServe(":8080", nil)
}
```

When the template is executed, a buffer is written instead of `http.ResponseWriter`. If any errors occur, those are handled before copying the contents of the buffer to the output. This approach can also be useful for running regression and fuzz tests, where you want to get a specific response under certain conditions.

In most cases, it makes sense to write directly to your `ResponseWriter`, but while developing and testing, a buffer prevents any confusion. If you're testing in the browser, a page may appear empty without any indication of an error. We can trigger this error pretty simply by breaking the template. If we go back to our `list.html` example, failing to close our range will give us a partial page:

```
<body>
  <h1>{{.Title}}</h1>
  <p>{{.VariableDoesNotExist}}</p>
  {{ range .Comments }}
  <div class="comment">
    {{.Text}}
    <div>by {{.Username}}</div>
  </div>
  {{ end }}
</body>
```

9.1.5 Mixing templates

The foundation of generating HTML output is the `html/template` package. It handles safely generating HTML output. But the documented use cases are simple. When building applications, you'll often want to mix templates together, have patterns for reusing and managing them, cache generated output, and more. In the following patterns, you'll see three ways to work with templates, built on top of the standard library, allowing you to use more-complex template handling. These patterns are nesting templates, extending a base template through inheritance, and mapping a data object to a specific template (a user object being mapped to a user template, for example).

NESTED TEMPLATES

Sharing and reusing sections of templates, like code reuse, is a common need. If you have an application with numerous web pages, you'll typically find that most elements are common across pages, and some elements are custom.

- *Problem*—You want to avoid duplicating the common sections of HTML markup in each template and the maintenance burden that goes along with that. Like the software you're developing, you want to take advantage of reuse.
- *Solution*—Use nested templates to share common sections of HTML, as shown in figure 9.2. The subtemplates enable reuse for sections of markup, cutting down on duplication.

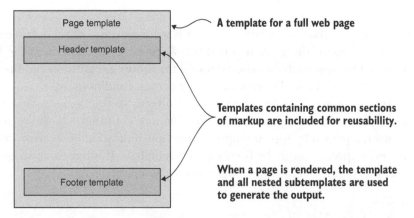

Figure 9.2   Using nested subtemplates to share common template code

- *Discussion*—The template system in Go is designed to handle multiple templates and allow them to work together. A parent template can import other templates. When the parent is executed to render the output, the subtemplates are included as well. The following listing shows how this works, touching on some important nuances.

Listing 9.8   Index template including head template

```
<!DOCTYPE HTML>
<html>
    {{template "head.html" .}}          Includes another
    <body>                              template in this one,
        <h1>{{.Title}}</h1>             passing in entire dataset
        <p>{{.Content}}</p>
    </body>
</html>
```

This nested template example starts out with index.html. This is similar to the simple template from listing 9.1. The difference is that instead of a `<head>` section, there's a directive to include another template.

The directive {{template "head.html" .}} has three parts. template tells the template engine to include another template, and head.html is the name of that template. The final part is the . after head.html. This is the dataset to pass to the template. In this case, the entire dataset from the parent template is passed to this template. If a property on the dataset contained a dataset for a subtemplate, that could be passed in. If {{template "head.html" .Foo}} were used, for example, the properties on .Foo would be the ones available inside head.html. See the following listing.

Listing 9.9 Head template included in the index

```
<head>
  <meta charset="utf-8">
  <title>{{.Title}}</title>        ◄─┤  Title is the same value
</head>                                  used in index.html.
```

When head.html, as shown in listing 9.9, is invoked by index.html, the entire dataset is passed in. When Title is used, it's the same Title used in index.html, as head.html has access to the entire dataset. The next listing brings the example together.

Listing 9.10 Using the nested templates

```
package main

import (
    "html/template"
    "net/http"
)

var t *template.Template
func init() {
    t = template.Must(template.ParseFiles("index.html
    ", "head.html"))          ◄─┐  Loads the two
}                                   templates into a
                                    template object
type Page struct {
    Title, Content string
}

func displayPage(w http.ResponseWriter, r *http.Request) {
    p := &Page{
        Title:   "An Example",
        Content: "Have fun stormin' da castle.",
    }
    t.ExecuteTemplate(w, "index.html", p)   ◄─┤  Invokes the template
}                                                with the page data

func main() {
    http.HandleFunc("/", displayPage)        │  Serves the page on the
    http.ListenAndServe(":8080", nil)        │  built-in web server
}
```

This listing starts by parsing the two templates to the same template object. This allows head.html to be accessible to index.html when it's executed. When the template is executed, `ExecuteTemplate` is used so that the template name to execute can be specified. If `Execute` had been used, as in the previous listings, the first template listed in `ParseFiles` would be used. `ExecuteTemplate` provides control over the template file when multiple ones are available.

TEMPLATE INHERITANCE

Many template systems implement a model with a base template and other templates that fill in the missing sections of the base template. They extend the base template. This is different from the previous technique, in which subtemplates were shared among a group of different top-level templates. In this case, the top-level template is shared.

- *Problem*—You want to have a base template and have other templates extend it. The templates would have multiple sections that can be extended.
- *Solution*—Instead of thinking of a file as a template, think of sections of a file as templates. The base file contains the shared markup and refers to other templates that haven't yet been defined, as shown in figure 9.3. The templates extending the base file provide the missing subtemplates or override those in the base. After they're combined, you have a fully working template with a shared base.

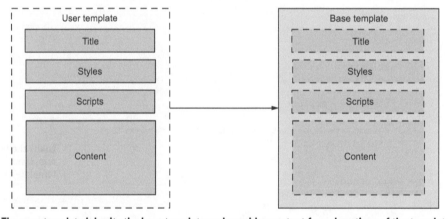

The user template inherits the base template and provides content for subsections of the template.

Figure 9.3   A shared based template

- *Discussion*—The template system enables some inheritance patterns within templates. It doesn't represent the full range of inheritance available in other template systems, but patterns can be applied. The following listing shows a base template for others to inherit from.

Listing 9.11   A base template to inherit from

```
{{define "base"}}<!DOCTYPE HTML>
<html>
```
◁─┐ **Starts a new base
   template with define**

```
<head>
  <meta charset="utf-8">
  <title>{{template "title" .}}</title>
  {{ block "styles" . }}<style>
    h1 {
      color: #400080
    }
  </style>{{ end }}
</head>
<body>
    <h1>{{template "title" .}}</h1>
    {{template "content" .}}
    {{block "scripts" .}}{{end}}
</body>
</html>{{end}}
```

Invokes the title template, which is defined elsewhere
Defines and immediately invokes the styles template
Defines and invokes the scripts template, which is currently empty. An extending template can redefine the contents of scripts.
End of the base template

Instead of the entire file being a template, the file contains multiple templates. Each template starts with a `define` or `block` directive and closes with an `end` directive. The `block` directive defines and immediately executes a template. This file opens by defining a `base` template. The `base` template, which can be referred to by name, invokes other templates but doesn't necessarily define them. Templates that extend this one, such as in listing 9.12, need to fill in the missing templates. In other cases, you may have a section with default content that you want to allow to be overridden by an extending template. Some sections may be optional. For those sections, you can create empty templates to be used by default.

NOTE Go 1.6 introduced the `block` directive and ability to redefine template sections that have content. Before this version, you couldn't redefine templates that had content.

Listing 9.12 Inheriting required sections

```
{{define "title"}}User: {{.Username}}{{end}}
{{define "content"}}
<ul>
  <li>Userame: {{.Username}}</li>
  <li>Name: {{.Name}}</li>
</ul>
{{end}}
```

←—— **Defines a title template**
Defines a content template

Templates extending the base need to make sure all the subtemplates without a default are filled out. Here, the title and content sections need to be defined because they're required. You'll notice that the optional sections with empty or default content defined in listing 9.11 don't need to have sections defined. The following listing showcases filling in an optional template in addition to the required sections.

Listing 9.13 Inheriting with optional section

```
{{define "title"}}{{.Title}}{{end}}
{{define "content"}}
```

```
<p>
  {{.Content}}
</p>
{{end}}
{{define "styles"}}
<style>
h1 {
      color: #800080          Defines a template to fill
}                             in an optional section of
</style>                      the parent
{{end}}
```

Here, the `styles` template is defined. This overrides the default supplied in listing 9.11. The following listing brings the templates together.

Listing 9.14　Using template inheritance

```
package main

import (
      "html/template"
      "net/http"
)                                              Invokes the template
                                               for the page
var t map[string]*template.Template
func init() {                                  Sets up the
      t = make(map[string]*template.Template)  template map
      temp := template.Must(template.ParseFiles(
      "base.html", "user.html"))
      t["user.html"] = temp                    Loads templates
      temp = template.Must(template.ParseFiles(    along with base
      "base.html", "page.html"))               into the map
      t["page.html"] = temp
}

type Page struct {
      Title, Content string
}                                   Data objects
                                    to pass into
type User struct {                  templates
      Username, Name string
}

func displayPage(w http.ResponseWriter, r *http.Request) {
      p := &Page{
            Title:   "An Example",                     Populates a dataset
            Content: "Have fun stormin' da castle.",   for the page
      }
      t["page.html"].ExecuteTemplate(w, "base", p)   Invokes the
}                                                    template for
                                                     the page
func displayUser(w http.ResponseWriter, r *http.Request) {
      u := &User{
            Username: "swordsmith",
```

```
        Name:      "Inigo Montoya",
    }
    t["user.html"].ExecuteTemplate(w, "base", u)
}

func main() {
    http.HandleFunc("/user", displayUser)
    http.HandleFunc("/", displayPage)          Serves pages via the
    http.ListenAndServe(":8080", nil)          built-in web server
}
```

This listing starts with creating a map to hold the templates. Each template is stored separately from the others. The map is populated with the template instances by using a key for the template name. When the templates user.html and page.html are loaded, the base.html file is loaded with each of them. This allows for the inheritance in each case.

Preparing to render a page happens in a manner similar to normal template use. A dataset is defined and populated. When it's time to render a response, the template to use is selected from the map of templates and the base template is invoked. The base is the root of the page and needs to be the one invoked. It will invoke the subtemplates defined in the inheritance.

Keeping your output tidy

In the previous examples we had our {{ define }} blocks jammed directly into the content within them. Although there's nothing wrong with this, you can also let Go trim the whitespace content of your templates to the left, right, or both using the hyphen (-) keyword before and/or after the variable.

As an example, if we wanted to leave the {{ define }} keyword on its own line and put <DOCTYPE> on the next but still want the latter to be rendered first on the page, we can do so like this:

```
{{ define "head" -}}
<!DOCTYPE HTML>
<html>
```

Similarly, we'd do this to remove preceding whitespace at the end:

```
  </style>
</head>

{{- end }}
```

This is useful for keeping the code more readable without affecting the output itself. For HTML, the practical implication may be limited, but if you need to generate whitespace-sensitive content at some point, this comes in handy. At bare minimum, it makes it easier to visually parse the template code without having the whitespace affect the final output.

MAPPING DATA TYPES TO TEMPLATES

The previous two template techniques rendered all the output together. A dataset consisting of the entire page needs to be passed in, and the template setup needs to handle the variations to the full page.

An alternative approach is to render parts of the page, such as a user object instance, on its own and then pass the rendered content to a higher-level template. The higher-level template doesn't need to know the data type or how to render it. Figure 9.4 represents this concept.

- *Problem*—You want to render an object to HTML and pass the rendered object to a higher-level template, where it can be part of the output.

- *Solution*—Use templates to render objects as HTML. Store the HTML in a variable and pass the HTML to higher-level templates wrapped in `template.HTML`, marking it as safe HTML that doesn't need to be escaped.

- *Discussion*—There are a couple of reasons to have multiple rendering steps. First, if part of the page is expensive to generate a dataset for or render to HTML, it's worth not repeating when each page is generated.

   Imagine that you have a directory listing for a user. The listing contains information about a user and their activity that can be viewed by many other users. Obtaining the dataset to render would require multiple data source lookups. If they were cached, you could skip loading this information whenever the page is viewed.

   Caching this dataset would still require the dataset being rendered on each page load, and you'd need to store a complicated dataset somewhere. Rendering the data would mean making sure that the template package handles rendering in the right format and everything is escaped properly. If the cache were instead populated with a rendered HTML snippet to reuse each time, more work on each page generation would be skipped due to better caching.

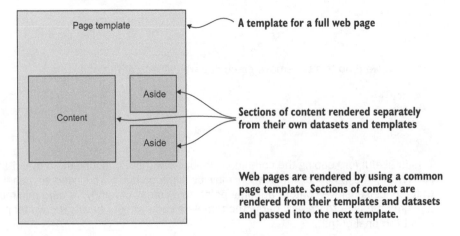

Figure 9.4   HTML rendered objects passed into the template

In a second case, suppose that you have applications with complicated logic and have many pages to render. You could have many templates containing a lot of duplicate markup. If each template were instead scoped to render one thing—whether it be the main content, a piece of the sidebar, or the page wrapper—the templates could be easier to manage.

The following listing shows how to render an object from a template, store the HTML, and later inject it into another template.

Listing 9.15   A `Quote` **object template**

```
<blockquote>
&ldquo;{{.Quote}}&rdquo;
&mdash; {{.Person}}
</blockquote>
```
| **Properties on the**
| **Quote object to be**
| **written to output**

This template, `quote.html`, is associated with a `Quote` object. The template is used to render the `Quote` object as HTML and has `Quote` object fields to render. You'll notice there are no other elements for a complete page here. Instead, those are part of `index.html`, shown in the following listing.

Listing 9.16   A generic page wrapper

```
<!DOCTYPE HTML>
<html>
  <head>
    <meta charset="utf-8">
    <title>{{.Title}}</title>
  </head>
  <body>
    <h1>{{.Title}}</h1>
    <p>{{.Content}}</p>
  </body>
</html>
```
| **Properties related**
| **to displaying a**
| **generic page**

The `index.html` file is a template for the page wrapper. It contains variables that make sense in the scope of a page. The variables printed out aren't specific to a user or anything else. The following listing pulls this together.

Listing 9.17   Bringing the templates together

```
package main

import (
    "bytes"
    "html/template"
    "net/http"
)

var t *template.Template
var qc template.HTML
```
| **Variables to hold persistent**
| **data shared between requests**

```
func init() {
    t = template.Must(template.ParseFiles("index.html
    ", "quote.html"))                                          ◁─┐  Loads the two
}                                                                 │  template files for
                                                                  │  later use
type Page struct {
    Title    string
    Content template.HTML
}                                            Types to store data for
                                             templates with differing
type Quote struct {                          and specific properties
    Quote, Name string
}

func main() {
    q := &Quote{
            Quote: `You keep using that word. I do not       Populates a
            think it means what you think it means.`,         dataset to supply
            Person: "Inigo Montoya",                          to template
    }
    var b bytes.Buffer                                 ◁─┐  Writes template and
    t.ExecuteTemplate(&b, "quote.html", q)               │  data structure to a buffer
    qc = template.HTML(b.String())             ◁──── Stores quote as HTML in global variable
    http.HandleFunc("/", displayPage)              │  Serves handler using built-in web server
    http.ListenAndServe(":8080", nil)
}
func displayPage(w http.ResponseWriter, r *http.Request) {
    p := &Page{
            Title:   "A User",                         Creates page dataset
            Content: qc,                               with quote HTML
    }
    t.ExecuteTemplate(w, "index.html", p)      ◁─┐
}                                                 │  Writes quote and page
                                                     to web server output
```

This code starts out in a fairly typical manner. It begins with parsing the two templates, quote.html and index.html, into a variable. In this case, you have two data structures for use. The first is for the output of a web page. The second is Quote, which can be converted to HTML.

To create a piece of content that's separate from generating the page, a quote is instantiated as part of the main function. Quote is passed into ExecuteTemplate along with the quote.html template to render the quote as HTML. Instead of writing the template to output, the template is written to Buffer. Then Buffer is converted to a string and passed into template.HTML. The html/template package escapes most of the data sent into it. An exception to that is template.HTML, which is safe HTML. Because the content was generated from a template that performed escaping, you can store the output of the quote.html template as safe HTML to use later.

In the Page type, you'll notice that the Content property is the type template .HTML. When the dataset used to generate the page is created, the HTML generated from the Quote object is set as the Content. When the index.html template is invoked with the dataset, the template system knows to skip escaping anything of the type `template.HTML`. The quote HTML is used as is. This provides a clean way to store and pass around HTML.

> **WARNING**   User input HTML should never be considered safe. Always escape user input information, such as information gathered from a form field, before presenting.

9.2   Using templates for email

Email is one of the staples of modern communication. It's often used for service notifications, registration verification, and more. Even services looking to take over where email is the predominant broadcast system of the internet, still end up using it in some capacity.

The Go standard library doesn't provide a special template package for email as it does for HTML. Instead, the `text` and `html` template packages provide what you need to send text and HTML email.

Email is another place where templates can be used. Email is sometimes generated as text, and at other times as HTML. These happen to be the two template packages provided by the standard library, and we can use one or more to generate email.

- *Problem*—When creating and sending email, you want to incorporate templates to produce formatted output the same way we did with web pages.
- *Solution*—Use the template packages to generate the email text into a buffer. Pass the generated email in the buffer to the code used to send the email, such as the `smtp` package.
- *Discussion*—Templates can be used for a wide variety of things, and email messages are great places to employ them for well-formatted emails. To illustrate this, the following listing creates email messages from a template and sends them using the `net/smtp` package.

Listing 9.18   Sending email from a template

```
package main

import (
    "bytes"
    "net/smtp"
    "strconv"               ◁─┐ Uses text templates
                               │ to send plaintext
    "text/template"         ◁─┘ email
)

type EmailMessage struct {
    From, Subject, Body string        The data structure
    To                  []string      for an email
}
```

```
type EmailCredentials struct {
    Username, Password, Server string
    Port                      int
}

const emailTemplate = `From: {{.From}}
To: {{.To}}
Subject {{.Subject}}
{{.Body}}
`

var t *template.Template
func init() {
    t = template.New("email")
    t.Parse(emailTemplate)
}

func main() {
    message := &EmailMessage{
        From:    "me@example.com",
        To:      []string{"you@example.com"},
        Subject: "A test",
        Body:    "Just saying hi",
    }
    var body bytes.Buffer
    t.Execute(&body, message)
    authCreds := &EmailCredentials{
        Username: "myUsername",
        Password: "myPass",
        Server:   "smtp.example.com",
        Port:     25,
    }
    auth := smtp.PlainAuth("",
        authCreds.Username,
        authCreds.Password,
        authCreds.Server,
    )
    smtp.SendMail(authCreds.Server+":"+strconv.Itoa
    (authCreds.Port),
        auth,
        message.From,
        message.To,
        body.Bytes())
}
```

The email template as a string

Populates a dataset with the email for the template and mail client

Populates a buffer with the rendered message text from the template

Sets up the SMTP mail client

Sends the email

The bytes from the message buffer are passed in when the message is sent.

This code sends a simple email generated from a template. You'll notice that the listing is using the text/template package instead of the html/template package used in the previous listings in this chapter. The html/template package is built on top of the text/template package. It provides HTML-specific features such as context-aware escaping on top of the text/template package.

Using the text/template package means the injected properties (such as .Body) aren't escaped. If you need to escape anything injected into the template, you can use escape functions from the text/template package.

When you execute the template with a dataset, pass in a buffer to store the rendered template. The buffer provides the source of the content to send from the mail client.

This concept can be expanded to send a variety of email in a variety of ways. You could use the `html/template` package to send HTML email, for example.

Using and extending template patterns for both HTML and email allows you to handle complexity in a more maintainable manner with better separation of concerns. This is useful as complexity grows within an application.

Summary

- Go's templating system can be extended via custom functions and a piping syntax for chain processing of output variables.
- Caching and buffering templates allows us to mitigate expensive parsing operations and prevent partial renderings in the case of template errors.
- Reusable sections within templates that can be shared across templates prevent code duplication and template complexity. For HTML templates, this includes having reusable sections such as a header or footer.
- We can use both the `text/template` and `html/template` packages in the standard library to generate emails or any other simple text/markup formatted document.

Sending and receiving data

10

This chapter covers

- Serving static files like CSS, images, and JavaScript
- Embedding static files directly in your compiled binary
- Handling HTML forms, including dealing with file uploads
- Working with raw multipart messages

In a way, the original web service was simply serving files. The kind of interactive web we enjoy today wasn't there when the HTTP protocol was publicly released to the internet in 1991. When it came, it did so through web forms. These constructs, created decades ago, are still the foundation of the web and continue to power modern web applications.

This chapter starts by presenting methods to serve static files for your Go application. Because what you create in Go is a web server, rather than running behind a separate web server such as Nginx, you need to set up how you want files such as Cascading Style Sheets (CSS), JavaScript, images, or other files to be served. You'll learn several ways to store and serve files that provide solutions for varying applications.

From there, we move to form handling, which we saw the basics of in Go in chapter 9, but for advanced cases such as handling files as multipart form data, more advanced techniques are required, especially if you want to work with large files.

File serving and form handling combined with template handling from chapter 9 lay a foundation for building web applications in Go. You can use these techniques with your frontend technologies of choice to build rich web applications.

10.1 Serving static content

As we've seen, a web application built with Go doesn't need to sit behind a separate web server. Unless you're using the default server, you can specify timeouts to reduce latency and leaking connections. Although there are some advantages to using a reverse proxy server, like built-in caching and load balancing, Go's `http` package is more than capable of serving all the content with its web server, whether that content is application pages or static files, such as CSS, images, or JavaScript. Figure 10.1 illustrates the difference between a Go application and one using a separate web server as a reverse proxy.

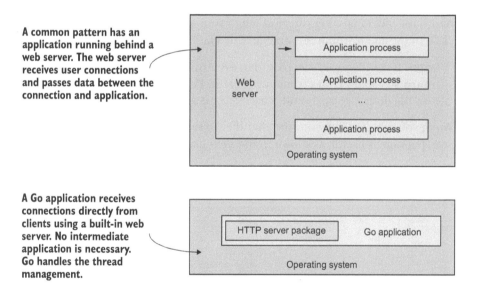

A common pattern has an application running behind a web server. The web server receives user connections and passes data between the connection and application.

A Go application receives connections directly from clients using a built-in web server. No intermediate application is necessary. Go handles the thread management.

Figure 10.1   A Go application communicating over HTTP compared to a common web server model

To handle static files, the `http` package in the standard library has a series of functions that deal with file serving. A single file server is built directly into the application, as demonstrated in the following listing.

Listing 10.1   Serving files via the `http` package

```
package main

import (
    "net/http"
)

func main() {
    dir := http.Dir("./files")                      Uses a
    if err := http.ListenAndServe(":8080",          directory on
    http.FileServer(dir)); err != nil {             the filesystem
        panic(err)
    }                                               Serves the filesystem
}                                                   directory
```

The `FileServer` handler in the `http` package is a semismart file server. From a directory on the local filesystem, `FileServer` will serve files following proper permissions. It's capable of looking at the `If-Modified-Since` HTTP header and responding with a 304 `Not Modified` response if the version of the file a user already has matches the one currently being served. Keep in mind the directory here, which may not work if you move your static files in another directory when your app is built and deployed. This is a good place to use an environment variable with a fallback, though failure will be easy to spot.

> **NOTE** If the directory you pass to `Dir` doesn't exist, you'll get no error but will return 404 status codes from any request. Prefacing this with a check to make sure the directory exists and is accessible is a good practice.

When you want to write your own handler to serve files, the `ServeFile` function in the `http` package is useful, as shown in the next listing.

Listing 10.2   Serving file with custom handler

```
package main

import (
    "net/http"
)
                                                        Registers a
                                                        handler for
func main() {                                           all paths
    http.HandleFunc("/", readme)
    if err := http.ListenAndServe(":8082", nil); err != nil {
        panic(err)
    }
}
func readme(res http.ResponseWriter, req *http.Request) {
    http.ServeFile(res, req, "./files/readme.txt")      Serves the contents
}                                                       of a readme file
```

This is a different approach to serving a single file. A basic web server has a single handler to serve all paths. This `readme` handler serves the content of a file located at

./files/readme.txt by using the ServeFile function. ServeFile takes a file or directory as its third argument to serve. Like FileServer, ServeFile looks at the If Modified-Since HTTP header and responds with a 304 Not Modified response if possible.

Of course, you can extend this by adding a path value to the route to enable matching multiple files using an endpoint like /readmes/{documentID} and r.Path-Value("documentID"). But you'd want to be careful about sanitizing input to prevent unnecessary path and file access, so if you went this way, FileServer is still a better option than ServeFile.

This functionality, along with some of its underpinnings, enables you to serve content a few different ways with varying degrees of control. If you have other routes and endpoints and want to mix and match with file servers, you can pass a file server as a handler to any route, like

```
http.HandleFunc("/comments", routeComments)

fileServer := http.FileServer(http.Dir("./static/"))
http.Handle("/static/", http.StripPrefix("/static", fileServer))
```

This also provides a directory view if you call the /static endpoint directly.

10.1.1 Serving subdirectories

A common practice in many frameworks and applications is to serve files from the local filesystem where the application resides. This allows other applications to mount external filesystems as though they were local or to have them local.

- *Problem*—You want to serve a directory and its subdirectories from the filesystem as part of your web application.
- *Solution*—Use the built-in file server or the file-serving handlers to serve these files from the local filesystem. For more control over error pages, including the case of a file not being found, you need to implement your own file server.
- *Discussion*—An easy way to understand file serving is to look at a simple example. Take the directory example_app/static/ and serve it from the path example.com/static/. This may seem straightforward, and in some cases it is, but if you want specific control over the experience, you need to bypass some of the built-in file serving to have that control. First, let's look at the simple example in the following listing.

Listing 10.3 Serving a subdirectory

```
func main() {
    dir := http.Dir("./files/")
    handler := http.StripPrefix("/static/",
    http.FileServer(dir))
    http.Handle("/static/", handler)
```

A directory and its subdirectories on the filesystem are chosen to serve.

The /static/ path serves the directory and needs to be removed before looking up file path.

```
    http.HandleFunc("/", homePage)
    if err := http.ListenAndServe(":8080", nil); err != nil {
        panic(err)
    }
}
```

**Serves a home page that may include
files from the static directory**

In this example, the built-in web server is serving the ./files/ directory at the path /static/ by using the file server from the http package. The directory on the filesystem could be any directory and doesn't need to be relative to the source for the application. Strip-Prefix is used to remove any prefix in the URL before passing the path to the file server to find. When serving a subpath in your application, you need this to find the right files.

10.1.2 *Using a file server with custom error pages*

The built-in file server in the Go standard library generates error pages, including the common 404 Not Found error for you. This is presented as the browser dictates, rather than a web page, and can't be changed. What if you want to build custom response pages with links to help people find the content they're looking for when they ended up with a Not Found error?

- *Problem*—How can you specify your own error pages, including a response to a file not being found, when your application is serving files?
- *Solution*—Use a custom file server that allows you to specify handlers for error pages. The https://github.com/Masterminds/go-fileserver package provides functionality to complement the built-in file server while enabling custom error handling.
- *Discussion*—FileServer and ServeFile both rely on the function ServeContent in the http package. That function calls private functions within the package that use the functions Error and NotFound to produce these responses. Error handling is included at the lowest levels. To alter these, you need to build your own file server. This can be something entirely new or a fork of the file server from the standard library.

The package https://github.com/Masterminds/go-fileserver is a fork of the file server in the standard library. This fork adds the ability to use custom error handlers, including the common 404 Not Found response. It's designed to be used alongside the http package in the standard library, providing only file-serving elements not already in the standard library. The following listing illustrates how this file server works.

Listing 10.4   Custom file server error pages

```
package main

import (
    "fmt"
    fs "github.com/Masterminds/go-fileserver"
    "net/http"
)
```

**Imports the
file server
package**

```
func main() {
    fs.NotFoundHandler = func(w http.ResponseWriter,
    req *http.Request)
            w.Header().Set("Content-Type", "text/plain;
             charset=utf-8")
            fmt.Fprintln(w, "The requested page could
            not be found.")
    }
    dir := http.Dir("./files")
    http.ListenAndServe(":8080", fs.FileServer(dir))
}
```

> Sets a function to call when no file is found

> Sets a function to call when no file is found

> Sets up a directory to serve files from

> Uses built-in web server and custom file server

This example is similar to the file server in the standard library, with a couple of differences. First, a handler function is set for the case when no file is found. Any time a file isn't found, this function will write the response. Although it's not used here, a custom function can be set for all error responses as well. The setup to serve a directory of files is the same as the file server in the standard library. An `http.Dir` instance is created for the directory of files to serve. The second difference has to do with serving the files. Rather than using `http.FileServer`, the function `fs.FileServer` is used. This function will make sure that the proper error handlers are called.

NOTE https://github.com/Masterminds/go-fileserver was created for this book. Because of the size of the codebase, which would have spanned many pages, and the useful nature of the file server, it was released as a package to be used in applications.

10.1.3   Embedding files in a binary

The question of where to store nonexecutable files can cause some confusion, particularly when it comes to deploying your application. They can sit alongside your binary, but often this demands some associated configuration both for the application to find them or for a web server to hide them from direct access. Sometimes, you'll want to include assets right inside the application binary. Then, instead of looking for them on the filesystem, they're included in the application itself. At this point, the binary is the only thing needing to be distributed, rather than a collection of files to accompany it.

- *Problem*—You want to include static assets, such as images or stylesheets, directly inside a Go binary.
- *Solution*—Starting with Go version 1.16, you can embed a filesystem directly in your application and include it directly. You can also assign these files' values directly to a string or byte slice.
- *Discussion*—The idea is simple. Convert a file to bytes or string, store that and the related information in a variable, and use the variable to serve the file via `ServeContent` from the `http` package. At this point, there's no need to include these files separately

The embed package gives you flexibility to keep your entire application self-contained. This is great for containerization, where you may want to limit the amount of associated resources that need to be managed and built into your final image.

Listing 10.5 Embedding files in binaries with `go:embed`

```
package main

import (                          Imports the embed
    "embed"                       package from the
    "net/http"       ◁────┘       standard library
)
                                  The go:embed
                                  compiler directive
//go:embed files    ◁────┐
var f embed.FS       ◁─────       Assigns the value
                                  to a variable
func main() {
    if err := http.ListenAndServe(":8088",
    http.FileServer(http.FS(f))); err != nil {    ◁──┐  Serves files from
        panic(err)                                      the go:embed
    }                                                   filesystem
}
```

You'll see that we wrap the resulting `go:embed` filesystem in `http.FS` to cast it, enabling it as a handler for the `http.ListenAndServe` method.

When you run or build the application, the files are built directly into the executable. Note that the directive for `go:embed` cannot exist inside of function directly. This is because the directives are similar to traits in Rust or #pragmas in C/C++. They exist purely for the compiler and are not part of the language itself.

It's not necessary to build a full filesystem using `go:embed`. If you need only a single file, such as for an HTML template, you should include only that file. The embed package will allow you to grab a string or byte slice from a single file. You can also use this to embed any configuration you might want to include but not necessarily deploy separately.

Listing 10.6 Templates as embedded files

```
package main
                                  Includes the embed package,
import (                          underscored so it can be
    _ "embed"        ◁────        used for its side effects
    "fmt"
    "log"
)
                                  Embeds a singular value
//go:embed files/example.html    ◁──┐
var myString string    ◁─────         The compiler assigns
                                      that value to the string.
func main() {
    log.Println(fmt.Sprintf("embedded value: %s",
```

```
        myString))
}
```
→ **The value is now available to the rest of the application.**

You're not necessarily limited to text files when using `go:embed`, but for other file types, it may be beneficial to take other approaches such as a content-delivery network (CDN), as they can increase the resulting size of your binary.

This has less utility for the templating system we saw in chapter 9, but `go:embed` can sometimes make deployment easier by enabling a single binary to contain your entire application.

10.1.4 Serving from an alternative location

At times, you'll want to store and serve the files separately from the application. A common example is serving a web application's JavaScript, CSS, and other assets from a CDN. This approach can reduce the overall load on your server and allow your application to focus on the more dynamic data.

- *Problem*—Instead of serving files through the same server as your application, you want to serve files through an alternative location. The alternative location needs to work with multiple environments, such as your production, testing, and development environments.
- *Solution*—Serve the files from alternative locations, such as a CDN in production. For each environment, manage the deployment of files alongside the application and pass the location into the application as configuration. Use the location within your template files to tell browsers where to get the files.
- *Discussion*—In each environment, you'll want to have a copy or a representative copy of the application's assets. Although these files may be served separately from the application pages, they shouldn't be used from a single source for all environments. This clean separation, illustrated in figure 10.2 allows any testing environments to be full testing environments, allows developers to be creative

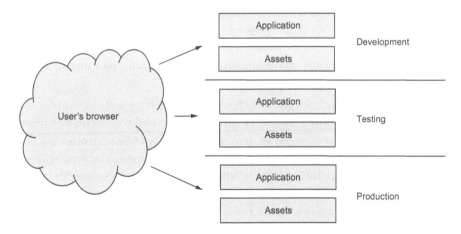

Figure 10.2 A browser fetches a different application and asset set in each environment.

in development environments, and enables safe development and testing whereby a slip-up in development or testing doesn't affect production users.

When the location of the files is different in each environment, the location needs to be passed into the application as configuration. This can happen via a shared configuration service such as etcd, in configuration files, as arguments passed into the application at startup time, or some other means of passing configuration. The following listing passes a location in as a command-line argument, making it dynamic for deployments across multiple environments.

Listing 10.7 Passing a URL location to a template

```
var t *template.Template
var l = flag.String("location",
"http://localhost:8080", "A location.")      ◁——  Gets the location of
var tpl = `<!DOCTYPE HTML>                         the static files from the
<html>                                             application arguments
  <head>
    <meta charset="utf-8">
    <title>A Demo</title>
    <link rel="stylesheet" href="{{.Location}}/styles.
    css">                                    ◁——  The path to the
  </head>                                          CSS is relative to
  <body>                                           the location.
    <p>A demo.</p>
  </body>
</html>`
func servePage(res http.ResponseWriter,
req *http.Request) {
    data := struct{ Location *string }{         An HTTP handler
        Location: l,                            passes the location
    }                                           into the template.
    t.Execute(res, data)
}
```

This simple approach takes a command-line argument for a location and uses it within a template. When no value is passed into the application, a default (empty string) is used.

This example serves to illustrate the general idea of passing specific configuration as an execution-time value. In production software, you might use something more complicated:

- *Pass the location in as configuration.* See chapter 2 for multiple ways you can do this, including configuration files, etcd, and command-line arguments.
- *If no value is passed in, it should be logged and possibly cause a panic.* The lack of a configuration value shouldn't allow production, and testing before that, to serve content pointing to an invalid URL. This is a case where defaults are harmful, as a lack of value may be technically wrong but still appear to work.
- *The location can be attached to a global configuration object and reused across responses in the application.* This could include storage in a database, distributed memory, or other data storage.

If the server handling these files is only serving the files, it should be optimized for serving static files. If you're using an Apache or Nginx web server, for example, you can turn off modules you don't need.

HTTP/2 and HTTP/3 provide features that may cause you to consider serving files along with application pages. When a browser requests a page, an HTTP/2 or HTTP/3 server can respond with the page and any associated files for the page. The associated files can be sent to the browser even before it requests them, and all the files can be sent over the original connection requesting the page. For this to happen, the server needs to serve the application and files.

> **NOTE** The HTTP/2 specification is documented in RFC 7540 by the Internet Engineering Task Force. You can read it at https://datatracker.ietf.org/doc/html/rfc7540. HTTP/3 extends the QUIC protocol and you can see its RFC at https://datatracker.ietf.org/doc/html/rfc9114.

Serving content is only half the process for modern interactive applications. To complete the cycle, the server needs to handle interaction from users. In the next section, we'll do that by processing some forms with user data.

10.2 Advanced form processing

In chapter 8, we did some rudimentary form processing, grabbing POST parameters and extracting their data. Working with HTML forms and POST or PUT requests in general is common in web applications and on websites. Go provides much of what you need in the `http` package within the standard library. Although the functionality is available under the hood, it's not always obvious how you should use it. The following patterns highlight methods for working with data, whether it's a form submission or a multipart POST or PUT request.

10.2.1 Handling form requests

When a request is made to a server and it contains form data, that request isn't processed into a usable structure by default. In listing 8.3 in chapter 8, we created a form and processed a singular, named form field.

As a quick recap, the first step in working with form data is parsing it (see listing 10.8). Inside a request handler are two methods on the `Request` object that can parse form data into a Go data structure. The `ParseForm` method parses fields that contain text. If you need to work with binary data or files from the form, you need to use `ParseMultipartForm`. As its name suggests, this method works on multipart form data (a form containing content with different MIME content types). `ParseMultipartForm` is called by `FormValue` in the preceding example if parsing hasn't happened yet.

Listing 10.8 Parsing a simple form response

```
func exampleHandler(w http.ResponseWriter, r *http.Request) {
    err := r.ParseForm()        ⟵  Parses a simple form containing only text-based fields
```

```
        if err != nil {
                fmt.Println(err)
        }
        name := r.FormValue("name")
}
```

Handles any errors that
occurred parsing the form

Gets the first value for the
name field from the form

This listing contains the handling for a simple form. This simple example works for forms with only text fields. If a file field were present, it wouldn't be parsed or accessible. Also, it works only for form values that have a single response. HTML forms allow for multiple responding values. Both of these are covered in the following techniques. The form data is parsed into two locations:

- The `Form` property of the `Request` value will contain the values from the URL query along with the values submitted as a `POST` or `PUT` body. Each key on `Form` is an array of values. The `FormValue` method on `Request` can be used to get the first value for a key. That's the value sitting in the `0` key of the array on `Form`.

- When you want the values from the `POST` or `PUT` body without those from the URL query, you can use the `PostForm` property on the `Request` object. Like `FormValue`, the `PostFormValue` method can retrieve the first value from `PostForm` for a key.

10.2.2 Accessing multiple values for a form field

Form fields can have more than one value for a single name. A common example is check boxes on a form. You can have a multiple select list using check boxes that, in the HTML, have the same name.

- *Problem*—`FormValue` and `PostFormValue` return the first value for a form field. When you have multiple values, how can you access all of them?

- *Solution*—Instead of using `FormValue` and `PostFormValue` to retrieve a field value, look up the field on the `Form` or `PostForm` properties on the `Request` object; then iterate over all the values.

- *Discussion*—When a form field has more than one value, you'll need to do a little more work to access it. The following listing shows how to parse a form and retrieve multiple values for a field.

> Listing 10.9   Parsing a form with multiple values for a field

```
func exampleHandler(w http.ResponseWriter,
r *http.Request) {
        maxMemory := 16 << 20
        err := r.ParseMultipartForm(maxMemory)
        if err != nil {
                fmt.Println(err)
        }
        for k, v := range r.PostForm["names"] {
                fmt.Println(v)
        }
}
```

The maximum memory to
store file parts, where the
rest is stored to disk

Parses a multipart form

Handles any error parsing the form

Iterates over all the POST
values of the names form field

The HTTP handler function opens by defining a number for the maximum amount of memory to use when parsing a multipart form. In this case, the number is 16 MB. When `ParseMultipartForm` is called, the maximum amount of memory for storing file parts needs to be specified. Parts of files larger than this number will be stored to disk. The default number used when `FormValue` or `PostFormValue` needs to call `ParseMultipartForm` is 32 MB.

Instead of using `FormValue` or `PostFormValue` to obtain the first value for a form field, all the values of the names form field are iterated over. The names field on the `PostForm` property is used, limiting the values to those submitted in the `POST` or `PUT` body.

> **TIP** When presenting forms to users and processing forms, use security elements such as a cross-site request forgery (CSRF) token. For more information, see https://owasp.org/www-community/attacks/csrf.

10.2.3 *Working with files and multipart submissions*

After you move from general form handling to file handling and multipart submissions that contain more than one type of content, the way you handle the processing changes. You can see this in its simplest form when you upload a file via an online form. The file has a content type, such as an image, and the other text fields on the form. That's at least two types of content that need dedicated handling.

In this section, you'll explore the handling of multipart submissions, often thought of as file handling. These submissions can come in via simple and fast file uploads or large files that need special handling.

This approach differs a bit from the last few sections. Instead of single, self-contained values, we're working with incremental pieces of a larger blob of data. Working with files is different from working with the input from text fields. Each file is a binary blob with surrounding metadata.

- *Problem*—When a file is uploaded with a form, how do you process and save it? How do you deal with large pieces of submitted binary data in a Go web server?
- *Solution*—When a file is uploaded, process the form as a multipart form by using `Process-MultipartForm` on the `Request` object. This picks up the file parts. Then use the `FormFile` method on the `Request` object to access and file fields, uploading a single file. For each file, you can access the metadata and a file object that's similar to `File` objects from the `os` package.
- *Discussion*—Handling a file's data is nearly as straightforward as handling text form data. The difference lies in the binary file itself and the metadata that surrounds it, such as the filename. The following listing presents a simple file-upload form.

Listing 10.10 A form with a single-value file-upload field

```
<!doctype html>
<html>
  <head>
```

```
    <title>File Upload</title>
  </head>
  <body>
    <form action="/" method="POST" enctype="multipart/form-data">
      <label for="file">File:</label>
      <input type="file" name="file" id="file">
      <br>
      <button type="submit" name="submit">Submit</button>
    </form>
  </body>
</html>
```

The form must be
multipart for file uploads.

A single-value
file field with
the name "file"

A button is
needed to submit
the form.

This form has some important parts. The form method is POST, and its encoding is in
multipart. Being multipart allows the text part of the form to be uploaded and processed as text while the file is included and handled using its own file type. The input
field is typed for a file, which tells browsers to use a file picker and upload the contents of the file. This form is served and processed by the handler function for the
http package in the following listing.

Listing 10.11   Handling a single file upload

http handler to
display and process
the form in file.html

```
func fileForm(w http.ResponseWriter, r *http.Request) {
    if r.Method == "GET" {
        t, _ := template.ParseFiles("file.html")
        t.Execute(w, nil)
    } else {

        f, h, err := r.FormFile("file")
        if err != nil {
            panic(err)
        }
        defer f.Close()
        filename := "/tmp/" + h.Filename
        out, err := os.Create(filename)
        if err != nil {
            panic(err)
        }
        defer out.Close()

        io.Copy(out, f)
        fmt.Fprint(w, "Upload complete")
    }
}
```

When the path is
accessed with a GET
request, displays the
HTML page and form

Handles any
errors retrieving
the form field

Gets the file
handler, header
information, and
error for the
form field keyed
by its name

Be sure to close the form
fields file before leaving
the function.

Creates a local location to
save the file, including the
file's name. In this case,
it's a temp location, but a
production application
would have a file store
location.

Copies the uploaded file
to the local location

Be sure to close the local
file before leaving the
function.

Creates a local file to
store the uploaded file

This handler, meant to be used with the web server in the `http` package, handles both displaying the form via `GET` and processing the submitted form. It opens by detecting the method for the request. When a `GET` request is submitted, it returns the form from listing 10.11. When another HTTP method is used, such as a `POST` or `PUT` request, the form submission is processed. In practice, it makes sense to restrict this to `POST`, as other verbs don't necessarily translate to the operation we're performing, but this makes for a good catchall.

The first step in processing the file field is retrieving it by using the `FormFile` method on the `Request`. If the form hasn't been parsed, `FormFile` will call `Parse-MultipartForm`. `FormFile` returns a `multipart.File` object, a `*multipart.File-Header` object, and an error if there is one. The `*multipart.FileHeader` object has a `Filename` property that it uses here as part of the location on the local filesystem to store the upload. To save the file locally, a new file is created on the filesystem, and the contents of the upload are copied into this new file.

This solution works well for a field with a single file. HTML forms allow for mul-tivalue fields, and this solution will pick up only the first of the files. For multivalue file uploads, see the next technique.

10.2.4   Uploading multiple files

File fields on forms can optionally have the `multiple` attribute. When this attribute is on the input element, any number of files can be uploaded. In this case, using `Form-File` won't work to process the form; instead, it assumes that there's only one file per input field and returns only the first file.

- *Problem*—How do you process the files when multiple files are uploaded to a sin-gle file-input field on a form?
- *Solution*—Instead of using `FormFile`, which handles single files, parse the form and retrieve a slice with the files from the `MultipartForm` property on the `Request`. Then iterate over the slice of files, handling each individually.
- *Discussion*—An input field handling multiple files needs to have only the multi-ple `attribute` on it. The difference between the following listing and the single file-upload form in listing 10.11, for example, is the `multiple` attribute.

Listing 10.12   A form with a multiple-value file upload field

```
<!doctype html>
<html>
  <head>
    <title>File Upload</title>
  </head>
  <body>
    <form action="/" method="POST" enctype="multipart/          The form must be
    form-data">                                                  multipart for file
                                                                  uploads.
      <label for="files">File:</label>                            A multivalue file field
      <input type="file" name="files" id="files"                  with the name "files" and
      multiple>                                                   the multiple attribute
```

```
        <br>
        <button type="submit" name="submit">Submit</button>      ◁
      </form>
    </body>
</html>
```

A button is needed to submit the form.

This form, with the multipart encoding, has an input to accept multiple files. The `multiple` attribute turns a single file-input field into one accepting multiple files. The following listing processes this form to handle multiple files.

Listing 10.13   Processing file form field with multiple files

```
func fileForm(w http.ResponseWriter, r *http.Request) {      ◁
    if r.Method == "GET" {
        t, _ :=
        template.ParseFiles("file_multiple.html")
        t.Execute(w, nil)
    } else {
        err := r.ParseMultipartForm(16 << 20)
        if err != nil {
            fmt.Fprint(w, err)
            return
        }

        data := r.MultipartForm
        files := data.File["files"]
        for _, fh := range files {      ◁
            f, err := fh.Open()      ◁
            defer f.Close()
            if err != nil {
                fmt.Fprint(w, err)
                return
            }

            out, err := os.Create("/tmp/" + fh.
            Filename)
            defer out.Close()      ◁
            if err != nil {
                fmt.Fprint(w, err)
                return
            }

            _, err = io.Copy(out, f)      ◁

            if err != nil {
                fmt.Fprintln(w, err)
                return
            }
        }
    }
}
```

http handler to display and process the form in file_multiple.html1

When the path is accessed with a GET request, displays the HTML page and form

Parses the form in the request and handles any errors

Retrieves a slice, keyed by the input name, containing the files from the MultipartForm

Iterates over the files uploaded to the files field

Opens a file handler for one of the uploaded files

Be sure to close and handle any errors when opening a file handler.

Creates a local file to store the contents of the uploaded file

Be sure to close and handle any errors when creating a local file.

Copies the uploaded file to the location on the filesystem

Handles any errors copying the uploaded file to the local file

```
                fmt.Fprint(w, "Upload complete")
        }
}
```

This listing contains a handler function for the web server in the `http` package. It opens by presenting the form if the request is a `GET` request rather than one posting a form. When a request other than a `GET` request occurs, it handles the form submission.

Before you can work with the form fields, the form needs to be processed. Calling `ParseMultipartForm` on the `Request` object causes the form to be parsed. This is handled internally by methods such as `FormFile` used in previous techniques. The value passed in sets the amount of memory to use for holding form data in memory to 16 MB, and the rest of the files will be written to disk as temporary files.

After the form has been parsed, the fields are available on `MultipartForm`. The uploads to the file-input field with the name files are available on the `File` property of `MultipartForm` as a slice of values. Each value is a `*multipart.FileHeader` object pointer.

Iterate over each of the files to process them sequentially. Calling the `Open` method on a `*multipart.FileHeader` object returns `File`, a handler for the file. To save the file to disk, you need to create a new file somewhere to save the contents. The name of the uploaded file is available in the `Filename` property on the `*multipart.File-Header`. After you have a local location to store the contents, copy the uploaded file to the local file by using `io.Copy`.

This solution requires moving a level lower in the package API. In doing so, you gain a little more power while needing to handle a little more on your own.

10.2.5 Verifying that uploaded file is of an allowed type

When a file is uploaded, it could be of any type. The upload field could be expecting an image, a document, or something else. But is that what was uploaded? How would you handle an improper file being uploaded?

Client-side detection is sometimes seen as an option. Input fields with a type of file can be annotated with an `accept` property with a list of extensions or MIME types, also referred to as content types. Unfortunately, the `accept` property isn't implemented in all browsers. Even in the browsers where it works, the ability to easily alter the value makes it unreliable, effectively making it nothing but an ornamental blocker. Type checking needs to happen in your application.

- *Problem*—How can you detect the type of file uploaded to a file field inside your application?
- *Solution*—To get the MIME type for a file, you can take one of several approaches, with varying degrees of trust in the resulting value:
  - When a file is uploaded, the request headers will have a Content-Type field with either a specific content type, such as `image/png`, or a general value of `application/octet-stream`.

  – A file extension is associated with a MIME type and can provide insight into
    the type of file being uploaded.
  – You can parse the file and detect its type based on its contents.
- *Discussion*—The three solutions have varying degrees of trust. The Content-
  Type field is set by the application doing the uploading, and the file extension is
  set by the user uploading the file. These two methods rely on outside parties for
  accuracy and trust. The third solution requires parsing the file and knowing
  what to look for to map to a content type. This is the most difficult method and
  uses the most system resources but is also the most trusted one. To understand
  how to use these methods, you'll look at each of them.

When a file is uploaded, as you saw in listing 10.13, a `*multipart.FileHeader` object
is available to interact with. This is the second of the responses from `FormFile` on the
`Request` object. The `*multipart.FileHeader` object has a property named `Header`
with all the uploaded header fields including the content type, as in this example:

```
file, header, err := r.FormFile("file")
contentType := header.Header["Content-Type"][0]
```

Here, `FormFile` is called on a field with the name file. Header fields can be multivalue. In this case, you'll need to get the first one even if there's only one value. The
content type will be a specific MIME type, such as `image/png`, or a generic value of
`application/octet-stream` when the type is unknown.

 An alternative to the uploaded header value, the filename's file extension can provide insight into the type of file. The `mime` package includes the function `TypeBy-`
`Extension`, which attempts to return the MIME type based on the file extension, as in
this example:

```
file, header, err := r.FormFile("file")
extension := filepath.Ext(header.Filename)
type := mime.TypeByExtension(extension)
```

Determining the type based on the file extension provides only some degree of accuracy. File extensions can be changed. The standard library contains a limited extension to MIME type mapping but can reach out to the operating system to retrieve a
larger list.

 Another option is to parse the file and determine the type from the file itself. You
can perform this type of operation in two ways. The `http` package contains the function
`DetectContentType`, which is capable of detecting the type for a limited number of file
types. These include HTML, text, XML, PDF, PostScript, common image formats, compressed files (such as RAR, Zip, and GZip), .WAV audio files, and WebM video files. The
following example showcases the `DetectContentType` function:

```
file, header, err := r.FormFile("file")
buffer := make([]byte, 512)
```

```
_, err = file.Read(buffer)
filetype := http.DetectContentType(buffer)
```

The buffer is only 512 bytes because `DetectContentType` looks at only up to the first 512 bytes when determining the type. When it isn't able to detect a specific type, `application/octet-stream` is returned.

The limited list of content types `DetectContentType` can detect means you need another method if you want to detect other common formats, such as Microsoft Word documents or MP4 files. To parse and detect these other formats, the easiest method is to integrate with an external MIME sniffing library such as the widely used libmagic. At the time of this writing, several Go packages provide bindings to libmagic, making it easy to use from within Go.

> **NOTE**   A specification to sniff MIME types is available at https://mimesniff .spec.whatwg.org.

10.2.6 Saving a file incrementally

Imagine that you're building a system meant to handle a lot of large file uploads. The files aren't stored on your API server but are instead stored in a back-end service designed for files. Using `ParseMultipartForm` is going to put those files into the temporary files directory on your API server while the uploads are in progress. To support large file uploads with `ParseMultipartForm` handling, your server would need a large disk cache for the files and careful handling to make sure it doesn't get full while parallel uploads are happening.

The Go standard library provides both high-level helper functions for common file-handling situations and lower-level access that can be used for the less common ones or when you want to define your own handling. The handler function for a request is executed when a request begins rather than when a request is completed. Many requests happen quickly, and the helper functions account for any delay. If you work with large files, you have an opportunity to act while uploads are happening.

Instead of using the `ParseMultipartForm` method on the `Request` object inside an `http` handler function, you can access the raw stream of the request by accessing the underlying `*multipart.Reader` object. This object is accessible by using the `Multipart-Reader` method on the `Request`.

- *Problem*—You want to save the file as it's being uploaded to a location of your choice. That location could be on the server, a shared drive, or another location.
- *Solution*—Instead of using `ParseMultipartForm`, read the multipart data from the request as it's being uploaded. This can be accessed with the `Multipart-Reader` method on the `Request`. As files and other information are coming in, chunk by chunk, save and process the parts rather than wait for uploads to complete.
- *Discussion*—Using an API server as a pass-through for data on its way to a final destination is a common model. You'll often see nonfile data being stored in a

database. Handling large files or handling a lot of files concurrently presents a problem in local resources in storing that much information as a cache on its way to the final location. An easy solution is to pass the problem on to the final destination, which should already be able to handle storing large files. Don't cache them locally if you don't need to.

The way to access the multipart stream directly, which is what `ParseMultipartForm` does, is to retrieve the reader from the `Request` with `MultipartReader`. After you have the reader, you can loop over the parts and read each one as it comes in.

When you process a multipart form, you'll often want to process file fields along with text fields. The following listing contains a simple form with a text field, file field, and Submit button.

Listing 10.14   HTML form containing a file and text field

```html
<!doctype html>
<html>
  <head>
    <title>File Upload</title>
  </head>
  <body>
    <form action="/" method="POST" enctype="multipart/form-data">
      <label for="name">Name:</label>
      <input type="text" name="name" id="name">        A text input field
      <br>
      <label for="file">File:</label>                  A file input field requiring
      <input type="file" name="file" id="file">        the form to be multipart
      <br>
      <button type="submit" name="submit">Submit</button>    A Submit button
    </form>                                                   also available as
  </body>                                                     a field
</html>
```

The next listing contains an `http` handler function to display and process the form and incrementally save the file's data.

Listing 10.15   Saving uploaded files incrementally

```go
                                                        http handler to display
                                                        and process the form
                                                        in file_plus.html
func fileForm(w http.ResponseWriter, r *http.Request) {
    if r.Method == "GET" {                              When the path is
        t, _ :=                                         accessed with a GET
        template.ParseFiles("file_plus.html")           request, displays the
        t.Execute(w, nil)                               HTML page and form
    } else {
        mr, err := r.MultipartReader()                  Retrieves the multipart
        if err != nil {                                 reader, giving access to
            panic("Failed to read multipart             the uploaded files, and
            message")                                   handles any errors
        }
```

A map to store form field values not related to files

10 MB counter for nonfile field size

Continues looping until all the multipart message has been read

```
values := make(map[string][]string)
maxValueBytes := int64(10 << 20)
for {
        part, err := mr.NextPart()
        if err == io.EOF {
                break
        }
        name := part.FormName()
        if name == "" {
                continue
        }
        filename := part.FileName()
        var b bytes.Buffer
        if filename == "" {
                n, err := io.CopyN(&b, part,
                maxValueBytes)
                if err != nil && err !=
                io.EOF {
                        fmt.Fprint(w, "Error
                         processing form")
                        return
                }
                maxValueBytes -= n
                if maxValueBytes == 0 {
                        msg := "multipart
                        message too large"
                        fmt.Fprint(w, msg)
                        return
                }
                values[name] = append(values
                [name],b.String())
                continue
        }
        dst, err := os.Create("/tmp/" +
        filename)
        defer dst.Close()
        if err != nil {
                return
        }
        for { #
                buffer := make([]byte, 100000)
                cBytes, err :=
                part.Read(buffer)
                if err == io.EOF {
                        break
                }
                dst.Write(buffer[0:cBytes])
        }
}
fmt.Fprint(w, "Upload complete")
```

Attempts to read the next part, breaking the loop if the end of the request is reached

Retrieves the name of the form field, continuing the loop if there's no name

Retrieves the name of the file if one exists

A buffer to read the value of a text field into

If there's no filename, treats it as a text field

Copies the contents of the part into a buffer

If there's an error reading the contents of the part, handles the error

Using a byte counter, makes sure that the total size of text fields isn't too large

Puts the content for the form field in a map for later access

Creates a location on the filesystem to store the content of a file

Closes the file when exiting the http handler

As the file content of a part is uploaded, writes it to the file

```
    }
}
```

This code opens with an `http` handler function. When it receives a GET HTTP request, it responds with an HTML form. When that form is posted, it processes the form.

Because the handler function parses the form, instead of relying on `Parse-MultipartForm`, you have a few elements to set up before working with the form itself. For access to the data on the form as it comes in, you'll need access to a reader. The `MultipartReader` method on the `Request` object returns `*mime.Reader`, which you can use to iterate over the multipart body of the request. This reader consumes input as needed. For the form fields not being handled as files, you need a place to store the values. Here, a map is created to store the values.

When the setup is complete, the handler iterates over the parts of the multipart message. The loop starts by attempting to retrieve the next part of the multipart message. If there are no more parts, an `io.EOF` error is returned, and the function breaks out of the parsing loop. *EOF* stands for *end of file*.

Now the parsing loop can start handling the parts of the message. First, it checks for the name of the form field by using the `FormName` method and continues the loop if there's no name. Files will have a filename in addition to the name of the field. This can be retrieved by using the `FileName` method. The existence of a filename is a way to distinguish between file and text-field handling.

When there's no filename, the handler copies the value of the content of the field to a buffer and decrements a size counter that starts at 10 MB. If the size counter runs down to 0, the parser returns and provides an error. This is put in place as a protection against text-field content being too large and consuming too much memory. 10 MB is quite large and is the default value inside `ParseMultipartForm` as well. If no errors occur, the content of the text form field is stored in the values map created previously, and the parsing loop continues on the next part.

If the parsing loop has reached this point, the form field is a file. A file on the operating system is created to store the contents of the file. At this point, an alternative location such as cloud storage could be used to write the file to. Instead of creating a file on the operating system, a connection to another storage system could be opened. After the destination is opened, the handler loops over the content of the part, iteratively reading it as it comes in. Until a notification of the end of the part, designated with an `io.EOF` error, comes in, the bytes are written to the destination as they arrive. If you use this to upload a large file, you can watch the data slowly being written to the output file while the upload is happening. When the loop completes, all the files are available on disk, and the text fields are available on the values map.

Summary

- Go has simple tooling to accept POST/PUT/PATCH data from forms or other methods, enabling backends to easily parse standard form data and/or binary uploads from clients.

- Dealing with files from a root or subroot as part of a web server or other applications is trivial with Go. Inside web servers, we can create routes or full server routers that serve files directly to clients.

- We can use files to serve unique error pages rather than browser defaults.

- Files can be embedded directly inside a Go binary, mitigating deployment problems and complexity around distribution and containerization.

- Advanced form processing lets us deal with binary data, multipart uploads, and duplicate named form fields.

- Streaming methods in Go allow us to take data incrementally and save it or escape partially if we encounter an error.

Working with
external services

This chapter covers

- Making REST requests
- Detecting request timeouts and resuming downloads
- Passing errors over HTTP, with additional metadata
- Parsing JSON, including arbitrary JSON structures
- Building a versioning system for maintaining different versions of REST APIs
- Using gRPC as an alternative to architectures like REST

In chapter 10, we explored how to receive data from users in the form of uploads via POST including binary data. We also demonstrated how to return different types of data to the client. When we are ready to be a client ourselves—a consumer of data—we need to know how to deal with different communication protocols and conventions.

This chapter begins with the basics of REST APIs, a cornerstone of the modern internet, and moves to handling cases that don't go as planned. You'll look at detecting timeout failures, resuming file transfers when timeouts happen, and you'll learn how to pass errors between an API endpoint and a requesting client.

Many APIs pass information as JSON, and you'll learn about handling JSON responses when you don't know the structure of the data ahead of time. This is useful when you need to work with poorly defined, undefined, or variable JSON data. When APIs change, they need to be versioned, and you'll also explore a couple of approaches for versioning your REST APIs.

Finally, you'll look at an alternative to REST that's had some traction within public APIs: gRPC. We'll see how this protocol allows us to better define our expectations for what an API produces, avoiding some of the problems that come with nebulous REST APIs. In this chapter, you'll learn how to move from the basics of API consumption to more robust functionality.

11.1 Consuming REST APIs as a full-featured client

The Go standard library includes an HTTP client that's sufficient for most common use cases. When you move beyond these common use cases, you may run into some problems for which there isn't a single built-in approach in the standard library. Before we touch on a couple of those, let's look again at how the HTTP client works in Go.

11.1.1 Using the HTTP client

The HTTP client is in the `net/http` library within the standard library. It has helper functions to perform `GET`, `HEAD`, and `POST` requests; can perform virtually any HTTP request; and can be heavily customized.

The most common helper functions for retrieval are `http.Get`, `http.Head`, `http.Post`, and `http.PostForm`. With the exception of `http.PostForm`, each function is for the HTTP verb its name suggests. `http.PostForm`, for example, handles `POST` requests when the data being posted should be posted as a form. To illustrate how these functions work, the following listing shows a simple use of `http.Get`. All the other HTTP methods exist as similar constants in the package.

Listing 11.1   A simple HTTP `GET`

```
package main

import (
    "fmt"
    "io"
    "net/http"
)

func main() {
    res, _ := http.Get("https://www.manning.com/")    ←── Performs a GET request
    b, err := io.ReadAll(res.Body)                      ←── Reads the body of the response into a buffer
    if err != nil {
        panic(err)
    }
```

```
        defer res.Body.Close()
        fmt.Printf("%s", b)                    ◁──┤  Prints the body to
}                                                    standard output
```

All the helper functions are backed by the default HTTP client that's accessible and can perform any HTTP request. The following listing shows how to use the default client to make a DELETE request.

Listing 11.2   DELETE **request with default HTTP client**

```
package main

import (
    "fmt"
    "net/http"
)

func main() {                                        Creates a new request
    req, err := http.NewRequest("DELETE",            object set up for a delete
    "http://example.com/foo/bar", nil)               HTTP method
    if err != nil {                      ◁──┘
        panic(err)
    }                                                Performs the request
    res, err := http.DefaultClient.Do(req)   ◁──┘   with the default client
    if err != nil {
        panic(err)
    }
    fmt.Printf("%s", res.Status)         ◁──┤  Displays the status code from
}                                              performing the request
```

In this case. you should receive a 404 (Not Found) or 405 (Method Not Allowed) error, but in standard REST architecture, an authenticated client can perform a deletion by hitting this endpoint. Making a request consists of two separate steps. The first is the request, contained in http.Request instances, which contain metadata about the request such as protocol and headers. The second part is the client that performs a request. In this example, the default client is used. By separating the request into its own object, you provide a separation of concerns. Then both of these instances can be customized. Other helper functions, such as http.Get, wrap by creating a request instance and executing it with a client in a single step.

The DefaultClient has configuration and functionality to handle things like HTTP redirects, cookies, and timeouts. It also has a default transport layer that can be customized.

Clients can be customized to allow you to set up the request any way you need. The following listing shows the creation of a simple client with a timeout set to 1 second.

Listing 11.3   A simple custom HTTP client

```
package main

import (
    "fmt"
```

```
    "io"
    "net/http"
    "time"
)

func main() {
    cc := &http.Client{Timeout: time.Second}
    res, err := cc.Get("http://www.manning.com")
    if err != nil {
        panic(err)
    }
    b, err := io.ReadAll(res.Body)
    if err != nil {
        panic(err)
    }
    defer res.Body.Close()
    fmt.Printf("%s", b)
}
```

Creates a custom HTTP client with a timeout of 1 second

Performs a GET request using the custom client

Handles any errors such as a client timeout

Custom clients allow numerous elements to be customized, including the transport layer, cookie handling, and the way that redirects are followed.

11.1.2 When faults happen

The internet was designed with fault tolerance in mind. Things will break or won't work as expected, and you try to route around the problem via retries or ultimately logging it, giving an alert system a chance to act against the error. When you're working with HTTP connections, it's useful to detect problems, report them, and try to fix them automatically when possible.

DETECTING TIMEOUTS

Connection timeouts are a common problem and useful to detect. If a timeout error occurs, especially in the middle of a connection, retrying the operation might be worthwhile. On retry, the server you were connected to may be back up, or you could be routed to another working instance.

To detect timeouts in the `net` package, the errors returned by it have a `Timeout` method that's set to `true` in the case of a timeout. Yet in some cases, a timeout occurs and `Timeout` doesn't return `true`, or the error you're working with comes from another package, such as `url`, and doesn't have the `Timeout` method.

Timeouts are typically detected by the `net` package when a timeout is explicitly set, as in listing 11.3. When a timeout is set, the request needs to complete in the timeout period. Reading the body is included in the timeout window. But a timeout can also happen when one isn't set. In this case, a timeout in the network occurs while the timeout checking isn't actively looking for it.

- *Problem*—How can network timeouts be reliably detected?
- *Solution*—When timeouts occur, a small variety of errors occurs. Check the error for each case to see whether it was a network timeout.

- *Discussion*—When an error is returned from a `net` package operation or a package that extends `net`, such as `http`, check the error against known cases showing a timeout error. Some of these will be for the explicit cases where a timeout was set and cleanly detected. Others will be for the cases where a timeout wasn't set but a timeout occurred.

The following listing contains a function that looks at a variety of error situations to detect whether the error was caused by a timeout.

Listing 11.4   Detecting a network timeout from error

```
                                          A function whose response is true or false
                                          if a network timeout caused the error
func hasTimedOut(err error) bool {        Uses a type switch to detect
    switch err := err.(type) {            the type of underlying error
    case *url.Error:
        if err, ok := err.Err.(net.Error); ok && err.Timeout() {
            return true
        }                                     A url.Error may
    case net.Error:                           be caused by an
        if err.Timeout() {                    underlying net
            return true        Looks for timeouts error that can
        }                      detected by the net be checked for
    case *net.OpError:         package          a timeout.
        if err.Timeout() {
            return true
        }
    }
    errTxt := "use of closed network connection"   Some errors, without a custom
    if err != nil && strings.Contains(err.Error(), type or variable to check against,
    errTxt) {                                      can indicate a timeout.
        return true
    }
    return false
}
```

This provides the capability to detect a variety of discrete timeout situations. The following snippet is an example of using that function to check whether an error was caused by a timeout:

```
res, err := http.Get("http://example.com/test.zip")
if hasTimedOut(err) {
    panic("request has timed out")
}
if err != nil {
    panic("something else has happened")
    }
```

As you may recall from chapter 4, we also could change this switch to use the `errors.Is()` method, but the idea is the same. Reliably detecting a timeout is useful, and the next technique highlights this in practice.

Timing out and resuming with **HTTP**

If a large file is being downloaded and a timeout occurs, starting the download from the beginning is wasteful. In some cases, you may be dealing with huge files a gigabyte or larger, and it would be ideal to avoid the extra bandwidth use and time to redownload data.

- *Problem*—You want to resume downloading a file, starting from the end of the data already downloaded, after a timeout occurs.
- *Solution*—Retry the download again, attempting to use the `Range` HTTP header in which a range of bytes to download is specified. This allows you to request a file, starting partway through the file where it left off.
- *Discussion*—Servers such as the one provided in the Go standard library can support serving parts of a file. This is a common feature in file servers, and the interface for specifying ranges has been a standard since 1999, when HTTP 1.1 came out.

This snippet creates a local file location, downloads a remote file to it, displays the number of bytes downloaded, and retries up to 100 times when a network timeout occurs. The real work is done inside the `download` function, spelled out in listing 11.5.

```go
func main() {
    file, err := os.Create("file.zip")     // Creates a local
    if err != nil {                        // file to store the
        fmt.Println(err)                   // download
        return
    }
    defer file.Close()
    location := https://example.com/file.zip
    err = download(location, file, 100)    // Downloads the remote
    if err != nil {                        // file to the local file,
        fmt.Println(err)                   // retrying up to 100
        return                             // times on timeout
    }
    fi, err := file.Stat()
    if err != nil {
        fmt.Println(err)                   // Displays the size
        return                             // of the file after
    }                                      // the download is
    fmt.Printf("Got it with %v bytes downloaded",  // complete
    fi.Size())
}
```

> **Listing 11.5 Download with retries**

```go
func download(location string, file *os.File, retries int64) error {
    req, err := http.NewRequest("GET", location, nil)   // Creates a new
    if err != nil {                                      // GET request for
        return err                                       // the file being
    }                          // Starts the local file   // downloaded
    fi, err := file.Stat()     // to find the current
                               // file information
```

```
if err != nil {
        return err
}
current := fi.Size()
if current > 0 {
        start := strconv.FormatInt(current, 10)
        req.Header.Set("Range", "bytes="+start+"-")
}
cc := &http.Client{Timeout: 5 * time.Minute}
res, err := cc.Do(req)
if err != nil && hasTimedOut(err) {
        if retries > 0 {
                return download(location, file,
                retries-1)
        }
        return err
} else if err != nil {
        return err
}
if res.StatusCode < 200 || res.StatusCode > 300 {
        errFmt := "Unsuccess HTTP request. Status
        : %s"
        return fmt.Errorf(errFmt, res.Status)
}
if res.Header.Get("Accept-Ranges") != "bytes" {
        retries = 0
}
_, err = io.Copy(file, res.Body)
if err != nil && hasTimedOut(err) {
        if retries > 0 {
                return download(location, file,
                retries-1)
        }
        return err
} else if err != nil {
        return err
}
return nil
}
```

Retrieves the size of the local file

When the local file already has content, sets a header requesting where the local file left off. Ranges have an index of 0, making the current length the index for the next needed byte.

An HTTP client configured to explicitly check for timeout

Performs the request for the file or part if part of the file is already stored locally

When checking for an error, tries the request again if the error was caused by a timeout

Handles nonsuccess HTTP status codes

If the server doesn't support serving partial files, sets retries to 0

Copies the remote response to the local file

If a timeout error occurs while copying the file, tries retrieving the remaining content

Although the download function can handle timeouts in a straightforward manner, it can be customized for your cases. The timeout is set to 5 minutes. This can be tuned for your application; a shorter or longer timeout may provide better performance in your environment. If you're downloading files that typically take longer than 5 minutes, a timeout longer than most files take will limit the number of HTTP requests needed for a normal download.

If a hash of a file is easily available, a check could be put in to make sure that the final download matches the hash. This integrity check can improve trust in the final download, even if it takes multiple attempts to download the file. Checking for errors and attempting to route around the problem can lead to fault-tolerant features in applications.

11.2 Passing and handling errors over HTTP

Errors are a regular part of passing information over HTTP. Two of the most common examples are Not Found and Access Denied errors, which are common enough that the HTTP specification includes the capability to pass error information from the beginning. The Go standard library provides a rudimentary but generally sufficient capability to pass errors. The following listing provides simple HTTP generating an error.

Listing 11.6 Passing an error over HTTP

```go
package main

import "net/http"

func displayError(w http.ResponseWriter, r *http.Request) {
    http.Error(w, "An Error Occurred",
        http.StatusForbidden)
}
func main() {
    http.HandleFunc("/", displayError)
    if err := http.ListenAndServe(":8080", nil); err != nil {
        panic(err)
    }
}
```

Returns an HTTP status 403 with a message

Sets up all paths to serve the HTTP handler displayError

This simple server always returns the error message An Error Occurred. Along with the custom message, served with a type of text/plain, the HTTP status message is set to 403, correlating to forbidden access. As we saw in chapter 10, surrounding an authentication with middleware via WithContext allows us to wrap logic to authenticate before possibly passing to our destination handler.

> **TIP** The http package in the standard library has constants for the various status codes. You can read more about the codes at https://developer.mozilla .org/en-US/docs/Web/HTTP/Status.

A client can read the codes the server responds with to learn what happened with the request. In listing 11.5, when the res.StatusCode is checked, the client is looking for a status in the 20x range, which signifies a successful request. The following snippet shows a simple example of printing the status:

```go
res, _ := http.Get("http://example.com")
fmt.Println(res.Status)
fmt.Println(res.StatusCode)
```

The res.Status is a text message for the status. Example responses look like 200 OK and 404 Not Found. If you're looking for the error code as a number, res.StatusCode is the status code as an integer.

Clients to a server like this need to know things like the status code to understand when requests can be retried. In a case where we get a status code like `429 Too Many Requests` or `500 Internal Server Error`, an incremental backoff retry strategy might be useful:

```
func requestUntil(url string, ops retryableRequest) (http.Response, error) {
    for i := 0; i < ops.maxRetries; i++ {
        // if succeeds, early return
    }
    return nil, nil
}
```

11.2.1 *Generating custom errors*

A plaintext error string and an HTTP status code representing an error are often insufficient. If you're displaying web pages, you'll likely want your error pages to be styled like your application or site. If you're building an API server that responds with JSON, you'll likely want error responses to be in JSON as well.

The first part of working with custom error responses is for the server to generate them. There isn't much room for customization when using the `Error` function within the `http` package. The response type is hardcoded as plaintext, and the `X-Content-Type-Options` header is set to `nosniff`. This header tells some tools not to attempt to detect a content type other than what was set. This leaves little opportunity to provide a custom error aside from the content of the plaintext string.

- *Problem*—How can you provide a custom response body and content type when there's an error?
- *Solution*—Instead of using the built-in `Error` function, use custom functions that send both the correct HTTP status code and the error text as a more appropriate body for your situation.
- *Discussion*—Providing error responses that are more than a text message is useful to those consuming an application. Someone viewing a web page might get a `404 Not Found` error. If this error page is styled like the rest of the site and provides information to help users find what they're looking for, it can guide users rather than provide a surprise (what they're looking for wasn't found, and they can't easily find it).

A second example involves REST API error messages. APIs are typically used by software development kits (SDKs) and other client applications. If a call to an API returns a `409 Conflict` message, more detail could be provided to guide the user. Is there an application-specific error code an SDK can use? In addition to the error message, is there guidance that can be passed to the user? Should the user retry as is or with new request options? Can we provide more context to the consumer of the API?

To illustrate how this works, let's look at an error response in JSON. We'll keep the same response format as for the other REST API responses that provide an application-specific error code in addition to the HTTP error. Although this example is targeted at API responses, the same style applies to web pages.

Listing 11.7 Custom JSON error response

```go
type Error struct {
    HTTPCode int    `json:"-"`
    Code     int    `json:"code,omitempty"`
    Message  string `json:"message"`
}
func JSONError(w http.ResponseWriter, e Error) {
    data := struct {
            Err Error `json:"error"`
    }{e}
    b, err := json.Marshal(data)
    if err != nil {
            http.Error(w, "Internal Server Error", 500)
            return
    }
    w.Header().Set("Content-Type", "application/json")
    w.WriteHeader(e.HTTPCode)
    fmt.Fprint(w, string(b))
}
func displayError(w http.ResponseWriter, r *http.Request) {
    e := Error{
            HTTPCode: http.StatusForbidden,
            Code:     123,
            Message:  "An Error Occurred",
    }
    JSONError(w, e)
}
func main() {
    http.HandleFunc("/", displayError)
    http.ListenAndServe(":8080", nil)
}
```

- **A type to hold the information about an error, including metadata about its JSON structure**
- **The JSONError function is similar to http.Error, but the response body is JSON.**
- **Wraps Error struct in anonymous struct with the error property**
- **Converts error data to JSON and handles an error if one exists**
- **Sets the response MIME type to application/json**
- **Makes sure that the HTTP status code is set properly for the error**
- **Writes the JSON body as output**
- **Creates an instance of Error to use for the response error**
- **Returns the error message as JSON when the HTTP handler is called**

This listing is conceptually similar to listing 11.6. The difference is that listing 11.6 returns a string with the error message, and listing 11.7 returns a JSON response like the following:

```json
{
    "error": {
        "code": 123,
        "message": "An Error Occurred"
    }
}
```

After errors are passed as JSON, an application reading them can take advantage of the data being passed in the same structured format. Using errors passed as JSON can be seen in the next technique.

11.2.2   *Reading and using custom errors*

Any client can work with HTTP status codes to detect an error. The following snippet detects the various classes of errors:

```go
res, err := http.Get("https://www.manning.com/")
switch res.StatusCode {
case 300 <= res.StatusCode && res.StatusCode < 400:
    fmt.Println("Redirect message")
case 400 <= res.StatusCode && res.StatusCode < 500:
    fmt.Println("Client error")
case 500 <= res.StatusCode && res.StatusCode < 600:
    fmt.Println("Server error")
}
```

The 30x range of messages has to do with redirects. You'll rarely see these in browsers because the default setting for the HTTP client is to follow up to 10–20 redirects. The 400 range represents client errors. `Access Denied`, `Not Found`, and other errors are in this range. The 500 range of errors is returned when a server error occurs; something went wrong on the server.

Using the status code can provide insight into what's going on. If the status code is a 401 or 403, you'll need to authenticate to see the request. A user interface could provide an opportunity to log in to try the request again, or an SDK could attempt to authenticate or reauthenticate and attempt the request again.

If an application responds with custom errors, such as those generated by listing 11.7, this presents an API response with a different structure from the expected response in addition to there being an error.

- *Problem*—When a custom error with a different structure is returned as an API response, how can you detect that and handle it differently?
- *Solution*—When a response is returned, check the HTTP status code and MIME type for a possible error. When one of these returns unexpected values or informs of an error, convert it to an error, return the error, and handle the error.
- *Discussion*—Go is known for explicit error handling, and HTTP status codes are no different. When an unexpected status is returned from an HTTP request, it can be handled like other errors. The first step is to return an error when the HTTP request didn't go as expected, as shown in the next listing.

Listing 11.8   Converting HTTP response to an error

```go
type Error struct {
    HTTPCode int    `json:"-"`
    Code     int    `json:"code,omitempty"`      Structure to
    Message  string `json:"message"`             hold data from
}                                                 the error
```

```
func (e Error) Error() string {
    fs := "HTTP: %d, Code: %d, Message: %s"
    return fmt.Sprintf(fs, e.HTTPCode, e.Code,
    e.Message)
}
func get(u string) (*http.Response, error) {
    res, err := http.Get(u)
    if err != nil {
            return res, err
    }
    if res.StatusCode < 200 || res.StatusCode >= 300 {
            if res.Header.Get("Content-Type") !=
            "application/json" {
                    sm := "Unknown error. HTTP status:
                    %s"
                    return res, fmt.Errorf(sm,
                    res.Status)
            }
            b, _ := io.ReadAll(res.Body)
            res.Body.Close()
            var data struct {
                    Err Error `json:"error"`
            }
            err = json.Unmarshal(b, &data)
            if err != nil {
                    sm := "Unable to parse json:
                    %s. HTTP status: %s"
                    return res, fmt.Errorf(sm, err,
                    res.Status)
            }
            data.Err.HTTPCode = res.StatusCode
            return res, data.Err
    }
    return res, nil
}
```

The Error method implements the error interface on the Error struct.

The get function should be used instead of http.Get to make requests.

Uses http.Get to retrieve the resource and return any http.Get errors

Checks whether the response code was outside the 200 range of successful responses

Checks the response content type and returns an error if it's not correct

Reads the body of the response into a buffer

Parses the JSON response, places the data into a struct, and responds to any errors

Adds the HTTP status code to the Error instance

Returns the custom error and the response

When there's no error, returns the response as expected

This code replaces the `http.Get` function for making a request to a server with the `get` function, which handles custom errors. The `Error` struct, which holds the data from the error, has the same structure as the error in listing 11.7. This custom error handling is designed to work with a server that emits errors in the same way. These two techniques could share a common package defining the error.

Adding the `Error` method to the `Error` type implements the error interface. This allows instances of `Error` to be passed between functions as an error, like any other error.

The main function in the following snippet illustrates using the `get` function instead of `http.Get`. Any custom errors will print the custom error details from the JSON and exit the application:

```
func main() {
    res, err := get("http://localhost:8080")
    if err != nil {
            fmt.Println(err)
```

```
            os.Exit(1)
        }
        b, _ := io.ReadAll(res.Body)
        res.Body.Close()
        fmt.Printf("%s", b)
}
```

Using this technique for getting and passing HTTP errors around applications allows these errors to get the benefits of other error handling in Go. Using switch statements to test the type of error and reacting appropriately, as listing 11.4 showed, will work for the custom errors.

11.3   Parsing and mapping JSON

When communicating over REST APIs, the most common format to transfer information is JSON. Being able to convert JSON strings easily and quickly to native Go data structures is useful, and the Go standard library provides that functionality out of the box via the `encoding/json` package. The following listing parses a simple JSON data structure into a struct.

Listing 11.9   A simple custom JSON-parsing example

```
package main

import (
    "encoding/json"
    "fmt"
)

type Person struct {
    Name string `json:"name"`     ◁   A struct that also represents information
}                                      in JSON. The json tag maps the Name
                                       property to name in the JSON.

var JSON = `{
  "name": "Miracle Max"          ◁   JSON represented
}`                                     as a string
                                                          An instance of the Person struct
                                                          to hold the parsed JSON data
func main() {
    var p Person                                    ◁
    err := json.Unmarshal([]byte(JSON), &p)    ◁        Parses the JSON data into the
    if err != nil {                                     instance of the Person struct
        fmt.Println(err)                     ◁   Handles any
        return                                   parsing errors
    }
    fmt.Println(p)            ◁
}                                Acts on the now populated Person
                                 object, in this case printing it
```

Although the standard library provides everything you need for the foundational JSON-parsing use cases, you may run into some known and common situations without an obvious solution.

The structure of JSON is often passed along via documentation, examples, and from reading the output response. Although schemas exist for JSON, such as JSON

Schema, they are not widely adopted. Not only is JSON schemaless, but API responses may vary the structure, and in some cases, you may not know the structure.

When JSON data is parsed in Go, it goes into structs with a structure defined in the code. If you don't know the structure when the structs are being created or the structure changes, that presents a problem. It may seem as though it's difficult to introspect JSON or operate on documents with a varying structure, but this can be done in Go by generalizing the data and inspecting its type.

- *Problem*—How can you parse a JSON data structure into a Go data structure when you don't know the structure ahead of time?
- *Solution*—Parse the JSON into an `interface{}` instead of into a struct. After the JSON is in an interface, you can inspect the data and use it.
- *Discussion*—A little-known feature of the `encoding/json` package is the capability to parse arbitrary JSON into an `interface{}`. Working with JSON parsed into an `interface{}` is quite different from working with JSON parsed into a known structure because of the Go type system. The following listing contains an example of parsing JSON this way.

Listing 11.10 Parsing JSON into an `interface`

```go
package main

import (
        "encoding/json"
        "fmt"
        "os"
)

var ks = []byte(`{
"firstName": "Jean",
"lastName": "Bartik",
"age": 86,
"education": [
        {
                "institution": "Northwest Missouri State
                Teachers College",
                "degree": "Bachelor of Science in
                Mathematics"
        },
        {
                "institution": "University of
                Pennsylvania",
                "degree": "Masters in English"
        }
],
"spouse": "William Bartik",
"children": [
        "Timothy John Bartik",
        "Jane Helen Bartik",
        "Mary Ruth Bartik"
]
}`)
```

A JSON document to be parsed and unmarshaled

```
func main() {
    var f interface{}              ←—    A variable instance of type
    err := json.Unmarshal(ks, &f)  ←—    interface{} to hold the JSON data
    if err != nil {
        fmt.Println(err)                  Parses the JSON data and puts it
        os.Exit(1)                        into the interface{} type variable
    }
    fmt.Println(f)                        Handles any errors, such as invalid JSON
}                                  ←—
                                          Accesses the JSON data
                                          now on the interface{}
```

The JSON parsed here contains a variety of structure situations. This is important because working with the interface{} isn't the same as working with JSON parsed into a struct. You'll look at working with this data in a moment.

When JSON data is parsed into a struct, such as the example in listing 11.9, it's easily accessible. In that case, the name of the person from the parsed JSON is available at p.Name. If you tried to access firstName on the interface{} in the same way, you'd see an error:

```
fmt.Println(f.firstName)
```

Accessing firstName like a property would generate an error:

```
f.firstName undefined (type interface {} is interface with no methods)
```

Before you can work with the data, you need to access it as a type other than interface{}. In this case, the JSON represents an object, so you can use the type map[string]interface{}. It provides access to the next level of data. Following is a way to access firstName:

```
m := f.(map[string]interface{})
fmt.Println(m["firstName"])
```

At this point, the top-level keys are all accessible, allowing firstName to be accessible by name.

To programmatically walk through the resulting data from the JSON, it's useful to know how Go treats the data in the conversion. When the JSON is unmarshaled, the values in JSON are converted to the following Go types:

- bool for JSON Boolean
- float64 for JSON numbers
- []interface{} for JSON arrays
- map[string]interface{} for JSON objects
- nil for JSON null
- string for JSON strings

Knowing these type conversions, you can walk the data structure and unpack each successive child. The following listing shows a function for recursively walking the parsed JSON, printing the key names, types, and values.

Listing 11.11   Walking arbitrary JSON

```
func printJSON(v interface{}) {
    switch vv := v.(type) {          ⟵—— Switch based on the
    case string:                          data type for a value
            fmt.Println("is string", vv)
    case float64:
            fmt.Println("is float64", vv)
    case []interface{}:
            fmt.Println("is an array:")
            for i, u := range vv {
                    fmt.Print(i, " ")
                    printJSON(u)
            }
    case map[string]interface{}:
            fmt.Println("is an object:")
            for i, u := range vv {
                    fmt.Print(i, " ")
                    printJSON(u)
            }
    default:
            fmt.Println("Unknown type")
    }
}
```

For each type of data from the JSON, displays information about the type and value. On objects and arrays from the JSON, recursively calls printJSON to display the properties inside them.

If all you're doing is printing raw data, Go's string formatter also provides %v as a default type-specific verb, but this gives us some display flexibility. Although it's handy to be able to parse and work with JSON when you don't know the structure, it's useful to have known, documented structures or to handle the version changes when those structures change. In the next section, you'll learn about versioning APIs that includes changes to JSON structures.

11.4   Versioning REST APIs

Web services evolve and change, leading to changes in the APIs used to access or manage them. To provide a stable API contract for API consumers, changes to the API need to be versioned. Because programs are the users of an API, they need to be updated to account for changes, which takes time after an update is released.

APIs are typically versioned by major number changes such as v1, v2, and v3. This number scheme signifies major, potentially breaking changes to the API. An application designed to work with v2 of an API may not be able to consume the v3 API version because it's too different.

But what about API changes that add functionality to an existing API? Suppose that functionality is added to the v1 API. In this case, the API can be incremented with a point version; feature additions can increment the API to v1.1. This tells developers and applications about the additions. The following two techniques cover a couple of ways to expose versioned APIs.

11.4.1 API version in the URL

A change in the API version needs to be easy to see and work with. The easier it is for developers to see, understand, and consume, the more likely they are to work with it and to fully use services.

Versioned APIs that easily work with existing tools are also important. The ability to quickly test API calls with cURL or Postman, a popular API extension for Chrome, makes it easier for developers to develop and test APIs.

- *Problem*—What is an easily accessible method to provide versioned APIs?
- *Solution*—Provide the API version in the REST API URL. Instead of providing an API of `https://example.com/api/todos`, add a version to the path so it looks like `https://example.com/api/v1/todos`.
- *Discussion*—Figure 11.1 illustrates an incredibly popular method for versioning APIs: via the URL. Google, OpenStack, Salesforce, and Facebook are a few examples that use APIs versioned this way.

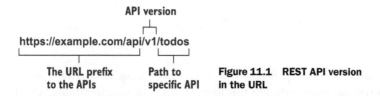

Figure 11.1   REST API version in the URL

As the following listing shows, implementing this URL structure is done when the mapping between path and handlers occurs.

Listing 11.12   Registering the API path including a version

```go
package main

import (
    "encoding/json"
    "fmt"
    "net/http"
)

type testMessage struct {
    Message string `json:"message"`
}

func displayTest(w http.ResponseWriter,
r *http.Request) {                              // An example handler
    data := testMessage{"A test message."}       // function returning a
    b, err := json.Marshal(data)                  // JSON response
    if err != nil {
            http.Error(w, "Internal Server Error", 500)
            return
    }
    w.Header().Set("Content-Type", "application/json")
```

```
        fmt.Fprint(w, string(b))
}
func main() {
        http.HandleFunc("/api/v1/test", displayTest)
        http.ListenAndServe(":8080", nil)
}
```

> When the handler function is mapped to the URL, the API version is included.

In this example, the way the handler function is mapped to the path doesn't allow you to easily handle different request methods such as POST, PUT, and DELETE. If an endpoint represents a resource, a single URL typically handles all these requests. You can find techniques for handling multiple HTTP methods being mapped to the same URL in chapters 2 and 8.

Although this is an easy method for passing an API version, it's not technically semantic versioning. A URL doesn't represent an object. Instead, it represents accessing an object within a version of an API. The tradeoff is developer ease; specifying an API version in the URL makes it easier for developers consuming the API.

11.4.2 *API version in content type*

Although the previous technique focused on a method that was easy for developers, the approach didn't give us semantic versioning. Part of the original theory of REST was that a URL represented some thing. That could be an object, list, or something else. Based on the details in the request, such as the requested content type or HTTP method, the response or action to that object would be different.

- *Problem*—How can API versions be handled in a semantic manner?
- *Solution*—Instead of referencing JSON in the request and response, use a custom content type that includes the version. Instead of working with application/json, use a custom content type such as application/vnd.mytodo.v1 .json or application/vnd.mytodo.json; version=1.0. These custom types specify the intended schema for the data.
- *Discussion*—To handle multiple API versions at a single path, as seen in figure 11.2, the handling needs to consider the content type in addition to any other

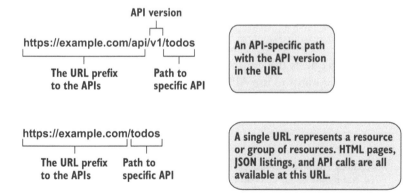

Figure 11.2 Differences between semantic URLs and API version in a URL

characteristics. Listing 11.13 showcases one method for detecting the content type and using that to generate the response.

Listing 11.13   Passing the API version in the content type

```
func main() {
    http.HandleFunc("/test", displayTest)       ◄──┤  Registers a path that can
    http.ListenAndServe(":8080", nil)                  have multiple content types
}

func displayTest(w http.ResponseWriter, r *http.Request) {
    t := r.Header.Get("Accept")                  ◄──┐  Detects the
    var err error                                       content type that
    var b []byte                                        was requested
    var ct string
    switch t {
    case "application/vnd.mytodos.json; version=2.0":
        data := testMessageV2{"Version 2"}
        b, err = json.Marshal(data)
        ct = "application/vnd.mytodos.json;
            version=2.0"
    case "application/vnd.mytodos.json; version=1.0":    Generates different
        fallthrough                                      content to return,
    default:                                             based on different
        data := testMessageV1{"Version 1"}               content types
        b, err = json.Marshal(data)
        ct = "application/vnd.mytodos.json;
            version=1.0"
    }
    if err != nil {                                   If an error occurs in
        http.Error(w, "Internal Server Error", 500)   creating the JSON,
        return                                        returns it
    }
    w.Header().Set("Content-Type", ct)    ◄──┐  Sets the content type
    fmt.Fprint(w, string(b))              ◄──    to the type that was
}                                                generated
type testMessageV1 struct {
    Message string `json:"message"`            Sends the content
}                                              to the requestor
type testMessageV2 struct {
    Info string `json:"info"`
}
```

When a client requests the content, it can specify no content type to get the default response. But if it wants to use API version 2, it will need to forgo a simple GET request and specify more details. The following snippet requests version 2 and prints out the response:

The content type with the API version to request

Creates a new GET request to the server created in listing 11.13

```
ct := "application/vnd.mytodos.json; version=2.0"    ◄──
req, _ := http.NewRequest("GET", "http://localhost:80
80/test", nil)                                        ◄──
req.Header.Set("Accept", ct)                          ◄──
```

Adds the requested content type to the request headers

```
res, _ := http.DefaultClient.Do(req)              ⟵── Performs the request
if res.Header.Get("Content-Type") != ct {
    fmt.Println("Unexpected content type returned")      Verifies that the
    return                                               response used the
}                                                        expected content type
b, _ := io.ReadAll(res.Body)             Prints the
res.Body.Close()                         response body
fmt.Printf("%s", b)
```

Although this method provides the capability to have multiple API versions from a single endpoint, you need to be aware of the following considerations:

- Content types in the `vnd.` namespace are supposed to be registered with the Internet Assigned Numbers Authority (IANA).
- When making a request for a nondefault version, you need to add extra steps to specify the content type for the version. This adds more work to applications consuming the API.

11.5   Working with gRPC

Although REST is the most common communication protocol on the web for dealing with API-level communication, there's another somewhat common alternative that has ebbed and flowed as an alternative. gRPC (a recursive acronym meaning gRPC Remote Procedure Calls) leans on the concept of Remote Procedure Calls (RPC), an old technique for distributed computing. RPCs were originally a system tantamount to breaking up a single application and storing various functions in different places, making them callable from a distributed system.

Google took to this approach early on in its architecture and in 2015 open sourced its concept of RPC designed for microservices and HTTP API communication. With it, they developed a system—protocol buffers—that attempts to bring formal, safer serialization for use across multiple languages. The main advantages are

- The serialization format creates, parses, and transmits faster than JSON, which can have a real effect at scale.
- Although Go can enforce strong typing through the unmarshaling process, it's not unusual to have to do so in a `json.RawMessage` or `interface{}` followed by some reflection when the input or output is unknown or variable.
- Some code generation boilerplate behind the scenes prevents you from having to build up the scaffolding to handle messages.

But it may be overkill for small projects because it has some disadvantages as well:

- By default, you can't process the input and output of requests as with REST, as they're usually not human readable or easily accessible. There are options that enable alternate encodings transcoding options, but out of the box, you get binary data.
- It's harder to test within a browser, which lacks the tooling to process and display, although the popular tool Postman does have support for gRPC.

- The gRPC protocol is intended to have guaranteed backward compatibility. You can extend it, but changing the contract can result in clients being unable to process input.
- It's more complicated to build out than REST APIs.

You can look at this list as somewhat metaphorical to strongly typed versus weakly typed languages. With a strongly typed language, you get safety and compile time but trade that for the flexibility and speed of development. For small projects, it's hard to argue for gRPC as a design choice if not planning for those advantages. But even if you don't choose gRPC for building your own APIs, you're likely to encounter it at some point when communicating with external services, and as a consumer, it's very nice to have a guaranteed communication and types coming from the upstream API's design.

- *Problem*—We want to use an API that has a precise, type-safe contract which is more reliable than RESTful APIs.
- *Solution*—When an API is available as gRPC, we need to communicate using protocol buffers, which give us a general definition for producing as well as deserializing well-typed data, which we can use as we might use parameters for local functions.
- *Discussion*—Although you'll sometimes see protobufs described as a schema, it's not self-encompassing. As a client, you'll need to understand the data that's coming from the server before attempting to unpack it.

Although plenty of APIs in the wild use gRPC, they almost always require some sort of authentication and possibly payment. So to demonstrate how we'd ingest this, we'll build a gRPC application in Python so we can see how to interact with it in Go using the same general framework. Let's do so using our chat/comments app from previous chapters. Using gRPC instead of REST will provide a more robust and reliable service and will have better defined data than using JSON messages across server-sent events or websockets. These are remote procedures, so there's some value in sharing generated code between different languages.

The basis of any server starts with a .proto file, which defines the API and payload, including message types and routes. This file is written in a syntax called proto3, the third version of the protocol buffer language. Its syntax will look very familiar to a Go programmer but can of course be used by any language with gRPC support. See the following listing.

Listing 11.14   A basic proto3 file for a chat server

```
syntax = "proto3";            ◁──── Defines the protobuf format
package chat;                 ◁──── Declares the package, used for namespacing

import "google/protobuf/timestamp.proto";     ◁──── Imports an external type

option go_package = "./ch11";     ◁──── Declares the Go-specific package
```

```
message CommentRequest {
    string username = 1;
    string text = 2;
    google.protobuf.Timestamp sent = 3;
}

message CommentResponse {
    int32 commentLength = 1;
    int32 previousCommentCount = 2;
}

service ChatService {
  rpc RouteComments(Comment) returns (CommentMeta) {}
}
```

Generalized type structures

Defines a gRPC service and methods

If that looks a lot like Go code, you can thank the common ancestry at Google. Notice the option line. There are various flags and options for each supported language, and this tells protoc which Go package the protoc must belong to.

First, we need to make sure we have protobuf and the Go plugins installed as described at https://grpc.io/docs/languages/go/quickstart. When we have protobuf installed, to generate our relevant file, we simply run protoc against our .proto file:

```
protoc - --go_out=. --go-grpc-out=._protos/chat.proto
```

For a server, we can use gRPC tooling to generate Python classes (or similar structures for any other language). This code generation reduces a lot of the boilerplate we'd have to write if we were building a server from scratch. When we generate our class, we can use it in our Python server. With Python (and other supported languages), you can switch or include in the out options, like --python_out=. You may need a Python library for support, which can be installed via the primary package manager, pip, through python -m pip install grpcio.

> **NOTE** The official gRPC has guides for the code generation for each language; among them, the Python example we worked from can be found at https://grpc.io/docs/languages/python/basics.

There isn't much to this Python example, and if you don't know the language well, don't worry about what it's doing specifically because it's leaning heavily on the gRPC generated code.

Listing 11.15   A gRPC server in Python

```
import concurrent.futures as futures
import grpc

import chat_pb2_grpc
import chat_pb2

class ChatServiceServicer(chat_pb2_grpc.ChatServiceServicer):
  def __init__(self, *args, **kwargs):
```

Defines a Python implementation of the method(s) for the service

```
        self.comments = []
        pass

    def RouteComments(self, request, context):
        response = { 'commentLength': len(request.text), 'previousCommentCount':
          len(self.comments) }
        self.comments.append(request)
        return chat_pb2.CommentResponse(**response)

def main():
    print("starting server")
    server = grpc.server(futures.ThreadPoolExecutor(max_workers=10))
    chat_pb2_grpc.add_ChatServiceServicer_to_server
    (ChatServiceServicer(), server)
    server.add_insecure_port("localhost:50051")
    server.start()
    server.wait_for_termination()

if __name__ == '__main__':
    main()
```

Starts the server and adds the implementation to it

Defines a Python implementation of the method(s) for the service

This will set us up with a gRPC endpoint. Now let's connect to it with Go to see how we might connect and send messages against this channel. We generate our Go code as we did with Python for listing 11.15. This will produce some .go files that you can look at to see the scaffolding gRPC produces. Obviously, don't modify these files (as the comments within the code will remind you).

Listing 11.16   Connecting to and using a gRPC service

```go
package ch11

import (
    "context"
    "fmt"
    "log"
    "time"

    "google.golang.org/grpc"
    timestamppb "google.golang.org/protobuf/types/known/timestamppb"
)

func ConnectToGRPC() error {
    conn, err := grpc.Dial("localhost:50051",
    grpc.WithInsecure())
    if err != nil {
        return err
    }

    client := NewChatServiceClient(conn)

    meta, err := client.RouteComments(context.Background(),
    &CommentRequest{Username: "Nick", Text: "Hello World!",
    Sent: timestamppb.
```

Creates the connection structure

Adds a new gRPC client with the connection

```
New(time.Now())})                        Calls the remote procedure,
if err != nil {                          sending a typed Comment
    return err                           structure as an argument
}

log.Println(fmt.Sprintf("Message length: %d,
previous comments: %d", meta.CommentLength,
meta.PreviousCommentCount))               Prints the response
                                          to stdout
defer conn.Close()
return nil
}
```

Although this is a simple request/response approach, it's already adding something we don't get from REST: a connection-level guarantee that the input and output is of the proper type or structure. Random JSON coming from a client is prone to failure in this regard. This is the same sort of type safety you would get from functions within the same application. This fixes a huge concern for microservice architectures using myriad languages.

But things get even more powerful when you realize that by leaning on HTTP/2, gRPC can use persistent connections and thus one-way or bidirectional streaming. Creating a service that accepts and/or returns a stream of data can be defined as simply as follows:

```
rpc GetComments() returns (stream CommentResponse) {}
```

Although the application logic is still up to you, the scaffolding for an endpoint that conforms to a rigid definition and keeps your application relatively type-safe is provided for you. You can think of gRPC as an HTTP framework that handles a lot of the requirements for a web service that would typically need to be written from scratch.

Summary

- When network connections fail, we can lean on a few techniques to detect errors like timeouts and recover, and we can retry connections and downloads when failures do occur.
- Response errors can be passed in a number of ways, and we're not limited to HTTP status codes. We can complement standard responses with custom messages, particularly for REST responses.
- We may encounter services that offer gRPC as an alternative to REST; similarly, we might implement gRPC in our own services to strengthen the reliability of our own API services.

Part 4

Go in the cloud, microservices, and advanced topics

The final part focuses on rounding out the details, edge cases, and deployment of applications built in Go.

In chapter 12, we'll dig into cloud deployment and discoverability, including containerizing your application with Docker. We'll also go deeper into protocol buffers and gRPC and offer tips for speeding up intracloud communication.

Chapter 13 looks at some advanced Go topics that you may not need on a day-to-day basis but are powerful tools in your development toolbox. You'll learn about runtime reflection, interoperability with C, and generating code with built-in Go code generation. A deeper look at struct annotations will allow you to create more user-friendly structures that can interface with network connections, configuration files, and more. We'll discuss some edge cases with the language, including fine-toothed control of garbage collection.

Cloud-ready applications and communications

This chapter covers

- Following best practices for containerization and deployment of Go applications
- Keeping microservices highly available in the cloud
- Speeding up communications among microservices
- Compiling to various operating systems and architectures
- Monitoring the Go runtime in an application
- Approaches to handling back pressure in services

In previous chapters, we worked toward building fully featured applications using Go. With development and testing covered, a natural next step is deployment. Although we can still deploy applications in myriad ways, sending an application to the cloud in some way is the standard. In this chapter, we'll start with an introduction to cloud computing that explores this question and what cloud computing looks like in a practical sense. You'll see how it relates to the traditional models working with hardware servers and virtual machines (VMs).

Cloud computing is a space filled with various cloud providers, which are easy to get locked into. You'll learn how to avoid vendor lock-in through generalization while architecting code in a manner that's easier to develop and test locally.

When you're ready to deploy and run your application in the cloud, you'll find situations you need to work with, such as learning about the host your application is running on, monitoring the Go runtime inside every application, and cross-compiling to various systems before deploying. You'll explore how to do this while avoiding pitfalls that can catch you off guard.

This chapter rounds out some key cloud and cloud deployment concepts. After you've completed this chapter and the previous chapters, you'll have what you need to build and operate cloud-based applications written in Go.

12.1 Cloud computing overview

As a marketing term, *cloud* is somewhat nebulous, a hand-wavy term that implies to corporate or business development folks something modern, cheaper, and easier. Given the way the term is thrown around, its meaning can be difficult for someone unfamiliar with the space to navigate. In this section, you'll learn about cloud computing in a way that you can apply to software development and operations.

12.1.1 The types of cloud computing

In the simplest form of cloud computing, part of a system is managed by another entity in an abstracted form. This can be someone else in your company, an outside service provider, an automation system, or any combination of these. If an outside service provider is providing part of the stack, what parts are they providing? Figure 12.1 shows the three forms of cloud computing and how they compare to an environment where you own the entire stack.

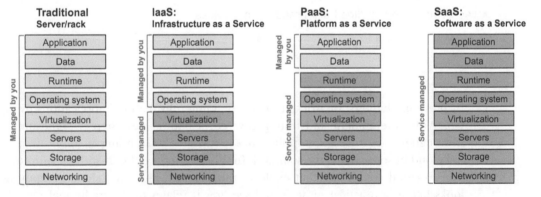

Figure 12.1   The types of cloud computing

With a traditional bare-metal server or rack of servers, you need to manage all the components of the stack. When changes are needed, someone needs to order the hardware, wait for it to show up, connect it, and manage it. Cloud computing exists to mitigate a bit of the cost of manual server management, although it often comes at a literal cost.

INFRASTRUCTURE AS A SERVICE

Accessing Infrastructure as a Service (IaaS) is different from previous forms of working with VMs. Services have been providing VMs and co-located servers for years, but when IaaS came into being, the change was the way those servers were used and accessed. Under an IaaS setup, virtual servers are created and destroyed as needed. When you need a server, an abstraction of one is created. Creating and working with IaaS resources happens via a programmable API, typically a REST API or command-line interface (CLI) app that can be used to manage the resources.

IaaS is about more than servers. Storage, networking, and other forms of infrastructure are accessible and configurable in the same way. As the name suggests, the infrastructure is the configurable part. The operating system, runtime environment, application, and data are all managed by cloud consumers and their management software. Examples of an IaaS include services provided by Amazon Web Services (AWS), Microsoft Azure, and Google Cloud.

PLATFORM AS A SERVICE

Platform as a Service (PaaS) differs from IaaS in some important ways. One of the simplest is how you work with it. To deploy an application to a platform, you use an API to deploy your application code and supporting metadata, such as the language the application was written in. The platform takes this information and then builds and runs the application.

In this model, the platform manages the operating system and runtime. You don't need to start VMs, choose their resource sizes, choose an operating system, or install system software. Handling those tasks is left up to the platform. You gain back the time typically spent managing systems so you can focus on other tasks, such as working on your application.

Heroku, DigitalOcean, and Engine Yard are three of the most widely known examples of a PaaS, although the major cloud providers AWS, Google, and Azure have competitive offerings in the space.

12.1.2 Containers and cloud-native applications

When Docker, the container management software, came into the public eye, using containers to run and distribute applications became an extremely popular way to spin up relatively lightweight environments without the bloat of traditional VM software. Containers are different from VMs or traditional servers in that they define exactly what's needed to build an application environment from start to finish and are deterministic when built and deployed.

Figure 12.2 compares VMs to containers. On the left is a system, going all the way down to the hardware server, that runs VMs. On the right is a separate system running containers. Each is running two applications as workloads, with App A being scaled horizontally to have two instances, for a total of three workload instances.

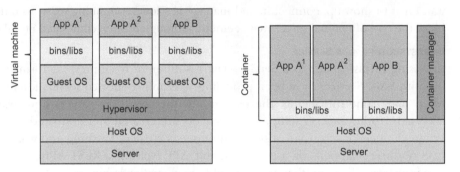

Figure 12.2   Comparing containers to VMs

When VMs run, the hypervisor provides an environment for an operating system to run in that emulated hardware or uses special hardware for VMs. Applications run in this environment. When two instances of an application run in parallel (which is how horizontal scaling works), the entire guest operating system, applications, libraries, and your application are replicated. Using VMs comes with certain architectural elements worth noting:

- When a VM starts up, the kernel and guest operating system need time to boot up.
- Hypervisors and modern hardware can enforce a separation between VMs.
- VMs provide an encapsulated server with resources being assigned to it. Those resources may be used by that machine or held for that machine.

Containers operate on a different model. The host server, whether it's a physical server or a VM, runs a container manager. Each container runs in the host operating system. When using the host kernel, its startup time is almost instantaneous. Containers share the kernel, and hardware drivers and the operating system enforce isolation between the containers and host. The binaries and libraries used, commonly associated with the operating system, can be entirely separate.

Cloud-native applications are often referred to when dealing with containerized deployments, abstracting away a lot of details closer to bare metal. Cloud-native applications take advantage of the programmatic nature of the cloud to scale with additional instances on demand, correct failures so that many problems in the systems are never experienced by end users, tie together microservices to build larger applications, and more.

One of the best approaches to containerizing your apps is to use a multistage build and compile directly inside the build process. Nothing is stopping you from compiling to your target virtual environment and copying into a Docker image, and Go supports this out of the box, but it's far more reliable to do compilation on the destination environment itself. In the very terse example `Dockerfile` in the following listing, we show such an approach to building an app.

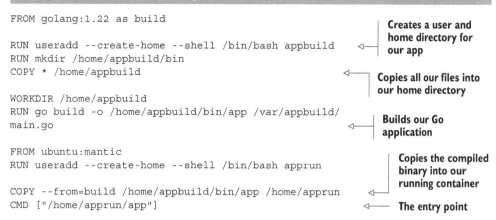

Listing 12.1 A simple multistage Docker build for Go

```
FROM golang:1.22 as build

RUN useradd --create-home --shell /bin/bash appbuild     ◁  Creates a user and
RUN mkdir /home/appbuild/bin                                home directory for
COPY * /home/appbuild                                       our app
                                                         ◁  Copies all our files into
WORKDIR /home/appbuild                                      our home directory
RUN go build -o /home/appbuild/bin/app /var/appbuild/
main.go                                                  ◁  Builds our Go
                                                            application
FROM ubuntu:mantic
RUN useradd --create-home --shell /bin/bash apprun          Copies the compiled
                                                            binary into our
COPY --from=build /home/appbuild/bin/app /home/apprun       running container
CMD ["/home/apprun/app"]                                 ◁  The entry point
```

With this approach, we can let our application get compiled directly as part of the build process, which allows Docker to cache steps and perform less data transfer as part of the build. Deployment might not always lead to a single application, of course, and multiple Dockerfiles can be used to create init and sidecar processes that can live in a clustering environment such as Kubernetes. That's beyond the scope of this book, but keep in mind that you may be containerizing multiple applications within a single codebase, as well as the interactions among them.

One of the most important elements of cloud services that we need to look at in more detail is the way you manage the services. The interface to manage cloud services provides a point of interaction for Go applications.

12.2 *Microservices and high availability*

One very common approach in the cloud, though certainly not necessary, is the microservice architecture. Applications built with a microservice architecture are created as collections of independently deployable services, each with its own specific purpose. The rise of complex systems, the desire to independently scale parts of an application, and the need to have applications that are less brittle and more resilient have led to the rise of these microservices. A good analogue for a microservice architecture is piped commands in *nix systems, where each process has a discrete, minimal task that can be performed arbitrarily or in a sequence. Microservices tend to have the following characteristics:

- *Can perform a single action*—They can store configuration or transcode media from one format to another, for example.
- *Are elastic and capable of being horizontally scaled*—As load on a microservice changes, it can be scaled up or down as needed.
- *Are resilient to failures and problems*—The service can be deployed so that it doesn't go offline, even when instances of the application have problems.

As demonstrated with shell commands, this is similar to and inspired by the UNIX philosophy "Do one thing and do it well."

Imagine that you're building a service that transcodes media from one format to another. A user can upload media, the format is transcoded, and later the media in the new format is available for download. This could be built as a monolithic application in which all elements are part of the same application, or as microservices with different functional parts that are their own applications. Figure 12.3 shows a simple transcoding application built using microservices.

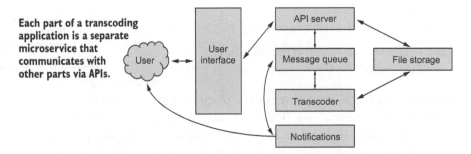

Each part of a transcoding application is a separate microservice that communicates with other parts via APIs.

Figure 12.3   A simple transcoding application broken into microservices

In this application, media is uploaded through the user interface to the API server. The API server puts the media in the file store and places a job to transcode the media in a message queue. Transcoders pull the job from the message queue, transcode the media into a new format, place the new file in file storage, and place a job in the queue to notify the user that transcoding is complete. From the user interface, the user can retrieve the transcoded file. The user interface communicates with the API server to retrieve the file from storage.

The following listing shows how a single microservice—in this case, the media retrieval job—can be tersely self-contained despite being a part of a much larger application in this architecture. In this toy example, we grab a media job from a Kafka message queue and consume it to perform another operation.

Listing 12.2   An example microservice

```
package main

import (
    "context"
    "log"
    "os"
    "time"

    kafka "https://github.com/segmentio/kafka-go"
)
```

```
func main() {
    topic := "media"
    kafkaHost := os.Getenv("KAFKA_HOST")
    if kafkaHost == "" {
        panic("KAFKA_HOST environment variable not set")
    }
    conn, err := kafka.DialLeader
    (context.Background(), "tcp", kafkaHost, topic, 0)    ←——  Connects to Kafka
    if err != nil {                                             instance via TCP
        panic(err)
    }
    conn.SetReadDeadline(time.Now().Add(30 * time.Second))     Creates a batch
    batch := conn.ReadBatch(10e3, 1e6)                   ←——  for consuming
                                                              messages within
                                                              a window of sizes
    message := make([]byte, 10e3) // 10KB max per message
    for {
        n, err := batch.Read(message)                   ←——  Consumes
        if err != nil {                                       messages
            break
        }
    }
    log.Println(string(message))
    // get details of media upload, transcode media
    // or pass to another service              ←——  Performs a next
    batch.Close()                                    step on the task
    conn.Close()
}
```

The last step in that process is something of a design decision. Relying on message queues means that sometimes the communication happens exclusively on them. But some microservice architectures eschew queues other than as a source of truth for logging and retries, and sequentially hand off jobs to a next step in a larger process.

Each of these microservices can be written in a different programming language, reused on different applications, and even be consumed as a service. File storage, for example, could be an object storage designed as its own Software as a Service (SaaS).

Scaling each of these services depends on the needs of the service. The transcoder service, for example, can scale up or down depending on how much media needs to be transcoded. The API server and notifications service can scale differently from the transcoder, depending on the amount of resources they need. These scaling requirements can change from hour to hour or minute to minute, so logging can go a long way toward designing approaches that most efficiently deal with these changes.

Users have the expectation that services will never go offline. The days of maintenance windows during which services aren't available are in the past. Accidental outages can reduce user trust and lead to lost income. One advantage of microservices is that each service can be made highly available in a method most appropriate for that service. Keeping an API server highly available is different from keeping a message queue highly available, for example.

12.3   Communicating among services

One of the key parts of a microservice architecture is communication among the microservices. If not done well, this can become a bottleneck in the performance of an application, as services will connect in a one-to-one or one-to-many system.

In the transcoding example in figure 12.3, four microservices are communicating with one another when uploading a new piece of media to be transcoded. If these used REST to communicate and the communications were over Transport Layer Security (TLS), which is typical, a significant amount of time would be spent in network communications.

The performance of these communications becomes more important when you use an increasing number of microservices. Companies such as Google, which are known for using microservice architectures, have gone so far as to create new, faster ways to communicate among microservices and build their own networking layer that outperforms what's being sold on the market. We saw that with the introduction of gRPC in chapter 11.

Faster communication is something you can bring to your applications. As you'll see in this chapter, it isn't that complicated to implement. We'll expand on previous examples to use REST in a more performant way.

12.3.1   Making REST faster

REST is the most common form of communication used in web and cloud services. Although transferring representational state data over HTTP is common, it's not efficient or as fast as other protocols. Most REST frameworks and approaches aren't optimized out of the box, either. This often makes the communication layer of a microservice architecture an easy place to speed up application performance.

REUSING CONNECTIONS

It's not unusual for each HTTP request to be made over its own connection. Negotiating each connection takes time, including the time to negotiate TLS for secure communications. Next, TCP slow-start ramps up as the message is communicated. Slow-start is a congestion-control strategy designed to prevent network congestion and to better distribute traffic. As a slow-start ramps up, a single message may take multiple round-trips between the client and server to communicate.

- *Problem*—When each request is transmitted over its own connection, a significant amount of time is lost to network communication. How can an application mitigate as much of this lost time as possible?
- *Solution*—Reuse connections. Multiple HTTP requests can be made over a single connection. That connection needs to be negotiated and ramped up for slow-start only once. After passing the first message, others pass more quickly over the persistent connection instead of requiring a new one.
- *Discussion*—Whether your application is using HTTP/2 (first available in Go 1.6) or HTTP/1 and HTTP/1.1 for your communications, you can reuse

connections. Go tries to reuse connections out of the box, and antipatterns in the application are most likely to bypass this efficiency.

When connections are reused, as shown in figure 12.4, the time spent opening and closing connections is reduced. Because TCP slow-start has already happened, the time to communicate future messages is faster as well. This is why the second, third, and fourth messages take less time when the connection is reused.

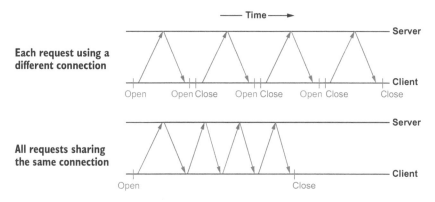

Figure 12.4   Messages being passed with and without connection reuse

The server included in the net/http package provides HTTP keep-alive support. Most systems support TCP keep-alive needed to reuse connections out of the box. As of Go 1.6, the net/http package includes transparent support for HTTP/2, which has other communication advantages that can make communication even faster.

> **NOTE**   HTTP keep-alive and TCP keep-alive are different. HTTP keep-alive is a feature of the HTTP protocol a web server needs to specifically implement. The web server needs to periodically check the connection for incoming HTTP requests within the keep-alive time span. When no HTTP request is received within that time span, it closes the connection. Alternatively, TCP keep-alive is handled by the operating system in TCP communications. Disabling keep-alive with DisableKeepAlives in Go disables both forms.

Most of the problems preventing connection reuse happen in the clients used to communicate with HTTP servers. The first and possibly most widespread problem occurs when custom transport instances are used and keep-alive is turned off.

When the basic functions in the net/http package are used, such as http.Get() or http.Post(), they use http.DefaultClient, which is configured with keep-alive enabled and set up for a default of 30 seconds. When an application creates a custom client but doesn't specify a transport, http.DefaultTransport is used. http.DefaultTransport is used by http.DefaultClient and instantiated with keep-alive enabled.

Transporting without keep-alive can be seen in open source applications, examples online, and even the Go documentation. The Go documentation has an example that reads as follows:

```
tr := &http.Transport{
    TLSClientConfig:    &tls.Config{RootCAs: pool},
    DisableCompression: true,
}
client := &http.Client{Transport: tr}
resp, err := client.Get("https://example.com")
```

In this example, a custom `Transport` instance is used with altered certificate authorities and compression disabled. In this case, keep-alive isn't enabled. There are myriad reasons someone might choose to disable keep-alive: to constrain resources, yield to a load balancer, or to mitigate denial-of-service attacks, to name a few. The following listing provides a similar example, the difference being that keep-alive is enabled.

Listing 12.3   Custom transport with connection reuse

```
tr := &http.Transport{
    TLSClientConfig:    &tls.Config{RootCAs: pool},
    DisableCompression: true,
    Dial: (&net.Dialer{                              The Dial function is configured
            Timeout:   30 * time.Second,             with a keep-alive and timeout.
            KeepAlive: 30 * time.Second,             This is the same configuration
        }).Dial,                                     as the http.DefaultTransport.
}
client := &http.Client{Transport: tr}
resp, err := client.Get("https://example.com")
```

One part of working with `http.Transport` in this way can be confusing. Setting its `DisableKeepAlives` property to `true` disables connection reuse. Setting `DisableKeepAlives` to `false` doesn't mean that connections are explicitly reused. It means you can opt in to either HTTP or TCP keep-alive independently.

Unless you have a reason to disable keep-alive, like the ones noted above, we suggest you use it. When making many HTTP requests to the same endpoint, it generally provides for faster performance.

The other behavior that can prevent connection reuse occurs when the body of a response isn't closed. Prior to HTTP/2, pipelining was almost never implemented or used. Pipelining allows multiple requests and their responses to be communicated in parallel rather than in serial, as you can see in figure 12.5. Prior to HTTP/2, one request and response needed to be completed before the next could be used. The body of the response would need to be closed before another HTTP request and response could use the connection.

The following listing illustrates a common case of one response body not being closed before another HTTP request is made.

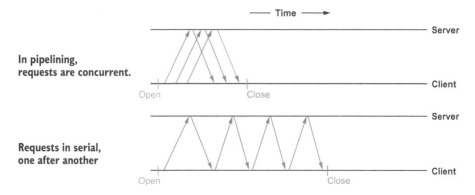

Figure 12.5   HTTP Pipelining compared to serial requests

Listing 12.4   Failing to close an HTTP response body

```go
func main() {
    r, err := http.Get("http://example.com")
    if err != nil {
        ...
    }
    defer r.Body.Close()
    o, err := ioutil.ReadAll(r.Body)
    if err != nil {
        ...
    }
    // Use the body content
    r2, err := http.Get("http://example.com/foo")
    if err != nil {
        ...
    }
    defer r2.Body.Close()
    o, err = ioutil.ReadAll(r2.Body)
    if err != nil {
        ...
    }
    ...
}
```

⟵ **Makes an HTTP request and gets a response**

⟵ **Defers closing the body until the main() function exits**

⟵ **Makes a second HTTP request. Because the body isn't yet closed on the first, a new connection needs to be made.**

In this case, using `defer` isn't optimal. Instead, the body should be closed when it's no longer needed. The following listing illustrates the same example, with the connection being shared because the body is closed.

Listing 12.5   Using and closing the HTTP response quickly

```go
func main() {
    r, err := http.Get("http://example.com")
    if err != nil {
        ...
    }
```

⟵ **Makes an HTTP request and gets a response**

```
o, err := ioutil.ReadAll(r.Body)
if err != nil {
        ...
}
r.Body.Close()
// Use the body content
r2, err := http.Get("http://example.com/foo")
if err != nil {
        ...
}
o, err = ioutil.ReadAll(r2.Body)
if err != nil {
        ...
}
r2.Body.Close()
...
}
```

Copies the response body to another instance and closes the body when done with it

Makes another HTTP request. This request reuses the connection made during the previous request.

This subtle change to the application can affect how network connections behind the scenes are happening and can improve the overall performance of an application, especially as it scales.

FASTER JSON MARSHAL AND UNMARSHAL

In general, most of the communication over contemporary REST involves passing data as JSON. The JSON marshaling and unmarshaling provided by the `encoding/json` package uses reflection to figure out values and types each time. Reflection, provided by the `reflect` package, takes time to discern types and values each time a message is acted on. If you're repeatedly acting on the same structures, quite a bit of time will be spent reflecting. We've touched on reflection a bit, and it's covered in more detail in chapter 13.

- *Problem*—Rather than figuring out the types of data whenever JSON is marshaled or unmarshaled, how can the type be figured out once and skipped on future passes?
- *Solution*—Use a package able to generate code that can marshal and unmarshal the JSON. The generated code skips reflection and provides a faster execution path with a smaller memory footprint.
- *Discussion*—Reflection in Go is fairly fast. It does allocate memory that needs to be garbage-collected, and there's a small computational cost. When using optimized generated code, those costs can be reduced, and you can see a performance improvement.

Several packages are designed to do this. The following listing looks at the package `github.com/ugorji/go/codec`, which is designed to work with Binc, MessagePack, and Concise Binary Object Representation (CBOR) in addition to JSON. Binc, MessagePack, and CBOR are alternative data exchange formats, though none is as popular as JSON.

Listing 12.6 A struct annotated for codec

A code comment for the go generate command to know how to generate code from this file

codec can't generate code for main packages. Here, the user functionality is in the user package.

```go
//go:generate codecgen -o user_generated.go user.go
package user
type User struct {
    Name  string `codec:"name"`
    Email string `codec:",omitempty"`
}
```

The User struct is annotated for codec instead of for JSON.

The Name property will be found as "name" in the JSON file. The difference is the case of the name.

The codec annotation will omit Email when it generates JSON output and the Email value is empty.

A struct marked up for the `codec` package is almost the same as for the `json` package. The difference is in the name `codec`. To generate code, the `codecgen` command needs to be installed. This can be done as follows:

```
$ go get -u github.com/ugorji/go/codec/codecgen
```

After `codecgen` is installed, you can use it to generate code on this file, named `user.go`, by executing the following command:

```
$ codecgen -o user_generated.go user.go
```

The output file is named `user_generated.go`. In the generated file, you'll notice that two public methods have been added to the User type: `CodecEncodeSelf` and `Codec-DecodeSelf`. When these are present, the `codec` package uses them to encode or decode the type. When they're absent, the `codec` package falls back to doing these at runtime.

When the `codecgen` command is installed, it can be used with `go generate`. `go generate` will see the first comment line of the file, which is specially formatted for it, and execute `codecgen`. To use `go generate`, run the following command:

```
$ go generate ./...
```

NOTE Chapter 13 covers generators and reflection in more depth.

After the `User` type is ready for use, the encoding and decoding can be incorporated into the rest of the application, as shown in the next listing.

Listing 12.7 Encoding an instance to JSON with codec

Creates a new JSON handler for the encoder. The codec package has handlers for each type it works with.

```go
jh := new(codec.JsonHandle)
u := &user.User{
    Name:  "Inigo Montoya",
    Email: "inigo@montoya.example.com",
}
```

Creates an instance of User populated with data

```
var out []byte
err := codec.NewEncoderBytes(&out, jh).Encode(&u)
if err != nil {
    ...
}
fmt.Println(string(out))
```

Creates a byte slice to store the output in. This will be the generated JSON from the instance of User.

Encodes the instance of User into the output using the JSON handle. The codec package does this in two steps that can be done together.

Converts the byte slice to a string and prints it

Here's the output of this code:

```
{"name":"Inigo Montoya","Email":"inigo@montoya.example.com"}
```

Notice that the name key is lowercase, whereas the Email key has an uppercase first letter. The User type, defined in listing 12.6, has uppercase property names leading to key names that directly reflect that. But the Name property has a custom key of name used here.

The byte slice with the JSON that was created in listing 12.7 can be decoded into an instance of User, as shown in the following listing.

Listing 12.8   Decoding JSON into an instance of a type

Creates a variable to hold the decoded JSON

```
var u2 user.User
err = codec.NewDecoderBytes(out, jh).Decode(&u2)
if err != nil {
    ...
}
fmt.Println(u2)
```

Decodes the JSON by using the JSON handler, both created in listing 12.6, into the new instance of the User type. The decoder uses two steps that can be used together. The decoder can reuse the JSON handler.

Prints the populated instance of User

Although the API to github.com/ugorji/go/codec is different from the encoding/json package in the standard library, it's simple enough to be easily used.

Code generation is a somewhat common approach to solving this problem, but you can see it adds more steps to your process. For something a little closer to optimizing the intent of the standard library, we can look to Sonic, from Bytedance, perhaps most known as the developer of TikTok. They noticed enormous amounts of time being lost to JSON processing and saw abnormalities in processing depending on input size(s). In short, their approach is a just-in-time (JIT) compiler that works as a drop-in replacement and can be a big boost when you need to handle the volume of JSON data that could create bottlenecks. Because no application is required to implement this, you can just add the package as normal:

```
$ go get github.com/bytedance/sonic
```

From there, the implementation is somewhat close to what you would expect. The next listing shows how we might process the JSON from listings 12.7 and 12.8.

Listing 12.9   JSON decoding with Sonic

```
package main

import (
    "log"
    "strings"

    "github.com/bytedance/sonic"          ← Imports the Sonic package
)

func main() {
    var receiver = []map[string]interface{}{}          ← Creates a receiver similar to a struct we might use for standard encoding
    jsonData := strings.NewReader(`
        [
            { "email": "inigo@montoya.example.com", "name":
            "Inigo Montoya" },
            { "email": "fezzik@example.com", "name": "Fezzik" },
        ]
    `)
    decoder := sonic.ConfigDefault.NewDecoder(jsonData)          ← Creates a decoder with our JSON data
    decoder.Decode(&receiver)          ← Decodes into the structure
    for k := range receiver {
        log.Println(receiver[k])          ← Iterates through the structure and prints the value to standard out
    }
}
```

There are some minor caveats to using a package like this. Build support is limited to certain processors, so building outside them, as with Apple's M-series chips, will be slower.

12.4   Running on cloud servers

When an application is being built to run in the cloud, at times you may know all the details of the environment, but at other times information will be limited due to the way the cloud provider implements virtualization. Building applications that are tolerant to unknown environments will aid in the detection and handling of problems that can arise.

At the same time, you may develop applications on one operating system and architecture but need to operate them on another. It's quite likely that you will develop an application on Windows or macOS and operate it on Linux in production. In this section, you'll explore how to avoid pitfalls that can come from assuming too much about an environment.

12.4.1   Performing runtime detection

It's usually a good idea to detect the environment at runtime rather than to assume characteristics of it in your code. Because Go applications communicate with the kernel, one thing you need to know is that if you're on Linux, Windows, or another system, details beyond the kernel that Go was compiled for can be detected at runtime. This allows a Go application to run on Red Hat Linux, Ubuntu, or any other supported OS. Or a Go application can tell you whether a dependency is missing, which makes troubleshooting much easier.

GATHERING INFORMATION ON THE HOST

Cloud applications can run in multiple environments, such as development, testing, and production environments. They can scale horizontally, with the potential to have many instances dynamically scheduled. They can run in multiple data centers at the same time. Being run in this manner makes it difficult to assume information about the environment or pass in all the details with application configuration. Instead of knowing through configuration or assuming host environment details, it's possible to detect information about the environment at the application level.

- *Problem*—How can information about a host be detected within a Go application?
- *Solution*—The os package enables you to get information about the underlying system. Information from the os package can be combined with information detected through other packages, such as net, or from calls to external applications.
- *Discussion*—The os package has the capability to detect a wide range of details about the environment. The following list highlights several examples:
  - os.Hostname() returns the kernel's value for the hostname.
  - The process ID for the application can be retrieved with os.Getpid().
  - Operating systems can and do have different path and path list separators. Using os.PathSeparator or os.PathListSeparator instead of hardcoded characters allows applications to work with the system they're running on.
  - To find the current working directory, use os.Getwd().

Information from the os package can be used in combination with other information to know more about a host. If you try to look up the IP addresses for the machine an application is running on by looking at all the addresses associated with all the interfaces to the machine, you can end up with a long list. That list would include the localhost loop-back and IPv4 and IPv6 addresses, even when one case may not be routable to the machine. To find the IP address to use, an application can look up the hostname, known by the system, and find the associated IP address. The following listing shows this method in action.

Listing 12.10   Looking up the host's IP addresses via the hostname

```
func main() {
    name, err := os.Hostname()
    if err != nil {                          Retrieves the
            fmt.Println(err)                 hostname per
            return                           the kernel
    }
```

```
addrs, err := net.LookupHost(name)
if err != nil {
        fmt.Println(err)
        return
}
for _, a := range addrs {
        fmt.Println(a)
}
```

Looks up the IP addresses associated with the hostname

Prints each of the IP addresses

The system knows its own hostname, and looking up the address for that hostname will return the local one. This is useful for an application that can be run in a variety of environments or scaled horizontally. The hostname and address information could change or have a high rate of variability.

Go applications can be compiled for a variety of operating systems and run in various environments. When applications can detect information about their environment rather that assuming it, it removes the opportunity for bugs or other unexpected situations.

DETECTING DEPENDENCIES

In addition to communicating with the kernel or base operating system, Go applications can call other applications on the system. This is typically accomplished with the os/exec package from the standard library. But what happens if the application being called isn't installed? We can sometimes get nebulous errors from the operating system. Assuming that a dependency is present can lead to unexpected behavior, and a failure to detect any problems in a reportable way makes detecting the problem in your application more difficult.

- *Problem*—How can you better predict success calling another application before doing so?
- *Solution*—Prior to calling a dependent application for the first time, check whether the application is installed and available for you to use. If the application isn't present, log an error to help with troubleshooting.
- *Discussion*—We've already talked about how Go applications can run on a variety of operating systems. If an application is compiled for Linux, it could be running on a variety of distributions with different applications installed. If your application relies on another application, it may or may not be installed. This becomes more complicated with the number of distributions available and used in the cloud. Some specialized Linux distributions for the cloud are small, with limited or virtually no commands installed.

Any time a cloud application relies on another application being installed, it should validate that dependency and log the absence of the missing component. This is relatively straightforward to do with the os/exec package. The following listing provides a function to perform detection.

Listing 12.11 Function to check whether the application is available

```
func checkDep(name string) error {
    if _, err := exec.LookPath(name); err != nil {
        es := "Could not find '%s' in PATH: %s"
        return fmt.Errorf(es, name, err)
    }
    return nil
}
```

Checks whether the passed-in dependency is in one of the executable PATHs. If not present, an error is generated.

Returns an error if the dependency isn't found

Returns nil if there was no error

This function can be used within the flow of an application to check whether a dependency exists. The following snippet shows an example of checking and acting on an error:

```
err := checkDep("fortune")
if err != nil {
    log.Fatalln(err)
}
fmt.Println("Time to get your fortune")
```

In this example, the error is logged when a dependency isn't installed. Logging isn't always the action to take. There may be a fallback method to retrieve the missing dependency or an alternative dependency to use. Sometimes, a missing dependency may be fatal to an application, and other times, it can skip an action when a dependency isn't installed. When you know something is missing, you can handle the situation appropriately.

Some of this can be mitigated in the containerization process as well. As part of a Docker build, we should attempt to gather and install all the needed dependencies. But this on its own won't ensure the build is functional, which is why building these types of checks directly into a cloud-ready application will give your application a stronger safety net.

12.4.2 Building for the cloud

There's no one hardware architecture or operating system for the cloud. You may write an application for the AMD64 architecture running on Windows and later find you need to run it on ARM8 and a Linux distribution. Building for the cloud requires designing to support multiple environments, which is easier handled up front in development and is something the standard library can help you with.

In addition to the variety of environments in cloud computing, it's not unusual to develop a Go application on Microsoft Windows or Apple's macOS and want to operate it on a Linux distribution in production, or to distribute an application via the cloud with versions for Windows, macOS, and Linux. Frequently, an application is developed in one operating system but needs to run in a different one.

- *Problem*—How can you compile for architectures and operating systems other than the one you're currently on?

- *Solution*—The go toolchain provides the ability to cross-compile to other archi-tectures and operating systems. In addition to the go toolchain, the third-party tool gox allows you to cross-compile multiple binaries in parallel. You also can use packages such as `filepath` to handle differences between operating systems instead of hardcoding values, such as the POSIX path separator /.
- *Discussion*—The compiler installed with the go toolchain can cross-compile out of the box. This is done by setting the GOARCH and GOOS environment variables to specify the architecture and operating system. GOARCH specifies the hardware architecture such as `amd64`, `386`, or `arm`, whereas GOOS specifies the operating system such as `windows`, `linux`, `darwin`, or `freebsd`.

The following example provides a quick illustration:

```
$ GOOS=windows GOARCH=386 go build
```

This tells go to build a Windows binary for the 386 architecture. Specifically, the resulting executable will be of the type PE32 executable for MS Windows (console) Intel 80386 32-bit.

> **WARNING** If your application is using `cgo` to interact with C libraries, complica-tions can arise. Be sure to test the applications on all cross-compiled platforms.

If you want to compile to multiple operating systems and architectures, one option is the aforementioned gox, which enables building multiple binaries concurrently, as shown in figure 12.6.

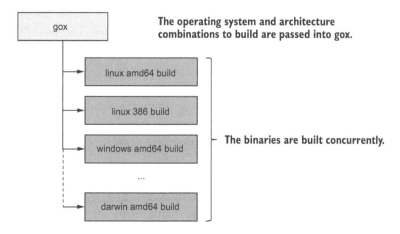

Figure 12.6 gox **builds binaries for different operating systems and architectures concurrently.**

You can install gox as follows:

```
$ go get -u github.com/mitchellh/gox
```

When gox is installed, you can create binaries in parallel by using the `gox` command, similar to `go build`. What gox brings to the table is the parallelized builds. If you don't need this, the `go` toolchain will work out of the box. The following listing provides an example of building an application for macOS, Windows, and Linux on both the AMD64 and 386 architectures.

Listing 12.12 Cross-compiling an application with gox

```
$ gox \
  -os="linux darwin windows " \
  -arch="amd64 386" \
  -output="dist/{{.OS}}-{{.Arch}}/{{.Dir}}" .
```

> Uses the os flag to specify multiple operating systems

> The arch flag is used to specify one or more architectures.

> A template is used to specify the output location. This way, binaries with the same name end up in different identifying directories.

When building binaries in other operating systems—especially when operating them in the cloud—it's a best practice to test the result before deploying. This way, any environment bugs can be detected before deploying to that environment. You can do this with multiple Dockerfile implementations, but compiling locally is definitely a faster and more lightweight approach.

Besides compiling for different environments, differences between operating systems need to be handled within an application. Go has two useful parts to help with that.

First, packages provide a single interface that handles differences behind the scenes. One of the most well-known is the difference between path and path list separators. On Linux and other POSIX-based systems, these are / and :, respectively. On Windows, they're \ and ;. Instead of assuming these, use the `path/filepath` package to make sure any paths are handled safely. This package provides features such as the following:

- `filepath.Separator` and `filepath.ListSeparator`—Represent the appropriate path and list separator values on any operating system the application is compiled to. You can use these when you need direct access to the separators.
- `filepath.ToSlash`—Takes a string representing a path and converts the separators to the correct value.
- `filepath.Split` and `filepath.SplitList`—Split a path into its parts or split a list of paths into individual paths. Again, the correct separators will be used.
- `filepath.Join`—Joins a list of parts into a path, using the correct separator for the operating system.

The go toolchain also has build tags that allow code files to be filtered, based on details such as operating system and architecture when being compiled. A build tag is at the start of a file and looks like this:

```
// +build !windows
```

This special comment tells the compiler to skip this file on Windows. Build tags (or build constants) can have multiple values. The following example skips building a file on Linux or macOS.

```
// +build !linux,!darwin
```

followed by a newline. These values are linked to GOOS and GOARCH options.

Go also provides the ability to name files in such a way that they're picked up for the different environments. `foo_windows.go` would be compiled and used for a Windows build, and `foo_386.go` would be used when compiling for the 386 (sometimes called x86) hardware architecture. These features enable applications to be written for multiple platforms while working around their differences and tapping into what makes them unique.

12.5 Performing runtime monitoring

Monitoring is a critical part of operating applications in production. It's typical to monitor running systems to find problems, to detect when the load has reached levels that require scaling up or down, or to understand what's going on within an application to speed it up.

The easiest way to monitor an application is to write errors, problems, and other details to a log. The log subsystem can write to disk and another application can read it or the log subsystem can push it out to a monitoring application.

Go applications include more than application code or code from libraries. The Go runtime sits in the background, handling the concurrency, garbage collection, threads, and other aspects of the application.

The runtime has access to a wealth of information. That includes the number of processors seen by the application, current number of goroutines, details on memory allocation and use, details on garbage collection, and more. This information can be useful for identifying problems within the application or triggering events such as horizontal scaling. As we did with file access, we could also generalize our logging process to store logs directly in the respective cloud provider's logging service.

- *Problem*—How can your application log or otherwise monitor the Go runtime?
- *Solution*—The `runtime` and `runtime/debug` packages provide access to the information within the runtime. Retrieve information from the runtime by using these packages and write it to the logs or other monitoring service at regular intervals.
- *Discussion*—Imagine that an imported library update includes a serious bug that causes the goroutines it created to stop going away. The goroutines slowly accumulate so that millions of them are being handled by the runtime when it should have been hundreds. Monitoring the runtime enables you to see when something like this happens.

When an application starts up, it can start a sidecar goroutine to monitor the runtime and write details of resource use to a log. Running in a goroutine allows you to run the monitoring and write to the logs concurrently, alongside the rest of the application, as the following listing shows.

Listing 12.13   Monitoring an application's runtime

```
func monitorRuntime() {
    log.Println("Number of CPUs:", runtime.NumCPU())
    m := &runtime.MemStats{}
    for {
        r := runtime.NumGoroutine()
        log.Println("Number of goroutines", r)
        runtime.ReadMemStats(m)
        log.Println("Allocated memory", m.Alloc)
        time.Sleep(10 * time.Second)
    }
}
func main() {
    go monitorRuntime()
    i := 0
    for i < 40 {
        go func() {
            time.Sleep(15 * time.Second)
        }()
        i = i + 1
        time.Sleep(1 * time.Second)
    }
}
```

A function to monitor the runtime

When monitoring starts, reports the number of processors available

Loops continuously, pausing for 10 seconds between iterations

Logs the number of goroutines and amount of allocated memory

Loops continuously, pausing for 10 seconds between iterations

When the application starts, begins monitoring the application

Creates example goroutines and memory use while the application runs for 40 seconds

It's important to know that calls to `runtime.ReadMemStats` momentarily halt the Go runtime, which can have a performance effect on your application. You don't want to do this often, and you may want to perform operations that halt the Go runtime only when in a debug mode.

Organizing your runtime monitoring this way allows you to replace writing to the log with interaction with an outside monitoring service. If you were using one of the services from a third-party monitoring service, you would send the runtime data to their API or invoke a library to do this. The runtime package has access to a wealth of information:

- Information on garbage collection, including when the last pass was, the heap size that will cause the next to trigger, how long the last garbage collection pass took, and more
- Heap statistics, such as the number of objects it includes, the heap size, how much of the heap is in use, and so on
- The number of goroutines, processors, and cgo calls

We've found that monitoring the runtime can provide unexpected knowledge and highlight bugs. It can help you find goroutine problems, memory leaks, or other problems. In the next chapter, you'll explore communicating between cloud services by using techniques other than REST APIs.

Summary

- We can work with various cloud providers while avoiding vendor lock-in.
- Go applications can be containerized with separated build and run steps.
- We can gather information about the host rather than assuming it.
- We can compile applications for varying operating systems and avoid operating system lock-in.
- We can reuse connections to improve performance by avoiding repeated TCP slow-start, congestion-control ramp-ups, and connection negotiations.
- If and when JSON marshaling and unmarshaling becomes a bottleneck, we have options in the form of third-party libraries to enable faster JSON processing.
- Monitoring the Go runtime detects problems and details about a running application.

Reflection, code generation, and advanced Go

- Using values, kinds, and types from Go's type reflection system
- Parsing custom struct annotations
- Working with other languages via C/C++ interoperability
- Writing code generators for use with the `go generate` tool

In chapter 12, we explored using Go in the context of tooling around deployment, looking at service communication and discovery. In this chapter, we turn our attention to some of Go's most interesting advanced features. We'll begin with Go's reflection system, which refers to a program's runtime ability to examine its own structure. Although Go's reflection subsystem isn't as versatile as Java's, it's still powerful.

Another feature that has enjoyed novel use is the annotation of structs. You'll see in the second part of the chapter how to write custom tags for struct fields. As useful as Go's reflection system is, though, it's sometimes cleaner to avoid complex and expensive runtime reflection and instead write code that itself writes code; this will be the third focus of the chapter. Finally, although Go now has generics, code generation has a niche role in developing in Go, and we will look at that in comparison with generics.

13.1   Three features of reflection

Software developers use reflection to examine objects during runtime. In a strongly typed language like Go, you may want to find out whether a particular object satisfies an interface, discover what its underlying kind is, or walk over its fields and modify the data—any task that might require more in-depth exploration of a type and its capabilities.

Go's reflection tools are located inside the `reflect` package. We've encountered them a few times earlier in this book. To understand those tools, we need to define a few terms. You need to understand three critical features when working with Go's reflection mechanism: values, types, and kinds.

You might approach the first term, *value*, by thinking of a variable and its underlying data. A *variable* is a name that points to a piece of data, as illustrated in figure 13.1. (The figure labels this "Variable name.") Depending on the type, the value may be `nil`; it may be a pointer, which in turn references a value somewhere else; or it may be a nonempty piece of data. With `x := 5`, for example, the value of x is 5. For `var b bytes.Buffer`, the value of b is an empty buffer. With `myFunc := strings.Split`, the value of `myFunc` is a function. In the `reflect` package, the type `reflect.Value` represents any of these values.

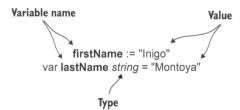

Figure 13.1   Variable and value declarations

As Go is a typed language, each value in Go has a single, specific type associated with it. With `var b bytes.Buffer`, that type is `bytes.Buffer`. For any possible `reflect.Value` in Go, you can discover its type. Type information is accessible through the `reflect.Type` interface.

Finally, Go defines numerous primitive kinds, such as struct, ptr (pointer), int, float64, string, slice, func (function), and so on. The `reflect` package enumerates all the possible kinds with the type `reflect.Kind`. (Note that in figure 13.1, the value of type `string` also has the kind `string`.)

The typical tasks you perform when working with reflection use these three concepts. Usually, reflection begins by taking a value and then inspecting it to learn about its contents, its type, and its kind. You can consider a broader description of what a type is comprised.

13.1.1 Switching based on type and kind

One of the most frequent uses of Go's reflection system is identifying either the type or kind of a value. Go has various tools for learning about the type and kind of a particular value.

- *Problem*—You want to write a function that takes generic values (`interface{}`s) and then does something useful with them based on underlying types.
- *Solution*—Go provides various methods for learning this information, ranging from the type switch to the `reflect.Type` and `reflect.Kind` types. Each has subtle strengths. Here, you'll look at type switches and then employ the `reflect` package to build a kind switch.
- *Discussion*—Suppose that you want to write a function with the signature `sum(...interface{}) float64`. You want this function to take a variadic argument of arbitrary types. You want it to convert the values to `float64` and then sum them.

  The most convenient tool that Go provides for doing this is the type switch. With this special case of the switch control structure, you can perform operations based on the type of a value, instead of the data contained in a value. As you read through common Go libraries, you'll frequently encounter type switches (though using kinds and switches, which you'll see later in this section, is rare). These also come up somewhat often inside generic functions, for obvious reasons. Let's start with a simple (though incomplete) example in the next listing.

Listing 13.1   Sum with type switch

```go
package main

import (
    "fmt"
    "strconv"
)

func main() {
    var a uint8 = 2
    var b int = 37
    var c string = "3.2"             Sums a uint8,
    res := sum(a, b, c)          ◁── an int, and a
    fmt.Printf("Result: %f\n", res)   string
}

func sum(v ...interface{}) float64 {
    var res float64 = 0.0
    for _, val := range v {          Loops through all the values given and
        switch val.(type) {          switches over them based on type
        case int:
            res += float64(val.(int))
        case int64:                      For each type that you
            res += float64(val.(int64))  support (int, int64, uint8,
        case uint8:                      string), converts to float64
            res += float64(val.(uint8))  and sum
```

```
        case string:
                a, err := strconv.ParseFloat
                (val.(string), 64)
                if err != nil {
                        panic(err)
                }
                res += a
        default:
                fmt.Printf("Unsupported type %T.
                Ignoring.\n", val)
        }
    }
    return res
}
```

For a string, you use the strconv library to convert the string to a float64.

If the type isn't one of the four you support, prints an error and ignores

If you were to run this code, you'd get `Result: 42.200000`. This code illustrates the basic use of a type switch, as well as one of its limitations compared to regular switches. If you had more non-numeric types, you might add some generic sugar, giving methods to various types:

```
type myString string

func (s myString) ToFloat() (float64, error) {
    fl, err := strconv.ParseFloat(string(s), 64)
    if err != nil {
        panic(err)
    }
    return fl, nil
}
```

In a standard `switch` statement, you might combine multiple values on a single case line: `case 1, 2, 3: println("Less than four")`. Combining types in a case statement introduces complications when assigning values, so typically a type switch has one type per line. If you were to support all of the integer types (int, int8, int16, int32, int64, uint, uint8, uint16, uint32, and uint64), you'd need 10 separate case clauses. Although writing similar logic for 10 kinds may feel like an inconvenience, it isn't a problem. But it's important to remember that type switches operate on types (not kinds). Let's add a new type to the preceding example, as shown in the following listing.

Listing 13.2   Type switch with extra type

```
package main

import (
    "fmt"
    "strconv"
)

type MyInt int64
func main() {
//…
    var d MyInt = 1
```

MyInt is an int64.

Creates a new MyInt and gives it the value 1

```go
    res := sum(a, b, c, d)
    fmt.Printf("Result: %f\n", res)
}

func sum(v ...interface{}) float64 {
    var res float64 = 0
    for _, val := range v {
        switch val.(type) {
        case int:
            res += float64(val.(int))
        case int64:
            res += float64(val.(int64))
        case uint8:
            res += float64(val.(uint8))
        case string:
            a, err := strconv.ParseFloat(val.(string), 64)
            if err != nil {
                panic(err)
            }
            res += a
        default:
            fmt.Printf("Unsupported type %T. Ignoring.\n", val)
        }
    }
    return res
}
```

This will not match for a MyInt.

This will catch the MyInt value.

Running this program generates the following output:

```
$ go run typekind.go
Unsupported type main.MyInt. Ignoring.
Result: 42.200000
```

The type of `var d` MyInt isn't int64; it's MyInt, which shadows int64. In the type switch, it matches the default clause instead of the int64 case. At times, this is precisely the behavior you'd desire. You want Go to assume that int64 might needed to be treated differently from MyInt. But for this case, it'd be better if `sum()` could tell what the underlying kind was and work from that instead.

The solution to this problem is to use the `reflect` package and work based on the broader kind instead of type. The first part of our example will be the same, but the `sum()` function is different, as shown in the next listing.

Listing 13.3   A kind switch

```go
package main

import (
    "fmt"
    "reflect"
    "strconv"
)

type MyInt int64
```

```go
func main() {
    var a uint8 = 2
    var b int = 37
    var c string = "3.2"
    var d MyInt = 1
    res := sum(a, b, c, d)
    fmt.Printf("Result: %f\n", res)
}

func sum(v ...interface{}) float64 {
    var res float64 = 0
    for _, val := range v {
        ref := reflect.ValueOf(val)
        switch ref.Kind() {
        case reflect.Int, reflect.Int64:
            res += float64(ref.Int())
        case reflect.Uint8:
            res += float64(ref.Uint())
        case reflect.String:
            a, err := strconv.ParseFloat
            (ref.String(), 64)
            if err != nil {
                panic(err)
            }
            res += a
        default:
            fmt.Printf("Unsupported type %T. Ignoring.\n", val)
        }
    }
    return res
}
```

Gets the reflect.Value of the variable

From the value, you can switch on the Kind().

reflect.Kind is a normal type, so you can switch on multiple values.

The reflect.Value type provides convenience functions for converting related subkinds to their biggest version (e.g., int, int8, int16...to int64).

In this revised version, you replace the type switch with a regular value-based switch, and you use the `reflect` package to take each `val interface{}` and get a `reflect` `.Value` describing it. One of the pieces of information you can learn from a `reflect` `.Value` is its underlying kind.

Another thing that the `reflect.Value` type gives you is a group of functions capable of converting related types to their largest representation. A `reflect.Value` with a uint8 or uint16 can be easily converted to the biggest unsigned integer type by using the `reflect.Value`'s `Uint()` method.

With these features, you can collapse an otherwise verbose type switch to a more concise kind-based switch. Instead of needing 10 cases for the integer types, you could accomplish the same feature with only 2 cases (1 for all the signed integers and 1 for the unsigned integers).

But types and kinds are distinct things. Here, you've produced two cases that perform approximately the same task. Summing numeric values can be more easily done by determining kinds. But sometimes, you're more concerned with specifics. As you've seen elsewhere in the book, type switches are excellent companions for error handling. You can use them to sort out different error types in much the same way that other languages use multiple catch statements in a try/catch block.

Later in this chapter, we return to examining types. In that case, you'll use the `reflect.Type` type to discover information about a struct. But before we get to that case, let's look at another common reflection task: determining whether a particular type implements an interface.

13.1.2 *Discovering whether a value implements an interface*

Go's type system is different from the inheritance-based methods of traditional object-oriented languages. Go uses composition instead of inheritance. A Go interface defines a pattern of methods that another type must have before it can be considered to implement that interface. A concrete and simple example might help here. The `fmt` package defines an interface called Stringer that describes a thing capable of representing itself as a string:

```
type Stringer interface {
        String() string
}
```

Any type that provides a `String()` method which takes no arguments and returns a string is ipso facto a `fmt.Stringer`.

- *Problem*—Given a particular type, you want to find out whether that type implements a defined interface.
- *Solution*—There are two ways to accomplish this. One is with a type assertion, and the other uses the `reflect` package. Use the one that best meets your needs.
- *Discussion*—Go's view of interfaces differs from that of object-oriented languages like Java. In Go, a thing isn't declared to fulfill an interface. Instead, an interface is a description against which a type can be compared. Interfaces are themselves types. That is why when you write types in Go, you don't declare which interfaces they satisfy. As you saw in chapter 4, it's common to write interfaces to match existing code.

  In Go, types express commonality, not inheritance. Go makes it easy to determine whether a given interface matches another interface type. Answering this question can be done at the same time as converting that type, as shown in the next listing.

Listing 13.4   Checking and converting a type

```
package main

import (
        "bytes"
        "fmt"
)

func main() {
        b := bytes.NewBuffer([]byte("Hello"))
```

```
        if isStringer(b) {                          Tests whether a *bytes.Buffer
                fmt.Printf("%T is a stringer\n", b)  is a fmt.Stringer. It is.
        }
        i := 123
        if isStringer(i) {                          Tests whether an integer is
                fmt.Printf("%T is a stringer\n", i)  a fmt.Stringer. It's not.
        }
}

func isStringer(v interface{}) bool {    Takes an interface{} value and runs a
        _, ok := v.(fmt.Stringer)        type assertion to the desired interface
        return ok
}
```

Type assertions are one way of testing whether a given value implements an interface. But what if you want to test whether a type implements an interface but determine which interface at runtime? To accomplish this, you need to use the `reflect` package and little bit of trickery.

Earlier in the chapter, you looked at the basic types in the `reflect` package. An astute reader might have noticed something missing. Go's `reflection` package has no `reflect.Interface` type. Instead, `reflect.Type` (which is itself an interface) provides tools for querying whether a given type implements a given interface type. To reflect on an interface type at runtime, you can use `reflect.Type`, as in the following listing.

Listing 13.5 Determining whether a type implements an interface

```
package main

import (                              Creates a Name type and
        "fmt"                         gives it a String() method,
        "io"                          then instantiates one
        "reflect"
)

type Name struct {                    Creates a nil pointer
        First, Last string            of type fmt.Stringer
}
                                      Tests whether n is a
                                      fmt.Stringer (has a
func (n *Name) String() string {      String() method)
        return n.First + " " + n.Last
}                                     Creates a nil pointer
                                      of type io.Writer
func main() {
        n := &Name{First: "Inigo", Last: "Montoya"}
        stringer := (*fmt.Stringer)(nil)            Tests whether n is
        implements(n, stringer)                     an io.Writer (has a
        writer := (*io.Writer)(nil)                 Write() method)
        implements(n, writer)
}                                                   Gets a reflect.Type
                                                    that describes the
func implements(concrete interface{}, target interface{}) bool {  target of the
        iface := reflect.TypeOf(target).Elem()      pointer
```

```
    v := reflect.ValueOf(concrete)
    t := v.Type()                              Gets the reflect.Type of the concrete type passed in
    if t.Implements(iface) {
        fmt.Printf("%T is a %s\n", concrete, iface.Name())      Tests whether
        return true                                             the concrete
    }                                                           instance fulfills
    fmt.Printf("%T is not a %s\n", concrete, iface.Name())       the interface
    return false                                                of the target
}
```

This example takes what may appear to be a roundabout method. The `implements()` function takes two values. It tests whether the first value (concrete) implements the interface of the second (target). If you were to run this code, you'd get the following output:

```
$ go run implements.go
*main.Name is a Stringer
*main.Name is not a Writer
```

Our `Name` type implements `fmt.Stringer` because it has a `String() string` method. But it doesn't implement `io.Writer` because it doesn't have a `Write([]bytes) (int, error)` method.

The `implements()` function does assume that the target is a pointer to a value whose dynamic type is an interface of some kind. With a few dozen lines, you could check that by reflecting on the value and checking that it's a pointer. As it stands now, it'd be possible to cause `implements()` to panic by passing a target that doesn't match that description.

To get to the point where you can test whether concrete implements the target interface, you need to get the `reflect.Type` of both the concrete and the target. There are two ways of doing this. The first uses `reflect.TypeOf()` to get a `reflect.Type` and a call to `Type.Elem()` to get the type that the target pointer points to:

```
iface := reflect.TypeOf(target).Elem()
```

The second gets the value of concrete and then gets the `reflect.Type` of that value. From there, you can test whether a thing of one type implements an interface type using the `Type.Interface()` method:

```
v := reflect.ValueOf(concrete)
t := v.Type()
```

The trickier part of this test, though, is getting a reference to an interface. There's no way to directly reflect on an interface type. Interfaces don't work that way; you can't just instantiate one or reference it directly. Instead, you need to find a way to create a placeholder that implements an interface. The simplest way is to do something we usually recommend studiously avoiding: intentionally create a nil pointer. In the preceding code, you create two nil pointers, and you do so like this: `stringer :=` `(*fmt.Stringer)(nil)`. In essence, you do this to create a thing whose only useful information is its type. When you pass these into the `implements()` function, it'll be able to reflect on the nil pointers and determine the type. You need the `Elem()` call to get the type of the nil.

The code in listing 13.5 illustrates how working with Go's reflection system can require thinking creatively about how to set up various reflection operations. Tasks that might seem superficially simple may require some thoughtful manipulation of the type system.

13.1.3 Accessing fields on a struct

Go structs are the most commonly used tool for describing structured data in Go. Because Go can glean all the important information about a struct's contents during compilation, structs are efficient. At runtime, you may want to find out information about a struct, including what its fields are and whether particular values of a struct have been set.

- *Problem*—You want to learn about a struct at runtime, discovering its fields.
- *Solution*—Reflect the struct and use a combination of `reflect.Value` and `reflect.Type` to find out information about the struct.
- *Discussion*—In the previous techniques, you've seen how to start with a value and reflect on it to get information about its value, its kind, and its type. Now you're going to combine these techniques to walk a struct and learn about it.

The tool you'll create is a simple program that can read a value and print information about it to the console. The principles will come in handy, though, in the next section, where you'll use some similar techniques to work with Go's annotation system. Let's start with a few initial types to examine in the following listing.

Listing 13.6 Types to examine

```
package main

import (
    "fmt"
    "reflect"
    "strings"
)

type MyInt int
type Person struct {
    Name    *Name
    Address *Address
}
type Name struct {
    Title, First, Last string
}
type Address struct {
    Street, Region string
}
```

Now you have an integer-based type and a few structs. The next thing to do is add some code to inspect these types, as shown in the next listing.

Listing 13.7 Recursively examining a value

```go
func main() {
    fmt.Println("Walking a simple integer")
    var one MyInt = 1
    walk(one, 0)
    fmt.Println("Walking a simple struct")
    two := struct{ Name string }{"foo"}
    walk(two, 0)
fmt.Println("Walking a struct with struct fields")
    p := &Person{
        Name:    &Name{"Count", "Tyrone", "Rugen"
        },
        Address: &Address{"Humperdink Castle",
        "Florian"},
    }
    walk(p, 0)
}
type MyInt int
type Person struct {
    Name    *Name
    Address *Address
}
type Name struct {
    Title, First, Last string
}
type Address struct {
    Street, Region string
}
func walk(u interface{}, depth int) {
    val := reflect.Indirect(reflect.ValueOf(u))
    t := val.Type()
    tabs := strings.Repeat("\t", depth+1)
    fmt.Printf("%sValue is type %q (%s)\n", tabs, t, val.Kind())
    if val.Kind() == reflect.Struct {
        for i := 0; i < t.NumField(); i++ {
            field := t.Field(i)
            fieldVal := reflect.Indirect
            (val.Field(i))
            tabs := strings.Repeat("\t", depth+2)
            fmt.Printf("%sField %q is type %q (%s)\n",
                tabs, field.Name, field.Type, fieldVal.Kind())
            if fieldVal.Kind() ==
            reflect.Struct {
                walk(fieldVal.Interface(), depth+1)
            }
        }
    }
}
```

Shows details for a simple type

Shows details for a simple struct

Shows details for a struct with struct fields

The walk() function takes any value and a depth (for formatting).

For your unknown value u, you get the reflect.Value. If it's a pointer, you dereference the pointer.

Gets the type of this value

Depth helps you do some tab indenting for prettier output.

If the kind is a struct, you examine its fields.

For each field, you need both the reflect.StructField and the reflect.Value.

If the field is also a struct, you can recursively call walk().

The preceding example combines just about everything you've learned about reflection. The depth in this case is just visual sugar for showing hierarchy. Types, values, and kinds all come into play as you walk through a value and examine its reflection data. If you run this little program, the output looks like this:

```
$ go run structwalker.go
```

Walking a simple integer looks like this:

```
Value is type "main.MyInt" (int)
```

Walking a simple struct looks like this:

```
Value is type "struct { Name string }" (struct)
        Field "Name" is type "string" (string)
```

Walking a struct with struct fields looks like this:

```
Value is type "main.Person" (struct)
        Field "Name" is type "*main.Name" (struct)
        Value is type "main.Name" (struct)
                Field "Title" is type "string" (string)
                Field "First" is type "string" (string)
                Field "Last" is type "string" (string)
        Field "Address" is type "*main.Address" (struct)
        Value is type "main.Address" (struct)
                Field "Street" is type "string" (string)
                Field "Region" is type "string" (string)
```

In this output, you can see the program examine each of the values you've given it. First, it checks a MyInt value (of kind int). Then it walks the simple struct. Finally, it walks the more complex struct and recurses down through the struct until it hits only nonstruct kinds.

The walk() function does all the interesting work for type/kind detection and output in this program. It begins with an unknown value, u, and inspects it. While you're walking through an unknown value, you want to make sure that you follow pointers. If reflect.ValueOf() is called on a pointer, it will return a reflect.Value describing a pointer. That isn't interesting in this case, although you might want to annotate that in some way in a real=world application. Instead, what you want is the value at the other end of that pointer, so you use reflect.Indirect() to get the reflect.Value describing the value pointed to. The reflect.Indirect() method is useful in that if it's called on a value that's not a pointer, it will return the given reflect.Value, so you can safely call it on all values:

```
val := reflect.Indirect(reflect.ValueOf(u))
```

Along with the value of u, you need some type and kind information. In this example, you get each of the three reflection types:

- The value (in this case, if you get a pointer for a value, you follow the pointer)
- The type
- The kind

Kinds are particularly interesting in this case. Some kinds—notably slices, arrays, maps, and structs—may have members. In this case, you're interested mainly in learning about the structure of your given value (u). Although you wouldn't need to enumerate the values in maps, slices, or arrays as they're just fundamentally basic type values, you'd like to examine structs. If the kind is `reflect.Struct`, you take a look at that struct's fields.

The easiest way to enumerate the fields of a struct is to get the type of that struct and then loop through the fields of that type by using a combination of `Type.NumField()` (which gives you the count of fields in the struct) and `Type.Field()`. The `Type.Field()` method returns a `reflect.StructField` object describing the field. From there, you can learn about the field's data type and its name.

When it comes to getting the value of a struct field, you can't get this from either the `reflect.Type` (which describes the data type) or the `reflect.StructField` (which describes the field on a struct type). Instead, you need to get the value from the `reflect.Value`, which describes that struct's value. Fortunately, you can combine your knowledge of the type and the value to know that the numeric index of the type field will match the numeric index of the value's struct field. You can use `Value.Field()` with the same field number as `Type.Field()` and get the associated value for that field. Again, if the field is a pointer, you'd rather have a handle to the value at the other end of the pointer, so you would call `reflect.Indirect()` on that field's pointer value. If you take a look at the output of the preceding program, you'll see this in action:

```
Field "Name" is type "*main.Name" (struct)
Value is type "main.Name" (struct)
```

The field Name is of type `*main.Name`. But when you follow the pointer, you get a value of type `main.Name`. This little program is dense, so to summarize what's happening:

- From `interface{}`, you can use `reflect.ValueOf()` to get `reflect.Value`.
- In cases where the value might be a pointer, to get the `reflect.Value` of the object pointed to, you call `reflect.Indirect()`.
- From `reflect.Value`, you can conveniently get the type and kind.
- For structs (of the kind `reflect.Struct`), you can get the number of fields on that struct by using `Type.NumField()`, and you can get a description of each field (`reflect.StructField`) by using `Type.Field()`.
- Likewise, with `reflect.Value` objects, you can access struct field values by using `Value.Field()`.

The `reflect` package also contains tools for learning about the methods on a struct, the elements in maps, lists, and arrays, and even information about what a channel can send or receive. A few of the most interesting tools include

- `MethodByName(name string)`—Returns a method and a Boolean indicating whether the method was found for a type
- `AssignableTo(theType Type)`—Returns whether a type can be assigned to another without type coercion
- `Comparable()`—Returns whether or not the type's values are comparable

For all of Go's elegance, though, the package can be difficult to learn and unforgiving to use: many of the functions and methods in that package will panic rather than return errors. In this case, it's best to lean on the panic recovery methods we looked at in chapter 4.

The example you've looked at here sets the stage for using one of our favorite Go features. Next, you'll look at Go's annotation system, which we briefly looked at in chapter 10 while discussing embedding files in a binary. Although there are many uses for tags in and outside the standard library, you'll see how to build and access your own struct tags.

13.2 Structs, tags, and annotations

Go has no macros, and unlike languages such as Java and Python, Go has only spartan support for annotations. But structs are one of the areas where tags are most frequently used. You've already seen this practice for providing JSON processing information, particularly in chapter 3. In this section, we'll look at more tag annotations for data validation.

13.2.1 Annotating structs

In previous chapters, you saw examples of using struct annotations with things like the JSON encoder, which are used to append final JSON tags to the output. You can begin with the struct from listing 13.5 and annotate it for the JSON encoder, as shown in the following listing.

> **Listing 13.8 Simple JSON struct**

```
package main

import (
    "encoding/json"
    "fmt"
)

type Name struct {
    First string `json:"firstName"`      Annotates struct fields for
    Last  string `json:"lastName "`      JSON encoding and decoding
}

func main() {
    n := &Name{"Inigo", "Montoya"}
    data, _ := json.Marshal(n)           Marshals n to JSON
    fmt.Printf("%s\n", data)B            and prints it
}
```

This code declares a single struct, Name, that's annotated for JSON encoding. Roughly speaking, it maps the struct member First to the JSON field firstName and the struct field Last to lastName. This is a very common usage because by convention JSON tags rarely include uppercase characters, but Go needs titleCase for public/private visibility of fields. If you were to run this code, the output would look like this:

```
$ go run json.go
{"firstName":"Inigo","lastName":"Montoya"}
```

The struct annotations make it possible to control how your JSON looks. Struct tags provide a convenient way to provide small bits of processing data to fields on a struct. Practically speaking, annotations are a freeform string enclosed in back quotes that follows the type declaration of a struct field.

Annotations play no direct functional role during compilation but can be accessed at runtime by using reflection. It's up to the annotation parsers to figure out whether any given annotation has information that the parser can use. You could modify the preceding code to include different annotations, as shown in the next listing.

Listing 13.9   A variety of annotations

```
type Name struct {
    First string `json:"firstName" xml:"FirstName"`
    Last  string `json:"lastName,omitempty"`
    Other string `not,even.a=tag`
}
```

All these annotations are legal in the sense that the Go parser will handle them correctly, and the JSON encoder will be able to pick out which of those applies to it. It will ignore the xml tag as well as the oddly formatted annotation on the Other field.

As you can see from the tags in listing 13.9, an annotation has no fixed format. Just about any string can be used. But a certain annotation format has emerged in the Go community and is now a de facto standard. Go developers call these annotations tags.

13.2.2 *Using tag annotations*

The sample JSON struct you looked at earlier contained annotations of the form `json: "NAME,DATA"`, where NAME is the name of the field (in JSON documents) and DATA is a list of optional information about the field (omitempty or kind data). Figure 13.2 shows an example of a struct annotated for both JSON and XML.

Annotations for validation

One of the most interesting uses for annotations that we've seen is for validating field data on a struct. By adding regular expressions in tags (`validate:"^[a-z]+$"`) and then writing code to run those regular expressions over struct data, you can write validation code easily and concisely. This could allow you to create very specific checks against what data can go into a struct.

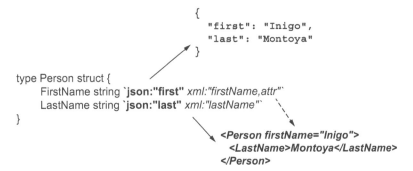

Figure 13.2   A struct marshaled to JSON and to XML

As with the `encoding/json` package, if you look at the `encoding/xml` package, you'll see a pattern similar to annotations for converting structs to and from XML. Tags for XML look like this: `` `xml:"body"` `` and `` `xml:"href,attr"` ``. Again, the pattern is similar to the JSON tag pattern `` `xml:"NAME,DATA"` ``, where NAME is the field name and DATA contains a list of information about the field (though XML annotations are more sophisticated than JSON annotations).

This format isn't enshrined in the definition of a struct annotation, though. You can use these tags any way you see fit in your own code. It's just a convention that has proved useful and thus enjoys widespread adoption. Go's reflection package even makes it easy to work with tags, as you'll see shortly.

13.2.3 Processing tags on a struct

Annotations can be useful in a wide variety of situations. The preceding examples show how they can be used by data encoders. Annotations can just as readily be used to describe how database field types map to structs or how to format data for display. We've even seen cases in which annotations were used to tell Go to pass struct values through other filtering functions. Because the annotation format is not rigidly defined, to build your annotations, you need only decide on a format and then write an implementation.

- *Problem*—You want to create your own annotations and then programmatically access the annotation data of a struct at runtime.
- *Solution*—Define your annotation format (preferably using the taglike syntax described previously). Then use the `reflect` package to write a tool that extracts the annotation information from a struct.
- *Discussion*—Suppose that you want to write an encoder for a simple file syntax for name-value pairs. This format is similar to the old INI format. An example of this file format looks like this:

```
total=247
running=2
sleeping=245
```

```
threads=1189
load=70.87
```

Here, the names are on the left side of the equal sign, and the values are on the right. Now imagine that you want to create a struct to represent this data. It looks like the following listing.

Listing 13.10   A bare `Processes` struct

```
type Processes struct {
    Total    int
    Running  int
    Sleeping int
    Threads  int
    Load     float32
}
```

To convert the plain file format into a struct like this, you can create a tag that fits your needs and then mark up your struct with them (see the following listing).

Listing 13.11   The `Processes` struct with annotations

```
type Processes struct {
    Total    int     `ini:"total"`
    Running  int     `ini:"running"`
    Sleeping int     `ini:"sleeping"`
    Threads  int     `ini:"threads"`
    Load     float32 `ini:"load"`
}
```

This tag structure follows the same convention as the JSON and XML tags you saw earlier. But there's no automatic facility in Go to handle parsing the file format and learning from the struct annotations how to populate a `Processes` struct. You'll do that work yourself.

As you design this, you can once again rely on existing conventions. Encoders and decoders in Go tend to provide `Marshal()` and `Unmarshal()` methods with a fairly predictable set of parameters and return values, so your INI file decoder will implement the same pattern, as shown in the following listing.

Listing 13.12   The `Marshal` and `Unmarshal` patterns

```
func Marshal(v interface{}) ([]byte, error) {}
func Unmarshal(data []byte, v interface{}) error {}
```

The bulk of both of these functions involves reflecting over the `interface{}` values and learning how to extract data from or populate data into those values. To keep the code concise, the following example deals only with marshaling and unmarshaling structs.

Reflection tends to be a little verbose, so you'll split the code for your program into smaller chunks, starting with a struct for your INI file and the `main()` function. In the first part, you'll create a new type (`Processes`) and then in the `main()` function a `Processes` struct, marshal it to your INI format, and then unmarshal it into a new `Processes` struct. See the next listing.

Listing 13.13 `Processes` and `main`

```
package main

import (                          ◁─┐  Most of these imports
    "bufio"                         │  are used later.
    "bytes"
    "errors"
    "fmt"
    "reflect"
    "strconv"
    "strings"
)                                      ┐  You saw this
                                       │  struct in
type Processes struct {           ◁────┘  listing 13.11.
    Total    int     `ini:"total"`
    Running  int     `ini:"running"`
    Sleeping int     `ini:"sleeping"`
    Threads  int     `ini:"threads"`
    Load     float64 `ini:"load"`
}

func main() {
    fmt.Println("Write a struct to output:")
    proc := &Processes{
        Total:    23,
        Running:  3,              Creates an
        Sleeping: 20,             instance of the
        Threads:  34,             Processes struct
        Load:     1.8,
    }
    data, err := Marshal(proc)    ◁──  Marshals the struct
    if err != nil {                    into a byte slice
        panic(err)
    }
    fmt.Println(string(data))                  ◁─┘  Prints the result
    fmt.Println("Read the data back into a struct")
    proc2 := &Processes{}                         ┐  Creates a new Processes
    if err := Unmarshal(data, proc2); err != nil {│  struct and unmarshals
        panic(err)                                │  the data into it
    }
    fmt.Printf("Struct: %#v", proc2)   ◁──  Prints out the struct
}
```

The top-level code is straightforward. You begin with an instance of your `Processes` struct and then marshal it into a byte array. When you print the results, they'll be in your INI file format. Then you take that same data and run it back through the other direction, expanding the INI data into a new `Processes` struct. Running the program produces output like this:

```
$ go run load.go
```

Write a struct to output:

```
total=23
running=3
sleeping=20
threads=34
load=1.8
Read the data back into a struct
Struct: &main.Processes{Total:23, Running:3, Sleeping:20, Threads:34, Load
:1.8}
```

The first section of output shows your marshaled data, and the second shows your unmarshaled struct. Next, you can look at the `Marshal()` function, which brings much of your reflection knowledge back to the forefront. See the following listing.

Listing 13.14   The `Marshal` function

```
func fieldName(field reflect.StructField) string {          ◀─┐  Simple utility function to
    if t := field.Tag.Get("ini"); t != "" {                    │  read tags from struct fields
        return t                                    Gets the tag off the struct field
    }
    return field.Name          ◀─┤ If there is no tag, falls
}                                 │ back to the field name
                                                               Gets a reflect.Value of
                                                               the current interface and
func Marshal(v interface{}) ([]byte, error) {                  dereferences pointers
    var b bytes.Buffer
    val := reflect.Indirect(reflect.ValueOf(v))    ◀─┐  For this program, you
    if val.Kind() != reflect.Struct {                 │  handle only structs.
        return []byte{}, errors.New("unmarshal can only take structs")
    }
    t := val.Type()                          ┌── Loops through all the
    for i := 0; i < t.NumField(); i++ {    ◀─┘   fields on the struct
        f := t.Field(i)
        name := fieldName(f)          ◀─┤ Gets the name
        raw := val.Field(i).Interface()  │ from tagName
        fmt.Fprintf(&b, "%s=%v\n", name, raw)    ◀─┐ Relies on the print
    }                                              formatter to print the
    return b.Bytes(), nil      ◀─┤ Returns the contents   raw data into the buffer
}                                │ of the buffer
```

This `Marshal()` function takes the given `v interface{}` and reads through its fields. By examining the type, it can iterate through all the fields on the struct, and for each field, it can access the annotation (via `StructField.Tag()`). As it loops through the struct fields, it can also fetch the relevant values for each struct field. Rather than manually convert these values from their native type to a string, you rely on `fmt.Fprintf()` to do that work for you.

Of note, the `fieldName()` function uses Go's automatic tag parsing. Although you can (if you desire) store any string data in an annotation, Go can parse tags for you. For any annotation tag that follows the format `NAME:"VALUE"`, you can access the value by using `StructField.Tag.Get()`. It returns the value unprocessed. It's a common idiom for tag values to contain a comma-separated list of params (`json:"myField,omitempty"`). For our simple tags, though, you allow only a single field in the `VALUE` space. Finally, if you don't get any tag data for the field, you return the struct field's name.

> ### Ignoring struct fields with annotations
> Sometimes, you want to tell encoders to ignore fields on a struct. The common idiom for doing this is to use a dash (-) in the name field of the annotation (`json:"-"`). Although we don't support this in the preceding code, you could extend the example to ignore fields whose name is -.

This `Marshal()` function isn't particularly robust. It will read only structs as it is. Maps, which could just as easily be converted to INI fields, aren't supported. Likewise, your `Marshal()` function is going to work well only on certain data types. It won't, for example, produce useful results for fields whose values are structs, channels, maps, slices, or arrays. Although those operations require lots switch code or generics, there's nothing particularly daunting about extending this `Marshal()` function to support a broader array of types.

In the next listing, you look at the process of taking an existing bit of INI data and turning it into a struct. Again, this uses annotations and the reflection subsystem.

Listing 13.15 The `Unmarshal` function

```
func Unmarshal(data []byte, v interface{}) error {
    val := reflect.Indirect(reflect.ValueOf(v))       ←─ Again, you begin with a
    t := val.Type()                                       (dereferenced) reflect.Value.
    b := bytes.NewBuffer(data)
    scanner := bufio.NewScanner(b)
    for scanner.Scan() {                               From data, you use a scanner to
        line := scanner.Text()                         read one line of INI data at a time.
        pair := strings.SplitN(line, "=", 2)       ←─ Splits a line at
        if len(pair) < 2 {                                the equal sign
            // Skip any malformed lines.
            continue
        }
        setField(pair[0], pair[1], t, val)         ←─ Passes the task of
    }                                                     setting the value
    return nil                                            to setField()
}
```

The `Unmarshal()` function reads `[]byte` and tries to convert the fields it finds there into matching fields on the supplied `v interface{}`. This INI parser is trivially simple: it iterates through the lines of the file and splits name-value pairs. But when it comes time to populate the given struct with the newly loaded values, you still have to do a fair amount of work.

The `unmarshal()` function relies heavily on the `setField()` helper, which uses most of the reflection strategies you've seen in this chapter. Again, you're going to switch on kinds, which makes for verbose code. See the next listing.

Listing 13.16   The `setField` helper function

Iterates through each field on the struct, looking for one whose name matches the INI field's name

setField takes the name and value from the INI data, and also the type and value of the struct itself.

Uses a kind switch to figure out how to take your value string and convert it to the right type

If you don't know about the kind, just skip the field, as this isn't an error.

This version supports only a few kinds of values. Supporting other types is usually easy, but requires highly repetitive code blocks.

Once a raw value is converted to its type, wraps it in a value

```go
func setField(name, value string, t reflect.Type,
v reflect.Value) {
    for i := 0; i < t.NumField(); i++ {
        field := t.Field(i)
        if name == fieldName(field) {
            var dest reflect.Value
            switch field.Type.Kind() {
            default:
                fmt.Printf("Kind %s not supported.\n",
field.Type.Kind())
                continue
            case reflect.Int:
                ival, err := strconv.Atoi(value)
                if err != nil {
                    fmt.Printf(
                        "Could not convert %q to int: %s\n",
                        value, err)
                    continue
                }
                dest = reflect.ValueOf(ival)
            case reflect.Float64:
                fval, err := strconv.ParseFloat(value, 64)
                if err != nil {
                    fmt.Printf(
                        "Could not convert %q to float64: %s\n",
                        value, err)
                    continue
                }
                dest = reflect.ValueOf(fval)
            case reflect.String:
                dest = reflect.ValueOf(value)
            case reflect.Bool:
                bval, err := strconv.ParseBool(value)
                if err != nil {
                    fmt.Printf(
```

```
                                    "Could not convert %q to bool: %s\n",
                                    value, err)
                                continue
                        }
                        dest = reflect.ValueOf(bval)
                    }
                    v.Field(i).Set(dest)        ◁─────  Sets the value
                }                                       for the relevant
            }                                           struct field
        }
```

The `setField()` function takes the raw name-value pair, as well as the `reflect.Value` and `reflect.Type` of the struct, and attempts to match the pair to its appropriate field on the struct. (Again, you restrict the tool to working only with structs, though you could extend it to work with map types.) Finding the matching field name is relatively easy because you can reuse the `fieldName()` function defined in listing 13.14. But when it comes to the value, you need to convert the data from the string form you were given to whatever the data type of the struct field is. For the sake of space, the code in listing 13.14 handles only a few data types (int, float64, string, and bool). And you didn't explore types that extend from your base kinds. But the pattern illustrated here could be extended to handle other types. Finally, you store the newly converted value on the struct by first wrapping it in `reflect.Value()` and then setting the appropriate struct field.

One thing becomes clear while examining the code written for this technique: because of Go's strong type system, converting between types often takes a lot of boiler-plate code. Sometimes, you can take advantage of built-in tools (such as `fmt.Fprintf()`). Other times, you must write tedious code. Instead of writing reflection code, you might find it useful to use Go's generator tool to generate source code for you. In the next section, you'll look at one example of writing a generator to do work that would otherwise require runtime type checking and detailed reflection code.

13.3 Generating Go code with Go code

Prior to generics, creating methods for types was arduous and required a lot of code duplication or reliance on reflection and type switching, which we just explored. It's worth mentioning that the runtime cost of reflection is high, adding up to real latency and overhead if you use it a lot in your programs. Generics should be used when necessary, but there exists a more performant way of creating code. As mentioned before, Go doesn't support macros, and annotations have only limited capabilities. Is there another way to transform code? How do you metaprogram in Go? Along with reflection and code duplication, there's another common approach to generating code in instances where generics aren't applicable.

An often-overlooked feature of Go is its capability to generate code. Go ships with a tool, `go generate`, designed exactly for this purpose. In fact, metaprogramming with generators is a powerful answer to the preceding questions. Generated code (which is then compiled) is much faster at runtime than reflection-based code. It's also usually much simpler. For generating a large number of repetitive but type-safe objects, generators can ease your development lifecycle. Although many programmers turn a jaundiced eye toward metaprogramming, the fact of the matter is that we use code generators frequently. As you saw in chapter 12, Protobuf, gRPC, and Thrift use generators. Many SQL libraries are generators. Some languages even use generators behind the scenes for macros, generics, and collections. In fact, prior to generics support in Go, generation was often the prescribed approach. The nice thing about Go is that it provides powerful generator tools right out of the box.

At the root of Go's embracing of code generation is a simple tool called go generate. Like other Go tools, go generate is aware of the Go environment, and can be run on files and packages. Conceptually speaking, it's shockingly simple.

The tool walks through the files you've specified, and looks at the first line of each file. If it finds a particular pattern, it executes a program. The pattern looks like this:

```
//go:generate COMMAND [ARGUMENT...]
```

The generator looks for this comment right at the top of each Go file that you tell it to search. If it doesn't find a header, it skips the file. If it does find the header, it executes the COMMAND. The COMMAND can be any command-line tool that the generator can find and run. You can pass any number of arguments to the command. Let's build a trivially simple example in the next listing.

Listing 13.17   A trivial generator

```
//go:generate echo hello
package main

func main() {
    println("Goodbyte")
}
```

This is obviously valid Go code, but with generation it operates a little differently than with a run or build command. If you compiled and ran it, it would print Goodbyte to the console. But it has a generator on the first line. The generator's command is echo, which is a UNIX command that prints a string back to standard out. It has one argument, the string hello. Let's run the generator and see what it does:

```
$ go generate simple.go
hello
```

All the generator does is execute the command, which prints hello to the console. Although this implementation is nearly the simplest you can think of, the idea is that you can add commands that generate code for you. You'll see this in action in the next technique.

Writing custom type-safe collections, generating structs from database tables, transforming JSON schemata into code, and generating many similar objects are some of the things we've seen developers use Go generators for. Sometimes, Go developers use the Abstract Syntax Tree (AST) package or `yacc` tool to generate Go code. Go itself comes with `parser` and `text/scanner` packages in the standard library. But we've found that one fun and easy way to build code is to write Go templates that generate Go code.

- *Problem*—You want to be able to create type-specific collections, such as a queue, for an arbitrary number of types. You'd like to do it without the runtime safety problems and performance hit associated with type assertions. If you have a lot of types you want to capture, using code generation reduces a lot of boilerplate, even if you use generics.
- *Solution*—Build a generator that can create queues for you and then use generation headers to generate the queues as you need them.
- *Discussion*—A queue is a simple data structure; you push data onto the front and dequeue data off the back. The first value into the queue is the first value out (first in, first out, or FIFO). Usually, queues have two methods: insert (or enqueue) to push data onto the back of the queue, and remove (or dequeue) to get the value at the front of the queue.

  If you recall our implementations of generics in chapter 3, you may have noted the amount of manual code duplication this sometimes requires. This can be optimized in some cases by using code generation.

You want to be able to automatically generate queues that are specific to the types you want to store in the queues. You want queues that follow a pattern like the next listing.

Listing 13.18   Simple queue

```go
package main

type MyTypeQueue struct {          // A simple queue backed
    q []MyType                     // by a typed slice
}

func NewMyTypeQueue() *MyTypeQueue {
    return &MyTypeQueue{
        q: []MyType{},
    }
}

func (o *MyTypeQueue) Insert(v MyType) {      // Adds an item
    o.q = append(o.q, v)                      // to the back of
}                                             // the queue

func (o *MyTypeQueue) Remove() MyType {       // Removes an item from
    if len(o.q) == 0 {                        // the front of the queue
        panic("Oops.")     // In production code, you'd
    }                      // replace the panic with an error.
    first := o.q[0]        // We simplify here to keep the
    o.q = o.q[1:]          // generator code smaller.
    return first
}
```

This code is a good representation of what you want to have generated for you but for a single type. There are certain bits of information that you want to be filled in at generation time. The obvious example is the type. But you also want the package name to be filled out automatically. Your next step, then, is to translate the preceding code into a Go template. The next listing shows the beginning of your queue generator tool.

Listing 13.19   The queue template

```
package main

import (
    "fmt"
    "os"
    "strings"
    "text/template"
)

var tpl = `package {{.Package}}          ◁─── .Package is your package placeholder
type {{.MyType}}Queue struct {         ◁─── .MyType is your type placeholder
    q []{{.MyType}}
}

func New{{.MyType}}Queue() *{{.MyType}}Queue {
    return &{{.MyType}}Queue{
        q: []{{.MyType}}{},
    }
}

func (o *{{.MyType}}Queue) Insert(v {{.MyType}}) {
    o.q = append(o.q, v)
}

func (o *{{.MyType}}Queue) Remove() {{.MyType}} {
    if len(o.q) == 0 {
        panic("Oops.")
    }
    first := o.q[0]
    o.q = o.q[1:]
    return first
}
```

Your template is almost the same as the target code you wrote previously but with the package name replaced with `{{.Package}}` and the MyType prefix replaced with a `{{.MyType}}` variable. From here, you need to write the code that performs the generation. This is a command-line tool designed to fit the `//go:generate COMMAND ARGUMENT...` pattern. Ideally, what you'd like is to be able to write something like this:

```
//go:generate queue MyInt
```

As a result, the generator would generate a MyIntQueue implementation. It'd be even nicer if you could generate queues for multiple types at once:

```
//go:generate queue MyInt MyFloat64
```

You should be able to easily accommodate that, too, as shown in the next listing.

Listing 13.20 The main queue generator

```
func main() {
    tt := template.Must(template.New("queue").Parse(tpl))    ⟵  Compiles the
                                                                 generator template
    for i := 1; i < len(os.Args); i++ {         ⟵  Loops through the args,
        dest := strings.ToLower(os.Args[i]) +       making a file named
        "_queue.go"                             ⟵  TYPE_queue.go for each
        file, err := os.Create(dest)
        if err != nil {
            fmt.Printf("Could not create %s: %s (skip)\n",
            dest, err)
            continue                         ⟵  Sets .MyType to the type specified
        }                                       in the passed-in argument
        vals := map[string]string{
            "MyType":  os.Args[i],           ⟵  Sets .Package to the
            "Package": os.Getenv("GOPACKAGE"),  ⟵  value of the environment
        }                                       variable $GOPACKAGE
        tt.Execute(file, vals)       ⟵
                                         Executes the template,
        file.Close()                 ⟵  sending the results to the file
    }

}
```

Because you want to accept multiple types at the command line, you start out by looping through os.Args. For each one, you automatically generate an output file with the name TYPE_queue.go, though to be consistent with the Go file-naming conventions, you should lowercase the type name.

Your template had only two variables. One is the Go type that you want to handle. But the other is the package. One nice thing that the go generate command does for you is populate a few environment variables with useful information about the location of the generator file. The $GOPACKAGE environment variable is set to the name of the package where the go:generate header was found.

When the template is executed, the vals map is used to populate the template, and a complete Go file is generated. To run this, you need to place the go:generate header in an appropriate file, as shown in the next listing.

Listing 13.21 Using the generator

```
//go:generate ./queue MyInt       ⟵  Allocates go:generate
package main                          header, creating a queue
                                      for type MyInt
import "fmt"

type MyInt int                    ⟵  Defines the
                                      MyInt type
func main() {
    var one, two, three MyInt = 1, 2, 3
```

```
    q := NewMyIntQueue()
    q.Insert(one)
    q.Insert(two)                              Uses the
    q.Insert(three)                            MyIntQueue
    fmt.Printf("First value: %d\n", q.Remove())
}
```

This is a good example of typical use of a Go generator. In this one file, you declare a generator, declare your type, and even use the generator. Clearly, this code will not compile until you've run the generator. But because the generator doesn't depend on your code compiling, you can (and should) run it before building your package.

That raises an important point about generators: they're intended to be used as development tools. The Go authors intended that generation was part of the development life cycle, not the build or runtime cycle. In many cases, you'll want to generate your code and then check the generated code into your VCS. You shouldn't require your users to run a generator (even if your users are other developers) except in cases where you want to expose the intervals of the generated code to end developers.

To run the preceding generator, you need to do a few things. First, compile the generator tool from listings 13.18 and 13.19. For the generator line to work, you need to have it in the local directory (because you called it as ./queue). Alternatively, you could store the queue program anywhere on your path ($PATH), often including $GOPATH/bin, and call it //go:generate queue.

With queue compiled and located where go generate can find it, you need to run your go generate tool, and then you can run the main program using the generated code:

```
$ ls
myint.go
$ go generate
$ ls
myint.go
myint_queue.go
$ go run myint.go myint_queue.go
First value: 1
```

After the generator has created your extra queue code, you can run the program shown in listing 13.21. Everything it needs has been generated.

The code you're using for this generator is basic. Instead of adding error handling, you let the queue panic. You don't handle the case where you'd want to queue pointers. But these problems are easily corrected by using the normal strategies. Adding pointers, for example, is just a matter of adding another template parameter that adds an asterisk where appropriate.

Again, Go templates aren't the only way to generate code. Using the go/ast package, you can generate code by programming the abstract syntax tree. For that matter, you could just as easily write Python, C, or Erlang code that generated Go. You're not even limited to outputting Go. Imagine generating SQL CREATE statements by using a generator that reads structs. One of the things that make go generate so elegant is the versatility within its simplicity, and generating SQL from types with struct annotations is a relatively common use for generation.

Taking a higher-level view, generators can be a useful way of writing repetitive code that would otherwise use reflection. Go's reflection mechanism is useful, but it's tedious to write and limited in capabilities, and the performance of your application will suffer. That's not to say that reflection is bad. Rather, it's a tool designed to solve a specific set of problems.

On the other hand, generating code isn't always the best solution either. Metaprogramming can make debugging hard. It also adds steps to the development process. Just like reflection, generation should be used when the situation calls for it. But it's not a panacea or a workaround for Go's strong typing.

13.4 Working with other languages

One final area we'd like to touch on is one that's become very common with modern languages: the ability to work with other languages, namely C. In recent years, Rust, Zig, Kotlin, and a few others have been released with this capability built in.

This isn't something you should need to do often (or ever), but the most common case is a C library you'd like to implement without rewriting. If resources are not limited, rewriting small libraries will almost always be a better approach, but for quicker prototyping or when rewrites would be prohibitively expensive, Go provides a language construct that allows you to "import" C code and use methods and variables between the two languages.

Ultimately, this is a lot closer to working directly in C than passing serialized data back and forth as we have with things like os.Exec.

As Rob Pike says, "cgo is not Go." In Pike's opinion, you won't be writing Go code when interfacing with C applications, even though it will look like it. In his Gophercon talk "Go Proverbs," he walks through some potential pitfalls and caveats with using cgo; see https://www.youtube.com/watch?v=PAAkCSZUG1c&t=757s.

To demonstrate how this works at a very basic level, let's pass some data from a Go application to C, as shown in the next listing.

Listing 13.22 From Go to C

```
package main
                                              Standard C import
                                              via #include
// #include <stdio.h>
// void delimiter(int num, int limit) {       A function that prints one of
//    if (num < limit) {                       two possible delimiters based
//        printf(", ");                        on iteration number
//        return;
//    }
//     printf("\n");
// }
```

```
// void fizz_buzz(int limit) {                      ◁────  A Fizz Buzz function
// for (int i = 0; i <= limit; i++) {               ◁──┐   declaration in C
//     if (i % 3 == 0 || i % 5 == 0) {                  │
//         printf("FizzBuzz");                          │
//     }                                                │   The main logic loop
//     else if (i % 3 == 0) {                           │
//         printf("Fizz");
//     }
//     else if (i % 5 == 0) {
//         printf("Buzz");
//     } else {
//         printf("%d", i);
// }
//     delimiter(i, limit);
// }
// }
import "C"           ◁────  The C import in Go

func main() {
    if _, err := C.fizz_buzz(15); err != nil {   ◁──┐   Execution of the C
        panic(err)                                   │   function, capturing
    }                                                │   a possible error
}
```

Here, we're calling a `fizz_buzz` function from C embedded in our Go file. We can also reference C header files from this Go file as well. In this case, all our cgo references need to be in comments specified above any packages being called, including `"C"`. Although obviously we could (and should) build `fizz_buzz` in Go, this gives a simple example of how the two languages can work together when you need.

Working with cgo is very much an edge case, but if you encounter C libraries that have no native Go counterpart which would be hard to integrate, and you don't plan to use the interoperability frequently, this can be a quick way to work with C libraries.

In advanced cases of interoperating with C, you may want to explore some of the runtime options around garbage collection. Go provides flexibility around the memory footprint of garbage collection by setting GOMEMLIMIT and the target percentage of garbage collection using the GOGC environment variable. In the latter, garbage collection can be disabled by setting GOGC to off. You won't need this often, if at all, so its use should be reserved for cases where garbage collection has become a bottleneck.

Summary

- Reflection in Go allows us to examine our data and its types and kinds. We can use this to determine at runtime whether a type implements an interface, is comparable or castable, and more.
- We can examine annotations in structs and parse tags to better extend functionality like runtime checks against data validity.

- Using reflection, we can create our own `Marshal` and `Unmarshal` methods to encode data in a way similar to built-in Go data encoders.
- Using `go generate`, we can avoid boilerplate code that would require a lot of repetitive declarations, especially when working with vast generics.
- We can work with C directly in our Go code to bring in various libraries that may not be natively available in Go.

index